Oleg Gordievsky was born in Moscow in 1938. He attended the Moscow State Institute of International Relations where he specialized in German. He was sent to East Berlin as a diplomatic trainee in August 1961. Two days after his arrival, the Wall went up. In 1962 he joined the KGB and was posted to Copenhagen and London. He worked as a secret agent for eleven years until his dramatic escape to the West in 1985.

PRAISE FOR NEXT STOP EXECUTION:

'Gordievsky's extraordinary courage, mental toughness and self-possession are heroic.' — *The Spectator*

PRAISE FOR OLEG GORDIEVSKY:

'Oleg Gordievsky, a KGB colonel widely regarded as one of MI6's most valuable Cold War assets' — *The Independent*

'The greatest spy story of the Cold War' — Ben Macintyre, *The Times*

'A true story more gripping than Le Carre.' — *Daily Mail*

NEXT STOP EXECUTION

The Autobiography of Oleg Gordievsky

Oleg Gordievsky

LUME BOOKS

LUME BOOKS

First published in 2018 by Lume Books
30 Great Guildford St,
London, SE1 0HS

ISBN 978-1-83901-179-5

Printed and bound in Great Britain by
Clays Ltd, Elcograf S.p.A.

www.lumebooks.co.uk

I am profoundly grateful to all my good friends during my co-operation with the British Intelligence, to all those who helped at my rescue, and to all who fought for my family to be reunited.

Author's Note

I wish to emphasize that this book is in no sense an official history of intelligence operations, and has not been endorsed by any government authority. Rather, it is a purely personal account of my life and career, and the opinions expressed are mine alone.

Oleg Gordievsky
March 1995

Foreword

This book was originally published over two decades ago, in the aftermath of the Cold War, which ended with the break-up of the Soviet Union and the liberation of the countries of Eastern Europe that had been under Soviet domination since the end of the Second World War. It was a time of huge change — and hope. After years of confrontation between two world systems — Soviet Communism and Western values — which had come at times dangerously close to catastrophic military conflict, it seemed a new era had arrived, in which the values of freedom, democracy and openness had finally overcome totalitarianism and oppression.

Many of us, especially those who had resisted the Soviet regime from within, were full of hope that real change was under way, even in Russia itself. That sense of optimism was reflected in the final pages of the first edition of *Next Stop Execution*. The communist system that I had come to despise, and against which I had fought in secret for so many years, was finally gone. The apparatus of tyranny by which the party, and its chief agency of oppression, the KGB, had kept the people in a state of fear and subjugation, was being dismantled. Russia began to open up, with a spirit of freedom not only in politics but in all spheres of society, not experienced since before the First World War. It was a heady, exciting time.

People were hungry for change, but also to understand what kind of system they had been living under; and, with that knowledge, to build strong institutions that would protect their new-found freedoms and create an open society. For a while, it seemed as if anything was possible, and perhaps it was.

It takes time to build democracy and accountable institutions able to limit the exercise of power, especially through independent media and a fair legal system. The new system of government which immediately succeeded Soviet rule was far from perfect, and this opened the way for a reversal of the gains which had been achieved. In the late 1990s and early years of this century Russia took a decisive step backwards, with the return to power of many of the individuals and institutions, albeit renamed, which had upheld the old Soviet tyranny. In particular, the former security and intelligence agencies succeeded in regaining their former positions of power and control, and now once again dominate the Russian state, including all the major political institutions, the economy and the military.

The old KGB, under its new names, now constitutes the real government in Russia. It is even more powerful, relatively speaking, than the KGB of old. The new Russia, shorn of the former communist ideology, and without its veneer of idealism for a better world, is interested only in power: power for Russia itself and unchallenged power for the new ruling class; those few individuals and their cronies who now dominate all spheres of Russian politics, society and life.

As in the Soviet era, this new regime will use any means to consolidate its authority, and to try to undermine those institutions and countries it regards as its enemies and rivals. So we are now seeing a return to the brazen methods and instruments of the past, including use of military force — (invasion of Eastern Ukraine, seizure of the Crimea, military adventures in the Caucasus and Syria) — and subversion of democratic processes and institutions in the West, including interference in elections and the criminal elimination of its enemies, including journalists, lawyers and oppositionists, some of whom have settled in the West, who dare to speak out against the regime. In its reckless choice of murder weapons, endangering innocent bystanders, it seems not to care whether its hand is revealed. Indeed, such brazen use of force seems now to be, as it was in the Soviet era, a deliberate part of the tactic to silence and to intimidate opposition and protest, just as terrorists seek to do.

Today, the former Soviet regime and its confrontation with Western values during the Cold War are fading in popular memory. But the challenges today, to continue to fight for freedom and openness, and to expose subversion and underhand methods to destroy the precious institutions of democracy, remain, sadly, all too real and pressing.

The dangerous situation we now face did not come about spontaneously: it grew out of the conflicts and struggles of the past. It is my hope that the retelling of my own story of struggle and opposition may have lessons for our present struggle, and remind us that it is by remaining true to our values that we have the best chance to protect our way of life from those who seek to destroy or undermine it.

It is over thirty years since I settled in the United Kingdom. Life has been good to me. I enjoy freedom and democracy, I enjoy openness and debate. I would like the same privileges and opportunities to be more widely available in the world. I am grateful for the support and protection I continue to be given; and I wish success to those who protect and safeguard the institutions and values of this country, and its international partners, both now and in the challenging years ahead.

Oleg Gordievsky, 2018

Chapter One – Escape or Die

Thunderstorms were rolling over Moscow, and occasional heavy showers sent people scurrying for cover. On Tuesday, 11 June 1985, the KGB net was closing round me, and I knew that if I did not break out of the great concentration camp of the Soviet Union within the next few weeks, I would die. The time had come to activate the escape plan which my friends in the British Secret Intelligence Service (SIS) had prepared for me and held in readiness for years.

The KGB had planted microphones in my flat, on the eighth floor of the tower block at 103 Leninsky Prospekt, in the south-western sector of the city known as Yugozapad. I feared that they might also have installed a secret television camera. I therefore had to be extremely careful about bringing out my escape instructions, two copies of which were bound into the hard covers of innocent-looking English novels. Taking one of the books, I went into the kitchen where I was doing some washing and put the book to soak beneath it. After a few minutes I was able to peel back the flyleaf and retrieve the sheet of Cellophane containing my secret instructions. Putting the remains of the book down the waste chute, I went into the small box-room, closed the door behind me, and read the instructions by the light of a candle beyond the reach of any probing lens.

The ease of that little operation reassured me, and it took only a few minutes to refresh my memory about what I must do. To warn the British that I was in danger, I had to appear on a certain street corner at 7 p.m. on a Tuesday, and stand by a lamp-post on the edge of the pavement holding a plastic Safeway shopping bag. Next, at 11 a.m. on the third Sunday after that, I would pass a written message by brush-contact in St Basil's Cathedral, on Red Square.

Normal methods of communication were impossible. Telephone lines into the Embassy were bugged, as were the lines into the compound where British diplomats lived. A visit to the Embassy itself was out of the question since the gates were guarded by KGB in police uniform, who would either chase a caller away or detain him in conversation while he was covertly photographed. The diplomats' compound was similarly guarded.

By then I was under such pressure that I had become obsessed by the need for secrecy. To preserve the sheet of escape instructions seemed intolerably dangerous, so I made cryptic notes on a piece of paper and burnt the original. Then I crumpled the paper into a tight ball and took it to the underground garage where my car was stored, a couple of kilometres from the flat. The garage was divided up into individual bays by partitions of brickwork with steel grilles across the front of each. It was the centre of much social activity, for it was warm and well lit, and the owners of the cars frequently held parties down there, bringing food and drink and listening to music. But what interested me was that the place had been built to good Soviet standards, and the bricks had been so poorly laid that there were large gaps between them. Assuming that in due course my own bay would be searched, I shoved the paper into a crack at eye level in the communal area, leading to the exit. Now, even if my flat were raided and the book containing the second copy of my instructions were confiscated, I would still have the rudiments of the plan.

On Tuesday, to reach the signal site on time, I prepared to set off at 4 p.m. Because the weather was so unsettled, I put on a grey raincoat and black rubber boots, as well as a peaked leather cap I had bought in Denmark and now wore as an aid to recognition. To make it look as if I had been shopping, I stuffed the two carrier bags with crumpled newspaper.

Luckily I was not a conspicuous figure: at 1 metre 58, or 5 feet 8 inches tall, I did not stand out in a crowd; and although, at the age of forty-seven, I had lost much of my hair, my cap concealed the bald patch on top of my head. Nevertheless, as I left the tower block, my first essential was to make certain that no surveillance was behind me, using the technique known to the KGB as *proverka*, and to the Americans as dry-cleaning.

Because my car was off the road, having failed its annual technical test, I had to use public transport, and went out on foot, walking five or six hundred metres to the nearest shopping precinct. As always, I steeled myself not to look back: it was a fundamental principle of KGB training that one should appear unworried, and give no sign of concern about being followed.

The first shop I entered was a pharmacist: I moved from one window to the other and then to the counter, apparently in search of some item, but in fact to check what was happening outside. My next stop — a savings bank — offered an even better vantage point, as it was on the first floor, and a window on the stairs gave a good view of the street. I hovered there for a couple of minutes, went on to call at a food shop, and walked up a footpath between some small blocks of flats, as if heading for home again. But then I turned quickly into one of the blocks, went up the communal staircase, waited, watched from a window, came down again, and continued.

I saw no sign of anyone following, yet it was still not safe to relax. I walked on, took a bus for a few stops, then hailed a taxi and went to the transport police station where I was supposed to make inquiries about my car. From there I moved on to the block in which my sister Marina lived, and went in, as if visiting her; but after a few minutes' observation from a window on the stairs, I came out again, caught the Metro, changed trains once, and so, after three hours' dry-cleaning, at last reached Kievsky tube station, within walking distance of my rendezvous.

By the time I took up position on the edge of the pavement, at 7 p.m. precisely, I was feeling exceedingly nervous. Official limousines were pouring past along the big avenue, taking Politburo members home from the Kremlin, with numerous KGB officers in cars behind them. More KGB were undoubtedly on duty in plain clothes, studying the operational situation.

Knowing this, I had to make a great effort to stand still and pretend to be looking for a friend — especially in that exposed position on the edge of the road. It would have been more natural to wait at the back of the pavement, against the wall. I held on for what seemed an eternity but was probably no more than three or four minutes. Then I thought: All right, I've done it. Whether or not anyone had picked up my message, I could not tell, but at least I had gone through the procedure laid down.

On the third Sunday, again after extensive dry-cleaning, I made my way to Red Square for the brush-contact. My first objective was the Lenin Museum, now closed, but then the best looked-after public building in Moscow, in its way a temple of Communism. I headed for the underground lavatories, which I knew were clean and spacious. Safely ensconced in a cubicle, with the door locked, I sat on the seat and wrote a note in block capitals on an opened-out envelope:

AM UNDER STRONG SUSPICION AND IN BAD TROUBLE. NEED EXFILTRATION SOONEST. BEWARE OF RADIOACTIVE DUST AND CAR ACCIDENTS.

The last sentence was a warning against two common practices of the KGB: that of smearing radioactive dust on the soles of shoes, so that they could follow a target more easily, and of staging car crashes, with which they could bring any operation to a halt and force those taking part into the open. Screwing the paper into a tight ball, I went on towards St Basil's. To make doubly sure that I had not picked up any surveillance at the last moment, I turned into GUM, the huge department store which runs the whole length of Red Square on the side opposite the Kremlin. There, in the complex of three main alleyways, with shops on three levels, I dodged up and down, back and forth, before I began to feel that I needed space around me, and went back out into the fresh air.

As always, the square was full of tourists, and there were KGB everywhere, especially in front of the Spassky Tower, the main entrance to the Kremlin. My instructions were to enter St Basil's and go up the spiral staircase to the first floor. I had been given a hint — no more — that my contact would be a woman: she would be wearing grey, and holding something grey in both hands. The idea was that I would slip her my message as we brushed past each other on the narrow staircase.

At the last minute I realized that my peaked leather cap was going to be an embarrassment: men are not supposed to wear hats inside Russian Orthodox churches. Besides, the day was hot, and I was pouring with sweat. But my instructions had been to wear the cap as a recognition signal, so I had to keep it on.

Then came a severe disappointment. I had hardly entered the cavernous ground floor of the cathedral when I saw a sign saying 'UPPER FLOORS CLOSED FOR REDECORATION'. Now what? For a few minutes I strolled about, hoping that my contact might be there among the crowd, and that if she was, I could slip her my note in the open. Yet after an apparently casual look round, I saw no one dressed in grey, and after twenty-five minutes I gave up. On the way home in the tube, I chewed my SOS into small pieces, and spat them out one by one.

*

That evening, when I thought things over in my flat, I realized that the failure of communication was my fault. I had not waited long enough at the signal site: because I had left prematurely, my message had not been picked up. I should have mastered my nerves and held on. Now my predicament was growing desperate, and as I lay awake that night, I racked my brains for the hundredth time, trying to work out who it could have been that betrayed me.

I had been a member of the KGB for more than twenty years, but for the past eleven years, since 1974, I had been working for the British Secret Intelligence Service, otherwise MI6, first in Denmark and then in England. In 1982 I had been appointed Counsellor at the Soviet Embassy in London — on the surface a diplomat, but in fact a senior member of the KGB station in the British capital. For more than two years, together with my wife Leila and our young daughters Maria and Anna, I had lived in Kensington, worked at the Embassy, and maintained regular contact with my British case officers. In Soviet eyes I had done well, and by the spring of 1985 I had become acting head of station, with the promise that I was to be promoted Resident, or head of the KGB in London, that summer.

Then suddenly the ground had opened under me. Summoned back to the Centre, ostensibly for high-level briefings about my new position, I flew to Moscow on 19 May, leaving Leila and the children in London. To my alarm, I found that my flat had been broken into — presumably by the KGB in search of evidence — and that I was suspected of treason. A week later I was taken to a KGB dacha, drugged with doctored brandy and interrogated. Afterwards, I could not remember how much or how little I had given away. I thought I had managed to hold my own — but soon I was told that, although I would be allowed to serve on in the KGB, my mission to Britain had been terminated. I would be granted leave until early August.

Had my colleagues discovered firm evidence of my treachery, or were they only working on a vague tip-off? I could not tell. Either way I was in acute danger: the KGB were searching for conclusive proof of my guilt. My only hope seemed to be to play for time, and pretend that everything was normal. So I agreed to go for a month's leave at a KGB sanatorium some sixty miles south of Moscow.

My family, meanwhile, had been flown back from London. Inevitably Leila realized that something was wrong, but I told her that my problems were due only to the intrigues which constantly raged within the KGB, and she took the children off as planned for their summer holiday at her father's dacha on the shore of the Caspian. Saying goodbye to her was one of the most difficult moments of my life. We parted in the doorway of a supermarket: with her mind already on the holiday, and on the clothes she was about to buy for the girls, she gave me a quick farewell peck on the cheek. I said, 'That could have been a bit more tender', and she was gone, not knowing that by the time she returned to Moscow I would be either dead or in exile.

Now, in the middle of July, I sensed that I had little time left. At the sanatorium, although kept under light surveillance, I had been free to return to Moscow whenever I wanted; but chance encounters with professional colleagues were unanimously disconcerting. In their faces, one after another, I saw my own fate reflected: even though they said nothing, I could tell from their demeanour that they knew the KGB hounds were hot on my scent.

Alone in Moscow, I had all too much time for self-analysis and examination. How had I made such a mess of my life? Where had I gone wrong?

I like to think that I am an easy-going person, without any physical aggression. The only time I retaliate is when I hear myself being insulted, or people making unfair remarks about me; then I am inclined to hit back verbally, and become forceful in argument. My main fault, I know, has always been a tendency to trust people too much. When I was a child, my mother used to tell me that just because someone was kind to me, it did not mean that he or she was a nice person. Several times colleagues had warned me that I was not very good at discerning the true nature of the people I met — a dangerous trait in an intelligence officer, who should see through everyone. Because I trusted too much, I was often deceived.

Yet this failing had nothing to do with my present predicament. As far as I knew, I had not been compromised by anything that I had said or done. When I am pursuing a long-term strategic objective, as I was then, my nerves are good: in all my dealings with the British, I had made no serious mistake. I know that in the short-term I am prone to attacks of panic — but I had not suffered any yet.

On the other hand, one of the penalties of leading a double life was that it had drastically inhibited my emotional development. Because Leila had grown up very much a Soviet girl, heavily indoctrinated by Communist propaganda, I had never dared tell her that I was working for the British for fear that she would denounce me. Inevitably this meant that we had never come as close as we might have in normal circumstances: always I had withheld a central feature of my existence from her. Is intellectual deception of one's partner more or less cruel than physical deception? Who can say? In any case, it was adding to my anxiety.

But now my overriding priority was to save my own skin, and I decided to stake everything on the third week in July. If I gave a correct signal on Tuesday 16th, my escape would be set up for the following Saturday. Once again, therefore, I planned to be standing on the signal site at 7 p.m. on Tuesday.

On Monday night I slit open my second specially bound novel, brought out the sheet bearing the second copy of my exfiltration plan, developed it, read it, studied it. The document would have meant little to anyone else for it appeared to refer to places in France; but in fact it contained detailed instructions for reaching a rendezvous in the forest near Viborg, on the border between the Soviet Union and Finland. The distances were all real, but for the sake of security the names of French cities and towns had been substituted for Russian originals — Paris for Moscow, Marseilles for Leningrad, and so on.

To calm my stretched nerves, I was taking sedatives and drinking rather too much Cuban rum, of which a good brand had recently appeared in Moscow. By 9 p.m. my head was not as clear as it might have been, and I wanted to go through the plan again in the morning, when I was fresh. Yet what was I to do with such an incriminating document? After some thought I barricaded the front and balcony doors with furniture, and went to sleep with the plan and a box of matches lying on a metal tray under a newspaper on Leila's side of the double bed, so that if the KGB did try to break in during the night, my makeshift blockade would at least give me time to burn the most dangerous evidence.

As luck would have it, on Tuesday morning I got a telephone call from my father-in-law, Ali Aliyevich, who was looking after me in avuncular fashion during Leila's absence. 'Come round to supper at seven tonight, and I'll cook a nice chicken in garlic,' he said. Seven o'clock! I knew the KGB were listening. Ali lived in Davitkova, on the outskirts of the city, in a direction which coincided well with my rendezvous. But if I suggested, 'Eight would be better,' the listeners would immediately wonder, 'Aha! What's he doing at seven?', and make quite certain they did not lose sight of me. So I just said, 'Thank you. I'll look forward to it.' All the same I was annoyed, for I knew that Ali, a most punctual man, would be irritated by my late arrival.

In the middle of the day I got out money for the journey. At that date there were no ordinary banks in Moscow, only primitive savings banks, and I reckoned that the most I could draw from my account without attracting notice was three hundred roubles (then worth three hundred pounds). Most of this I intended to leave for Leila: eighty roubles would be plenty for my train ticket, a couple of taxis and meals during my journey. At the end of it, roubles would be of no further use to me: I would either be out of the Soviet Union or in gaol.

Tuesday evening was clear and warm, but not too hot — a lovely

Moscow summer's evening. This time I was full of resolve not to make mistakes. Wearing a smart, lightweight pale-grey suit and tie, and carrying a Safeway supermarket bag, I left the flat at 4 p.m. and went through my full repertoire of dry-cleaning tricks: to the shops, to the police station, and on to my sister's block, where I watched from the staircase window. When all seemed clear, I continued to the rendezvous, arriving early at 6.45.

Purely to kill time, I went into a shop, bought a packet of cigarettes, opened it and put one in my mouth. As I discovered later, this proved a mistake for the contact who came to meet me knew that I did not smoke, and the sight of the cigarette made him doubt my identity. Never having seen me in the flesh, he was relying on photographs for identification, and when he saw a man smoking he immediately wondered if this was not a KGB provocation, designed to entangle British intelligence officers.

By 6.59 I was on station, at the edge of the pavement, by the lamp-post. Hardly had I reached the spot when a black Volga pulled out of the traffic and stopped half on the pavement: it looked exactly like a police or surveillance car, and when two men jumped out of it, I felt certain they were members of a police arrest group. They disappeared through the crowd, but the driver, who had stayed behind, began looking at me with great suspicion. I stared back at him — and suddenly I realized that his companions were doing nothing more sinister than picking up money from the shops. When I saw what was happening, I relaxed and winked at the driver, who returned my wink and grinned back at me.

All that took only a few seconds, and I had to remain in my exposed position for, once again, what seemed an age. People flocked past on foot, heading home from their offices, and government limousines sped by along the main road. My instructions were to stay there long enough to be noticed, then to withdraw to the corner and stand outside the window of a bakery. After seven minutes I moved back, watching out all the time for someone of typically English appearance, and someone who would show that he had seen me by chewing something.

Time crawled past: ten minutes, fifteen. An endless stream of faces flowed along the pavement, but none looking English, and none munching. Then at last, after twenty-four minutes, I saw him: a man with an unmistakably British look, carrying a dark-green Harrods bag and eating a Mars bar. As he passed within four or five yards, he stared straight at me, and I gazed into his eyes shouting silently, 'Yes! It's me! I need urgent help!' He walked on, giving no other sign, but I knew without any doubt that contact had been made. I forced myself to stroll off casually for several hundred metres. Then I took a taxi to my father-in-law's, and found him rather annoyed that I was so late but I invented some story to account for the delay, and although his special chicken was slightly spoiled, I felt elated that one important stage of my escape was behind me.

Wednesday brought proof positive that my habitual dry-cleaning was not superfluous. My most urgent task now was to buy a railway ticket for Leningrad, and this meant a trip to the Leningrad station on Komsomolskaya Square. I set off on foot as usual, heading for my local shopping centre and, after calling into a couple of shops, walked slowly along the footpath leading to the small blocks of flats, which were staggered in two groups of three. Once round the corner and out of sight, I sprinted twenty or thirty yards, darted on to the nearest staircase and up a flight.

From a window I saw a fat man hurry round the corner, almost running, then stop and search about him. He looked hot and uncomfortable in jacket and tie, but he was clearly no fool, for he realized that I had done something unusual. He began to scrutinize the windows on the staircases, of which (luckily for me) there were twelve in all. Hanging back in the shadow, I felt cold sweat break out on my back. Oh, clever chap! I thought. Then he began to speak into a small microphone fastened to his lapel. After hesitating for a moment he hurried on — and five or six seconds later a coffee-coloured Lada nosed into view, crawling along the footpath. The track was supposed to be for pedestrians only and was barely wide enough for a single car, but here was the motorized surveillance, coming down it! In the front a man and a woman, both in their early thirties, were speaking simultaneously into a microphone.

When the car disappeared between the blocks, I waited half a minute, came down, and hurried back on my tracks till I reached the main road. There I leapt into a bus, rode it for a couple of stops, took a taxi to the traffic police station, went in, came out, made sure no one was behind me, and continued slowly to the Leningrad station, where I bought a fourth-class ticket with a reservation for a train due to leave Moscow at 5.30 p.m. on Friday. That night I slept with the doors of the flat barricaded once more, the ticket and a box of matches lying on the tin tray beside me. To catch a glimpse of a single man or woman on your tail is one thing, but to see a whole carload of surveillance behind you — that gives you a terrible feeling.

Thursday I spent with my sister Marina and, as part of my general deception plan, I made a date to visit her early the next week. It felt odd and uncomfortable to be deceiving members of my own family, but for the benefit of KGB listeners I had to maintain the pretence that I was going to be around beyond the weekend. Yet, at the same time, some devil made me deliberately taunt the unseen eavesdroppers. I rang my old friend and colleague Mikhail Lyubimov, who had been dismissed from the KGB for marital indiscretions, and in the course of a general conversation I reminded him of the short story by Somerset Maugham called 'Mr Harrington's Washing'. This concerns a maddeningly fastidious and self-centred American businessman, Mr Harrington, who falls in with the British secret agent Ashenden on the Trans-Siberian railway as they travel west-wards from Vladivostok in 1917, and then are trapped in Petrograd by the Bolshevik coup. Ashenden is intriguing to keep Russia in the war against Germany, but everyone advises Harrington to escape to Sweden while he still has the chance. He is shot dead in the street, however, when he insists on trying to recover the clothes he had sent to the hotel laundry. The reader is left to assume that Ashenden, together with his overpowering ladyfriend, Anastasia Aleksandrovna, slips away through Finland.

Lyubimov had forgotten the story, but I knew that he had Maugham's collected works and I told him, 'It's in Volume Four. Look it up, and you'll see what I mean.'

Soon he returned my call, saying, 'Oh, yes, I see' — but of course he did not.

In a way it was a risk to draw the KGB's attention to a story about someone trying to escape through Russia's northern frontier but I wanted to insult their intelligence or, rather, lack of it, and I felt confident that they would not pick up the reference in time to do anything about it. To throw the listeners still further off the scent, I made a precise rendezvous with Lyubimov for the following Monday. When he invited me to join him and his girlfriend Tanya for lunch in their dacha at Zvenigorod, outside Moscow, I said I would be in the last carriage of the train which reached his station at 11.30 a.m.

On Thursday night I again slept with the doors barricaded and my railway ticket under a napkin on the tin tray. On Friday, feeling emotional and overexcited, I spent the morning cleaning the flat. I knew I would probably never see the place again, but I wanted to leave everything in perfect order. I did not doubt that the KGB would study every detail, and I was anxious that they should find things shipshape — washing-up done, crockery put away, documents in place, spare cash on the shelf. Having calculated that eighty roubles would suffice for my journey, I left two hundred and twenty in a neat pile — enough, at that date, to keep Leila going for a couple of months. In spite of all the care I took, I forgot one special item: the snuff I had bought in case I had to deal with inquisitive search-dogs at the frontier.

At last, about 4 p.m., it was time to leave. Although the flats were modest, the foyer of the block was huge and portentous, with marble walls, tall windows, and plants scattered about in tubs. A concierge, one or other of a rota of middle-aged women, was always on duty at the desk in the corner, and I knew that she was bound to see me as I went out. I therefore made myself look as ordinary as possible, in a thin green sweater, old green corduroy trousers and scuffed brown shoes. I rolled up a light jacket and put it in the bottom of a carrier bag, together with my Danish cap, essentials for washing and shaving, and a small road atlas covering the area of the Finnish border. Knowing that Soviet maps were deliberately falsified in border regions, to confuse and mislead would-be escapers, I was not sure how much use this would be but it was all I could get. Everything else I left behind — and when I closed the door, I knew that I was closing it not only on my home and my possessions, but on my family and my life.

I went down from the eighth floor in the lift. Sure enough, the concierge was at her desk but, if she noticed me at all, she probably mistook my green clothes for the tracksuit in which I often went jogging, and thought I was going for a run. Outside, I presumed that one surveillance car would be close to the small blocks of flats, with two others somewhere in support. But this time, instead of heading in that direction, I walked off into the wood on the far side of the main road, and as soon as I was hidden in the trees, began to run. In a couple of minutes I reached the shopping precinct, but from a different direction. The place was busy, and I was soon lost in the crowd. It took only a minute to buy a cheap hold-all made of artificial leather, a poor-quality bag but authentically Soviet. Having transferred my sparse luggage into it, I went on, dry-cleaning myself in classic fashion all the way to the Leningrad station, and continuing the process even as I crossed the expanse of Komsomolskaya Square.

By then I was so nervous that everything appeared highly sinister: an incredible concentration of police and internal anti-riot troops seemed to be patrolling the station. The whole place was seething with men in uniform. I felt threatened by this totalitarian display, and for a moment my overheated imagination made me think they were looking for me. Then I remembered that young people from all over the world were pouring into the city for an international youth festival, which was due to open on Sunday. The first event of that kind, held in 1957, had seemed to me a marvellous occasion, lit up by the spontaneous excitement of the Khrushchev era; but this was different, artificial, over-organized and unattractive. Yet I saw that it might work to my advantage, for the great influx of foreigners coming across from Scandinavia would surely help to distract the frontier officials.

On the train my fourth-class ticket gave me a top bunk in an open-fronted compartment with room for six. There was little privacy, as people were constantly walking past, but I got clean sheets from the conductor — a nice-looking girl, obviously a student earning money during her vacation — and made up my bed for the night. The train pulled out punctually at 5.30, and for the first hour or two people sat around on the lower bunks, chatting and reading out the clues of a crossword. At that time, in the era of stagnation two years before *glasnost*, strangers never talked to each other in public about politics or anything contentious: doing the crossword was a harmless and neutral activity in which everyone could take part without risk. I must have had something to eat: probably I bought bread and sausage in the station, but I do not remember. In any case, I went to bed about 9 p.m. and took a double dose of sedatives.

The next thing I knew, I woke up to find myself no longer in the top bunk, but in the one below. It was 4 a.m., and already light. For a few seconds I lay feeling stunned. Never before in my life had I lost control. Looking up, I saw a young fellow in the bunk above — my bunk! When I asked what had happened, he said, 'Don't you remember? You fell out.'

Checking myself over, I found one cut on my temple, another on my shoulder, and blood inside my green sweater. Considering that I had fallen a metre and a half on to the hard floor, it was not surprising that my head and neck were aching. I was in a bad way — dirty, dishevelled, unshaven, and looking like a vagabond in my shabby old clothes.

With some fresh air from the corridor, I started to feel better and, in any case, the train was already approaching Leningrad, so I sat on the bottom bunk and waited. In the next section were some lively young students from Kazakhstan, beautiful, long-legged girls, full of life and conversatioh. Presently one of them made some remark on which I wanted to comment, but as I opened my mouth the girl next to me drew back and gasped, 'If you speak one word to me, I'll scream.'

That made me realize how awful I must look. Grabbing my bag, I stood up and went along to the little compartment occupied by the guard. She could have made trouble and reported me to the police, or had me taken to hospital, so I handed her five roubles and said quietly, 'Thank you very much for your help.' At that date it was a colossal tip — ten times what she might have expected — but she took the money, giving me a reproachful look, and I went on into the open area at the end of the carriage, where I stood for the rest of the journey.

As the train pulled in, I jumped out and disappeared into the crowd. Outside, the huge square was empty, looking pretty and clean in the early-morning light; people were waiting for taxis in a long line, but there were also some private cars touting for hire, so I went up to one of the drivers and asked, 'How much to go to the Finland station?'

'Ten roubles,' he said. It was an incredible amount, more than my fare for all the eight hundred kilometres from Moscow, but I was in such a fever to keep moving that I did not argue.

When we reached the Finland station at 5.45, I found that the first train in the direction of the frontier would run in twenty minutes. I took it, and arrived in Zelenogorsk, ninety kilometres north-west of Leningrad, at 8.30 a.m. My judgement must have been clouded by excitement and anxiety, for I then made the first of many mistakes.

My rendezvous with the British was near the main road to the border, but several kilometres short of it: the most sensible course would have been to take a train to Viborg, the frontier town, and make my way back to the pick-up point by bus or on foot. If I had done that, it would not have mattered even if I had been seen on the road: at least I would have been proceeding southwards, away from the border. Yet something made me tackle the last stage of my journey the other way round: I decided to take one bus to Terioki, half-way to Viborg, and another on from there. I knew of Terioki only as the place where, in December 1939 during the early stages of the Soviet-Finnish war, a worker-peasants' Finnish government had been formed. At least the station buffet was open by the time I arrived, and I bought a piece of fried chicken and a cup of tea for breakfast. That Saturday morning the station was busy, with plenty of casually dressed people around so that I no longer looked out of place.

As I ate, I hoped fervently that the British side of the operation was proceeding on schedule. The plan was that at the meeting place, by a large stone in the forest, a team would pick me up, hide me in the boot of a car, and go on through the frontier into Finland. Everything depended on the drivers managing the journey successfully, avoiding KGB surveillance, and reaching the rendezvous point on schedule.

I would have been even more worried if I had known how awkward the timing of my departure from Moscow had proved: precisely coinciding, as it did, with the arrival of a new British Ambassador, it created severe problems. Clearance for my exfiltration had to be obtained from the Foreign Office in London: in his memoirs *Conflict of Loyalty*, published in 1994, Geoffrey Howe, then foreign secretary, described how at the last minute, on Saturday 20 July, 'two senior officials (one from the FCO, the other from SIS)' attended on him at Chevening, the Foreign Secretary's official country residence, and how he 'gave authority for the plan to go ahead' — a decision endorsed by the Prime Minister, Margaret Thatcher.

That Thursday the new British Ambassador, Sir Bryan Cartledge, flew to Moscow to take up his appointment, and on Friday he marked his arrival by throwing a large evening reception at the Embassy. Since many of the guests were targets of KGB surveillance, the whole area of the Embassy was boiling with undercover agents. Later, the KGB leaked to the Western press a story that I had been smuggled into, and out of, the Embassy during the disturbance caused by the reception. In fact, as I have shown, I never went near the Embassy, and I was on the train before the party began. Now, on Saturday morning in Terioki, my thoughts were concentrated on the rendezvous ahead. At the bus station I discovered the number of the service I needed, and bought a ticket to the furthest stop. Then, as I consulted my atlas during the journey, I discovered that this bus would terminate short of my destination.

Another bus, then, and one going all the way to Viborg. This time the main hazard was a couple in their thirties, both drunk enough to be excessively sociable. 'Where are you from?' they asked in friendly but slurred voices. 'Where are you going?' I said I was visiting friends in a village whose name I had seen on the map. I was encouraged to see coaches full of students coming the other way, clearly on their way to the youth festival. I reassured myself again: the frontier would be busy, the officials preoccupied. From the number of armoured personnel carriers and artillery pieces on the move, I deduced that there must be some major military base nearby.

In due course the drunks got out — and so, in ones and twos, did all the other passengers, until I was the only person left on board. Suddenly I seemed to recognize my surroundings, which matched the description given in the escape plan. At that point the main road was running due north through a forest, and a loop-road went off to the right, like the curve of a capital D. All at once the scene seemed familiar. When the bus came to a stop, I hesitated, not sure whether this was my halt or not. As we rolled forward again, I realized I should have got off, so

I hurried forward up the aisle, calling to the driver, 'Sorry, I'm feeling sick. Can you put me off?'

The man gave me an odd look, as if not sure what I was up to: like everyone else in frontier areas he was on his guard, but he stopped and opened the doors. Once on the road, I crouched with my head held low as if throwing up, and then walked a few steps backward, in case he decided to wait. After a moment he revved up his engine irritably and moved off, leaving me alone.

Silence descended on the forest. Tall conifers were mixed with smaller, scrubby trees like birch and aspen. On the edges of the road and in the glades rank grass grew to a height of almost two metres. With water lying in pools among the undergrowth, the humidity was unbelievable — and so were the mosquitoes, which came whining at me in dozens when I stood still for a few seconds.

I began walking round the loop-road, and soon found a huge rock, which I took to be the rendezvous point. Yet it was still only 11 a.m., and my friends were not due to arrive until 2.30. What was I to do? Wait there for three and a half hours? I felt taut with nervous excitement, but also disorientated and irresolute. All the time I was thinking: if the KGB come after me and try to trace my route, who will remember me? The girl guard on the train, for one, and now the bus driver. My best course was to keep out of sight, to curl up in the undergrowth and wait for time to pass; yet the mosquitoes made the idea intolerable, and I decided to go on into Viborg where I could get something to eat.

Out on the main road again, I fell in with some sort of a tramp: a friendly fellow, courteous and well-spoken, wearing an ancient jacket full of holes, who reminded me of the alcoholic old beggars who frequent Waterloo Station. What he was doing out there, ambling through the forest, I did not ask, but I liked him instinctively, and because I was so excited, got into conversation. For a while we walked together, that harmless crank and I; then I heard a car coming up from behind, hailed it, and got a lift, leaving him alone on the road.

The car was a Lada, private and well-kept, and the driver looked an interesting character: young, obviously successful, probably an official of the KGB or the Ministry of the Interior. Luckily for me he did not feel like talking, but kept one of his many cassettes of Western pop music playing loudly. That suited me fine — but he was not too rich or too proud to accept the three roubles I gave him when he set me down in the southern outskirts of Viborg.

The town looked a typical Soviet settlement, faceless and colourless with a barracks and badly built blocks of flats. But there was also a plastic-and-glass cafeteria, which was just what I wanted, so I went in and bought myself lunch — chicken again. I also got two bottles of beer, one to drink with my meal, and one to take with me.

As I was finishing, in came a group of three young men who immediately struck me as sinister. In my overwrought state I assumed they were KGB surveillance, on the look-out for potential defectors — as teams constantly were in border areas. There they sat in their smart jackets, not buying anything, scanning round — and soon their attention settled on me, the alien.

Leaving the café without a backward glance, I began to walk southwards, in the direction of Leningrad. Only after four hundred metres or so did I allow myself to look round. The road was empty. On I went, pouring with sweat, partly from the heat, partly from anxiety. Already it was after 1 p.m. Instead of having too much time, I began to fear being late. I had nearly twenty kilometres to go. The traffic seemed to have died away in the noonday heat, as if everybody was having a long lunch or a Saturday siesta. Then, at last, as I was becoming desperate, I heard an engine behind me, and saw a lorry approaching.

The driver had a pleasant, open Russian face, friendly and attractive. 'What do you want to go *there* for?' he asked, when I named the bus stop. 'There's nothing within kilometres of that.'

'Ah!' I said craftily. 'You don't know. There are some dachas deep in the woods there, and I've got a nice lady waiting for me in one of them.'

'That's different, then!' he cried enthusiastically. 'In you get.'

My heart went out to that driver: a really nice man, ordinary, relaxed, not obsessed by the proximity of the border, he was simply enjoying his job. After all the sinister people in Moscow, and the hostile youngsters in the train, it was a glorious relief to be with somebody normal. I was so glad to be back on schedule, with food and drink inside me, and another bottle of beer to look forward to, that when he put me out at the bus stop I offered him four roubles.

'*Bratik*,' he said, 'Little Brother, it's too much. Three's more than enough.' So I gave him three and said goodbye.

Back in the undergrowth by the marker stone, I found my nervousness building up again, and I conceived the idea that I had too many things in my bag. One object which I certainly did not need any more was the atlas, so I took it out and threw it away under the stone. A few seconds later I realized what an idiotic move that was: if the KGB found the map, it would give everything away. So I nipped across, recovered it, and put it back in my luggage.

Mosquitoes tormented me, whining round my head in a continuous swarm: I swatted and cursed them, and one by one the minutes ticked away. Then, just before 2 p.m., I heard the sound of an engine. Peering out through the tall grass, desperately hoping to see a car, I found that the vehicle was a bus, evidently carrying wives to the military base.

When I glimpsed their faces in the windows, I knew that, from their vantage point, they could see down into the grass, so I hurled myself flat on the marshy ground until the vehicle had gone.

The second bottle of beer tasted wonderfully refreshing. I enjoyed every drop, then threw the bottle away — only to realize that, for the second time, I might be presenting the KGB with giveaway evidence. The bottle must have my fingerprints on it. Quickly retrieving it, I smeared it all over with mud, and then jettisoned it once more.

The magic pick-up moment came and went: 2.30, 2.35, 2.40. At 2.45 my impatience reached breaking point. Crazy as it was, I decided I must go to meet my rescuers, so that they could sweep me up a few seconds earlier. I came out of the grass, walked quickly round the loop-road, and set off along the highway in the direction of Leningrad. Yet I had gone only a few yards when, thank God, my brain started to function again. I saw that what I was doing was an act of real madness: almost certainly my rescuers would have a KGB tail. If they spotted me waiting by the road, all would be lost.

It was as if I had woken from a nightmare. Running back, I dived into the grass and said out loud, 'Control yourself!' I resolved to wait indefinitely: after all, I had no alternative.

At last I heard the sound of engines. Peering out, I saw two cars pull up right opposite. Two men got out, one of them the fellow who had passed me munching at the signal site in Moscow. To my surprise, I saw that two women had come as well.

To me, in my frenzy to get going, they all seemed extraordinarily lethargic, moving slowly and jerkily, as though they, too, were in the middle of a nightmare. In fact they were almost as tense as I was, but their nervousness expressed itself in a different way. The man I recognized stared at me, not certain that this unshaven creature with blood on his temple was really their target. But in a few seconds my sense of urgency got through to them.

'Keep these separate, please,' I said, handing him my shoes. 'They may have radioactive dust on them.' He put them into a plastic bag, and opened the boot of the second car, for me to climb in. Then he closed the lid, and I was imprisoned in stifling darkness. At once the car began to roll, and loud pop music burst out over the stereo system. Normally I hate that kind of noise, but the British had accurately divined that in these extraordinary circumstances loud, obvious rhythms would have a soothing effect and prevent my mind becoming too active.

I knew from my instructions that I would have been furnished with sedative pills, a flask of cold water, a container into which I could urinate if need be, and an aluminium space-blanket, to pull over me when we reached the frontier, in case any of the guards turned an infra-red heat-detector on the car. Feeling round, I found all these items, and immediately took one of the sedative pills. I also began trying to remove my jacket; but, pinned down as I was on my right side in that constricted space, I had a dire struggle.

While I was thus engaged, the convoy survived a minor crisis. As I expected, the cars indeed had a surveillance vehicle on their tail; but by clever timing they had gradually increased speed and pulled away from it over the last few kilometres before the pick-up point until they had a lead of some ninety seconds, so that when they pulled off on to the loop road, they were out of sight, concealed by the dense undergrowth of the forest and by the bulk of the marker stone. The KGB team went on ahead until they reached the next GAI (traffic police) checkpoint. There they asked if two other cars had been past, and were disconcerted when the answer was 'No'; but just as they were trying to work out what had happened, along came the convoy after all. After such a short time-lapse, the KGB concluded that the party must have popped into the forest to answer calls of nature.

Inside the boot I was battling against claustrophobia. I had at last succeeded in divesting myself of my jacket, but the battle had left me hotter than ever. Then the first of the sedatives began to take effect, and I settled down as best I could. I knew when we were passing through Viborg from the unevenness of the road-surface and the sound of other traffic, and I took advantage of the noise to clear my throat a few times — something I knew I would not be able to do when we reached the border.[1]

To cut short a saga of desperate uncertainty, we went through five frontier barriers in less than half an hour. At the first, I pulled the space-blanket into position over me and lay like a baking corpse while negotiations proceeded outside. The pop music was still playing, and after only three or four minutes we went forward once more. At the penultimate stop the engine was switched off, and the music died with it. In the silence I began to hear women's voices speaking in Russian, and deduced that, having passed safely through the KGB border controls, we were now with the customs. Both Englishmen spoke some Russian, and I heard them chatting to the officials about the problems incurred by the youth festival. The customs women were complaining about how exhausted they were at dealing with the huge influx of Finns, many of them drunk. Then I heard the whining and snuffling of dogs, too close for comfort. Little did I know that one of my rescuers' wives

---

1 I heard later that, at that moment, in London, a high-powered meeting concerned with my escape was taking place in the Foreign and Commonwealth Office. The atmosphere was extremely tense. At midday London time David Goodall, then Deputy Under-Secretary of State with responsibility for Russian affairs, looked at his watch and said, 'Gentlemen, they're crossing the border about now. Let's have a moment's silence and pray for the success of the operation.'

was carefully feeding the Alsatians with potato crisps to divert their attention from the car.

All the time I was thinking, *What happens if someone opens the boot?* The British, I knew, would have to disown me. They would feign amazement and cry, 'By God, a provocation!', claiming that they had no idea who I was. They would say they knew nothing about me, and that I must have been secretly foisted on them while they were having breakfast in a Leningrad hotel. If that happened, they themselves might well be thrown into gaol. As for myself, I had no plan but to surrender.

Six or seven minutes seemed like an hour. My clothes were sodden with sweat. Breathing had become a labour. I had to concentrate all my resources on keeping still. Then, to my inexpressible relief, I felt the car rock as people climbed back into it: the engine started, the music blasted on again, and we began to roll once more. At least I could shift my cramped limbs…but already we were slowing down again. One more brief halt, and we were off, accelerating hard. Abruptly the pop music stopped, and in its place there burst out the brooding grandeur of Sibelius's *Finlandia*. I recognized the piece at once, and knew it was a signal: we were through and into Finland.

Before the good news could sink in, there came one final scare. The car slowed, stopped and began to reverse. My spirits dived. I felt sure we were being summoned back to the frontier. In fact the driver had overshot a side-road. In a few seconds I felt the vehicle turn, and then it began to bump along the uneven surface of a track. When at last it stopped, I heard voices call out in English.

When someone opened the boot, I saw blue sky, white clouds and pine trees above me. Best of all, in the middle of that glorious view was the face of Joan, the architect of my escape plan, the wonderful friend who had been my case officer in England. Seeing her, I knew that my troubles were over. Thanks to the courage and ingenuity of my British friends, I had outwitted the entire might of the KGB. I was out! I was safe! I was free!

Chapter Two – Origins

My origins were as humble as could be.

I never met my paternal grandparents, but I know that they lived at Razyezd Yeral, a tiny siding where a few houses stood beside the railway linking the Volga and the southern Urals. My grandfather, Lavrentiy Gordievsky, worked as a ganger on the line, and was responsible for coupling and uncoupling the trains. Family legend recalled that he was once severely injured when he was crushed between buffers, and the accident may have led to his premature retirement. What I find fascinating about him is that he, an ordinary working man far out in the wilds of Tsarist Russia, sent his son Anton Lavrentiyevich, my father, to a college for teachers. No doubt it was a modest establishment, but it was a college of sorts, and it put my father on the road to a successful career.

He was born at Razyezd Yeral in 1896; all round were enclaves of Bashkirs and Tartars, both of Turkic origin, but that particular district was Russian-speaking, and he grew up with a good command of the language. He must have gone to school locally, and then, when he was eighteen or so, to the college, which I assume was in Chelyabinsk, the nearest large town. There he obtained a sound general education, read widely, and developed an interest in Russian literature. Returning home at the age of twenty-one in 1917, not long before the Bolshevik revolution, he became headmaster of a country school, where he taught all subjects in company with only one other teacher. At that time in the depths of the provinces 80 per cent of the population were peasants, most of them illiterate and without education, so the school must have been fairly basic. All the same, I imagine that my father taught well, since he had a good delivery and a gift for addressing audiences. He was also, I was amazed to discover many years afterwards, leader of the church choir, and later in life, when he had long since rejected all religious beliefs, his early training would surface when, with a good supper and a few glasses of vodka inside him, he would sing traditional hymns in his fine baritone.

The revolution of October 1917 changed the course of his life. He became an ardent, committed Communist, and remained one till the end of his days. Exactly what part he played in the events of 1917 and 1918 I have never been able to discover, but I believe that he joined the Socialist Revolutionaries, the biggest left-wing party which was particularly strong in the countryside. The SRs were not merely socialist, but also agrarian: their leaders did not agree with the Marxist principle that the industrial proletariat must be in the vanguard of the revolutionary movement. On the contrary, they proclaimed that it was the Russian peasants in the country who mattered most, which made them strong in rural towns. During 1917 the party split into left and right wings, and it was the left wing that joined the Communist Party. From the end of 1917 until the middle of 1918 Lenin's government was a coalition of Bolsheviks and left-wing SRs (many of whose extremist radicals were members of the Cheka, forerunner of the KGB). For those few months the SRs were an acceptable party in their own right, but after complications in the summer of 1918, the Bolsheviks dissolved them.

My father never gave any clear account of his role in these events but he told me that he joined the Communist Party as a candidate member in 1919, and then as a full member in 1920. (If, in official eyes, he had remained a member of the proletariat, which he was, he would have been entitled to full membership straight away; that he had become a teacher made him bourgeois and he had to take up candidate membership first.)

In 1920 he was sent to Ohrenburg, in Kazakhstan, to organize the expropriation of food from the peasants. Because this was a brutal operation, often carried out violently, he never cared to speak about it in detail, but essentially it consisted of the forcible seizure of grain, which was needed to feed the army and the population of the big cities where the Bolsheviks were strongest. Later, he said only that he had taken part in the food-collecting operation. Certainly for years afterwards he remained a functionary in the food sector — the central collection of grain, and the sale of it to the West — but he was never an economist or agricultural specialist. Rather, he was an exceptionally conscientious member of the Party, ideologically strong, with a gift for public speaking, who happened to be drafted into food.

Later, in the 1960s and 1970s, almost everyone in State service became a member of the Communist Party, which at its zenith claimed 20 million members. People signed up not out of ideological conviction but simply because it was impossible to make any worthwhile career without joining; but to my father as a young man Communism was a religion, and the Party was like God. Just as for Roman Catholics the Church is always right, so for Soviet Communists in the 1920s the Party was supreme — a man's father, mother and god all rolled into one. To doubt its authority or wisdom was to go against every notion of duty, honour and commitment, and my father dedicated himself to an ideal in which he believed passionately.

For us, his children, much of his early life remained cloaked in mystery. Just as he preferred not to talk about the food-gathering, so he said little about his own family. My mother once mentioned that he had a brother and a sister, but by the time I was born they had disappeared, and I never met this phantom uncle and aunt. The same was true of his parents, who seem to have vanished in the mighty upheavals that followed the revolution and the civil war.

At some date in the 1920s he got married for the first time — but to whom, I never knew, for he concealed the details from us. Uncertainty about this key event tantalized my elder brother Vasilko and me for years: once, just after I had joined the KGB, I was thrilled by the chance discovery of another Gordievksy, who seemed the right age to be my half-brother. Suddenly coming on his file, I whipped it open in the hope that I had stumbled on a long-lost relation — but no, he was Anatoli Georgiyevich, a Far Eastern specialist born in Vladivostok, whose patronymic showed that he had no connection with us. Whether or not my father had a child by that first marriage we never discovered; no doubt he concealed these details of his past so as not to upset his second family.

Obviously he did well at his job in the food sector, for in 1931 he was sent as deputy leader of an expedition to Georgia, which was then relatively unknown in Moscow. The aim of the team — part scientific, part practical — was to assess the agricultural potential of an area recognized as a valuable source of citrus fruit, but also producing other fruit, tea and cotton. The expedition was led by a prominent Polish Communist who had been gaoled in his own country for subversive activities, and then swapped for Polish Catholic priests held prisoner in Russia: a Jew, he was an able man, and he got on well with my father, who generally liked Jews, finding them warm, intelligent people whose lack of political rights in Russia gave them a leaning towards the Bolsheviks.[1]

Not that the 1931 expedition was taxing for its leaders. They must have made various research trips to the interior of Georgia, but they also spent several summer months based at Gagra, a lovely resort on the Black Sea coast, with a fine beach, luxuriant vegetation and mountains rising steeply behind the little town. In those romantic surroundings my father fell in love with one of the junior members of his team, Olga Nikolayevna Gornova.

My mother also had far-flung antecedents. In the second half of the nineteenth century her family lived in the Cossack-dominated territory near Rostov, south of the Don; but there the Cossacks were the elite, difficult and arrogant, and my grandparents belonged to the second tier of relative newcomers, who were not readily admitted to the higher echelons of society. This they found uncomfortable — so when, in the 1890s, they heard that the Tsarist government was offering free land to Russians prepared to settle as colonists in Central Asia, they seized the chance, piled all their possessions into a cart, and trekked eastwards for several months into the wilds of what was then called Turkestan (it is now Kazakhstan). There they were allocated some land near Chimkent. My grandmother always, and my mother often, spoke of Turkestan rather than Central Asia.

For a while they worked their new patch, but then my grandfather made some kind of a deal, as a result of which he became manager of a stud farm on the outskirts of the city. The owner of the establishment, a retired army officer, was known as the *pomeshtchik*, or landlord, and

---

1   Many prominent Bolsheviks, like Lenin, and outstanding intellectuals such as Korolenko and Gorky, had a high regard for Jews, and tried to help them. Later I found that I had inherited my father's sympathy for them.

it may be that my grandfather allowed him to use some of our land in return for being appointed manager of the stud. He and my grandmother both loved horses: even the smell of manure was wonderful to them, for horses were their life. Some of the stud's output was sold to the Russian army, but every now and then my father would take the latest batch and herd them across the steppes to Urumchi, in Sinkiang, where they sold at a good price. (At that time Russia had close ties with Sinkiang, but the Chinese government were not much interested in their remote western province.)

The *pomeshtchik*, being a good-natured man, paid for several of my grandparents' seven children to go to school. First came Anna, Aleksandr and Yevgenia, with my mother, Olga, fourth, in the middle, and then Konstantin, Valentina and Faina. Anna and Aleksandr were born early enough to receive a full education; Yevgenia got all but one year, but my mother had been at school for only two years when the revolution swept away the entire system of private education. After an interval she began again at the United Soviet School in Chimkent.

In Kazakhstan, as elsewhere, the Bolshevik uprising threw everything into chaos. The stud farm was destroyed and my grandfather lost his job. When the civil war began in 1919, boys who had been good friends at school rushed off aged eighteen or nineteen to fight on opposite sides. Most of the students from the Gymnasium turned out for the Whites, fighting for Admiral Kolchak, partly because they were naturally patriotic, and partly because they sensed a tyrannical tendency among the Bolsheviks; but, according to my grandmother, the situation became so confused that it was often difficult to remember who was on which side.

Somehow my grandparents survived, and in the early 1920s when Lenin launched his New Economic Policy, which aimed to restore agriculture and get some small private industries going again, my grandfather was one of the many people who took the initiative seriously. Having long dreamed of owning a water-mill, which would grind corn for the farmers of the district, he now put all his savings into just such an enterprise. For a year or two it flourished, but then, in 1928, the government seized it from him, and he was classified as a *kulak*, or rich peasant. He died in 1931, a broken man.

My mother, meanwhile, had gone to Moscow, probably in 1927 when she was twenty, to train at the Moscow Economic Institute, with the aim of becoming a statistician. For a girl brought up in the provinces, this must have been a drastic change; but she persevered with her studies, and was in the fourth year of her course when, as a trainee, she gained a place on the expedition to the Caucasus. At the age of twenty-four she had fine black hair and handsome dark eyes — in photographs I see resemblances to my own daughter Anna — and when she met Anton Lavrentiyevich Gordievsky, they quickly fell in love.

Not that they got married: it was regarded as bad manners for a Communist to go through any form of wedding ceremony. The fashionable leftist ideology then prevalent held that it was both unnecessary and undesirable for a man to marry: if he loved a woman, and she bore his children, it was purely a matter of honour that he should stay with her and support her. There was no need for any such foolish and archaic ceremony as a marriage service. So in 1932 my parents began to live together in a flat in Moscow, and my brother was born in 1933. (They did eventually get married in 1945, after Stalin had issued a new set of laws in an attempt to restore family life and increase the number of children being born. By then they had three children, and had been together thirteen years. Because both their surnames began with G — Gordievsky and Gornova — I believed for years that only men and women with the same initials married each other.)

Until 1932 my father had continued working in food production, distribution and trade, always more as a member of the Party than as an economist. He used to recall, with some sadness, that in the 1920s he had been considered as a candidate to be sent on a Soviet trade mission to Hamburg, and if he had gone, he might well have remained in the Ministry of Foreign Trade for the rest of his career. Yet it was probably fortunate for him that he did not go since, during the Great Terror of the 1930s, officials of that ministry suffered badly from Stalin's repressions, and he could easily have been liquidated.

Instead, he was called up into the OGPU, forerunner of the NKVD, which itself was the forerunner of the KGB. For ease of reference, I shall describe him, henceforth, as a member of the NKVD or KGB, which was already a huge organization, and growing fast, an independent department with influence and power as great as that of the Red Army — in effect an empire within the State. At that date the Party was sending its best sons to strengthen the Soviet armed forces, and my father became an officer of the Polit Directorate of the Borderguard Troops, his job being to act as the eyes and ears of the Party among the soldiers, lecture members of the armed forces on the political situation, and carry out political indoctrination. I imagine he cut rather an academic figure, for he wore steel-rimmed pince-nez and followed the German custom of keeping his head completely shaved — perhaps to conceal that he had lost most of his hair in early middle age.

Membership of the NKVD brought valuable privileges, not the least of which was a place to live. Like everything in Moscow, accommodation was short: before the revolution the city had had a population of about 800,000, but after rapid social, economic and industrial development it grew to 8 million in the 1970s. During the 1920s and 1930s there was no mass-building programme, no answer to the population explosion: the only new blocks being built contained flats for senior officials and officers, and most people were crammed into the big old apartments from which the bourgeois inhabitants had been evicted. A normal flat, which before the revolution had had four bedrooms, a sitting room, dining room and servants' room, now had a different family living in each room and sharing common facilities. My parents were lucky enough to be in a flat shared with only two other families.

All the same, their life in the 1930s was a dire struggle. In the famine of 1933-34 food ran out: people arriving in Moscow from the Ukraine and the centre of Russia told appalling stories of death from hunger. The Ukrainians, in particular, felt that the starvation was deliberate, that Stalin was punishing their nation. Certainly troops were sent out to the villages to exact the norm of grain and other produce from every *oblast* (province) and *rayon* (district); most of the soldiers were NKVD, well fed, with their own weapons and uniforms, and commanded by brutal, ideologically dedicated officers. Yet so awful were the scenes of devastation — mothers dying with babies in their arms, people resorting to cannibalism — that even some of these officers committed suicide or had mental breakdowns after directing raids.

All this, of course, was deeply repugnant to my father: he tried to believe that most of the stories were not true, and that those which were true were somehow inevitable. From later conversations with my mother, I know that he was reluctant to discuss the famine with her, but she, being a more practical and down-to-earth person, talked about it a good deal, especially with her own mother, my grandmother, Lukeria Grigoriyevna.

In Moscow all food was rationed, and ration cards were issued for basic commodities, including soap and flour. The system was particularly tough on old people such as my grandmother, for they were simply left out, and received no cards or rations. Our own family life was made easier with my father being a member of the armed forces. Besides their normal rations, NKVD officers were entitled to something called *payok*, a share of food available in special shops closed to outsiders. There they could buy small quantities of basic supplies such as eggs, butter, sugar and meat. In spite of this, I often wondered whether my brother, who was born in 1933 and grew up in the worst of the shortages, may have suffered from malnutrition for he was never robust, and even as a young man tired easily.

Still more difficult for my father to stomach than rationing were Stalin's political purges, which reached their nadir in the second half of the 1930s. The first show trial took place in Moscow in 1936, another in 1937, and that of Stalin's old rival Mikhail Bukharin in 1938. The dreaded new phrase 'Enemy of the People' was on everyone's lips, and victims began to disappear at a terrifying rate as the NKVD conceived the notion of 'concrete results'. Years later, when I was an officer in the KGB, a concrete result was the recruitment of a foreign citizen as a spy for the Soviet Union. In the 1930s the term was the equivalent of *vyshka*, literally a tower or jumping-off point, but figuratively capital punishment: from on high came the highest penalty, *vyshka*. NKVD officers were assessed according to the amount of capital punishment they were able to bring about: the number of people shot as a result of their investigations.

For my father, the worst period came when not merely outsiders but men from within the NKVD itself began to disappear, and the arrests seemed random. The process gathered a momentum of its own as prisoners made wild confessions to escape further torture. When interrogators kept demanding, 'Who was in the conspiracy?' men gave any names they could think of, even of people in no way involved, and each new list would feed the flames. You could never tell who might betray you: someone with whom you had had a trivial argument, years before, might denounce you as an Enemy of the People, a terrorist, a spy, an anti-Soviet, a secret Trotskyist — the NKVD had any number of categories of traitor. One of the victims closest to my parents was the Pole who had led the 1931 expedition to the Caucasus. Like most of the Polish Communist Party, who were in exile in the Soviet Union, he was arrested and executed as a foreign spy.[2]

My father never talked to me about that time, but my mother and grandmother often told me how terrified they were, not least at night when they lay awake listening for the tramp of boots as arrest parties stormed up the communal staircase of the building in which they lived. Of the twenty-eight flats in the block, a quarter were raided. Usually the team took away the man first, and returned for the rest of the family later. In the worst period of all, from the spring of 1937 to the autumn of 1938, there were at least fifteen visits by secret police and their henchmen, torturers and butchers, coming to seize people in the middle of the night. The victims were led out and driven away in black cars known as *voronki*, or little black ravens, a scene memorably caught by the poet Yevgeny Yevtushenko with the line:

I remember that little van with the slogan BREAD written on it.

My mother was far too sensible to accept propaganda at face value. Not being brainwashed by going to an office or sitting through interminable speeches at Party meetings and seminars, she retained her

---

2 One minor consequence of his downfall was that all trace of him had to be expunged from official records, and group photographs of the expedition were destroyed. In the same way, numerous political books published in the 1920s and 1930s had to be expurgated to remove references to figures who had been declared enemies of the people. One prominent victim was Lev Kamenev, a chief editor of the first edition of Lenin's works, whose long introductions and supplementary articles suddenly became suspect.

sense of proportion and realized that there could not possibly be as many genuine Enemies of the People as the authorities were claiming: criminals and traitors simply could not exist in such numbers. Yet when she protested to my father, he brushed her worries aside and sometimes became indignant. He would quote the slogan, 'The NKVD is always right!', and claimed that there must be some good reason behind every arrest. Much later, when I asked him about the techniques of the NKVD in those days, he would say, 'Oh, I understand the main method was recruiting agents, or secret informers.' That was true, as far as it went, for in the 1930s the network of contacts became immense, and it was rumoured that the NKVD's ambition was to turn every third adult into an informer. All the same, I believe my father's faith in Communism must have been severely tried by the savagery of Stalin's campaign.

Even though our immediate family remained intact, retribution fell on my uncle Aleksandr (my mother's eldest brother), an agronomist, who was arrested in 1938, declared an Enemy of the People, and sentenced to ten years at a prison camp in eastern Siberia — somebody must have denounced him for making critical remarks about the collectivization of agriculture. He managed, however, to turn his ill luck to advantage, for, being a skilled gardener, he began to grow vegetables and became one of the most influential inmates of the camp, producing fresh vegetables for the tables of the KGB bosses. In 1948, when his time was up, he was in theory a free man; but he was not allowed to return home and in effect was an exile. No matter: he became head of an enterprise growing vegetables in greenhouses, and made himself, by Soviet standards, a wealthy man. Then, after Stalin's death in 1953, he was allowed to come to Moscow, and I saw him for the first time — a lively, amusing and energetic man, looking forward to whatever was left to him. He told me how he had always loved beer but how, during his ten years in the camp, he had never had a drop of alcohol. The prison town was so far from civilization, cut off without roads or railways, that to import beer (which is 95 per cent water) or even vodka (60 per cent water) would have been prohibitively expensive: the only liquor available was *spirt*, 96 per cent alcohol brought in from Khabarovsk, or sometimes purloined from hospitals and airforce bases. In spite (or perhaps because) of his long deprivation, Aleksandr became a connoisseur of beer, and when he came to Moscow, he made a point of seeking out every variety he could find.

Alas, after only two years he died of a heart attack, his health undermined by life in the camp. After his arrest in 1938, his wife had been left behind in Samarkand; in due course he heard that she had disassociated herself from him, so he took up with a woman who had also been a prisoner, and began to live with her. She survived him, and became more or less a member of our family, a friendly and kind woman who visited us often.

After his death my grandmother decided to fight for his rehabilitation so we could clear his name and recover any confiscated property that might remain. Inevitably the process was slow, because the authorities — in any case bureaucratic and unsympathetic — were besieged by thousands of similar claims; but Lukeria Grigoriyevna pursued the case indefatigably, writing letters, filling in forms and visiting government offices. By then her back was severely bent with arthritis, and she walked leaning forward almost horizontally, with her hands folded on the base of her spine — an attitude which made people ask us why we did not get her some treatment. We had tried but nothing could be done, and I am afraid she must have suffered great pain; but her will was indomitable, and in the end she secured Aleksandr's certificate of exoneration. By the time I was fifteen I knew his whole story, which I found illustrative and educational.

Another strong influence was my uncle Konstantin, my mother's younger brother, a humble, modest man, but one of earthy common sense, who became a veterinary practitioner. At the time when the charlatan biologist Trofim Lysenko was all the rage, with his quack theories that genes did not exist in plants, Konstantin would come to us saying, 'This is nonsense! It's incredible. How can anyone listen to him? Of course genes exist. We knew about them before the war.' Listening to such obvious good sense, I began moving towards the rejection of a society which could habitually commit crimes like persecuting scientists because they told the truth.[3]

*

I was born in Moscow on 10 October 1938, just as the blackest period was ending, but my first faint memory dates from the autumn of 1941 when I was nearly three. By then the Germans were bombing Moscow, and together with my brother I was taken down into an unfinished Metro station, which was being used as a shelter. The escalators were not working, so we had to walk down a long flight of steps to a tunnel packed with people.

My father was working all out as a political lecturer to the troops. When Hitler's armies invaded the Soviet Union on 22 June 1941, he was too old (at forty-five) and too short-sighted to be sent to the front, and he never took part in any fighting, something of which he was secretly ashamed. Yet when I grew up I learned from my cousin Valentin what a brilliant orator he was. As a boy of sixteen Valentin went to one of my father's lectures, which was given in a summer theatre — an open auditorium with benches all round. For

---

3 Lysenko was president of the Lenin Academy of Agriculture until the early 1950s, when he was denounced and dismissed by Nikita Khrushchev.

forty-five minutes he held forth on the international situation and the latest position at the front. He spoke with unfaltering brilliance, beginning on a high note, but raising his tone steadily all the time until he finished in a crescendo with two slogans coined by Stalin which had become a ritual: 'OUR CAUSE IS THE RIGHT ONE!' and 'VICTORY WILL BE OURS!' By then the audience was ready to explode, and it did: people leapt to their feet and roared out a standing ovation. Valentin was immensely impressed by my father's ability to rouse his listeners and ignite their fervour. He may have been dishing out propaganda to the masses, but clearly he did it with exceptional panache.

As the Germans advanced rapidly towards Moscow in the late summer of 1941, government departments and foreign embassies began to pull out and evacuate themselves to Kuybyshev, a town on the Volga once (and now again) called Samara. On 16 October there was panic in the capital when people thought that the Germans were going to take the city: widespread looting broke out, and a special regiment of NKVD troops was formed to defend the place to the last, like kamikaze warriors.

Our own family was evacuated to Kuybyshev, where my father was working temporarily, but the town became so crowded with refugees that, after a short period there, he arranged for us to be sent on to Przhevalsk, in Kirgizia, almost on the Chinese border. There, in the town named after the explorer and geographer Colonel N. M. Przhevalsky (an officer of the Russian army who discovered a species of wild horse), a unit of Borderguard troops was stationed to look after the families of officers who remained in Moscow or were at the front.

Przhevalsk is the first place of which I have any clear recollection. A typical Russian colonial town, it had beautiful streets of brick houses painted white, and the tall, slim poplars which smell so sweet after rain. Lying nearly a thousand metres above sea-level, the place had a comfortable climate, with crisp, dry frost in the winter, and temperate summers. My father never came there, because it was too far away from his work, and I imagine that my mother must have been lonely, but for two years we lived comfortably enough in lodgings allocated to us. The owner of the house kept a pig, of which my brother and I became fond, and when it was about to be killed for the New Year, my mother made us stay in our room so that we did not witness its slaughter. But then, as soon as it was dead, someone spread a rug over its body, and Vasilko and I sat on it without worrying.

Other odd recollections filter back through the mist of time. I remember being embarrassed by my shoes, which were old, with torn uppers. I remember going to play among the wooden benches of an outdoor theatre in which, because there was nobody to keep it tidy, wild flowers were growing. On our way to Frunze (now Bishkek), to catch the train back to Moscow, we were driven round the end of the Issuk Kul lake, and I was astonished by the mountains rising steeply from the shores of that vast expanse of water. Then in Frunze flowers again made a strong impression: as we waited for something, we sat in a well-kept square, and the warm September evening air was loaded with the smell of tobacco plants. To this day the sweet, almost sickly scent of nicotiana brings back the scene in every detail. Finally, when we reached Moscow and emerged from the Kazan station into Komsomolskaya Square, I was enormously impressed by the sight of a train crossing above the lower tracks on a viaduct — a train high up in the sky.

By then, the autumn of 1943, Moscow seemed relatively safe. After the great battles of Stalingrad, in January and February, and Kursk, in the summer, the German armies were on the retreat, and it was clear they would never return or bomb the Soviet capital again. My father had managed to secure us a flat, close to the notorious Butyrky prison, in a solidly built Tsarist barracks which had once housed soldiers guarding the gaol. It was there that I grew up. The surroundings were hardly salubrious, for Butyrky was to Moscow what Moabit was to Berlin: a prison with a hideous past. Often, as we walked round it, we would watch a car approach the entrance and marvel at the way in which, as the guard pressed a button, the huge metal gate would slide back into one wall. Beyond that gate was another of the same kind, so that every vehicle going in or out was caught in a lock. From the little balcony of our flat we could see the circular eighteenth-century brick tower containing cells, in which countless people had suffered.

In spite of our proximity to the gloomy prison, for a boy of five Moscow seemed a fine place. There were few people — so many having gone away to, or because of, the war — and practically no traffic. The city was clean, and there were still some streets of wooden houses, with gardens in front and behind, where lilac bloomed in the spring. In the main thoroughfares, though, all the trees had gone, cut down on the orders of Stalin and Kaganovich, who regarded trees as unnecessary and got rid of them when they started trying to rebuild the capital. Our own road was Lesnaya Ulitza, or Wood Street, so called because it had once been a timber market.

The building next door to ours contained a curious relic. On one wall was an ancient, pre-revolutionary sign, including some of the letters which the Bolsheviks abolished, and proclaiming KALANDADZE WHOLESALE COMPANY FOR CAUCASIAN FRUIT. The place had been a clandestine print shop, in which Bolshevik leaflets were produced from a press hidden in the basement. In my day it was kept as a little museum, and the ground floor looked like an old-fashioned merchant's office, where you could put in an order for fruit from the south.

One of my most vivid childhood memories dates from the winter of 1944, when I was just over six. The authorities, having decided to stage a major propaganda event, announced that on a certain day German prisoners of war would be paraded through the city. The newspapers carried preliminary articles describing how these men had invaded a peaceful country, but were now beaten, and inciting Muscovites to turn out to see them.

Out we went with my mother to watch — and an unforgettable event it proved. On a dry, cold day, with no snow lying, an endless column of men marched past, most still wearing some sort of uniform, and shepherded by a few guards with machine-guns. The crowd stood silent: nobody jeered or threw anything, and nobody even muttered, for people simply did not know how to react. Later it occurred to me that they were struck by the sudden realization that these Germans were human beings caught in an unpleasant situation, trapped, guarded and led like animals. Many had nice faces, but their expressions were sad as death. Obviously they knew that the parade had been laid on to humiliate them and whip up anti-Nazi hatred, but the crowd could not feel that these men were their bitter enemies, and the spectators remained inert. All the same, the march was a propaganda success, since films of it were shown in numerous countries abroad, demonstrating once and for all that Moscow had never surrendered to Hitler's invading horde.

*

Vasilko and I got on well, but because he was five years older we were never particularly close. Even so, we spent a good deal of time together, and one of our favourite resorts was the colossal wreck of the Aleksandr Nevsky church in Miussky Square, not far from our home.

The authorities had tried to blow up the building, but so massive was its construction that they had failed to demolish it, and its ruin, full of crumbling brick arches, furnished us with a thrilling playground, extensive by any standards but positively immense to a small boy. (The ruins remained until late in the 1960s; then at last they were demolished and a Young Pioneer house of pretentious modern design went up in their place — a typical, shabby Soviet building covered with coloured plastic panels, which made a sad contrast with the grandeur of the church.) We also loved going to Gorki Park, where German tanks, guns, aircraft, cars, motorcycles and other equipment were permanently exhibited along the river front.

Vasilko's favourite place, however, was the garage in the courtyard behind our block of flats. The yard housed a car workshop, with some spaces for the vehicles of KGB officers who lived in the next block; there were also rows upon rows of German motorcycles, together with a mass of spare parts — wheels, gearboxes, and a whole mountain of tyres over which we used to climb. The place was used as a base by a few professional motorbike racers, including the legendary Korol (Russian for King), then the Soviet champion, who occupied one of the ground-floor flats. At the age of twelve my brother became fascinated by motorbikes, and developed a passion for everything mechanical and technical — cars, typewriters, radios. He was naturally good with his hands, and the courtyard confirmed his bent.

Looking back, I know that we must have lived on a basic diet: we regarded sugar, for instance, as a rare luxury, so hard was it to come by. But I never remember going hungry, and I believe that as a family we owed a great deal to my grandmother. A resolute woman with the true common sense of a peasant, she was determined not to become a parasite in middle and old age; she therefore travelled from one daughter to another, giving help to whatever branch of her family needed it most.

Being semi-literate, and knowing no better, she wrote whole letters without any division between the words — luckily her children could decipher them. She was a sound Christian: she knew a good deal about the Gospels and the life of Jesus, and quietly tried to introduce her grandchildren to Christianity. It was alleged that she had my brother baptized in secret, and had been on her way to church to baptize me when she was intercepted by my father. The discovery gave him an awful shock: for one thing, he was by then an atheist, and for another, 1938 was the year of the worst purges. If word had got out that his child had been baptized, the authorities could easily have had him shot: the secret practice of religion would certainly have been a capital offence. When he caught her in the act, he told her off in the most forceful terms, and she was terrified. As a result, I was never baptized. Nevertheless, my grandmother persisted in her faith: as I grew older, she told me about religious ceremonies, and extolled the beauty of Russian Orthodox services, and her words gave me a long-lasting interest in religion. She was fascinated by the life of Christ, and knew every detail of it: she had a particularly soft spot for donkeys, because Jesus had ridden into Jerusalem on an ass.

Not the least of Lukeria's virtues was her excellence as a cook. No one could make better *pirogi*, the big open pies filled with spiced meat which all Russians adore, or *piroshki*, tiny pancakes stuffed with meat, fish, cabbage and egg. She also produced wonderful *pilmeni*, or little dumplings, with a wide variety of fillings. Our family had some connection with the Urals, where people made a special type of Siberian dumpling, and our grandmother knew everything there was to know about making them. If we had company, she would have at least three pots of them on the boil. When the first lot were ready, out they would come: each person would get a dozen or so, and we would eat them with salt, pepper, mustard and vinegar, the men washing them down with vodka. As soon as the first helping had been eaten, the next would be served — and when we were growing boys, we could put away incredible numbers.

'*Bratik*,' I would gasp at Vasilko, 'I've eaten forty!'

'That's nothing,' he would groan. 'I've eaten fifty-five!'

Another vivid snatch of memory dates from the end of the war. One day I was sitting in the courtyard of our block when some boy came running and shouting, 'Have you heard the news?'

'No, what?'

'You've got a sister!'

That was Marina, born on 31 March 1945. Five weeks later, on 9 May, we celebrated Victory Day, one day behind Western Europe as a result of difficulties caused by Stalin's demand that the Germans should surrender to him as well as to the rest of the Allies.

One man who brought fun and excitement into our lives was our cousin Igor Yashkin, son of Aunt Yevgenia. An airforce navigator, who flew in some of the first jets, he served in the squadron commanded by Vassily Stalin, son of the dictator; and twice a year, on 1 May and 7 November, this crack unit took part in the ceremonial fly-past over Red Square. After each big occasion the members of the squadron went on leave and blew their pay on drink and debauchery: it was on those leaves that Igor would visit us, always sparkling with life and jokes, a marvellous raconteur, especially at table. Alas, drink got the better of him in the end, and he finished his career as an impoverished air-controller.

During our stay in Kirgizia I had escaped kindergarten, because my mother was not working and was at home to look after me. But by the age of five or six I had learned to read — taught by her, I imagine — and from my earliest days I was fascinated by the written word. In 1945, while still only six, I began to read a weekly magazine called *British Ally*, published in Russian by the British Embassy in Moscow, and I also made a start on the *Literary Gazette*, which, although of course I could not appreciate it, was much better written than most Party publications. Thus when the time came for me to start school in September 1946, I was eager to begin learning properly.

Chapter Three – School Days

School No. 130 lay within easy walking distance of home, only a couple of blocks along Lesnaya Ulitsa, which was one of the reasons my mother chose it. The building, put up in the 1930s, was like dozens of others in Moscow erected at that time: plain, with four storeys and basic classrooms. The classes were very large — between thirty-seven and forty-two — and the standard of the pupils varied widely. When I joined, they were all boys, and about a third of them were from the *lumpen* proletariat: they lived in slums directly behind the building, and had little interest in learning.

By Moscow standards our school was only medium-sized, with just over a thousand children, but the building was used to capacity, with everybody, pupils and staff alike, working in two shifts. The first started at 8.30 a.m., and the second at 2.30 p.m., each working day being of six hours, with short breaks between periods. There was a small canteen, and some boys had a few kopeks with which they bought sausages and bread rolls, but most of us regarded such expenditure as folly, and saw no need to eat while at school: after all, we had breakfast or lunch before we started, and another meal when we got home.

When I first went to school, almost all the teachers were women;

the male population had been so drastically diminished by the war that there were very few men teachers left. Our own form teacher was a girl of twenty-two, just out of university. Thousands of women were without husbands, and although the prospect of finding a partner was so poor, many were desperate to have children, purely so that they would not be lonely in old age. I suppose, therefore, it was hardly surprising that in the middle of my school career one of the teachers, aged almost forty, became pregnant by a sixteen-year-old pupil. Nevertheless, the news caused a sensation, and made me start to think seriously about relations between the sexes. I am glad to say that in this instance the authorities, who were often brutally censorious over moral issues, decided to damp the affair down: the teacher had the baby and was allowed to keep her job.

Our school facilities were simple. The only commodity of which we had a good supply was ink, which came in powdered form, and had to be mixed with water. Apart from blackboard and chalk, the staff had no equipment — nothing so up-to-date as a slide projector or magic lantern. Luckily for me there were two exceptionally intelligent boys in my form. One was Alfred Shmelkin, like his physicist father a brilliant mathematician; the other, Viktor Pismenny, was the son of an army officer who had died during the Finnish war, and had been posthumously decorated with the highest order of the Soviet Union. We three formed a nucleus in our class and drove each other on, the other two leading in scientific subjects, I in history and languages. Our teacher was glad to have at least three boys who showed real interest in their work, and she gave us more than our share of attention. (Viktor later became an engineer but because his father was Jewish, he was never allowed to join the operational KGB, and could only work in the organization's maintenance and administrative Directorate.

That his father was a Hero of the Soviet Union could not defeat the entrenched anti-Semitism. Alfred Shmelkin, however, who was also Jewish, managed to defeat the system. Even in the mathematics faculty of Moscow University the authorities tried to create obstacles for Jews, but Alfred's gifts were so outstanding that he overcame them, and worked there with distinction.)

Once a week we had a physical culture period, but facilities for sports were minimal: the sports hall was only the size of two classrooms put together and, apart from gymnastics, we could only play basketball. Instinctively I felt deprived: although too young to realize that I needed regular exercise, I wanted to play more games and now I much regret that I did not discover badminton when I was ten or so. Had I made an early start, I might have become quite good at the game, because it suited me well: tactics are subtle and complicated, as the shuttlecock, slowing down in the final few seconds of its flight, gives a player the chance to use his wits and change his shot at the last moment. This I enjoyed, but as I did not try the game until I was thirty, I never achieved my full potential at it.

When I was ten or eleven my mother took me along to the Dynamo stadium (Dynamo being the sports club of the KGB and the Ministry of the Interior). There I belatedly discovered that she was not well educated in certain areas, for I found that she knew nothing about sport. Rather than telling me about the choices available, she simply asked which club I would like to join. I, being even more ignorant, showed no initiative and let her put me down for the most obvious, gymnastics, which I soon found I hated. One day I was sitting in the gym, waiting for my turn on the rings, when a group of boys ran into the room with glowing cheeks and the aura of the great outdoors about them: they were members of the Track and Field Club, and I looked at them longingly, thinking, '*That's* what I'd like to do — to run.' But I was much too timid and well disciplined to speak up.

In winter the opportunities for outdoor exercise were better. We could ski cross-country through the woods outside Moscow, and within the city there were numerous places where we could skate, among them Gorky Park, where extensive areas were covered with ice, and particularly the huge monument to the achievements of the Soviet Union's economy, a vast, Stalinist edifice like a cluster of temples, where the flat spaces between buildings were flooded to make rinks. In the basement of the main building there were changing-rooms, and we would skate for two or three hours at a time to music blaring out over loudspeakers. Even in our own courtyard winter snow gave us endless free entertainment; one year it was so deep — maybe as much as 2.5 metres where it had been shovelled off the paths and piled against the walls — that we dug ourselves a whole system of chambers, tunnels and vertical shafts, and spent many happy hours down there, like moles.

At home we were poor. Our flat was on the top floor, and the roof constantly leaked in spite of frequent repairs. My father wore his military uniform day in, day out, simply because he had no decent civilian clothes, even though he held the relatively senior rank of lieutenant colonel. I see him now in his mid-green tunic, with blue piping on the epaulettes and lapels. My mother owned only a couple of the most ordinary dresses, and, with three children to bring up, she had to calculate and save every kopek. This habit of economizing made her modest and self-effacing in all she did.

For the first two years after the war food remained scarce, and we were short of many basic necessities; in summer my mother worked on a collective farm near Moscow, so that at least we had potatoes and other vegetables, and in autumn we went into the forest to pick mushrooms, holding competitions among ourselves to see who could find most, especially boletus, which we regarded as the most delicious kind.

My father was a voracious reader, and he passed on his habit to me by reading aloud to us in the evenings. He was also a strict disciplinarian, and insisted on the highest standards of honesty: he never raised a hand against us children but when necessary gave us a severe verbal dressing-down. In later life it struck me as strange that a man who had such a clear perception of right and wrong could be so blind about the monstrous injustice of Stalin's regime.

Throughout all their difficulties my parents remained unquenchably optimistic, and whenever we boys complained, my mother would say, 'Never mind! Things are getting better all the time. Soon there's going to be a money reform, and after that rationing will be abolished. Then we'll be able to buy white bread, and as much sugar as you want. Think of that!'

We did think of that, all the time. 'Mum,' we would beg, 'just buy us a kilo of sugar, and we'll eat the whole lot!' We spent hours dreaming not of luxuries such as chocolate, which we had never seen, but of something as ordinary as plain sugar.

In 1947 the authorities did indeed bring in a money reform — a clever one, in which many people lost their savings. Soon after that rationing ended, and citizens could spend what money they had on things they wanted. On the day after the reform my mother went to the bakery and bought the most beautiful loaf of white bread; after the grey and black bread on which we had been living this seemed a miracle of deliciousness, and somehow the sugar we had craved became of lesser importance. Yet the flour shortage persisted into the 1950s. Muscovites knew that some days before every New Year a fresh consignment of flour would arrive in the shops, and immense queues would form, often of more than a thousand people. On the whole discipline was good: everyone in the queue would have a number written in ink on his or her hand — 1227 — and you could go away from time to time, without losing your place. All the same there was a certain amount of cheating: each person was supposed to get a three-kilo packet, but sometimes, having queued once, we would join the line again at the end.

By the time I was ten I had become a fluent reader, helped by the fact that our flat was always full of newspapers, magazines and books. Out of ignorance, my mother kept me reading children's books for too long, so that I fell behind in my knowledge of fiction. In political matters, on the other hand, I was way ahead: by the age of ten I was keenly interested in Marshal Tito's defiance of Stalin in Yugoslavia. My father was obliged by KGB rules to subscribe to at least three political periodicals — *Pravda*, *Bolshevik* (later renamed *Communist*), and *Pogranichnik*, the organ of the Borderguard troops, so that I never had any shortage of solid reading material. While still at school I began to study the third edition of the collected works of Lenin, published between 1929 and 1933. The notes in these volumes contained fascinating information about all the characters involved, most of which was removed from the fourth edition, published after the war.

Both at school and at home, various factors pushed me in the direction of the German language. My brother began to learn it, and started to take a German newspaper, which I tried to puzzle out. Then in my third year of school, when I was ten, I started to study German. In a cupboard at home I found a number of children's books in German, published before the war in the Republic of the Volga (the most prosperous administrative territory in the Soviet Union until 1941 when Stalin destroyed it by sending its inhabitants to Siberia). One day at school my teacher saw me trying to write in Gothic *Schrift*: she was amused, and asked me to write my homework in it. Only then did I realize that she could read it, and I asked her how she had learnt. 'Oh,' she said, 'it was my job during the war. Like many people who spoke German, I spent months sitting in camps for prisoners-of-war, and it was my task to read through their letters home.'

The school library was poor, but when I was eleven or twelve my father managed to get me accepted as a student member of the Central House of the Soviet Army, even though he was a KGB officer rather than a regular soldier. There I found an excellent library, and started to read more widely. The centre also organized conferences, at which boys and girls would talk about books they had read, and a writer of children's stories would give talks. In my time the most popular speaker was Lev Kassil, a leading author of the day, who always attracted big audiences.

There was also a small element of speech and drama, and I much enjoyed taking part in two plays, once in Gogol's *The Government Inspector*, and once in a sketch which we put together out of Chekhov's short story *The Transgressor*. In this an interrogator is questioning a peasant who has been caught unscrewing a bolt from the railway line to act as a weight for his fishing tackle. 'Don't you realize?' the interrogator asks. 'You could have weakened the track and caused an accident. You might have killed somebody.' But the peasant is so simpleminded, so utterly incapable of abstract thought, that he cannot grasp the chain of events presented to him. This seemed to me hilarious — so much so that I got the giggles, and was reprimanded.

Our school holidays were unevenly spaced: we got twelve days off over the New Year, three months in the summer and, apart from two-day breaks between terms, that was all. Our four terms were arbitrarily divided up. One ran from 1 September to 6 November, the next from

9 November to 29 December. Then came our winter holiday, from 30 December to 12 January, followed by a term which ran until early April, with the fourth succeeding it after a couple of days.

Christmas, which had been abolished in the 1930s after a series of artificially staged demonstrations and rallies against religion, did not feature in our lives. Even so, I was aware that the subject had caused problems among the Party theorists. Until the revolution Russians had celebrated Christ's birth exactly as people do in the West, with decorated trees, Nativity plays, special church services and so on. Then came the Stalinist ban; but later one of the Communist hierarchy suggested that everything to do with the festival should be reintroduced, bar Christ and all religious connotations. So trees and decorations were allowed again, but the paraphernalia of the European Christmas were transferred to the New Year, which was always the occasion for a great feast.

Presents would be bought, and stocks of favourite food laid in — cold meats, smoked salmon, home-made fish and meat jellies with plenty of garlic and, above all, sturgeon, cold-smoked, hot-smoked or fresh and poached. Some people might buy a goose, and cold chicken might feature as part of the *zakuska*, or hors d'oeuvre, but on the whole birds played little part in the festival. Dinner would start about 9 p.m. on New Year's Eve, the food being washed down with vodka, beer and wine. Most families had relatives in the Urals, Central Asia or Siberia, so there was always the excuse to drink *their* New Year in as well, an hour or two ahead of Moscow time. Thus there might be one round of toasts at 10 p.m. and another at 11 p.m., before the real moment came at midnight. Then we would say goodbye to the old year: generally somebody had a radio on (or later television), and there would be a short speech from one of the political leaders. Most people hated this: what they wanted to hear were the chimes of the big clock on the Spassky Tower of the Kremlin. Nobody was quite sure which chime signalled the New Year — the first or last stroke of twelve. No matter: they would drink a toast in cheap, sweet Soviet champagne, and then go back to vodka or brandy (which, being twice the price of vodka, was regarded as a sign of prosperity).

As children we were never allowed spirits, only a glass or two of wine, and now, looking back, I remember how abstemious my father was. He certainly liked his food, but he drank very little: he used to pour a bottle of vodka into a decanter, add some slices of lemon peel, and stand the mixture on the sideboard. It would remain there for weeks, with the level scarcely going down, because he would have a tot only now and then, on special occasions. Other people, of course, drank much more, but nothing like they did in the 1970s and 1980s, the era of stagnation, when religion and ideals alike were lost, the future was obscure, and people consoled themselves so heavily that alcoholism became a national catastrophe.

*

From 1946, when I was nearly eight, we began going out of Moscow for summer holidays. I do not think my parents ever had a holiday together before the war: my father had gone once or twice to some sanatorium in the Crimea, but always on his own. (In about 1950 the KGB reached its zenith, with a strength of more than a million, and it was proud of the six sanatoriums it maintained on the Black Sea coast: three in Sochi, one in Batumi, one near Yalta and one at Odessa.) With the children growing fast, my father started to rent modest dachas in the countryside near the city. In 1946 we went to the village where my mother was working on the communal farm, and the next year my father took a room for a month in a wooden cottage some thirty kilometres north of Moscow. In those days the landscape still consisted entirely of woods and lakes, fields and streams, with the Moscow-Volga canal striking past. Life was slow and simple: we drew our water from a well, and swam in the lakes and streams. If we wanted to wash more thoroughly, we would heat up water and pour it over ourselves standing in the middle of the wooden floor, secure in the knowledge that it would drain straight through.

Later we went further north, and for a couple of summers we hired a room at almost exactly the point where the invading German army crossed the Moscow-Volga canal on the ice as they moved to encircle Moscow in the winter of 1941. To children the canal seemed enormous — it was wide enough for two barges to pass each other — and sometimes when a tug came past, pulling a long raft of timber, Vasilko would swim out, scramble up on to the logs, and take a ride before diving off again. One year, going for a walk along the towpath, I noticed something strange: along the banks were numerous small, oblong humps in the ground, many with young trees growing by them. Belatedly I realized that they were the graves of people who had died building the canal: thousands of peasants and political prisoners had expired from cold and starvation during the construction of the waterway.

During our holidays my father would come out to join us every weekend but, because of the long hours he had to work, his visits were short. The lives of everyone in the KGB were dominated by the crazy schedule which Stalin maintained: a night owl, he preferred to work during the hours of darkness, and the senior bosses of the KGB were obliged to stay on in their offices until two or three in the morning, in case a call came from on high. Lower down the scale, at my father's level, people worked until about 10 p.m., and then slept late in the morning.[1]

On Saturdays my father was privileged enough to go off duty at 6 p.m. whereupon he would take a train and arrive at the dacha on foot, carrying bags full of food, at about 8 p.m. Then, in a form of ritual, he would immediately go for a swim: he would strip off and wade straight into the water with his thumbs in his ears and his hands stuck out, palms forward, on either side of his head. After the sticky heat of Moscow offices, those evening swims were clearly a wonderful release. He had two particular fads about his health, both harmless: one, that a vigorous rub-down after a swim or a shower was good for him, and the other that he ought to eat a lot of raw onions.

Some years we travelled further afield, once to Georgia, to visit an Ossetian woman who owned one of the dachas in which we stayed near Moscow. Having taken the train to Tbilisi, we went on to stay in an Ossetian village, where I had one of the most beautiful experiences of my life. The local people were Orthodox Christians, and on their saint's day they all came in from the surrounding villages, processing through the mountains. We joined in the throng, with people singing all round us, and walked for several hours to a chapel deep in the forest. The pilgrims went inside to pray, and afterwards held a huge picnic: they had all brought food and drink with them, and tucked into bread and salty white goat's cheese, washed down by fresh, dry white wine. It was a time of relaxation for the Church, as a result of Stalin softening his opposition to religion, and the local authority, far from seeking to spoil or suppress the celebrations, sent up a number of lorries loaded

1 When Khrushchev came to power in 1956, one of his first actions was to return government offices to normal working hours. He also made Saturday part of the weekend — a revolutionary innovation for which people are grateful to this day.

with more food and wine so that anyone who ran short could buy extra supplies. As for me, even though I had no religious feeling, I developed deep respect for those people who so obviously did, and sang so splendidly in honour of their God. I found the whole ceremony full of meaning and beauty.

Another distant destination was Akhaltsikhe, an Armenian town near the Turkish border, but administratively part of Georgia. There, too, I witnessed a religious ceremony, as we happened to be present on a day when local people were honouring their dead. Our host's brother suggested that we should join everyone else and go along to the event. In an extensive cemetery on the outskirts of the town we found hundreds of people sitting on the graves of their loved ones and lighting candles for them. After spending some time in silent remembrance, they opened baskets of food and wine, and began to enjoy picnics there on the tombstones. As dusk came on, they started to sing, low, sad, haunting songs, which rose and fell from the various groups as candle flames flickered in the twilight.

The following year, 1953, we went to Zaporozhye, in the Ukraine, and there I caught a fish with my bare hands — a young *shchuka* or pike, which was delicious, if rather bony. But I myself was also hooked, falling in love for the first time. I was fourteen, and she was only twelve, a local girl who was rather simple, not well developed either mentally or physically. Her family still treated her as a child — I remember her climbing trees wearing nothing but shorts — but I thought she was wonderful, and told her so. Infatuated as I was, I decided I must buy her a present, and, being a bookworm, I could think of nothing to give her but a book. In the village where we were staying the only books on sale were in Ukrainian; after a hunt I found one that looked interesting, but when I gave it to her, all she said, in an off-hand voice, was, 'Oh, you know very well that I prefer books in Russian!' With that we parted, and my innocent little romance came to an end.

*

My political awareness, already precocious, was much heightened by an event that took place in the autumn of 1952, when I was not quite fourteen. Several prominent doctors were arrested together in Moscow, accused of the murder of Zhdanov, Sherbakov and other leading Communists. Everyone suspected that the case was a sham for of the fifteen or so general practitioners seized, all but one were Jewish, and the operation was obviously an anti-Jewish plot hatched by Stalin. The woman who wrote the denunciation, Lydia Timashuk, was ostentatiously decorated, and other Jews started to lose their jobs.

I followed all this with close interest but then, suddenly, the anti-Semitic operations of the government came closer to home. In a flat across the landing from ours lived a Jewish family, father, mother and child. The father was a lieutenant colonel in the KGB, deputy head of the medical centre, and the mother was a major, head of the Party organization. Both had joined the Party in the 1920s and served it loyally, two among thousands of Jews who hoped that the Communists would win political rights for their race and open up real possibilities for them. Unlike many Russians, who merely paid lip-service to Communism, these two strongly believed in the system — and now lost their jobs simply because they were Jews. The same thing happened to another family on the ground floor of our block. The father, a major, had a boy about Marina's age — they were the first people in our block to own a television set, and they kindly let me watch it for an hour or so in the evenings. That man also lost his job for no reason: he went to Kiev, where he hoped life would be easier, and I never saw him again. Young as I was, I could not help being struck by the stupidity and injustice of these dismissals. The people involved were clever, dedicated and serious, specialists who had lost their livelihoods because of their racial origins. I began to feel critical of a system which could treat innocent citizens so badly.

Then, early in 1953, came a shattering event which gave me another firm push down the road to freedom: the death of Stalin. Towards the end of February, official radio and television bulletins began to carry disquieting reports on the great leader's health, and it became clear to everyone that the end was near. Sure enough, on 5 March he died, and the nation was temporarily stunned. That day, when my mother took me along Gorky Street, in the centre of the city, to do some shopping, everything seemed completely normal: people were going about their business as if nothing had happened, and it struck me as odd that the death of such a mighty statesman had had so little impact. In fact, the citizens were in shock, and within days they had begun killing each other in their frenzy to gain access to the House of Unions, in which Stalin's body lay in state. Unlike thousands of fellow Muscovites, I had no wish to see his corpse. Neither did I feel — as countless people did — that Stalin had been so wise, so great, that no other political leader could manage the affairs of the Soviet Union. Such had been the strength of his personality cult that everyone began saying plaintively, 'We are all orphans, abandoned. How can we live without him? Who will lead us?'

On the evening of the day he died, back at home, I was fiddling as usual with my primitive radio, a Baltika, when suddenly through the roar of jamming I heard a voice saying in Russian, 'He was the worst tyrant in the history of mankind, the greatest criminal and executioner the world has ever known…His victims number millions.'

Incredible statements! I listened spellbound. Never in my life had I heard anything like this — it was so different, so dramatic, so sensational.[2] And yet, I had a vague feeling that such ideas were not entirely new. Instinctively I felt I knew the truth of them already, even if I had never dared to articulate it. I started to remember the discussions between my father and mother, all those years ago, about Enemies of the People, neighbours disappearing, my own uncle sitting for ten years in a labour camp, without reason. Now I recalled how a couple of Father's acquaintances had come to supper, and how in their conversation they had dropped hints that the camps were full of perfectly ordinary people — not thugs or criminals, but political prisoners. Suddenly everything made sense.

The death of Stalin was thus a great eye-opener for me, and I began to look for confirmation that my ideas were right. But my mother was careful, and too scared to answer the questions that burned within me: the dictator might be dead, but the system still existed. However, within a few days we heard on the radio that the case of the doctors had been reviewed: the accusations had been found to be unsubstantiated; proceedings had been stopped, and all the detainees released. The author of the denunciation was stripped of her decoration, and the anti-Semitic campaign eased off. Yet the Jews who had lost their jobs never got them back, and official policy remained not to employ Jews in government organizations.

If the death of Stalin was like an earthquake, powerful aftershocks soon followed it. That summer in the village near Zaparozhye where I fell in love, my mother received a letter from my father which made her

---

2   Although I did not know it at the time, that was the first transmission by Radio Liberty, broadcasting from Munich, which by chance had taken to the air on an historic day.

gasp. When we asked what the trouble was, she read out the sentence, 'There are rumours that our boss has been demoted and is under arrest.'

'Who's "our boss"?' I asked.

'He must mean Beria,' she said.

Beria! We were astounded. After Nikita Khrushchev, he was the second most powerful man in the Soviet Union. How could he have been demoted and arrested? It seemed impossible — and yet it proved true, for Beria became a victim in the power struggle that followed Stalin's death. Not long afterwards, my father told us, a strange letter went out to Party organizations: it was supposed to be read aloud, in closed sessions, and sought to discredit Beria by claiming that he had had links with the British and Turkish intelligence services, that he had become morally corrupt, kept mistresses and had taken to seducing young girls beneath the age of consent. All this was nonsense, of course, but what we could not know at the time was that Khrushchev and his cronies were trying to finish off Beria, whom they regarded as a major threat. (Later they executed him.)

To teenagers like myself, every pronouncement that came from the Kremlin was of consuming interest, for, politically and ideologically, we were highly aware. We knew the names and records of every important member of the Politburo, and we recognized their faces, either from photographs in the newspapers, or increasingly from seeing them on television, or from their appearances on Lenin's red marble mausoleum during the parades in Red Square.

These, unintentionally, were a perfect paradigm of Soviet Communism in that they were a gigantic fraud, a deliberately misleading façade. For boys, they were genuinely exciting occasions — as any large parade with thousands of people, music, bands and high spirits must be — but behind the apparently spontaneous enthusiasm lay a high degree of planning and manipulation.

In Stalin's lifetime the military parade always began at 10 a.m. exactly, and lasted for fifty minutes. Then came a parade of sportsmen, lasting twenty minutes, and finally the immense civilian parade, with people pouring past the mausoleum in endless columns, flooding Red Square, and shouting patriotic slogans. To anyone listening on the radio, it seemed that the noise and enthusiasm of the crowd were colossal, that everybody present was roaring out the slogans; but this was an illusion, produced by skilful use of pre-recorded tapes.

Somewhere out of sight, probably in one of the windows of GUM department store, on the side of the square, lurked an official with a microphone whose duty it was to produce the right noises at the right time, like a town crier. As the head of each column approached, he would call out, 'Long live the vanguard of the Soviet people, the Communist Party! *URRAH!*' Then his operator would press a button, and a terrific '*URRAH!*' would burst from every loudspeaker, followed by rousing music. (For the military and sporting parades, an orchestra had played live, but now all the music was recorded.) As each column reached the middle of the square, he would call, 'Glory to the victorious armed forces of the Soviet Union — *URRAH!*' and again a colossal, answering, electronic '*URRAH!*' would erupt from the loudspeakers. As the front of the column drew near St Basil's, he would proclaim, 'Long live the unbreakable friendship of the peoples of the Soviet Union!', whereupon the massed '*URRAH!*' would blare out once more. Of course, some of the young people in the columns would also yell, '*URRAH!*', often derisively, to let off steam, particularly if they had had a few vodkas beforehand, but the millions listening in from all over the Soviet Union had no idea of how phoney the performance was.

Neither could they know that the columns and crowds had been thickly planted with KGB, whose task was to prevent terrorism and stamp on any trouble before it grew out of hand. Even I, when I joined the KGB, had no idea for a long time of the extent to which the occasion was planned in advance. Then one year I was required to be present at the security rehearsal, a couple of evenings before the parade itself — and an amazing spectacle it was. The run-through took place at 8 p.m., after dark, and when I arrived at Red Square I found the entire area sealed off by KGB. A duty-ticket got me through the cordon, and on the square more KGB were dotted about, many of them on the stands. Loudspeakers had begun to blast out the traditional slogans, and the recorded crowd-roars of '*URRAH!*' Then something extraordinary happened.

All along the side of GUM, basement doors burst open, and out sprinted hundreds of soldiers armed with sub-machine-guns. They appeared to race in all directions, but they were highly trained and, in a few seconds, had taken up predetermined positions so as to divide the open area up into a grid of human lines, each little square about ten metres along the sides, with one man facing outwards, the next inwards, and so on. Even as it was happening I thought of the chaos and injury that would have ensued if the manoeuvre had ever been executed in earnest — for the soldiers would have fought and kicked and beaten their way through the massed crowd. At another signal the men broke ranks and jogged back to their starting places, only to repeat the procedure a few minutes later. Clearly the Soviet leaders lived in fear that a major disturbance, even a rebellion, might start in the middle of the parade. At last I saw the significance of all the lines painted on the tarmac in the square.[3]

---

3   Under Stalin the parade grew out of hand until it was taking six hours. Khrushchev cut it down to two and a half, and this was regarded as a tremendous step towards democratization.

One inescapable element in every Soviet child's upbringing was the Young Pioneer Organization, of which every boy and girl had to be a member from nine or ten until fourteen. In the third year of school there was a ceremony in which all were expected to join. Each of us stood up and pronounced the solemn oath: 'I, a Young Pioneer of the Union of Soviet Socialist Republics, hereby give my promise that I will remain loyal to the cause of the Communist Party and to the cause of Lenin and Stalin.' Then a red scarf was tied round every neck, and we had to wear it until we came of age at fourteen or fifteen. Every class was called a Unit of the Young Pioneers; someone was supposed to be chairman, and to arrange occasional meetings.

In the early 1920s, when the Pioneer Organization was formed out of the Scout movement, some life survived in it because it still behaved in the way the Scouts always had: members went out into the woods on proper excursions, built huts, lived in tents and sang songs round camp-fires. Later, however, it became like everything else in Soviet ideology, an empty ritual. Summer camps were still held, and worthwhile activities went on there — excursions, swimming and so on. I remember being cold, sleeping in a tent, but enjoying the fresh smell of pine trees. Yet in school the Pioneers were no more than a hollow front in which children were expected to act out a charade, to please those who thought it necessary. Pioneer activities were intensely boring and pointless, but we had to go through with them because we were told that if we didn't we would never achieve any success in life.

It was through the Pioneers that we received much of our early political education. Politics was taught in primitive, black and white terms. Countries were either socialist or capitalist, and much was made of the cult of personality: we were supposed to know the names of the leaders of the Communist Party in every country — Wilhelm Pieck in East Germany, Klement Gottwald in Czechoslovakia, Harry Pollitt in England...To poorly educated Russian children, the most insignificant Communist parties were presented as powerful and important. We had no idea how weak they were.

The history of Russia had been rewritten so that the main story was one of 'productive' or 'progressive' forces — whatever forces were 'progressive' in a particular period, and led on to the next. Thus we were taught how slavery developed into feudalism, and feudalism into capitalism. All the movements or uprisings which led to more progressive social forms were given much space in our textbooks: all major strikes and revolutions which led to the establishment of the socialist order were, of course, thoroughly progressive, and had to be very well known. The superiority of the Marxist approach and the Socialist-Communist order was emphasized: the only true form of social science was Marxism, all other approaches were wrong, and their objective was simply to conceal the depth of the divide between classes in capitalist countries.

All this dogma was spiced by a virulent surge of chauvinism, deliberately whipped up by Stalin soon after the Second World War. For a while the Soviet leaders continued to pay tribute to the role of the Western Allies during the conflict with Germany, but gradually their tune changed. By 1947 they had begun to claim that it was the gallant Red Army and Air Force alone who had defeated the Nazis. The implication was that the war in North Africa had been insignificant compared with the struggle on the Eastern front. The opening of a second front in 1944, through the Normandy landings, came too late to make any difference since Germany was already shattered and the victory as good as won. As for the Pacific, that was a sideshow in which only small forces were involved. That Hitler's and Stalin's representatives had signed a non-aggression pact in August 1939, and that Britain had fought the Nazis on her own for more than eighteen months, from September 1939 to June 1941, were barely mentioned.

At fourteen we had to transfer to the Komsomol, or Young Communist League. This was more or less the same as the Pioneers but worse, because every unit had to elect a bureau, the bureau would elect a chairman, and the chairman was supposed to issue a protocol or report of every monthly meeting, one of the unit and one of the bureau. The whole thing was bureaucracy, as unnecessary as it was tedious, and served no purpose whatever.

This sham democracy was carried on in the annual Komsomol conferences, to which each organization was supposed to send a number of delegates. I was regarded as an active element, and took part several times in these meetings, which were held in a beautiful theatre. A great show of goodwill was made, with every member receiving a pad of paper and a nice new ballpoint pen, but all we did was sit and listen to excruciatingly dull speeches, and anyone with the slightest intelligence could see that this alleged democracy was not democracy at all, since everything was set up in advance, with the lists of people to be elected made out beforehand. The same thing happened at the annual Congress of the Young Communist League: candidates were supposed to be elected by secret ballot but, in fact, the representatives were appointed in advance.

A more sinister facet of the organization was its work in the Lenin mausoleum. We learnt from delegates at Party conferences that at any one time a hundred and fifty members of the Komsomol were detailed for duties concerned with the preservation of Lenin's mummified body. If a hundred and fifty young people were on the staff of the mausoleum, how many adults did the place employ? My guess was two hundred and fifty. Maybe four hundred people were servicing that one corpse. Some of the work went on underground, around and beneath the mausoleum itself, and some was done in a secret laboratory, where scientists were endlessly trying to devise ways of preserving Lenin for posterity.

My early experience in the Young Pioneers and the Komsomol opened my eyes to the way in which the Communist Party worked. I learnt that it was an authoritarian organization run entirely by the leadership, a body in which no ordinary member had any say. I saw that in the Soviet Union there was no democracy, no free elections, and no chance of anything unpredictable happening in the political field. Nobody was allowed to suggest a different candidate; nobody could start up a faction; nobody could propose alternative ideas. Anyone who tried to do so would be quickly suppressed and destroyed. With all its protocols and secret ballots, Soviet political life was a series of dead rituals. And yet, extraordinarily, throughout all seventy-odd years of the Soviet era, the authorities managed to preserve a façade of democracy.

My contemporaries and I discerned this clearly by the time we were sixteen or seventeen, but most people accepted it as part of their lives, and decided to play by Soviet rules. I could not, because I considered the game insufferable. At sixteen I had absolutely no knowledge of the West, but I saw that the Soviet system was neither sincere nor honest. More and more I wondered how people could behave in the way they did.

Doing my homework, at least, seemed a worthwhile exercise: I was learning, and my teachers gave me marks according to merit. Work was something real. Similarly, men and women employed in factories were producing things and that was real, too. But all the proceedings of the Komsomol were utterly unreal, an empty show in which everyone was obliged to take part.

*

The next milestone in my development came in March 1956, when, in secret session at the Twentieth Party Congress, Khrushchev delivered his epoch-making denunciation of Stalin. My father, as a senior Party official, was given a copy of the speech and allowed to bring it home for the night. He arrived lit up by the excitement of events, but although he lent me the twenty-five-page text to read, he never discussed his feelings about Khrushchev's revelations. He must have found the speech exceedingly disconcerting, for it went a long way towards destroying the ideological and philosophical foundation of his life. Yet he must have felt relief, for he now saw that many of the friends and colleagues who had disappeared in the 1930s had been not criminals but victims of the State.

As for me, I read the secret text three times that night, and felt wildly excited. Khrushchev's words backed up everything I had heard on the Radio Liberty broadcast three years earlier, and from that night I became a conscious, active anti-Stalinist. For the time being, however, I remained pro-Communist, believing, as the Czechs did in 1968, that it was possible to build socialism with a human face. I knew no better, being still profoundly ignorant about the West and believing much of the propaganda with which we had been force-fed at school.

*

At the start of my second-last year in school, girls appeared for the first time in our ranks, the authorities having decided that segregation of the sexes was a bad thing after all. The change was entirely beneficial: until then there had been a lot of bad behaviour — even outright hooliganism — but the arrival of the girls had a civilizing effect, and the boys calmed down.

No prizes were given for merit in school, but we worked on a system of marks: one was the bottom, and hardly ever awarded, except to show that a pupil's work was so bad that he or she had better not be at school at all; two was the worst that most people could normally get; three was satisfactory; four good, and five excellent. The best pupils, like Alfred, Viktor and myself, were always fighting for fives, and we usually managed to secure them. But real competition started only when we reached level nine, and some features of the pre-revolutionary curriculum were revived, including the award of gold and silver medals. These not only offered an incentive and reward: they also brought an important privilege for the future, in that those who won a gold medal — by scoring the top mark in all ten disciplines — automatically gained free admission to any college or university. Those who won silver enjoyed relatively simple access to higher education, having to sit only one long exam and one interview. Those who failed to win a medal had to sit five exams, all quite tough, and score high marks — 23 out of 25 — to make any further progress.

So the best three or four in each class started to compete for medals and, of course, the teachers, being secretly interested in winning a good medal-count, used various harmless tricks to help their favourites. History, literature and languages had always come easily to me, and in these I was pretty well guaranteed straight fives. Geography also posed no problem. In physics and chemistry I also scraped fives, thanks to a little massaging of the papers by my teacher (which made me feel guilty). My weakness lay in maths, which I disliked intensely, and I managed only fours in trigonometry, algebra and geometry. Thus I had to be content with a silver medal.

By the end of my last year, when I was seventeen, I had become head of the Komsomol organization within the school. The girl who took over from me when I left was supposed to write a recommendation for me to take to college and, in due course, she did so — but because there was so little to be said about Komsomol affairs, she inflated one small item out of all proportion to its worth. During my last month at school a decision had been taken in principle to set up a radio system, which would make broadcasts in the breaks between lessons. Planning had begun, and I was enthusiastic about the idea, but I left before the equipment arrived. Nevertheless, the girl wrote a long paragraph about how active I had been in the school broadcasting organization — an out-and-out exaggeration, entirely typical of Soviet life.

One incident from that year has haunted me ever since. A knock on the door of our flat: a man standing there — a man of my father's age (then fifty-nine), but looking older, very thin, and dressed in strange clothes made of poor cotton, with a rucksack on his back. He said he was an old friend of my father (who was at work), from the days before the Bolshevik revolution. Speaking carefully, and almost in riddles, he gave us to understand that he had recently been released from a concentration camp for political prisoners and altogether had spent eighteen years in camps or exile. He seemed thrilled that my father was still alive, but when he learnt that he was in the KGB — which had ruined and wasted his own life — he went quietly away, never to reappear.

When my father came home that evening, he was dreadfully agitated — almost in a panic — over the return from the dead of this old friend whom the system had treated so cruelly. The man's sudden arrival was worse than the visitation of a ghost, for my father was still serving in the KGB, and still afraid of being associated with an Enemy of the People, no matter how thoroughly any crime had been expiated. Even when his former comrade showed compassion and joy at finding him again, he was terrified.

Chapter Four – Coming of Age

I left school in June 1956 and, after a summer holiday, went to college in September, a few weeks before my eighteenth birthday. The building, with the imposing name of the Institute of International Relations, was near the Krimsky Most, one of the most attractive bridges over the Moscow river, near Gorky Park; it had once been a hotbed of Bolshevism, for in the years after the revolution it had been the Institute of Red Professors, the elite academy for Marxist ideologues. First Trotsky and his associates, then Bukharin had studied, taught and argued there, but in the end most of them proved too clever for their own good. The students at the college in the 1920s and 1930s paid lip service to Stalin and his leadership, but he saw that they were more interesting people, more imaginative and inventive, than his own clique. When he realized that they were becoming a threat to him, he dissolved the academy and had more than half of them imprisoned or shot.

The Red Institute closed down, and for several years the building stood empty. Then, at the end of the war, the government decided that a new college was needed specifically to bring on students as future members of the Ministry of Foreign Affairs. Before the war the Ministry had lost many of its people during the purges, so that it needed rebuilding; but

Stalin and the leadership also saw that, with the Soviet Union becoming a superpower, they would need a larger diplomatic service than in earlier years. The Institute of Foreign Affairs was opened and, because of its special role, came under the Ministry of Foreign Affairs, rather than under the Ministry of Higher Education.

To gain entry, I had to sit one examination, in German, and one interview. The exam was no problem, and I got a good mark, but during the interview I made a couple of elementary mistakes — giving wrong dates, for instance, for the reign of Peter the Great (they should have been 1689-1725). My interviewer was Mr Gonionsky, a leading specialist in Spanish and the history of South America, and head of the Western Department in the college.[1] He noticed my errors, but luckily did not take them seriously: he merely grinned and said, 'I see dates aren't your strong point.'

I liked the Institute from my first day: everything there suited me, not least because I arrived to find the place seething with excitement over Khrushchev's denunciation of Stalin. His secret speech, given to the Twentieth Party Congress in March, still seemed incredibly powerful six months later. Until his revelations burst on them, people had known so little about the true scale of the Great Terror that Khrushchev's words made a tremendous impact, particularly on the creative intelligentsia who, of course, included students. The country was flooded by new hope: all through that spring and summer the atmosphere in Moscow was one of relaxation and renewal, as people talked and argued with a freedom they had never known.

At the Institute this sense of spiritual and cultural liberation was

---

1   Gonionsky's wife spoke perfect Italian, and during the war had worked as an illegal — a buried agent — in Italy, adopting Italian identity. In due course she became my sister Marina's main teacher at the college.

exhilarating, infectious. We could criticize, print leaflets, organize rallies, put up posters, make speeches. Numerous meetings were held, particularly by the older students in their fourth, fifth and sixth years, who were, of course, more experienced, knowledgeable and eloquent than us. Until then the only posters displayed in public places had carried State propaganda: now all sorts of irreverent notices appeared, touting revolutionary ideas. We youngsters watched with admiration, often carried away, especially by the evenings of sketches on stage, which included much political satire. I particularly remember Gonionsky — who was clever, Jewish and probably liberal at heart — joking and laughing as he sat on the platform and answered accusations. Yet even he had to be careful, and although he did not discourage the students, he could not encourage them much either.

My own academic unit of twelve was divided into two language groups of six students apiece. Within our group four of us formed a nucleus: myself, Stanislav 'Slava' Makarov from Astrakhan, Valentin Lomakin from Kuybyshev, and a girl called Ada Kruglyak. Working intensively at my German in the language laboratory, with tape recorders, I conceived the idea of recording a speech of my own, about freedom, democracy and other such heady topics. As soon as I had finished it, I called the group together to hear it, not in any expectation of winning praise but in the hope that it would provoke discussion. The experiment proved disastrous: the tape lasted only five minutes or so, but as my colleagues sat listening, their expressions grew increasingly grim. I saw terror steal over their faces, and before my eyes they became almost paralysed by fear. When the tape finished, Slava Makarov, the only one who could speak, whispered, 'Oleg, *destroy it immediately*!' Feeling like a pricked balloon, I sensed my friends' terror spreading to me and I did as they ordered, erasing my revolutionary words before they could do serious damage.

It was a sobering moment. Son though I was of a KGB colonel, I had not realized the extent to which that organization had penetrated the college. The KGB were watching us on two levels: on one, for potential recruits to their own ranks, and on another, for any sign of dissidence or reactionary, pro-Western ideas. My colleagues were wiser and understood the system better than I did. It was not until six years later, when I was entering the KGB, that I knew how lucky I had been. At one point the officer who interviewed me consulted his file and asked, 'What are your views on abstract art?' I managed to concoct some harmless answer, but with a chill feeling inside: someone must have denounced me at college where, for a while, I had expressed decadent approval of avant-garde painting. I held my breath to see what further questions might follow but it seemed that, by the grace of God, nobody had reported my foray into tape-recording.

In any case, within a few days our new-found freedom was abruptly curtailed: in the last week of October Hungary rose in revolt against Soviet oppression, only for the rebellion to be brutally crushed by tanks rolling into the heart of Budapest. It was hard for us to discover exactly what had happened, since the official propaganda was overwhelming. The Soviet press reported that there had been a Fascist rebellion and that, in an action of fine proletarian solidarity, Soviet troops had gone in to help the long-suffering Hungarian people. The scraps of genuine news which I managed to pick up on our primitive shortwave radio told a different story, but it was impossible to form a coherent picture of events.

Nevertheless even in Moscow it was soon apparent that a terrible disaster had occurred, for our temporary release from censorship ended overnight. The atmosphere changed entirely: all warmth disappeared, and an icy wind set in. Life, in other words, returned to normal: we had gone back into the cold, and all the thousands of *Homo sovieticuses*[2] carried on as they had before, toeing the Party line.

After that dramatic start, my career at the Institute settled into an enjoyable and satisfactory pattern. Besides 120 Russian students, there were sixty foreigners, and the college was divided into two main departments, Western and Oriental. In those days the majority of the home students had gained their places through honest effort. Later, official corruption became ramp-ant, as the KGB, Ministry of Foreign Affairs, Central Committee, Ministry of Defence and other bodies all put in their lists, and places went to the names on them, regardless of merit; in my time perhaps only 10 or 15 per cent were admitted because they had special connections. One such was the adopted son of General Agayants, a powerful KGB official. The father was a clever, imaginative Armenian, who founded and ran the Department of Disinformation, but his son had no brains or will to work. When I heard the answers he gave in his final exam in international law, in 1962, I could scarcely believe my ears: it was clear that in six years he had learnt nothing. He had evidently thought that because he was the son of somebody important he could cruise through college without making any effort. He was awarded Mark 3, which was just enough for a pass but even that was a travesty for he had no clue about his subject.

The system was heavily loaded against girls, who were outnumbered ten to one, because the authorities knew that it was almost impossible to provide jobs for women in the diplomatic service. For the sake of appearances, they had to have girls in the college, but it was only a token presence. One of the lucky few was Ada Kruglyak. How she gained admission, we never knew, but she was a nice character and got married

2   Strictly speaking, the plural of Homo sovieticus should be Homines sovietici; but the form used here has gained widespread recognition.

at the age of twenty-one to a history teacher of thirty-four. To us that seemed ancient, and we wondered if the union could possibly work —but it did, for ten years anyway. By a curious chance Ada's husband later played an interesting role in my life in Denmark.[3]

Although the Institute's building was old, its facilities were far better than those at school. It had a language laboratory, with individual cabins and tape recorders, three separate libraries — for academic titles, foreign language books and newspapers — and a much bigger sports hall. The sports facilities were incomparably superior, and at last I began to realize some of my potential as an athlete, playing basketball and, above all, running.

I had wasted so much time earlier that at the beginning I achieved little, not least because I tried to compete in races too short for me. For a while 800 and 1500 metres seemed my best distances, but then I grew to enjoy cross-country, and the 3000-metre steeplechase became my favourite.

One advantage of the Track and Field Club was that it put me in close touch with some outstanding Czech and Slovak students, who were by far the liveliest of the East European contingent. After only eight years of Communism at home, their individuality had not been stifled: they were normal students, with the ebullience and casually nonconformist outlook of intelligent young people in the West. Prominent among them was Jan Handoga, an exceptional middle-distance runner, active, energetic, always laughing, a man who embraced life with both hands

---

3   In the mid-1960s he began to sign protests against the persecution of intellectuals in Moscow, and became a non-person. In 1967 he came to Copenhagen, where he had been invited to lecture on the Soviet Union's Winter War against Finland, and, in a private meeting, told me that news of Western support for Russian intellectuals and dissidents percolated through to Moscow, information which made a deep impression on me.

and was full of zeal, always wanting to change things. So good was he that we did something definitely not recommended by the authorities: we elected him chairman of the club, and he held office successfully for a couple of years.

Another leader in his field was Standa Kaplan, outstanding at the 400 metres — and as a man. Dark, good-looking — a killer among the girls — and always fun, he became one of my closest friends. In May every year we held a traditional relay race round the Institute building. Each circuit was about 400 metres, and some people ran one lap, some two. I generally went off as No. 1 in our team, but Standa always took the last slot, and was so fast that he could snatch victory for us even if he had a lot of ground to make up.

My own athletic improvement was steady rather than spectacular. During my fifth year we took part in a mass-meeting of all the colleges and institutes in Moscow, and my coach entered me for a heat of the 1500 metres which he said was about my level. Off we went, but I found it more than usually difficult to stay with the group. I started to struggle and, try as I might, I fell back over the final 150 metres, finishing in the last three. I was overcome with disappointment, but my coach took me in his arms, laughing, and when I asked what there was to be so pleased about, he said, 'Haven't you looked at the times? That was the best you've ever done.' Without telling me, he had put me into the strongest heat. Later, at the KGB school, I won the 3000-metre cross-country, and then, in the KGB itself, came second out of thirty in a cross-country ski race, helping my team to win. That was the extent of my career in track and field events: I was never much of a runner, but the exercise was character-building and good for my physical development.

In purely material terms, life was comfortable enough. I lived at home, travelling in and out by Metro, morning and evening. (Those living outside Moscow were housed in a special block, and it may be that their existence was enriched by the amount of time they had for talk in the evenings — but there was also a great deal of drinking and disturbance, so that the system also had its bad side.) As for grants, the State did us well, paying each student 450 roubles a month. During the summer months anyone who wanted to earn extra was invited to work on the building, doing decoration and repairs. For this we were paid five roubles a day and, if we did overtime, we got three roubles an hour for a maximum of three hours — fourteen in all for an eleven-hour day, which was not as tough as it sounds: all the hard work, such as carrying bricks up ladders, was done in the morning, while not much went on in the afternoons.

By today's inflated standards those amounts of money seem small but, at the time, prices were so ridiculously low that we were quite well off. A loaf of bread cost twenty kopeks, a bottle of milk eighteen. You could go anywhere you liked on a tram for three kopeks, and fares on trolleybus, bus and Metro — four, five and five kopeks respectively — were so low that public transport was virtually free. Sometimes it *was* free, because the bus or train was so packed with people that it was physically impossible to buy a ticket. (The minimal rates were, of course, heavily subsidized by the State, which took money from peasants and industrial workers who were paid tiny salaries.) One of our favourite extravagances was to go to a Czech restaurant in Gorky Park where we would buy excellent beer, much better than Russian, and eat thick little Czech sausages, accompanied by bread with large salt crystals on it — a treat that cost us all of eighty kopeks apiece.

Having been through numerous periods of terrible deprivation — the revolution and the civil war, the upheavals of the 1920s, the famines of the 1930s, collectivization, the Second World War and its after-math — Soviet people regarded poverty as a more or less normal state, and expected intermittent shortages of essential foodstuffs. Yet it was a constant annoyance that the shops had so little for sale. During my first years at college my wardrobe was modest in the extreme. Everyone else was the same, and everyone longed for something better. Then, in the middle of my time, a German student sold me his raincoat, only an old beige trench-coat but made in European style and, therefore, in my eyes a miraculous garment. I wore it until it fell apart. Only when I reached East Germany in 1961 did I manage to buy a couple of shirts and a new suit.

Among the attractions of the Institute was our barber, Grigory Abramovich, a middle-aged man of artistic appearance who was said to have won competitions and to have trained in Germany during the 1920s. Whatever his true background, he was an excellent barber, and generations of students remember him with gratitude; he was also a bit of a wit, and I have never forgotten one exchange that took place while I was awaiting my turn in the chair.

'Grigory Abramovich,' said the student whose hair he was cutting, and who was already going a bit thin on top, 'can you recommend any effective treatment that will cure baldness?'

'Young man,' said the barber, 'you study international relations, and read foreign newspapers and magazines, do you not?'

'Why, yes,' said the student, a bit surprised.

'Well, then, you've seen numerous pictures of Western millionaires. Haven't you noticed how many of them have lost their hair? And don't you think that, if there were any cure for baldness, they'd have been glad to pay a million or two to have the treatment?'

During my second year at the Institute I stayed in a winter camp some ninety kilometres north of Moscow, and there I met an exceptionally attractive girl. With her dark curly hair, lovely eyes and easy, natural behaviour, Natasha Afanasyeva appealed to me more strongly than anyone else I had met. When I found that she lived close to me, I thought, Wonderful! It will be easy to meet. But it was not that simple. It turned out that she had a full-time job as a clerk in the office of a factory, and also went to classes in a technical college five nights a week, so that she had practically no time for private life.

In spite of the difficulties, we did meet from time to time, and I remained fascinated by her — not only was she a beautiful girl, but a hard-working and serious one who seemed to enjoy my company. Nevertheless, something seemed to inhibit her — and, after about a year, a bombshell burst.

One evening she telephoned, and in a strange, strained voice, said, 'Can you come quickly? I need to have a word.'

'Where are you?'

'Outside our flat.'

I set off at once, full of apprehension, and found her standing on the pavement in the drizzle, obviously distressed, on the point of tears.

'Something's happened!' she gasped. 'And now I've got to tell you the truth.'

'What are you talking about?'

'Can you imagine? My name's Natasha Afanasyeva yet I'm not Russian.'

'What are you, then?'

'I'm German.'

'German!'

'Yes, I'm perfectly German.'

In a torrent of staccato sentences she revealed that her father was a leading German Communist who had come to Moscow in the 1930s, bringing his wife and five children 'to help build socialism'. Life had proved harder than he expected but he had persevered, got a good job, and done well for a couple of years. Then came 1937 and the purges, and he was declared a German spy.

'At least he wasn't shot,' Natasha rushed on, 'but he got ten years' concentration camp in the north. We were put into an orphanage. Then we were distributed among different Russian families, and I happened to land with the Afanasyevs. I grew up with them for ten years. I like them because they've been very kind to me, but they were never as loving as my parents would have been.'

Eventually, she said, her father had been released, but — just like my uncle — he had been kept in exile, and had taken up with another woman. Natasha's mother, who had remained loyal to him, was bitterly upset, and would not have him back, so he went to live in Rezun, in Central Russia, where he had become the city's chief architect.

As I listened, I felt that I was watching a film: that it was someone else, not me, standing there in the rain and hearing all this. But the story was far from over.

'The worst thing is that ever since I was first at school a boy called Aleks has been in love with me. I've always regarded him as a friend. I found it impossible to see him as lover and husband. But he's remained my loyal knight, always at my side, waiting for his chance. The other night I had a terrible row with my adoptive parents — so bad I had to get out. I had nowhere to go except to Aleks — and he was there waiting, so I went to his parents' flat. In the morning his mother made a solemn scene in the kitchen. "Natalya," she said, "you slept with him. You slept in the same room. There's only one thing for you to do and that's to get married — "' She broke off and gave me a stricken look, then cried, 'For me, there's no other way. I'll have to go with him.'

With that she burst into tears. I took her into my arms and kissed her, for the first and last time. Then she said, 'Goodbye,' and was gone. I felt stunned. There was nothing I could say or do, it was all so sudden, so sad. I kept her photograph for ages, the only memory I had left.

My brother Vasilko had grown thoroughly cynical and when I told him the story a month later, his reaction was characteristic. 'You don't realize how lucky you are,' he told me. 'You would have ruined your life. First, she's the daughter of an Enemy of the People.'

'Rehabilitated!' I protested.

'That makes no difference. The stigma will remain. Second, her father's a German, a foreigner.'

'Not a foreigner!' I cried. 'He's a Soviet citizen.'

'All the same, he'll be a foreigner for ever. And third, she's Jewish. A total disaster.'

*

The academic standards of the Institute varied from high in languages to rock-bottom in Marxist philosophy, which was utter nonsense. The level of language tuition would have been impressive in any country, and its spread was enormous: besides French, German and other European languages, students were learning Mongolian, Korean, Swahili, Bengali and other Indian languages, Greek, Hebrew, Serbo-Croat, and so on. In our first year we German specialists had sixteen hour-long periods a week, and were taught by first-class teachers, who were knowledgeable, enthusiastic and highly professional.

Languages apart, our main subjects were geography, law, military affairs and history. The geography was quite straightforward, covering the whole world and including economic geography but concentrating (for my group) on West Germany. Law was less satisfactory — because there had never been any real law, as such, in the Soviet Union — but we were given some idea of the subject, including international law, and international economic relations: how contracts are signed and how foreign trade is carried out. This last we found very difficult, as we were all weak on economics.

Military matters were more clear cut. During our first four years we had to go through military training as part of our main academic course and this relieved us from active service in the armed forces, which otherwise would have been compulsory. We began with general theory, tactics and strategy, and progressed to practical exercises, firing live ammunition on ranges outside Moscow. One day, as we blasted off with rifles and automatic weapons, supervised by the head of the military department at the Institute, who held the rank of general, a sergeant sitting on a little hill cried: 'My God! When *we* shoot, we have a sergeant in command — and here comes this lot with a bloody general!' Since we wore no uniforms but went to the ranges in our everyday clothes, we must have looked a real rabble.

Nevertheless during our third and fourth years we became, in a way, professionals, because our subject was military translation and interpreting. In this we grew expert, learning hundreds of advanced technical terms in German. Soon we could translate the most complicated military texts, and expressions like *eine Zwanzigstezentimeterdoppelschnellfeuerflugabwehrkannone*[4] became second nature to us. When we received a document stating that we were accomplished military translators and interpreters, it was not an exaggeration: we could have gone to work immediately in the event of war, or if called up by the army, and performed well.

---

4   20cm double fast fire air-defence cannon.

History, however, was regarded as our main subject, first the history of Russia and the Soviet Union, then of the rest of the world, starting with Ancient Egypt, Greece and Rome, progressing to medieval Europe and slowly up to modern times. Of course, everything was presented with a Marxist slant. In dealing with Ancient Greece, for instance, our teachers had none of the wide-eyed admiration that flourishes in the West: instead of worshipping Athens and Rome as the cradles of democracy and European civilization, they emphasized class aspects and 'progressive elements'. Spartacus, the Roman gladiator who led a slave revolt, was, of course, tremendously progressive. The democracy championed by Pericles was no more than a front — and anyway, was it not quickly succeeded by the Greek Empire? The classical Greek experience was just a phase of society and not the great ideal which became so important to Pushkin and his friends early in the nineteenth century at the lycée of Tsarskoe Selo, near St Petersburg.

For several years we studied the history of international relations of Russia and the Soviet Union, that is, a history of diplomacy with Russia at the centre. Treaties and wars featured strongly, especially those concerning the Ottoman Empire, Turkey, Greece, Napoleonic France, the Treaty of Vienna, Metternich and into the twentieth century. Also, inevitably, we were crammed with huge doses of Marxism/Leninism. After two years of the history of the Communist Party of the Soviet Union, which meant an account of all progressive social movements from early in this century, we went on to a tedious, heavily doctored and wildly inaccurate account of the Party since the revolution. Even the revelations of the Twentieth Party Congress were not enough to change the attitude of the teachers, who continued to use traditional distortions, with right- and left-wing threats inflated by Stalin to discredit his enemies. According to this unrevised version of events, Trotsky was still a demon.

Along with history proper, we worked on the history of ideas. An introductory course on world philosophy was excellent, and after it we spent six months on the philosophers of Greece and Rome. But Marxist philosophy was patent rubbish, and nothing could disguise that Lenin was a hopeless philosopher: his only book, *Marxism and Imperial Criticism*, was poor and derivative, and its importance was grossly inflated.

By our third or fourth year we had the measure of Soviet life. We knew the rules and how we had to behave; but for me the great challenge, while showing dutiful interest in my studies, was to discover what really *had* happened. My parents' flat was full of political books published in the 1920s and 1930s, and as I read them I began to see how false and worthless the official accounts were.

With my German improving fast, I also started reading books by former officers of the *Wehrmacht* who had been taken prisoner during the war and had spent years in the Soviet Union between 1943 and 1947. That proved another eye-opener — as did my chance to read West German newspapers. This was a unique period in the Soviet Union in that students at the Institute were free to read Western newspapers and magazines. Later such publications were banned, but I was lucky enough to hit the open period, and I seized on everything with insatiable appetite — one of the few people in the Soviet Union able to do so.

Gradually I began to see that the West was another world. Everything there was different. The political, social and moral systems were quite unlike ours. The open approach to the mass media and to the democratic process made the West another planet. At the age of twenty I started to feel that I was penetrating this different, exciting territory. All through my childhood and growing-up the non-stop refrain of Soviet propaganda had told us that ours was the only correct society. The Soviet Union was doing everything right. The capitalist world, with all its imperialist bourgeois circles, was a world of exploitation, of violence, of aggression. The capitalists had evolved a sophisticated system for exploiting the working class. Democracy was no more than a façade designed to conceal the real forces at work behind it.

Now a feeling began to steal over me that all this was lies, that things were the other way round. The propaganda insisted, 'We are the world of sanity, they of insanity,' but as I read the West German papers it dawned on me that exactly the opposite was true. The discovery was immensely exciting but so dangerous that, for the moment, I dared not speak to anyone else about it. What I could do, though, was to bolster my slender knowledge of the West by listening to foreign broadcasts: Radio Liberty was heavily jammed by a loud roaring noise, broadcast from towers all round Moscow, but I could sometimes pick up the Voice of America and the BBC World Service. Radios were not very efficient then, and those produced in the Soviet Union deliberately ended on the 25-metre wavelength, so that broadcasts on 21, 19 and 16 metres, used frequently by European stations, were unavailable. Other wavelengths were accessible, among them 49, 41 and 25, but the jammers concentrated on these, and often made it impossible to pick them up. With practice, however, I discovered that the transmitting stations would surreptitiously ease off one wavelength and on to another so that unless the KGB operators were constantly alert they would be left jamming thin air, while the signal came through and could be heard slightly further round the dial.

Why more of my contemporaries did not respond to this first faint scent of the truth, of reality, I do not know. I can only think that I was uniquely fortunate in having learnt German, which gave me the chance to read Western newspapers, magazines and books.

*

At the end of our second year an announcement went up on the noticeboard: 'Please put in your requests for your second foreign language.' At that time I had a great fear of English. My apprehension was entirely irrational, and due to lack of understanding, but I felt that the language was *so* complicated that I would never master it. The spelling looked difficult, and all the constructions seemed different from German, which I was enjoying so much. However, I put in for English, which I felt I must start to learn sooner or later.

A couple of weeks later, a clerk told me that dozens of people had applied for English, and that places on the course were being allocated by the administrators on a basis which only they understood. 'You, Gordievsky,' the man said, 'can choose between Czech and Swedish.' Because I had Czech and Slovak friends, my immediate reaction was to go for Czech, especially as I had already made some progress teaching myself from a textbook.

My brother had other ideas. At that stage he was just beginning his training for the KGB, but he had enough knowledge of the world to give me some sensible advice. 'Don't be an idiot!' he said fiercely. 'If you take Czech, you'll spend the rest of your life sitting in the pathetic consular departments of the Soviet embassies in Prague and Bratislava, and you'll never see any more of the world than that. Go for Swedish! There's no option. For one thing, Sweden's a nice country, and for another it's the doorway to the rest of Scandinavia. From there you can go anywhere in Europe.'

Vasilko was always more cynical and materialistic than I was. Being that much older, he had grown up among boys brutalized by war, and was completely career-minded, whereas many of my companions were more idealistic, and had some spiritual values. Yet with those

111

words he changed the course of my life. I took Swedish — and the consequences which flowed from the decision were incalculable. Not that I much enjoyed learning my second foreign language for, unlike Norwegian in which the instructor was first-class, it was poorly taught. Not enough hours were allocated to it, yet the instruction was dreadfully serious. The result was that although I was keen to master Swedish, I never did.

Much more congenial was a half-year course on Western European literature, which included some study of English and also an introduction to the economic geography of European countries. One book to which this course introduced me, and which made a strong impression, was *Gulliver's Travels*. I found the text so fascinating and witty that I read parts of it aloud to friends and to my mother. Later, in England, having read it three times in Russian, I bought an English edition, to see how the Russian translation compared with the original. Swift's earthy sense of humour appealed to me strongly, not least in the story of the blind academic who is teaching apprentices how to identify colours by the senses of smell and taste. I also enjoyed the account of the man who tried to reproduce the original substances — corn and vegetables — out of human excrement, and the reaction of the narrator to his greeting: 'When I was presented to him, he gave me a very close embrace (a compliment I could well have excused).'

All our academic disciplines were permeated by Marxist ideology. At school our knowledge of the history of the Soviet Union had been sketchy; now we learnt more and more about the revolution and the history of the Communist Party, including what was known as its prehistory — the development of the first Marxist organizations in Europe and Russia. We still did not know the full truth about the purges: I had read Khrushchev's secret speech, of course, but its text was not yet officially available for the rewriting of history books, which had been only partially recast. Even so, reading about the 1920s and 1930s, we saw how Lenin's supporters and colleagues, the best and cleverest revolutionaries, had disappeared one after another. One perennially fascinating topic was the Seventeenth Party Congress of 1934, when the Central Committee was elected for the first time. Legend — still not confirmed to this day — claimed that in the secret ballot Sergei Kirov had received more votes than Stalin because the majority of delegates hated Stalin and wanted to get rid of him. Kirov was assassinated in December that year, on Stalin's orders, and by the end of 1938 more than 70 per cent of those who had taken part in the congress were dead. Stalin never knew who had voted for whom, but he liquidated two-thirds of them just the same.

Such facts and legends we discussed at length, but at that stage my mind was not developed enough to reject Communism outright. Rather, I wanted to believe that there had been something good and noble in the movement at the beginning, but that it had gone wrong in a welter of brutality and terror. The collectivization of agriculture should have been a social improvement, but it had ended in catastrophe. My understanding of what had happened was limited: I was still within the system, but my feelings of disillusionment were growing by the day.

*

Among my friends in the Track and Field Club, none was more inter-esting than Li, a tiny Chinese athlete, who ran well but was clearly suffering from chronic undernourishment. Behind his spectacles his eyes were friendly and intelligent, and he had a strong sense of humour; yet he was a fanatical Communist and, although we became good friends, we had phenomenal political arguments. I used to tease him by saying,

'Now you've got a cult of personality in China. You've got Mao just as we had Stalin until four years ago. Don't you realize that when Mao dies you'll have a de-Maoization campaign?'

Li did not like such remarks. 'You don't seem to understand what Mao has done for the nation,' he would say furiously. 'We owe him a tremendous debt.'

'That's exactly what everyone said about Stalin,' I would retort. 'He was a great leader. We owed everything to him.'

In an attempt to build Li up a bit, I used to take him home for meals, and at the flat he got into endless arguments with my father. At that time — 1957 — unpleasant border incidents were flaring up between India and China, and Li attributed these to capitalist provocation. My father told him he was talking nonsense — and so they wrangled on.

In spite of Li's intransigence, I could not help liking him — and the curious thing about him was that, although he seemed bigoted, he often proved right. This happened once when we found ourselves together at a holiday camp in Karelia, on the Finnish border, a glorious area of mountains, lakes and rivers, and islands covered with pine trees and huge volcanic boulders. In these idyllic surroundings I had one of the best holidays of my life.

After five days' training, we set off in small boats for a ten-day voyage through the lakes, camping on islands where we pitched tents and lit fires to cook supper. Li often criticized Russian food as being unimaginative, and lamented the lack of spices. Then one evening, to his great excitement, he spotted that the bottom of a crystal-clear lake was covered with freshwater mussels. 'Look!' he cried. 'Delicatessen right under our feet!' In a flash he got several of us to fill buckets with mussels, which he then boiled, having already concocted a brew of onions, salt, pepper and vinegar to go with them. None of us had ever eaten such shellfish before, and several people refused to try them, but those who did were rewarded with a feast of rare deliciousness.

In our flotilla of boats we had no radio, so for days on end we were cut off from any news. Then one morning we came to a village where we could buy a newspaper, and all over the front page we saw the headline ANTI-PARTY CLIQUE UNMASKED IN LEADERSHIP OF CPSU. We found that the old Stalinists — Kaganovich, Malenkov and Molotov among them — had tried but failed to topple Khrushchev. The news thrilled me. Being such a militant anti-Stalinist, I welcomed Khrushchev's victory, almost dancing with delight, and called out, 'Li, how wonderful! Progress at last! All those old Stalinists have been sent packing into the wilderness.'

Li, however, looked anything but happy. 'Comrade Molotov expelled?' he said in a voice of doom. 'Practically a co-founder of the Soviet State, and they've got rid of him? I don't like it.'

His seriousness brought home to me that some people really did support old ideas and structures. Li was not paying lip-service to Communist ideals: he believed in them fervently. I saw that the Soviet Union would have to keep a close eye on China: if the ruling class were as fanatical as he was, things could become very dangerous.

Li was learning Persian, and if I challenged him as to the usefulness of the language — at a time when China had been ostracized by almost every country in the world as a result of American pressure — he would say, 'You'll see, Oleg, the time will come. China will be recognized as a great power all over the world. We'll have embassies everywhere. That's why we're learning diplomacy and languages.'

Once again he proved right — in the long term. But in 1959 relations between China and the Soviet Union deteriorated, and a year later all Chinese students were recalled from Moscow. I often wondered what happened to Li, especially at the time of the Cultural Revolution.

*

During my fourth year both my German and my knowledge of the West took a big step forward when I began to work as an interpreter for visiting German delegations. Most were East Germans, but after only twelve years of Communism, and before the Wall went up, they were still close to the West, both geographically and in spirit, and I found it refreshing to have contact with them. West Germans and West Berliners came as well, either as tourists or as part of official groups.

For students the best-paid jobs were those we did for the Ministry of Health: the delegations they invited seemed small, and they went to more interesting places. I travelled with several of them, but my most fantastic trip was one devoted to what the Germans called *Kurortologie*, or the study of how to treat patients in health spas and sanatoria. Our destination was Georgia, where people were then exceedingly hospitable, not spoilt by too many delegations. In Tbilisi, Gagra, Borzhumi and Sochi we were lodged in the best hotels, driven about in fast cars, and plied with every kind of food and drink. So high did we live, on wine, champagne and Georgian brandy, that by the time we reached Sochi some of the visitors' constitutions were feeling the strain. One morning, as we walked along the main avenue, we came to a souvenir shop and bought a few things. The people in the shop, seeing that their customers were foreigners, took the trouble to wrap up the purchases in paper and tied the parcels with string.

A few minutes later one of the Germans suddenly had to answer an urgent call of nature; luckily there was a public toilet close by, and soon he emerged looking much relieved, but with his souvenir no longer wrapped. 'You know the problem round here?' he said. 'No paper in the lavatory. But luckily I had my parcel!' A few minutes later we all boarded a trolley bus, and each put two kopeks through the slot into the money box (there being no conductor). Among the party was a doctor, and as he shoved his fare through the slot, the extra coin tipped a balance inside, so that a mass of change fell down with a crash into the bottom of the box. The doctor burst into roars of laughter, and the man who had been taken short remarked mock-sourly, 'What's so funny about that? It reminds me of my experience a few minutes ago.'

Besides improving my German, these tours gave me some polish, and also offered me a glimpse of how we, the Russians, appeared to people outside, especially to visitors from the West. Once at the end of a trip to Moscow and Leningrad a West Berliner said in a heavy, sarcastic voice: Now we know what the Russian national costume is.'

'What do you mean?' I asked. He replied: 'It's military uniform.'

The remark annoyed me and brought out all my patriotism. 'What makes you think that?' I demanded.

'Because the streets of Moscow and Leningrad are full of soldiers and officers, all in uniform.'

The German saw this as an expression of militarism and imperialism — and later, when I began travelling to the West and saw trains full of servicemen, and soldiers on the frontier, on the platforms, in restaurants, everywhere, I thought, Yes, it's true. This is a heavily armed, militaristic empire. Yet at the time I took the German's remark as a deliberate insult, and thought bitterly of how my father, who gave his salary to my mother to keep the household and the family, wore uniform all the time because he had no civilian suit. What the German did not know was that many of the uniforms he saw were the product not of any desire to show off or demonstrate aggression, but of poverty, and of the way in which the Communist system ran the country.

There was one way in which we could get our own back on Germans, and that was by taking them to the museum of the siege of Leningrad, which showed in graphic detail how people had lived and died while the Nazi forces surrounded the city from 1941 to 1943. During each visit we ran a tough, moving film. It only had a Russian soundtrack, so the guide sat at the back and translated simultaneously through headphones. One morning after I had done this, putting as much feeling as I could into it, some members of my group came up and protested, 'Oleg, you're being very hard on us today.'

'Me?' I said. 'Hard? All I did was read you the script.' But because they had been listening to my voice, they assumed the ideas it expressed were mine.

In my fourth year my enthusiasm for interpreting gave me a fantastic summer at Artek, on the coast of the Crimea. Every citizen of the Soviet Union knew Artek — a Tatar name — for it was the site of the best and most luxurious holiday camp ever built for the Young Pioneers. That year the authorities had arranged an international athletics competition between schools from the East European countries, and a high standard was guaranteed because every team taking part had already won national competitions. I was appointed guide-interpreter to the team from Leipzig, and asked to stay for twenty-five days.

Artek turned out to be more a village than a camp, with wooden cottages housing a dozen visitors apiece, all fully equipped with running water, showers and proper lavatories. The camp was beautifully laid out with facilities for all kinds of sports, games, films and other entertainments, not to mention easy access to the beach. The organizers also laid on excursions, on one of which I made my first visit to Sevastopol, a place of high interest to me because of its role in the Crimean and Second World Wars.

When I saw the team from Leipzig, I was amazed. The boys were more or less still boys, but the girls, aged fourteen or fifteen, were stunningly attractive with beautifully developed bodies. Of course, they won every event with one hand tied behind them, but I found it almost impossible to treat them as children, so adult did they look. They were supposed to be chaperoned by their teacher, but he had fallen ill and had been replaced at short notice by the sports correspondent of the Young Pioneer newspaper in East Germany, a former paratrooper who had fought in the war. A man of enormous energy, he was given to describing his experiences in the present tense: 'We are dropping over Greece! The earth is coming up to meet us! We spray everything in sight with our Schmeissers! What a day we are having!' There was also a Hungarian teacher, the oldest person present, who lusted mightily after the girls, and chased them round the camp after dark. They would provoke him deliberately, lurking in the shadows until he almost caught them, then running off with shrieks of laughter. The presence of those young Germans raised the temperature at Artek to fever pitch.

*

In Moscow I became aware that two representatives of the KGB spent much of their time in the Institute building: they had a little office, and kept out of sight, slipping in and out through the ground floor while the students were upstairs. For a long time I didn't really know what they were doing, but it gradually dawned on me that they were looking for potential recruits — and that the man representing the First Chief Directorate had his eye on me.

What was I to do? I liked the idea of making my career with the KGB, partly because I would be following in my father's footsteps, but also because it offered a good chance of serving and living abroad, one of the principal aims of almost every student in the Institute. We all knew that the Soviet Union was a prison, and that the only way to escape from it for any length of time was to join one of the organizations that worked in other countries — the Ministry of Foreign Affairs, journalistic agencies such as TASS and APN, or the KGB. (To join the GRU, the military equivalent of the KGB, one had to be a member of the armed forces.)

Ordinary Soviet citizens had no chance of going abroad for nobody was allowed to leave the country without special permission from the government, and every individual application had to be passed by the Cadres Abroad department of the Central Committee. Foreign travel was an impossible dream for almost everybody — and this made the lure of working in the KGB especially strong. Besides, in our eyes the organization had many uniquely glamorous and attractive advantages: the secrecy, the paraphernalia of espionage, the peculiar methods used and the specialist knowledge needed. A further incentive was that pay in the KGB was slightly better than in most other spheres. What none of us thought about much were the drawbacks: we brushed aside the many restrictions on our personal freedom, much checking-up on our backgrounds, and stricter discipline than in most other forms of service. We preferred not to think about what would happen if one of us were expelled from a foreign country; we ignored the fact that it was almost impossible to move from the KGB to any other organization — the Ministry of Foreign Affairs, for instance, would never take on former KGB men.

In making up my mind what to do, I had one advantage over my fellow students: I could discuss things with my brother, who was already training to be a *nelegal*, or illegal. Through Vasilko I knew a good deal about how the illegals operated: how they assumed a foreign identity and went to ground in the country to which they were assigned, living as nationals of that state. My German was already good — better than his — and I liked the idea of life in some Western country. I asked Vasilko to send a tip about me to Petr Grigoriyevich, who represented Directorate S (which controlled illegals) in the Institute, and one day early in 1961 he invited me to his little office for a talk. When he asked me if I was interested in his department's work, and I said, 'Yes', he told me I would be invited to an interview in the building known as the Pass Office, in Kuznetzky Most, a little old street near the KGB headquarters in Dzerzhinsky Square.

There, a more senior officer spoke to me about my academic progress, my plans, my German; and a couple of weeks later I was interviewed in German by a nice-looking woman in her fifties, who spoke the language so impeccably, and looked so like a typical German *Tante* (auntie) that I assumed she must be German. When I asked, she turned out to *be* Russian, but she seemed impressed by my German, and gave me the highest possible recommendation. I became a definite candidate for Directorate S, and from that moment no other KGB department was allowed to approach me.

*

By far the most formative period of my time at college was my stay in East Berlin, which began in August 1961, between my fifth and sixth years. It was the generous habit of the college and the Ministry of Foreign Affairs to send students abroad for six months, to gain practical experience — something which no other educational establishment in the Soviet Union did at the time. In my year there were thirty foreign slots for sixty students: this meant that half would go abroad, and the rest would join either the Ministry or some journalistic agency such as TASS, and do their practical work there.

Luckily I was one of the thirty destined for other countries; less fortunately, I was not well enough connected, and had not managed to ingratiate myself with the right people, to be sent to one of the prime destinations — the rich, capitalist countries alleged to exploit their workers so cruelly. Perhaps because my father was already a pensioner, I was allocated to a Communist country, but at least East Germany was a frontier state — and, as things turned out, there could then have been no more interesting place in which to be posted.

It was pure chance that we set out from Moscow on 10 August 1961, a little group of four trainee diplomats, all rather nervous, but proud and excited to hold green diplomatic passports, which few Soviet students possessed. One of my companions, Nikolai Starikov, was eight or nine years older than me, and already in his thirties. The other two members of the group, Stanislav Makarov and Vladimir Shcherbakov, were my age, but all of us were going abroad for the first time, so everything was new.

Sharing a four-berth compartment on the train, we left Moscow in the afternoon and rumbled comfortably westwards through the night. Like all Russians, we enjoyed eating on trains and I munched my way through a cold boiled chicken my mother had cooked for me. The others, too, had picnics, and we washed our food down with beer sold in corridors by vendors who came along from the restaurant car.

At 11 o'clock next morning we reached the frontier town of Brest-Litovsk. Innocents that we were, we thought that the ritual of going through the border was quite normal, something that happened between all countries. Only later, looking back, did it occur to me how sinister the whole performance was.

First teams of Borderguard officers and men in bright-green uniforms hurried aboard the train and took up position to seal off all the carriages simultaneously. No one was allowed to leave or move along the train as they inspected our documents. Next the soldiers lifted the bench-seats to make sure there were no stowaways in the luggage spaces beneath, and undid the ceiling panels with screwdrivers to check the roof space. Then they hung about, preventing any movement of the passengers, while customs officials in grey uniforms checked everyone except those, like us, with green passports. Most people, we noticed, had blue passports, indicating that they were on State business. Naïve as I was, I thought it odd that a totalitarian regime, which paid no attention to human rights, should allow some of its citizens this special privilege of exemption from customs searches. (In theory the privilege was for foreigners only, but Soviet diplomats enjoyed it for years until, after my own escape, it was suddenly withdrawn.)

After a while the customs men went, but the Borderguards remained. The train moved off a short distance and stopped under the roof of a huge factory-like building, where the wheels were changed, from wide gauge to narrow. It was a slick operation, in which the replacement wheels, hanging on chains, were swung down and fitted into place, the whole train being completed in less than an hour. Then we rolled back into Brest station, but to a different platform, with a three-metre chain-link fence sealing us off. The area was heavily patrolled. There we waited, as soldiers stood guard outside. At last we started towards the West, and in only a kilometre or so we crossed the frontier. On either side, at right-angles to the track, parallel fences struck off into the distance, separated from each other by wide cleared zones, with watch-towers rising at intervals above them.

On the Polish side of the border, things became a little less grim. Once again army officers and customs officials boarded the train, but the soldiers, though Communists, had a lighter, more elegant look, and wore more stylish uniforms. The customs officers were an even greater

123

improvement, since many were girls in tight-fitting uniforms, and all they did was glance round smiling. Then, at the East German border, it was like plunging back into Russia, only worse, for the military, in their grey uniforms, looked Prussian and serious, and uncomfortably reminiscent of the Nazis. So strongly did they resemble what we had seen in war films that we all got quite a shock.

Late in the evening of 11 August, we reached Berlin, a thrilling moment for a young man who had read about Germany since childhood. The imperial capital; the First World War; the artistic glories of Berlin in the 1920s; the adventures of the German Young Pioneers helping the Communist Party in its underground resistance against the Nazis in the 1930s; the burning of the Reichstag parliament building in 1933; the Nazi Olympics of 1936. All these were familiar to me from books, and now here was Berlin for real.

Immediately I was fascinated by the complexity of the city. Russia was huge, but it was all empty spaces and steppes. Here everything was far more concentrated — a highly developed infrastructure, with tracks crossing each other over bridges and in tunnels as the S-Bahn suburban railway wound between buildings. The traditional German architecture looked strikingly different from anything I had seen before. However, the closer we came to the centre of the city, the more the evidence of war-damage stood out — open spaces, gaps in rows of houses, blank side-walls.

At the Ostbahnhof we were met by a car and driven to Karlshorst, the suburb in which the KGB maintained a large enclave, like a military base, surrounded by a security fence with a guard on the gate. Inside, everything belonged to the Soviet Union, and we found we had been allocated a flat in a small block only three storeys high. The place was plain but adequate for four young men: a good kitchen, a sitting-room, two bedrooms, a bathroom. Yet what seized our attention was the television set and, within minutes of our arrival, we were greedily switching from one channel to the next, mesmerized by five being available simultaneously, and delighted to find that natural, everyday German — rather than the German of tapes and teachers — was perfectly comprehensible.

Tired after the long journey, we had supper and went to bed early. But then an entirely Russian event occurred. A few minutes after we had settled down, there was a sudden shout and we all leapt out of bed, rushing for the light switches. A shocking sight was revealed: both bedrooms were alive with bed-bugs, attacking us from all directions. Where they had come from it was impossible to say, but now they were everywhere, on beds, floor, walls, ceiling. Scratching and slapping at bites, we snatched the sheets off the beds and tipped the live cargo of each into the bath, flushing it down the plughole. For the next couple of hours we fought the invaders, catching and killing hundreds. Then, exhausted and determined to get some proper sleep, we took one bed from each bedroom and stationed it in the sitting room, with plenty of space round it, and pulled the remaining beds away from the walls. In the kitchen we mustered sixteen containers — saucepans, bowls, dishes — and deployed them so that every bed-leg was standing in water. Thus protected, we gradually settled down again and went to sleep. In the morning we complained bitterly to the administrator, who called in a German fumigation squad — and they must have done a truly Teutonic job, for when we returned to the flat in the evening, we found a slight smell of disinfectant but every bug had gone.

On our first morning in Berlin we began to get our bearings. Our base was the Soviet Embassy in Unter den Linden, the main thoroughfare which had been the heart of the capital before the war; the Embassy was a huge building put up by German prisoners, only a couple of hundred metres from the Brandenburg Gate. There our mentor was Vladimir Lomyeko, then personal assistant to the head of the Bloc Department, the instrument of the Central Committee which ran the East European countries. I knew Lomyeko already from the Institute, where he had been a couple of years ahead of me, so now I met him again as an old friend: tall, confident, energetic and immediately impressive, he obviously had great ability, and was determined to carve out a successful career for himself (later he held many senior posts, and became the Ministry of Foreign Affairs' representative at UNESCO). Another high-flyer in the making was Yuli Kvitsinsky, who was working as personal secretary to the Ambassador.

At that time, however, these two found themselves caught up, like everyone else, in a mighty historical event. From the way that people were gossiping urgently, in low voices, it was clear that we had arrived at a fraught moment; and hardly had Lomyeko briefed us about what we would be doing when he confided that something terrible was happening outside. 'In the last couple of weeks, and the last few days in particular, the citizens of the German Democratic Republic have been fleeing westwards by the thousand,' he told us. 'They've been going all the time, but for some reason the movement's suddenly accelerated. If you asked me for my impression of East Germany at the moment, I could put it very simply. It's as if the whole of the GDR is sitting on its suitcases.'

That phrase seized my imagination and has haunted me ever since. Within minutes its accuracy was confirmed by another of the Embassy officials, a choleric first secretary, who popped into the room and said in a conspiratorial voice: 'Chaps, something incredible's about to take place. I can't tell you what it is, but it's my duty to warn you. The important thing is that you should be on your guard tonight and tomorrow night. Don't go out anywhere. Don't go for walks. Don't stay in the city centre. When the office closes, go back to Karlshorst and remain in your quarters. Watch television, listen to the radio — but don't whatever you do go out. Then in the morning come to the office, like everyone else.'

Of course, that left us boiling with curiosity but we did as we were told, and remained unenlightened by various evening broadcasts. Next morning we found the city in a frenzy, with soldiers on guard everywhere, people and vehicles rushing in all directions. All along the line between the Soviet sector and the West barbed-wire barricades were going up: Berlin was being divided in half by the first version of the Wall.

In the Embassy the staff were so busy reporting events to Moscow that we were left to ourselves, and we spent the day glued to television sets, watching with incredulity and horror the shots of people desperately clambering over barricades and jumping out of windows into canals in their efforts to escape. Even with all this first-hand evidence, it was hard to believe what was happening but, whenever we ventured out into the street, reality was still closer. Within a few hundred metres of us Unter den Linden itself had been severed by barricades of wire blocking the Brandenburg Gate. One of the city's main arteries was cut off.

The building of the Wall created an electric atmosphere but somehow we had to settle down. After a while the people in the Embassy decided that no room could be spared for us so we were given desks on the fourth floor, in the corridor that led to the splendid great hall used for conferences and speeches. Since the corridor was wide there was plenty of space, but it was guarded by a dragon of a secretary, a smartly dressed woman who sat outside the door of an office, and much resented our arrival since we undermined her privacy and the luxury of her position. Soon we learnt that she worked for Colonel Slavin, head of the KGB section stationed in the Embassy. The main force of KGB was at Karlshorst, where more than five hundred officers were based. A couple of dozen worked from the Embassy under the guise of diplomats.

Before I left Moscow, I had been set various small tasks by my contact in Directorate S, and the first of these was to make contact with my brother. He was living in Leipzig but he came to Berlin to meet me one evening during my first week and, although we both much enjoyed our reunion, it landed me in deeper water than I had bargained for. Vasilko was in excellent spirits: to celebrate my arrival he took me to several late-night bars in East Berlin and bought me one or two German liqueurs, with the result that I did not arrive back at our flat in Karlshorst until nearly midnight. By then our minder had become worried about my safety: evidently he smelt alcohol on my breath, for he gestured to my companions that I had been drinking and angrily asked where I had been. Since I was already imbued with one of the KGB's fundamental principles that you must never reveal what you have been doing, I told him I had been to the cinema. 'Oh, yes?' he said nastily. 'And what did you see?' When I gave him the name of a film that I knew was on, he said, 'All right, we'll discuss it in the morning. Now go to bed.'

I went to my room feeling depressed. I did not want to let down the KGB by revealing my connection with them, but neither did I want to go back to the Institute with a bad report. I knew that in the morning our minder would start asking questions about the film I claimed to have seen…and the more I thought about my predicament, the clearer it became that there was only one solution. At dead of night I got dressed, crept out of the house and walked back into the city centre — a distance of at least three kilometres, which took three-quarters of an hour — to find the cinema at which my film was showing. There, on the pavement, I picked up not only a programme which gave a full synopsis of the plot but also a discarded ticket, and trudged wearily back. Only a young man would have gone to such lengths. My dogged endeavour paid off, for when I produced the programme and the ticket the minder swallowed my story. Later, when I mentioned the episode to the KGB, they were delighted: I had cleverly covered my tracks, had not mentioned my brother, and instead had carried out a minor operation to gain material support for my fiction. All this struck them as a major coup. I had shown that I possessed 'operational skills'. I had demonstrated 'spontaneous operational reaction'. 'We've found a good candidate!' they said to each other. 'The lad's doing well.'

The second task the KGB had set me proved less simple. They had given me the name of a woman with whom, they said, they wanted to renew contact. I was to approach her and find out her feelings about the Soviet Union — whether or not she was prepared to work for the KGB again. At first everything seemed very difficult but, after nerving myself to the task, I went to a police station and invented some pretext for getting her address. Armed with the details and some flowers, I went straight round without telephoning, in case I put her off. When I knocked at the door, taut with nerves, out came a good-looking woman in her forties. I blurted out some story about a friend in Moscow asking me to call on her, and she invited me in, apparently not at all surprised. It seemed to me that we had a useful conversation: obviously she had spent some time in the Soviet Union during the war, and she spoke about those years with warmth, remarking sadly that people were no longer as idealistic as they had been in the 1930s and 1940s. When I asked if she would like to resume contact, she gave me carefully to understand that she would not mind.

All this I wrote in a report, and at the time I thought I had done well. Later I realized that the whole thing must have been a try-on: that she must have been an active agent, and that it was I, rather than she, who was being tested. The KGB wanted to find out if I seemed presentable, if I had an easy manner when approaching strangers, whether I asked good questions. If they had wanted to resuscitate a useful contact, they would not have sent a naïve twenty-year-old to do the job. All the same, it was exciting to have an early taste of the kind of work I might do if I joined the KGB.

As the days went by, it turned out that we students had little to do, apart from sporadic translating. Our main task, we were told, was to work on our theses, which we would have to hand in when we returned to Moscow and finished our courses at the Institute. The man appointed to act as an academic tutor wanted me to write about the collectivization of agriculture in the DDR (East Germany); but I found the idea exceptionally boring and, while pretending to work at it, I pressed on with a subject which fascinated me: relations between Church and State in East Germany.

Our leisurely life left plenty of time for reading — and we read voraciously, not only West German newspapers, which were freely available to us, but also the secret reports compiled by the various political parties about morale among the East German population (the DDR retained puppet parties, but they were only sub-departments of the SED, or Sozialistische Einheitspartei Deutschland, the official body). Most reports began with a rush of platitudes — 'The population of the DDR greeted the decisions of the Plenum of the Central Committee of the Sozialistische Einheitspartei Deutschland with great enthusiasm' — but once the claptrap was out of the way, much of the truth would come out in a torrent of bitter and cynical complaints, which showed how angry and frustrated people were. The rumours in circulation, political jokes, comments about the Soviet Union, new nicknames for leading personalities — everything was here, along with the latest satirical rhymes:

Keine Butter, keine Sahne,
Aber hoch die rote Fahne![5]

In the flat we took it in turns to cook simple meals for supper — macaroni, potatoes with butter or sunflower oil, and plenty of vegetables. Then one evening Starikov introduced a new custom. Returning from the shops, he produced a neat little bottle embellished with the word 'Korn'. As he poured out the clear liquid into four glasses, he said, 'After all, we should mix business with pleasure now and then!' Drinking the smooth spirit down, we voted it much the same as vodka but better, and soon it became a regular habit.

Another day, when I was on my own in the apartment, I decided to give the others a surprise. Ever since our arrival I had been worried by the lavatory-bowl, which had become encrusted with scale through lack of thorough cleaning, and I was determined to do something about it. I could find no better instrument than an ordinary table-knife, but for two solid hours I scraped away, using the back of the knife to dislodge the scale flake by flake. In the end the bowl was snowy white and good as new. When the others returned, they admired it very much, so I said, Now keep it clean, and we'll be all right.' But, in the middle of supper, Starikov suddenly asked how I had managed the transformation.

'It was tough going,' I said. 'I had to use the back of a knife.'

'*What?*' Starikov jumped to his feet. 'One of the knives we're eating with? How disgusting!' With that he threw all the cutlery on the floor, seriously upset.

'Don't be silly,' I told him. 'I boiled it for half an hour in a saucepan of water. It's cleaner than it's ever been in its life.' It was days before Starikov could face using any of the knives, for fear he got the one I had

---

5   No butter, no cream — but never mind:/ The Red Flag's flying high.

contaminated. Even though he came from the humblest background of any of us he was by far the most finicky.

In a personal sense, the building of the Wall was a bitter blow to me as it meant that I could not visit the Western half of Berlin or see any of the sights on which I had set my heart: Charlottenburg, the Kurfürstendamm, the Tiergarten, the Olympic stadium. At weekends, though, we were allowed to take a commuter train and travel out to any destination within half an hour of the city centre among the lovely lakes and woods to the east and south.

The Wall had a far more profound effect on me than that of restricting physical movement: it stimulated another leap in my mental development. At first hand I saw how repugnant Communism was to ordinary people. I saw that only a physical barrier, reinforced by armed guards in watch-towers, could keep the East Germans in their socialist paradise and stop them fleeing to the West. For the first time I saw what the Soviet Union was doing to Eastern Europe.

Why, after witnessing all this, did I go ahead and join the KGB only a few months later? Dozens of people have put the question to me, and I do not find it easy to answer. I can only say that at the age of twenty-three my ideas were still confused, and I had not fully made up my mind about what was right or wrong. At the time my best policy seemed to be to remain an internal rebel: to keep my dissent to myself. Every day I was thinking: All right. I see how the system works, and it stinks. But what can I do against it? The only sensible way to behave is to remain an opponent in my mind. Later, of course, I realized that this attitude was dishonest and weak. Unlike most of the citizens of the Soviet Union, I had been lucky enough to go abroad and be in the right place at the right time to see the truth — and yet I did nothing about it.

It was no consolation that thousands of intellectuals and officials had also chosen to remain kitchen rebels, to sit in their kitchens condemning the system to family and friends while they drank their wine or vodka. In Russia there is a gesture which denotes that you are expressing contempt but keeping it in your pocket: the showing of the thumb between the knuckles of the first and second fingers (a cousin of the Western V-sign). Countless people were giving that signal, and they went on doing so for another thirty years, till the very end of the Soviet regime — only to discover, with dismay, that they could not then prove to anybody that they had always held strong anti-Communist views. At least, after a while, I took action. But in 1961 I was in no position to do so.

*

The longer we stayed in Berlin the more we felt we were men of the world. Now that we had learnt something about the KGB, we knew what had to be taken seriously, and what could be joked about for, in spite of the general greyness of life, we enjoyed some amusing interludes. One such occurred when Anastas Mikoyan, then number three in the Politburo, came on a State visit, a grand tour on which I was asked to act as interpreter for the two Soviet cameramen making an official record of the trip. I joined the entourage, and we travelled all over the country, going to the opera (where we saw *Fidelio*) and eating lavish meals in the best hotels and restaurants. For the cameramen, the climax of the operation was an invitation to a Soviet military base where they became excited, hoping to film all kinds of modern weapons. Alas, when the long line of cars drove on to the base, there was not a gun or tank in sight as everything had been hidden away in hangars. The Germans joked that the only weapon on display was the ceremonial dagger worn by the officer in charge of the guard of honour.

Things improved when we repaired to the canteen to find that a magnificent lunch had been laid out: red caviar, excellent soup, many kinds of cold meat — everything a Russian could wish for. The food and vodka brought out all that was coarse and bohemian in the cameramen, whose jokes demonstrated the typically irresponsible, flippant attitude of Russians to the conventions of European life. 'You know how we clean our shoes while travelling?' one of them asked. 'On the curtains, of course!' Then he said, 'You must have heard one of our favourite rhymes:

"Tolko pokoynik

Ne ssit v rukomoynik."[6]

In December, towards the end of our stay, we four students were dispersed to four different consulates. Everyone wanted to go to Leipzig, the second most interesting city in the country, but luckily my special secret pleading, that my brother was already there, won the day for me, and to my delight I found myself in Leipzig in time for Christmas.

Until then my interest in religion had been intellectual; no doubt it had been planted by my grandmother, and I had rarely had a chance to witness or feel religious faith for myself. Now I got one — and a thrilling experience it was. The atmosphere in Leipzig was particularly intense. The end of the war had left people shattered and depressed, but at least they had been able to travel wherever they wanted, to visit their families and friends at important festivals. Now, suddenly, they were cut off, with no definite prospect of ever again being able to hold a family reunion. Under Communism, life had become dark and poor and primitive — and all this, I felt, had intensified their religious

---

6   Only a dead man doesn't pee in the basin.

feelings. With little to buy in the shops, and not much light, everything depended on the fervour with which they sang in church and played brass instruments from the church balconies.

It was in this intense atmosphere that I heard Bach's *Christmas Oratorio* given in one of the concert halls. It was the first time I had heard Bach live — few of his works were ever played in the Soviet Union, and none with religious connotations — and it was a revelation to be in an audience of Germans, who listened with such awe and emotion. I was intensely moved, and have tried to listen to the *Christmas Oratorio* every year since, if not at a live performance at least on radio or television.

A day or two later I went to a service in the Tomaskirche, with which Bach had close connections. The church was packed, but I found a place at the back and had just sat down quietly when a deacon wearing a cassock came up and offered me a prayer-book.

'I'm a foreigner, you know,' I said.

'That doesn't matter,' he replied. 'You speak German. You can read it.'

So he gave me a book, and I took part in the service, which I very much enjoyed. The fusion of German national behaviour with the European spirit struck me as incredibly strong, and stirringly different from anything in the Soviet Union. The experience helped me realize that Communist Russia was a spiritual desert, and it made me want, all the more, to join the European world.

If the KGB had discovered that I had attended a church service, they would have taken a poor view; but already I was becoming crafty, and ready with my explanations. 'Oh,' I would have said, 'I went to the Tomaskirche purely to extend my cultural education. The church is a monument connected with the composer Johann Sebastian Bach, and I thought I ought to know about it.'

Moving around Leipzig, listening to conversations in trams, I began to feel upset on behalf of the German people. I saw that, having long been unhappy about Communism, they were now filled with hatred of it. I felt pity for them, and shame at being a Soviet citizen. I was ashamed that we, who were culturally so far behind, should keep such people down. At least in the old Russia there had been a fine élite, the aristocracy of intellectuals and artists. Now we had little compared with Europe. How could we lecture Europeans and tell them how to live? In spite of our manifold and obvious deficiencies, we were forcing our terrible system on them.

The boorishness of ordinary Soviet citizens was rammed home one day in Erfurt, which the Embassy had arranged for me to visit. One evening I was walking with a friend when we saw some people, obviously Soviet tourists, coming along the street. From their dowdy appearance it was clear that they were provincials, but they were our countrymen so we advanced towards them and merrily called, 'Hello!' The reaction was pathetic: after staring at us for a moment with fear and horror, they ran away. They had been so heavily indoctrinated and intimidated by their Party bosses, so filled with idiotic warnings, that when two young men approached them in the dusk and spoke in Russian, those provincial simpletons immediately assumed that this was a provocation and took to their heels.

Not that they were entirely wrong in supposing that underground activity was in progress everywhere. In Leipzig I met my brother again, and one morning, walking through the concourse of the main railway station, I suddenly saw another man I recognized: it was Leonid Kozlov, who had gone through the Institute in Moscow two years ahead of me with a high profile, always leading in political matters, a vociferous Party activist. In due course he had left, and I had not seen him again, but

now here he was, striding along, looking every inch a German bureau-
crat in a German overcoat, and carrying a typically German briefcase.
I opened my mouth to greet him, but he, obviously recognizing me,
quickly averted his face and kept walking. As I stared after him, it
dawned on me that, like Vasilko, he must be training as an illegal. (He
did become one but was exposed, and after some difficulty was swapped
for another prisoner.)

More surreptitious activity was needed for the third of the tasks the
KGB had set for me: to find somebody whom I could recommend as
a potential special agent. There was one obvious candidate — a tall,
blond, handsome East German called Erik, who had been a member of
our Track and Field Club at the Institute, but had had to return home
prematurely because of family problems. I found him in a pretty little
town south of Leipzig, and he, not knowing that I was cultivating him
as a potential recruit rather than just as a friend, asked me to spend
Christmas with him and his parents.

The first time Erik spoke of his family, he told me that the Russians
had made his father suffer after the war, but that his involvement in
the conflict had been entirely innocent. He was, Erik said, only an
accountant, a financial clerk, who had been called up and put into the
Waffen SS. The Russians had thrown him into Buchenwald concentration camp and kept him there for five years; many inmates died, and
he came out emaciated and ill.

That was Erik's first version of his story, but a week or two later, after
a couple of drinks, he let fall that his father was a Hero of the Defence
of Frankfurt-am-Oder, the last fortress before Berlin. Some accountant!
When I went to the family house just before Christmas, sure enough,
there opening the door for me was a man who personified the SS: square
jaw, close-cropped head, thick-framed glasses, with an Alsatian at his

heel. Yet in spite of his appearance he was kind, and we had a most enjoyable German Christmas, with presents round the tree, an elaborate cold meal on Christmas Eve, and traditional carp on Christmas Day.

The KGB seemed pleased with my discovery of a candidate, but later, when Erik visited me in Moscow, still not knowing that I belonged to the organization, he complained bitterly that the Russians had been playing spy tricks on him. Evidently things had reached the stage at which they wanted to recruit him but he was not keen and sent them packing, without ever realizing that I had been involved.

In Leipzig, apart from my other commitments, I caught up with some of the young people whom I had looked after in Artek eighteen months earlier. Having brought some addresses with me, I made contact with Hans, one of the more intelligent boys, who invited me to dinner with his parents and one of the girls who had been at the camp. The evening proved fascinating: it was fun to see the children again and hear about their progress at school, and I had a good talk with the parents about the state of Germany. Even to see a flat that had been built in the 1930s was an experience because the standard of construction was much higher than anything I had come across in Russia.

That evening, however, was tame compared with one that soon followed. I had been put to live in a building containing workshops, attached to a school for Soviet children. On the top floor was a huge dormitory, full of beds, but luckily I was the only person using it. One day there was a knock on the street door: the elderly couple who looked after the building did not hear it, so I went down myself — and who should I find but Olga, the most glorious of all the girls in the athletics group, looking even more sexy than I remembered her.

'Oleg!' she cried. 'I heard you were in town, and got the address. I just had to see you!'

Without ceremony she led the way upstairs and sat on the edge of my bed, brimming with confidence and vitality. It was perfectly clear that she had come with one object only — that of going to bed for the evening. So brazen was she that, under pretext of sewing a button on to her trousers, she took them off, and sat there with her fantastic legs swinging. I felt as if I was in a dream, for here was easily the most attractive girl I had ever seen sitting half-naked on my bed. Why did I not take advantage of her overtures?

All I had to do was run a hand up one of her thighs and that would have lit the fire. Instead, I did nothing but talk and talk, until in the end I suggested that we should go for a walk. We walked miles through the icy streets until we reached the block in which she lived, and there, outside the door, we kissed — but that was all. Ever since, I have cursed myself for being so timid, so backward. Partly I was put off by the knowledge that I was not supposed to associate with foreigners, but really it was my own inhibitions that held me back. When I saw Hans again, and mentioned that I had caught a glimpse of Olga, he gave me a sly look and said, 'Ah! She's become very naughty, you know. She goes out with Russian soldiers.' That made me feel slightly better — but, all the same, I bitterly regretted missing such an opportunity.

Stirred up by it, I wrote to another German girl, Charlotte, who lived somewhere near Leipzig, suggesting that we should get together. We had met in Moscow, when she had come as a tourist and I was acting as interpreter-guide: we had gone for walks in the evenings, and embraced passionately in dark courtyards, and she had been keen to start a full relationship. Now, though, she wrote back saying, 'Oleg, you're too late. I'm married, and to a Russian officer.'

We set out for home on 20 January 1962, leaving Berlin a few days before our full six months were up. I could happily have stayed longer.

We had all learnt an immense amount, and thoroughly enjoyed ourselves, for life in East Germany was more interesting and more comfortable than in Russia. Yet we had to return for our last term at the Institute lay ahead with final exams at the end of it, and also we had to write our theses. We were supposed to have collected enough material to dash off the papers quickly — and, indeed, I had assembled a good deal. My problem was that I still had no authorization to do the subject I wanted. In the end I simply started to write about relations between Church and State in the DDR, without anyone giving me the go-ahead.

With my natural interest sharpened by my own first-hand experiences in Leipzig, I had plenty to say. I collected material from newspapers and magazines on both sides of the German border, and picked up ideas during my travels. Also, in the Embassy, I had read the secret reports sent in by the research departments of the puppet political parties, which furnished good material.

In East Germany the Church was the only element of society openly opposing the State: diplomacy, intrigue and negotiation went on non-stop. The picture was complicated because four different units were involved: East Germany, West Germany, East Berlin and West Berlin. In each the structure of religious life was quite different: in West Germany, for instance, Protestants and Catholics were evenly balanced, with half the population belonging to each, but in the East 90 per cent of the people were Protestant. Strong regional differences had also to be taken into account. In Thuringia, for instance, things seemed to be much the same as in the days of Hitler: people in the Church were much more eager to support the regime than those anywhere else. East German students had no idea how important a force the Church was in their country: they told me that to write about it was a waste of time, as there were so few believers left. But they were wrong — as was made clear when the DDR finally crumbled, and it emerged that the Church had played a vital part in the collapse.

I wrote the thesis by hand, had it typed and, at over a hundred pages, it came out one of the longest papers of my year. Each of us was supposed to have a tutor, who in theory supervised our theses; still without anyone, I approached Mr Rozonov, one of the liveliest lecturers who always drew full audiences. He, however, declined to help, because when he had suggested I should study under him as a postgraduate student, I had declined his offer on the grounds that the KGB had already offered me a job when I finished my student course, and I wanted to start work as soon as possible.

Becoming more and more worried, I went to the history department one day, and outside the office of the department's head, I saw the boss himself. I must have looked harassed, because he asked, 'What's the matter? What's up?' I explained that I needed someone's name to put on my thesis as my tutor.

'What's the paper about?' he asked, and when I told him, he immediately said, 'OK, put my name on it. But I tell you what, let's not stick our necks out. Change the title. Call it something like "History of Religious Organizations in the DDR".'

That was the only stipulation he made. I felt enormously relieved. I knew that as head of the department he needed a number of names to justify his claim that he was supervising students, and also that he got extra money for every paper he sponsored. It did not worry me that he was making a double gain: I had my mentor, and that was all that mattered.

Then he said, 'As your tutor, I'm supposed to produce a review of your paper. But look' — he riffled through my pages —'you've written a whole book! Do me a favour and draft the review for me.' So I did that too: I wrote a 1000-word summary, which he signed, and that was the end of it.

Our final exams in June were tough. Everyone became nervous, especially about international law, which was the hardest, a real discipline, which had to be learnt properly and in which we had had relatively little instruction. The other subjects were the history of international relations and Marxism and Leninism: the whole month was devoted to the exams, with eight days of preparation building up to each one.

To a Westerner, the exam procedure would have seemed very odd. Everything was done orally, each student appearing for about twenty minutes before a panel of three teachers. Called into the room one at a time, we were issued with a piece of paper bearing a number and three questions. We would then sit at a desk equipped with pencil and paper, and have about an hour to prepare our answers, while other candidates were grilled ahead of us. It was highly distracting to have the sound of voices rising and falling at the front of the room: students were supposed to speak for seven minutes on each question, but if someone started to give exceptionally good answers, the examiners often hurried him on to his next subject so that he might be finished altogether in eight or ten minutes.

Clever students would try to take advantage of this practice by starting with the cream of their knowledge, in the hope that they would be stopped. There was a great deal of cheating: people brought in cribs which they consulted under their desks once they had seen the questions. A few were so brazen that they brought in textbooks concealed beneath their jackets, and others went to incredible lengths to manufacture long, narrow concertinas of paper, densely covered in notes, which could be folded down to nothing and then brought privily out of a pocket.

One teacher, Professor Epstein, who taught medieval history, was both so kind and so wise — an unusual combination — that he managed to outwit the cheats. He dressed in the shabbiest old clothes but was so deeply in love with the Germany of the fourteenth and fifteenth centuries that when he spoke of it he went into a trance-like state. When it came to exams, he ignored the surreptitious importation of textbooks and gently spread his questions on to a wider front — 'What do you consider were the wider effects of the Thirty Years' War?' — so that mere parrot knowledge of dates was useless.

Yet it was not only students who cheated. Besides the exams, we also had a kind of check called *zachyot* and *ni zachyot* — accepted or not accepted — in which we had to answer a couple of quick questions, and the teacher would say, 'All right, you're through,' or 'I'm sorry. That's not satisfactory. Please come again.' One day Slava Makarov, who was among the ablest students, went in to what should have been a formality for his questions on states law, only to emerge crimson and humiliated with an expression of shock on his face. The tutor, Sidorov, had political ambitions, and Slava's second question had been about the legal status of the Berlin Wall. We all knew that subject backwards, but when Slava gave what he thought was a perfectly adequate answer, Sidorov merely asked if he had read issue no. 9 of the magazine *States Law*. Slava said, 'I'm sorry, I haven't', and was told he had failed. Indignant on his behalf, we all went round to the library, and at once everything was plain: there, in issue no. 9, was an article on the Wall by none other than Sidorov.

In spite of such hazards, everything turned out well for me: I had a job to go to, which gave me a feeling of stability and stopped me being nervous, with the result that my marks were satisfactory. I received a handsome diploma, enclosing a certificate which listed all the subjects I had taken during my six years at the Institute, together with the marks

I had scored — a welcome souvenir of my time in college. Then came another interview with a KGB officer, who told us that we new recruits would become members of the organization from 1 August, but that we could count the month as a paid holiday and report for duty on the 31st, when we would be driven to School 101. In the meantime our monthly grant would go up from 450 roubles a month to 1500 — a handy increase.

Knowing that the Institute had acquired a holiday camp on the coast of the Black Sea, not far from Artek, I managed to get a place there, and travelled south to find an enchanted spot, with tents pitched beneath pine trees and a fantastic view out over the sea. My happiness was compounded because Standa Kaplan was also there. Rather than go straight home to Czechoslovakia when the term ended, he arranged to stay on for another month, and during that idyllic August our friendship, already strong, became even closer.

Every day we ran though the hilly woods, up and down paths of earth as red as that in Australia. We sunbathed and swam in the sea, diving off the rocks. We ate our meals outdoors under the pines, the food being passed out through the open window of a ruined villa, which had been covered with tarpaulins to make a temporary kitchen. With his European good looks, Standa had always enjoyed great success with women, and now he had a mistress somewhere near Yalta, a few kilometres down the coast. In the evenings he would talk about her, and we chatted for hours about life in general. He, too, was liberal-minded, and held strongly sceptical views about Communism, which he was not afraid to express when in the right company.[7]

---

7   Later he joined the intelligence service in Czechoslovakia — but only in order to be sent abroad so that he would be able to defect. This he did, in 1968 or 1969, not during the Soviet invasion of his country but some time afterwards.

As for me, my drawback with girls was that I was not only timid but choosy. At the camp there was a girl who often ran with me, and was obviously in search of an affair. She was lovely, long-legged, slim and attractive, yet somehow I thought she was not my type, and did not fancy her. So although we ran and talked together, and I was kind to her, there was no more to it than that.

I returned to Moscow in the autumn of 1962 with a healthy tan. I was slightly less green about the world, but I still had a great deal to learn about the KGB and its peculiar methods.

Chapter Five – KGB Pupil

On 1 August 1962, 120 young men, almost all strangers to each other, reported to an office in central Moscow. There we were put straight on to coaches and driven out to School 101, in the woods fifty kilometres north of the city. Sixty of us were on a one-year course, and sixty were beginning a two-year programme. With the same number left over from the year before, the total strength of the school was nearly two hundred. My presence in the draft was largely due to the advice of my brother, who had insisted that I should go through the school. A classical institutional KGB training, he said, would earn me a certificate entitling me to work in any part of the organization, whereas if I failed to get a certificate, and something then went wrong, my future would be uncertain.

I am now ashamed to admit it but I found School 101 idyllic: the year I spent there was the best time of my life. Later, under Yuri Andropov, the place was inflated into the Red Banner Institute of the KGB, and became a colossal academy of espionage; but in my day it was only a modest establishment, of three large wooden buildings standing in the middle of a lovely forest. Two were accommodation blocks, and the third the centre for studies. The bedrooms, for two people each, were rather basic, but the place had a number of features which I found attractive. One was the excellent sports hall, another the swimming pool, a third the tennis courts and a fourth the *banya*, or sauna bath, which was the best I had seen, spotlessly clean and heated by a wood-burning stove, with big stones on to which you could throw water to produce steam. The woods were ideal for running, and although the school was surrounded by a perimeter fence, it was easy enough to get permission to go for long runs outside it.

Soon after we arrived, we gathered for an introductory speech from the head of our faculty, Colonel Vladykin, who turned out a bit of a surprise. I think we had all secretly dreaded finding ourselves in the charge of big, tough, coarse officers, but here was a small, thin, insignificant-looking man, physically unimpressive, dressed in a smart civilian suit. He was courteous and spoke softly, with the mannerisms inculcated by good upbringing.

'Dear friends,' he began, with thoroughly un-Soviet warmth, 'the first thing you must remember is that you are all here under assumed names. You'll be known by the names I give you — I have a list here. Don't ask each other your real names. You're not supposed to know them.' He warned us not to speak about the school to anyone outside, not to reveal its address or how to find it, not to disclose its size, or any information about the teachers, or the curriculum. Even our parents were not supposed to know exactly where we were or what we were learning.

Next Vladykin announced: 'Now that you're officers, you must swear the oath which is an absolute condition of being a member of the armed forces. As you're all together, I'll read the text out loud. Then I'll distribute leaflets with a box for your signature, and collect them afterwards.'

This he proceeded to do, reading out in an expressionless voice, 'I, entering the ranks of the armed forces of the USSR, commit myself to defend my country to the last drop of blood, and to keep State secrets.'

147

With that, he handed out the leaflets, which we signed and returned to him. I remember feeling glad that he was not rude or pompous, but natural and rather avuncular. He then invited us, one at a time, into his little office. To make things easier, he had chosen pseudonyms with initial letters the same as those of our real surnames. I became Guardiyetsev — a name I found very silly, but one which, since it had already been entered in the records, I had to accept. I was also granted the rank of lieutenant — a pleasant surprise as I might have become only a second lieutenant with lower pay.

I was immediately struck that everything seemed so civilized. This was the first chance I had had to observe officers of the First Chief Directorate in action, and I noticed at once how different they were from everyone I had seen before. They never wore uniform, always good civilian clothes. The teachers and practical instructors all spoke well: former KGB officers, who wanted to go on earning full salaries as long as possible, they were fairly intelligent, obviously had interesting experience behind them, and worked with dedication. Several had a good sense of humour, and they gave the impression of enjoying their jobs. Altogether, the school was well run.

Once again, languages formed an important part of the curriculum. I put in for English, only to be rebuffed once more. 'English?' said the authorities. 'Everyone wants to learn English. Why not carry on with Swedish, now you've started it? We can give you a finishing course in Swedish with no trouble.' So I found myself in a tiny group of three: myself, Feliks Maier (whose real name was Meyner) and Yuri Vesnin (actually Voznesensky). No two young men could have been more different. Yuri was a typical Russian peasant from Petrozavodsk, square and solid, who neither looked nor was sophisticated. Feliks, in contrast, was a tall, elegant Estonian, careful, phlegmatic, a great planner, the personification of a European. As Solzhenitsyn once wrote, 'I have never in my life met an Estonian who was a bad person' — and Feliks lived up to this encomium. Yet he had an unusual background, in that he had been born in Siberia or, rather, what is now northern Kazakhstan: in the nineteenth century his family had been one of the thousands who settled in the East, along with Swiss, Polish and German migrants, just as my mother's family had gone to Central Asia. Although he still spoke Estonian and knew all about its culture, he had become so firmly attached to the Soviet system that this now meant far more to him than his roots.

He and I hit it off well, but we had some blistering political arguments. The Twenty-second Party Congress of 1962 proved hysterically anti-Stalinist, even to the extent of taking a decision to erect a monument to the victims of Stalinist repression, but many traditional Communists felt that Khrushchev and his colleagues had gone too far, and that Soviets should not criticize themselves so harshly. Feliks was one of these moderates. I, on the other hand, became a fervent advocate of the ideas put forward at the Congress. At one point he said, 'They can't put up a monument. How can we have a monument to the victims of our own regime? It's a contradiction in terms.' Of course he was right, and soon the idea was conveniently forgotten.

Lectures began as soon as we had settled in and, for people completely new to the KGB, there were some unpleasant revelations. Through my father I knew a good deal about the organization, and other students also had some previous experience; but some were shocked by the discovery that the entire work of the intelligence service was based on various forms of deception. Naïve young men imagined that intelligence-gathering was an activity that KGB officers carried out on their own; they supposed that they would travel alone to foreign countries, collect information and take photographs, exactly like journalists. Now, suddenly, they found that all such tasks were regarded as secondary, and that our primary role would be to *recruit agents*: to find suitable citizens of other countries and somehow to turn them, to persuade or force them to break the law of their country under our leadership and become secret servants of the Soviet intelligence service.

Our teachers knew from experience that some students would be shocked by this concept and might not be able to cope with it. In most years, I learnt later, one or two dropped out right at the beginning. Ours proved a robust intake, and nobody fell at this first hurdle but several were so bad at languages that it was clear they would never become fluent enough to work as intelligence officers, no matter how many hours they put in.

We were issued with one main textbook, *The Foundation of Soviet Intelligence Work*, which contained sections on all aspects of tradecraft (jargon for tricks of the trade): acquisition of contacts, targets of cultivation, recruitment, running agents, agent communications, personal meetings, use of deadletter boxes, signal sites, brush-contacts, surveillance, identification of hostile surveillance, use of impersonal communications, shortwave radio communications. We would have a lecture — say, on signal sites — then read the relevant chapter in the textbook and follow up with study of more books specified on lists of additional reading, which we took out of the library.

Most of these were strange-looking, for they had been run off through copying-machines on poor-quality paper, and even those properly printed had been turned out on primitive equipment. The short texts developed the ideas of tradecraft: they were written by veteran officers, and included case histories which were often interesting, but so thoroughly sanitized that it was impossible to tell in what country they had taken place. They would start off, 'In an Asian country there was an embassy of a major Western power…' and never became any more specific than that. The names, also, were falsified, so that 'Mr Johnson' featured in many of them, and the operational officer was often 'Mikhail Krotov'. In spite of these limitations, the case histories were often quite complicated, illustrating not merely techniques of cultivating contacts, but what were known as operational combinations, which involved the use of several techniques simultaneously. In the evenings we were supposed to read further textbooks, written by former officers about individual operations. These were absolutely riveting but still secret: we had to read them in the library and were not allowed to take them to our rooms.

On the sports side, I was in my element. Most of the students were interested in running, and regular training — for which the woodland tracks were ideal — greatly improved my fitness. (When the snow came in winter, we switched to cross-country skiing.) On one of my first days I noticed a man lifting weights in a primitive outdoor area under a roof beneath some trees. I fell into conversation and discovered that, although he spoke perfect Spanish, the KGB, for some mysterious reason, had ordained that he should learn Indonesian. He had a ribald sense of humour and adopted as his personal slogan, which he quoted frequently in a loud voice, Freud's dictum, '*Der Mensch sexualisiert den All*' — Man sexualizes the universe. His enthusiasm for body-building appealed to me and I joined in, later doing a lot of work with weights, which improved my physique steadily over the winter. One of my best days came at the end of October, when every student in the school had to enter a 3000-metre race. It was a wonderful crisp morning, with frost thawing, and I ran the race of my life. Everyone had expected a second-year student, a professional cross-country skier, to be the fastest but he took part in a different heat and, because his time was one second slower than mine, I came out the winner. (By an extraordinary coincidence, this man was one of the team who investigated me on suspicion of being a British spy in 1985.)

Each group of twenty-five students had a tutor and, under him, we began to tackle problems in which we were presented with a situation and a number of characters. In an office, for instance, are a girl secretary and her boss; in touch with them are an intelligence officer, an agent, another contact, and one person not in any operational position but burdened with debts. Given the position and the characters, how would we penetrate such a set-up? A simple problem of this kind would take up one lesson of fifty minutes, but more complex ones would occupy two hours. All the students would write their solutions, which would be collected, read and analysed by our tutor. He would then go through them with us a day or two later.

Within a couple of weeks it was clear that we had one outstanding student in our group: Misha Ilyushin to us, Mikhail Ilyinsky in real life, a young man of Latin good looks and exceptional ability, with such a quick mind that he would finish a one-hour problem in thirty-five minutes, leave his paper on our tutor's desk and disappear to the gym for a workout, secure in the knowledge that, next day, his solution would be judged the best. He had a marvellous gift for languages: brought up speaking French, he also learnt Italian and English, and when at the Institute of International Relations he had been put into the Asian section to study Vietnamese. He was also a fine athlete, skilled at football and ice-hockey, and dedicated to keeping fit. Altogether he seemed a brilliant prospect for the KGB, especially as an illegal: he would have made a perfect Frenchman.

And what happened? One day a message reached School 101 from the parents of a girl who complained that their daughter had been seduced a few months previously by a student at the Institute. Now she was pregnant, and claiming that the father of the child was Mikhail Ilyinsky. Nobody was much surprised, because, with his looks and intellect, he swept girls off their feet. Many thought they were in love with him, but he never took them seriously, considering himself too young for any long-lasting relationship. Yet this sudden challenge struck him like a knife in the back. He tried to parry it by claiming that he had not seduced the girl: she had demanded it. 'And by the way,' he added, 'if she is pregnant, it can't be by me, because that night, if I remember right, she was in the middle of her period.'

He may have been right. Girls often used such ploys to get the men they wanted — and this one probably believed that the KGB would force Misha to marry her. If he had done so, everything would have quietened down. As it was, he refused — and by sheer bad luck his own little affair coincided with the arrest and exposure of Oleg Penkovsky, the GRU officer who had been secretly working for Western intelligence agencies. This led to a tremendous shake-up in both the GRU and the KGB. The message passed round was that all immoral behaviour, all loss of moral principle, was to be severely punished. So the KGB, hypocritical as it was, set out to humiliate poor Ilyinsky: they interviewed him at length, held a Party meeting to discuss his behaviour, and eventually decided to dismiss him — the most brilliant student in School 101.[1]

Another student in line to become an illegal was Vladimir Myagkov.

---

1 Fortunately he had the resilience to succeed in another career. A natural writer, he became a journalist and worked for Trud, the organ of the trade union movement, before joining Izvestiya as the paper's leading foreign correspondent and being sent to Vietnam, an important post during the war, and from there to Italy. He soon married — a different girl — and had a son, of whom he was extremely proud, referring to the toddler by its first name and patronymic: 'Vladimir Mikhailovich is doing well.'

Compared with Ilyinsky, he was nobody — a grey, provincial type who never excelled at anything — and even though he survived School 101 a nasty experience befell him during his later training. The authorities decided to test him by sending him to Kazakhstan without proper documents to see if he could survive for a couple of days with no identity cards. If he had managed to avoid arrest, or if, in custody, he had behaved cleverly, sidestepping difficult questions from the police, he would have earned high marks, but in the event he had to be evacuated. Dismissed from training to be an illegal, he served at a lower level in the KGB, only to be demoted yet again. (In spite of these failures, he later rendered me a useful turn by surreptitiously obtaining somebody else's file, a service for which I was most grateful.)

I found most of our lessons fascinating, but was less interested in the practical sessions on photography, the creation of microdots and so on. In sport, also, there were two areas I disliked: shooting and unarmed combat. We were taught to use hand-guns, but I was never very good with them, and I was particularly bored by the stripping, cleaning and assembly of weapons. Wrestling and self-defence also left me cold — perhaps because at heart I am unaggressive, and do not like the idea of attacking people. The KGB had developed its own form of unarmed combat, which we practised during one period every week; but although I am fairly well co-ordinated — as I discovered later when I started to play badminton — I could not master all the holds.

It was a measure of our absorption that I missed the Cuban missile crisis, which brought the world to the brink of nuclear war in October 1962. One of our teachers' aims was to make us concentrate, and this shows how successful they were. Khrushchev's confrontation with President Kennedy was barely reported in the Moscow papers, and in the school we had no means of hearing about it. Had I been living at home, I would probably have picked up something on the radio; as it was, we were so wrapped up in our studies that our contact with the outside world was minimal. Not until much later did I find out how close we had come to catastrophe.

I enjoyed the training even more when, in November, as the cold weather was setting in, we moved on to practical exercises. For five or six days at a time we left the school and moved to a building in central Moscow known as the Villa, a folly built by some wealthy capitalist at the beginning of the century. There we stayed for the working week, carrying out what were known as *gorodskiye zanyatiya*, or city exercises, in an intense programme that we found both stimulating and exhausting.

After only three months' training, we were still very green, and at first everything seemed terribly difficult. Imagine an impoverished student from the provinces, not used either to having money or to spending it, not familiar with bars or restaurants, being required to order drinks or a meal for a contact who, until that first meeting, he had never seen. Imagine the mental pressure on a twenty-four-year-old faced with the task of trying to influence or direct someone far his senior. What we did not know at first was that most of our contacts were retired KGB officers, supplementing their pensions by turning out to act as agents; all we could be sure was that they were senior citizens, and therefore rather inhibiting. We had already learnt that all KGB contacts are divided into the following groups: *agents* (people actively working for the organization), *confidential contacts* (low-grade agents not entirely attached, but still doing something), *targets of cultivation* (people to whom you are talking and whom you hope to recruit) and *other contacts* (who are useful but sporadic in their assistance).

As a start, we were let loose in Moscow and told to look for operational sites — for posting signals, meeting people, making brush-contacts.

Then we began exercises in counter-surveillance — fascinating games of cat-and-mouse. For these we worked in pairs, one student acting as the target of surveillance, while his partner reconnoitred sheltered positions from which he could watch his friend and see if anyone was following him.

The surveillance was carried out by professional teams from the KGB, who themselves were in training. The minimum team would be one car and three people, one to drive, the other two to help each other keep a suspect in sight. Sometimes, wanting to increase the pressure both on us and on themselves, they might have three cars, each carrying three officers, some of them women, and all competent drivers, so that they could exchange jobs freely. To confuse targets further, they might change hats, wear different coats at different times, put spectacles on or take them off, and even sport false beards.

Every surveillance man or woman had a personal radio, with a microphone under shirt or tie, and a transmitter in a pocket. This kept them in constant touch with a car, which carried a more powerful set. One of the strangest facts we learnt was that every Metro station in Moscow is fitted with a special aerial, coming up to ground level in a tube, so that an officer can send a signal up to a car the moment he arrives at any platform down below.

The student acting as target would move along a predetermined route through the city, while his partner was supposed to find three sheltered positions from which he could watch him and anybody following. If I was the target, the surveillance team would tell me where to start, and I would be required to give them certain information: my time of departure from the start-point, and details of how to identify me. I would telephone the number given me and say, 'I'm wearing a brown jacket. At 10.05 a.m. precisely I will appear on the corner of Metrostroyevskaya and Sadovaya. I'll stand there on the corner for three minutes, with newspaper rolled — not folded — under my left arm. Then I'll start walking.' The voice at the other end would say, 'Thank you. That's fine', and everything was set.

The exercise was scheduled to last three hours, and during it I would have some task to perform — meet an agent, post something in a deadletter box, or make a brush-contact; but the first requirement was to carry out *proverka* — dry-cleaning — a combination of manoeuvres designed to establish with certainty whether or not you were under hostile surveillance. (If you did find you were being followed, the rule was that you should never take sudden evasive action, since this would only attract attention and arouse suspicion.)

The most difficult task of all, it seemed to me, was to place a container in a deadletter box under the eyes of a surveillance team without them spotting your action. After much thought, I selected a place I had known from childhood, a spot where a footbridge of steel girders went over a railway, but where many people were too lazy to climb the steps and simply walked across the tracks. At the point where the steps went up, the underneath of the bridge was low overhead, so that anyone walking under it disappeared for a moment as he was about to cross the line. In that instant, I thought, I should be able to attach a matchbox, which was fitted with a magnet, to the underside of a girder, without being seen, and walk on as if I had done nothing.

For me, the bridge had the added advantage of being on the way to my parents' flat: if challenged, I could justify my route by saying that I had been going home for a chat. It turned out, however, that the surveillance team were sharp that day: when I made the drop, they were close to me, and although they did not see me place the box, they deduced that I was up to something. They searched the bridge and found what I had left.

The teams were not usually briefed in advance about what we had been told to do: they followed a target, watched what he did, and were on their guard, trying to spot the sheltered positions from which the target's partner might be watching them. Having identified a possible lookout station, they would send one man on ahead to keep the target in view, and then rapidly search the shop or office or staircase they suspected. Usually they were very efficient, and whenever they caught someone spying on them, there was great jubilation.

Meanwhile, the target would be moving on; if he met anyone, it was the surveillance team's task to describe both the contact and the scene — how long the two remained together, what they were doing, whether they exchanged anything. If it was good fun being the target, it was no less fascinating to guard a target's tail. I remember once taking up station in the Museum of Architecture, where a colleague had found a good position in the window of a first-floor hall full of exhibits. Watching from there, I saw my partner approach and work his way along the street, but then suddenly whip round, as though aware of someone behind him. I just caught a glimpse of a man following, but the road was so busy that I did not see him well enough to make a positive identification.

All these exercises, of course, were for training only. In real life the KGB rule was, and is, that if you think you are under surveillance, you do not go through with any operation. In this the Russians are quite different from the intelligence officers of other services, who carry on even if they know they are being followed.

Our most complicated exercise consisted in meeting an agent, and then reporting the encounter. Before we started, we were supposed to know what our contacts looked like, more or less; we also knew that, being retired KGB officers, they would all be sixty or over. But to achieve positive identification each of them would be displaying a prearranged signal — a magazine folded in one or other hand, or sticking out of a pocket. A typical rendezvous would be a restaurant, a modest cafeteria or wine bar, where one could sit talking over a drink and a snack without attracting unwelcome attention.

The old KGB men knew that we were all beginners, so never tried to be unpleasant. If they set traps, the traps were according to the script, prepared by the staff of the school. A man might casually mention, for instance, that his niece was applying for a job in the Ministry of Foreign Affairs and then move the conversation on to some other topic. But that one remark represented an important operational opening — the key moment of the entire meeting — and if the student missed it, he would lose much credit later. Afterwards, we had to write two reports. The first described the operation itself — how we had found the rendezvous, whether or not surveillance had been present, how long the meeting had lasted, what sort of a mood the agent was in, happy, relaxed, nervous. In the second report we gave details of any information gleaned from him, perhaps about American policy towards the Middle East, or some similar question.

Naturally the reports threw up many discrepancies. The surveillance might describe the target as having behaved in a particular way, and he might not agree. An agent, similarly, might give an account of a meeting which struck the student as unfair — although the former KGB officers had no vested interest in the proceedings, we all wanted to present ourselves in the best possible light. Sometimes students gave detailed reports of surveillance where none had existed for often we could not be certain whether or not there was anybody behind us.

Another major preoccupation of the KGB was the use of signals. These were of two kinds: one, the signal of personal identification, as in the carrying of a magazine or newspaper, folded or rolled in a particular fashion; and the other, the cryptic signal posted at a prearranged site. Later, in the 1970s, the KGB introduced the use of disposable items, such as a crushed cigarette packet, a bent nail or a banana skin, left in certain places, for example on a particular window-ledge or balcony. As you passed such a ledge, you could casually lob the marker object on to it, and the site was supposed to be checked within half an hour. In the 1960s, however, the most usual signal was a chalk mark, put up on lamp-post, wall, noticeboard or signpost. It could take many forms — a numeral, a cross, a V inside a circle — and could mean many things: I have put something in the deadletter box; I have emptied the deadletter box; I need a meeting urgently; I am leaving the country tomorrow. (There was a condition that the signaller should come back after a certain time to remove the mark with a damp cloth.) For every illegal working abroad, there was a file of 'contact conditions', on which his case officer could check sites, times and meanings of messages at a glance.

I am aware that to Western readers all this may sound rather childish — and indeed we ourselves saw the childish side of it. We sometimes felt it was fairly ridiculous that intelligent people, who had spent six years at college studying academic subjects, reading serious books and learning languages, should now be playing elaborate games of barely adult hide-and-seek, and surreptitiously scratching up chalk marks on lamp-posts. It had hardly penetrated our consciousness that this might later be a matter of life or death. Yet we reassured ourselves by saying, truthfully enough, that there was an element of adventure in intelligence work, and that we had chosen careers in the KGB because they held out the prospect of action. We knew that for most of our working lives we would sit about reading and doing paperwork: why not have a few little adventures while the chance was there? We were a motley collection of young men with different cultural and educational backgrounds, all trying to make good, so, of course, there were a lot of high spirits and jokes, but we took the work seriously.

As there were nearly two hundred students in School 101, and a similar number in the spy school of the GRU Military Diplomatic Academy, all doing practical exercises in Moscow, the surveillance teams received an immense amount of practice, and became expert at their job. During one exercise I went into a cafe to have lunch, well aware that people were almost certainly close behind me. I queued at a counter, took my food to a table, sat down, ate, and returned my plates, all the time keeping the sharpest possible lookout. Never in all those moves did I see anything to arouse my anxiety, yet at the debriefing afterwards the surveillance described my every move — and still I could not work out who or where they had been.

'You looked at the person at the next table with great suspicion,' one of them told me. 'Surely you didn't think that was one of us?'

'Well, as a matter of fact, I did.'

'You really thought we'd come and sit right beside you? Of course not, we'd never do that.'

Two years later, while preparing for my first posting abroad, I went through some of the exercises again, but this time as part of a surveillance team. For three hours we worked behind a student target, and it was like being in a film, chasing him through the centre of Moscow, a thrilling adventure.

Apart from constantly teaching students new tricks, all this intensive training yielded one direct benefit in the real world of espionage. Because generation after generation of aspiring KGB officers had been all over the capital in search of sites for signal and deadletter boxes, there was hardly a street or square, hardly a bridge, tunnel, courtyard or flight of steps that had not been used at some time or other. The result was that the surveillance knew every convenient place by heart. When foreign intelligence services like the CIA went looking for sites they kept resorting to ones already familiar to the authorities, and it was easy for the KGB to catch Americans red-handed.

One exercise that struck me as largely a waste of time — it was so rarely used — was the brush-contact. I never understood why so much was written and said about it because in real life its possibilities were so limited. The most normal place to try it was in the space between the two sets of doors with which many Moscow shops are fitted for insulation in winter. If possible, one made a signal through the window to the incoming contact, then went out and slipped him some small object as he brushed past in the air-lock. Sometimes on exercises we quickly exchanged briefcases — one fundamental rule being that all our briefcases were supposed to be identical.

Our curriculum contained relatively little in the way of indoctrination and, really, none was needed, for most of the students were so thoroughly indoctrinated already that they were like professors of Marxism. As for my own mental development, I have to admit that I was so absorbed in this new work, so carried away by the thrill of the material, that I worried less about ideology than in other periods. Nevertheless, one function of the school was to ensure that all students became members of the Communist Party, another element in the overall plan to ensure our loyalty and discipline.

Towards the end of the academic year all those who had not yet joined but were members of the Komsomol, or Young Communist League, were obliged to sign on as candidate members. In theory every student needed three recommendations: one from the Komsomol organization, and two from full members of the Party who had known the candidate for at least a year. In practice this was impossible, since we students had known each other only since August; there had to be a minor violation of the rules. But, in my case, two older members were available, in the form of Feliks and Yuri, and someone from the Komsomol was found to sponsor me, so that in June 1963 I became a candidate member of the Party. From that moment I was supposed to pay 1½ per cent of my income into Party funds, more if my salary became very high, in a form of minimal income tax. (A year later, in the KGB itself, three colleagues gave their recommendations, and I became a full member.)

Joining the Party was something that no Soviet citizen employed by the government machine could avoid, but by the 1960s membership was not regarded as any form of commitment or ideological belonging. All the meaning it had held during the 1920s had long since vanished, and people signed on automatically. It was like having to be in your office by nine o'clock, or having to lock your papers in the filing cabinet when you went home — a routine action, bereft of emotional significance. At Party meetings people had to pay lip service to ideology, but everyone knew that it was just a show, and the way that life was organized in the Soviet Union. I joined without any sensation of unease: I did not feel I was deceiving anyone, least of all myself. If I wanted to join the intelligence service, to work abroad and have an interesting life, it was what I had to do.

On the moral front, the attitude of the Party and the KGB was old-fashioned. Students were not supposed to sleep around or have strange friends: if anybody made a peculiar approach, we were supposed to report it immediately. On the other hand the authorities knew that most single young men were looking for girls, and encouraged them. 'Look for a friend for life,' was the slogan. As for homosexuality, that was never officially mentioned: both then and later, the intelligence service remained incredibly ignorant about it, and somehow the notion did not exist, except in the minds of the officers of the Second Chief Directorate who deliberately exploited it by recruiting young men as agents to seduce and blackmail foreign visitors. If people spoke about it at all, it was as if they were relating anecdotes rather than talking about real life.

In the school the emotional lives of our own small language group were complicated by the proclivities of our teacher, Nadezhda Aleksandrovna, an attractive woman of nearly forty, slightly plump but with pretty blue eyes and curly dark hair, whose husband, I guessed, had been posted to Sweden, where she had picked up a smattering of the language. She neither spoke nor taught Swedish well but because there were only three of us in the group, we made progress all the same.

Then she began bringing us Swedish novels, which we soon found had a strong erotic content. They were, in fact, some of the front-runners in the wave of sexual liberation which had begun surging through Scandinavia, and our teacher clearly enjoyed discussing the contents with us. After a while Feliks said, 'Friends, I reckon our Nadezhda Aleksandrovna's getting obsessed with sex.' A few days later he remarked, 'I find that Nadezhda Aleksandrovna isn't entirely happy with the way her husband treats her.' Later again he said, 'My friends, I suspect that our dear teacher actually wouldn't mind having a closer relationship with one of us.'

'Well, Feliks,' I said, 'you're a fine, upstanding fellow. Why not have a go?'

'No, no.' He sighed. 'I fancy her all right, but I'm a married man, and I love my wife.'

Then he tried Yuri, but the answer was the same, for Yuri, though utterly unsophisticated with his hair poorly cut and sticking out in all directions, was a tender and loving husband. So Feliks turned to me and said, 'What about you, Oleg? You're our only hope.'

True enough, I was still single but I was timid, and, at twenty-two, had no idea how to deal with a woman of maybe thirty-nine. So — no doubt to her secret disappointment — none of us was prepared to perform.

Matters came to a head in February and March, with two of the important festivals of the Soviet calendar. The Day of the Soviet Army, on 23 February, commemorates the creation of the Red Army in 1918, and is sometimes marked by the giving of presents to men. Nadezhda Aleksandrovna sought to seize the initiative by presenting each of us with a gift.

We should have made a joke out of it, of course, but, being modest and embarrassed, we declined to accept the offerings. She saw this as an insult, and took it very hard. Then, barely a fortnight later, International Women's Day, 8 March, was upon us, the occasion for *all* women to receive nice presents. We duly produced tokens of our esteem but she refused to accept them on the grounds that we had rejected hers. In vain we assured her that our sole motive in all this manoeuvring was to show our respect for her, our revered teacher. Our relationship was irretrievably wrecked — but it had been full of exciting tensions. Obviously she was aroused and frustrated by the close proximity of three young men and hoped that it might lead to an adventure. For our part, it was a novelty to have a teacher who was sexually motivated and passed on such spicy books under the guise of work.

Because we were encouraged to go in search of girls at weekends, I tried diligently to find someone I liked but had little success until one day I came across a student who attracted me. We spent much of Saturday evening chatting in a cafe, where we had a couple of glasses of wine — but these went to her head and, when we kissed goodnight outside, she deliberately bit my lip, leaving a blood blister. Not only did it hurt, it was still very much in evidence on Monday morning, and Nadezhda Aleksandrovna, being the sort of person she was, went on and on about it. 'What's happened to *you*?' she kept asking. 'Oh, yes, I can imagine!'

At the end of the course we sat three exams: in languages, Marxism/ Leninism and tradecraft. For our little Swedish-speaking family, the language paper was a formality. So was the one on Marxism/Leninism. That left tradecraft, and even here we found the questions relatively simple. Our tutor had taken so much trouble with us that we all went through without casualties. By then he knew us well, having set us our problems, read our reports, organized our recruitment to the Party, and spent time in the homes of married students to find out what kind of feeling existed in the family.

During our final few days there was a good deal of talk about the end-of-term parties held by previous courses and how some of them had ended in riots of drunkenness and debauchery. We were a sober crew, however, and when the time came to leave, we went quietly, eager to launch on our careers. I graduated as an operational officer, one rung higher up the ladder than the junior operational officer I might have been, and went to join the KGB in the summer of 1963.

Chapter Six – Among the Illegals

I reported for work on 20 August 1963, wearing my best suit and tie. After being issued with a pass in the little building which housed the Pass Office, I walked to the KGB headquarters, known throughout the world of espionage as the Centre. The main building is not one but three, all connected. The earliest structure was the one taken over from the Rossiya Insurance Company, the Lubyanka, which became the headquarters of the Cheka in 1918, but the hulk which dominates all photographs was built by German prisoners after the Second World War. Yet the most impressive section is the one at the back, made of dark grey granite, with black marble on the ground floor, built during the 1930s when the NKVD was fast expanding.

My first impression was of corridors and rooms brightly lit and spotlessly clean: the whole place had the air of being well run. Yet appearances were deceptive. Because the KGB is supposed to be a military unit, action can be initiated only on receipt of a signed order from the head of the appropriate department and, needless to say, no order had arrived appointing me to any particular job. The personnel officer, a kindly fellow, said, 'Well, until it comes, you'd better do something. You can help them sort out the books in the library.'

I soon found that there was not one library but several: one for operational literature, textbooks and pamphlets, a smaller one belonging to the First Chief Directorate, and the main library, which had an immense stock of foreign reference books and dictionaries, atlases, encyclopedias, school textbooks, as well as works of history and fiction. Never in my life had I seen so many books! The first that my eyes lit on, lying on a round table in the middle of the big hall, was a coffee-table volume on the Spanish surrealist painter Joan Miró. I had never heard of him, and I was impressed. Then I saw that whole shelves were full of books on modern artists, Picasso among them, all unknown to most Russians, and thrilling to encounter for the first time. Also I saw the autobiography of General Wrangel, the White Russian commander who defended the Crimea during the civil war, and memoirs by Russian refugees published in the West. Well! I thought. It was worth joining the KGB just to read all these fantastic books. I did not know that the libraries were little used because most people were afraid of being seen devoting time to the study of banned literature.

There was plenty of work to do, as the library was being reorganized, but after a day or two I began to feel uneasy. I had expected to make an immediate start on my training as an illegal. I imagined that I would be taken to a safe flat, and shown various other flats in which to learn my trade, one for operational activities with my tutor and the Party secretary, another for photography, a third for radio work, a fourth for wardrobe, where clothes and disguises would have been found for me. Instead of this, I was stuck in the main building arranging books.

When I saw the man from the personnel department, I said, 'Look, what's happening? When I joined School 101, the whole idea was that I was going to become an illegal. What am I doing here?'

The officer looked slightly embarrassed and said, 'I'm afraid there's been a change of mind. They've decided not to take you as an illegal. Instead, you're to work in the superstructure of Directorate S [for Special], the organization which deals with the illegals' affairs.'

I said, 'I'm sorry, I wanted either to become an illegal or to go into political intelligence. I don't want to go into the superstructure.'

'I'm afraid you've no choice,' he said. 'You've already been recruited by the Second Department, so you have to go there.'

I was appalled. I discovered that the department for which I was destined dealt with documentation. I protested vigorously but was told that they needed people like me and that I had no alternative. My euphoria drained away: I had thought I was launching into a sunny new life, and suddenly the sky had clouded over. I would hardly be using my languages; instead, I would be training people whose languages were probably not as good as mine. As a student, I had been more or less a free man. Now I was going to be a galley-slave.

Because my appointment order still had not come through, the personnel officer said that I could move into his room for a few days and give him a hand. He was a timid fellow of thirty-one or so, who had been recruited to the KGB seven years earlier. Because he had trained as an engineer, he was put into T (for Technology) Department and sent to Britain as a member of the permanent trade delegation in London, but the authorities must have realized that he was too limited to develop into an intelligence officer, and when he returned to Moscow he was dumped in the personnel department, which only handled paperwork.

While I was working with him, he told me a good deal about England. He had certainly enjoyed being there, but his view of London was simplistic. The traffic was terrible, he said, and people were mad about dogs, of which there were many varieties. English people — women particularly — went to great lengths to impress others. 'If they've got good legs,' he said, 'they display them as much as possible. Breasts the same. Dresses, shoes, the same.' He shot me a peculiar look. 'I can tell you more. There was one woman in our street who had nothing to show off but her crotch — and she worked out her clothes so that she could display it!'

This fellow put me to work on the thick, brown record cards kept at the back of each file. I was supposed to write down the numbers and dates of the orders by which each man had been promoted, all the details of his career. It was a terrible job, and one day, through not paying attention, I made a mistake. The engineer noticed it immediately, and said, 'Don't you understand? It's absolutely unacceptable to leave a single figure out. They may be just numbers to you, but to others they're all-important data. They're the man's career — his salary and pension are all based on those figures. You mustn't omit a single one.

In the middle of that dreary chore came a sudden moment of excitement. Among the old blue files, with 'Committee of State Security' and the Soviet insignia on the outside, I saw a familiar name jump out at me from the little window in the cover: GORDIEVSKY. My own file? Surely I couldn't have such a thick one already? My brother's, then? No. This was Anatoli Georgiyevich Gordievsky, a Japanese specialist, and a veteran of the Second World War. From some of his banal pronouncements, which people had copied out of his reports to use as anecdotes, I could see that he was not very clever. All the same, I was fascinated, and so was Vasilko: when I spoke to him about it, and he heard the name Georgiyevich, he said, 'Ah, yes…' in a way that made me think he knew more about my father's background than he had let on.

At last my own order came through, and I was taken on to the staff of the Second Department of Directorate S. Each department had its function: the Second (mine) created identities for illegals; the Third trained them and prepared them for going abroad, while the Fifth dealt with security and the recovery of agents who had been exposed. Others, however, were more shadowy. For instance, at that date the ultra-secret Thirteenth Department, formed during the Second World War to carry out sabotage behind enemy lines, was still in existence. When the Cold War developed, it was supposed to recruit agents who would set up cells of sabotage workers in the countries that lined up against the Soviet Union.

Such people were difficult to find, of course: in the 1930s, when Europe was full of dedicated Communists, it would have been easy enough but in the 1950s and 1960s fewer and fewer dissidents were prepared to blow up bridges and power-lines just to please the Kremlin. Also, as intercontinental weapons were perfected, it became less and less likely that a Third World War would be a protracted struggle so the role of the Thirteenth Department declined still further. But it was also responsible for carrying out assassinations abroad, and illegals trained as hitmen were allocated to it. (It was dissolved in 1971 when one of its members, Oleg Lyalin, defected from the KGB station in London thereby provoking a mass expulsion of Soviet intelligence agents.)

I found that at the time of my joining the KGB the function of the illegals was changing. They were peculiar creatures, who combined the qualities of an agent or member of the public with those of a trained, full, conscious member of the KGB. Soviet nationals, they assumed foreign identities — became Germans, Dutch, French, Belgians and so on — by taking over the papers of either a real person who had died, or a fictitious one. Between the wars the KGB and GRU had been imaginative and bold, and had had many officers who spoke foreign languages fluently. They were able to deploy illegals all over Europe and the Near and Middle East, sending men back and forth between

Turkey, Egypt, Greece, wherever. After the war, however, the system became bogged down in a mass of documentation: because the KGB expelled all Jews, the quality of their people fell, and it became necessary to employ Russians from peasant backgrounds who did not understand the West. The result was a vast bureaucracy, with something called a *ligenta biografia*, or invented biography, being laboriously compiled for every man before he went abroad.

This set out an entire fictitious life, with short paragraphs in two columns. On the left were alleged details of the man's career, and opposite the fabricated evidence supporting them:

Michael Smith's parents were both born in London.

The birth and wedding certificates will be in his pack of documents.

He spent his childhood in Halifax, Nova Scotia, when his parents emigrated there for a while.

The period in Halifax is invented. No traces survive. The story is that his documents were destroyed in an office fire in 1951. MS has visited Halifax briefly, studying places alleged to do with his childhood.

So it went on for several pages. After the war the typical role of an illegal was simply to live in the country of his adoption and wait for the Third World War to erupt. He had a buried radio, which he would exhume when hostilities broke out, and then, assuming that all conventional communications had been destroyed, his hour would come. What he would report back to the Centre was never clear to me — presumably the number of nuclear mushrooms that he could see on the horizon.

In my time, the 1970s, things began to change, and people talked about activating the illegals, to make them work more. Some were regarded as hopeless and told to carry on with their waiting game, but the better men and women were instructed to find contacts and cultivate them, though not to recruit anybody, a job which would be done by a special envoy so that the illegal could remain hidden.

Some of the most dynamic operators, who, for various reasons, found it impossible to continue living abroad in the same place, were brought back to Moscow and attached to a mobile unit known as the Nagayev Group, after its first commander. Like the journalists on British national newspapers called 'firemen', they were despatched to all parts of the world when a job needed to be done. Something similar happened to my brother, whose wife found that she could not stand living abroad: he was attached to the mobile group in East Berlin, and carried out valuable assignments in Mozambique, South Africa and South Vietnam, where there was no regular Soviet representation. Once he had to recover an illegal who had gone mad in Sweden. Far-ranging operators like him moved about with the greatest care, always ensuring that they had the means of making a quick getaway. If, for instance, the Directorate had identified a potential target in Egypt, perhaps an American businessman with a weakness for drink or girls, an illegal who knew Cairo well would fly in with a well-prepared plan of approach. He would also have with him an air ticket to Cyprus so that if a meeting went wrong, and the target threatened to report him, he could immediately fly off and disappear into thin air.

*

In this strange world the Second Department's work consisted largely in the physical creation of the necessary papers for illegals, and we specialized in what was known as *perebroski*, a much-used term which meant the transfer of an illegal from one country to another — from the Soviet Union to the West, from Austria to Hungary or vice versa. It was a complicated exercise which had to be done thoroughly, with every document changed and every loose end woven in.

The most secure area of the department was the section occupied by the forgers: a pair of sealed rooms with one door only. In there worked three or four men (backed up by another three in East Germany), and although they never invented anything, because they were always copying drafts or original documents, they were highly skilled artists. The store of forged documents and samples, managed entirely by women, was amazingly rich: thousands upon thousands, constantly replenished. The blank papers and forms were produced at a KGB laboratory somewhere outside Moscow, and the details of identities to be created — name, forenames, date and place of birth, numbers — would be presented to the forgers. They created the new documents. They had many shelves full of typewriters, for various languages and typefaces, including some of the primitive dot-printers used in Germany, but they executed all the calligraphy themselves, mixing their own inks and, if necessary baking documents in a special oven to make them look old. They went to extraordinary lengths — for instance copying a whole page stolen from a church register and rewriting dozens of entries in Gothic *Schrift* so that they could respace the lines and insert one new name. They used ultraviolet lamps to look for watermarks and other traces in the paper on which foreign documents were printed, and turned out forgeries so skilful that they were indistinguishable from the originals, including blank passports of every conceivable nationality from Finnish to Iranian and Japanese.

Sometimes they came up against problems that seemed almost insoluble — for instance, the covers of Finnish passports, made from a blue plastic compound which they could not imitate. Then one of the three Directorate S officers on service in Finland went into a stationery shop to buy some small item and saw large rolls of blue plastic stacked above the counter. When he asked to see one, he realized that it was exactly the material they were looking for, so he bought the whole roll and sent it back to Moscow, enough for several hundred passports.

If I had been less interested in history, politics, ideology and languages, I might well have been fascinated by my new work because it was full of the paraphernalia of espionage, highly secret, the heart and soul of the KGB intelligence service. Such was the importance of Directorate S that the chairman of the KGB, Vladimir Semichastny, several times addressed its staff while I was a member.

On payday every month all members of the Communist Party would go to the Party secretary's office to put in the regular 3 per cent levy from their wages, but, in a little ceremony, the secretary would take his papers and rubber stamp and go down to Mr Semichastny's office to receive the boss's 3 per cent in the holy of holies.

The entire Directorate was a hive of activity. The Anglo-American section was studying possibilities in the United States, Britain, Australia and New Zealand, with a lesser interest in Canada and Africa. Britain was regarded as particularly important, because documentation there was so lax: nobody was required to carry identity cards, and there was no central registration bureau like the *Meldeamt* in Germany. Also it was relatively simple to obtain a British passport, and this was the dream of many a KGB officer: 'Somerset House' was one of the most popular phrases in Directorate S. People on assignment to London would go there, search the records, find a birth certificate that looked potentially useful, obtain a copy, and then assemble the other documents needed for a passport. Three guarantors were needed, and three signatures were forged. The great question was whether the Passport Office would check these through. Sometimes they did, but often they did not — a loophole exploited profitably by the KGB.

The Directorate was looking for opportunities all over the world — in India, Pakistan, Iran, Japan, China. Cuba was important, because it provided a large number of false identities. In West Germany, officers were seeking people with Swiss or Austrian connections, since a man speaking German with a slight foreign accent could plausibly claim to originate from one or other of those countries. 'Europe' meant all of the continent except Britain, Germany and Austria, and we had agents working on our behalf in every country. In France and Italy they had probably been recruited in left-wing circles soon after the war. In Finland they were similarly drawn from the left, but also there were a couple of Orthodox priests who had been bribed to allow the KGB to make extra entries in their church registers. In Belgium there were a number of former Communists, plus a few Russian or Ukrainian women who had married Belgians and pressured their husbands to help. Thus, by a combination of industry, patience and stealth, the European section was slowly building up its strength.

And yet, in spite of its high rating, the work did not appeal to me. I was put into the German section, where my fluency in the language made things easy for me, but I found that all I was doing was dealing endlessly with sheets of paper. I had no interest in all those wretched passports and attests and certificates. Besides, I found that 95 per cent of the work concerned East Germany. Although the main flow of political refugees was from East to West, there were always a few people returning, either disillusioned with life beyond the Iron Curtain or lured back by the pull of their families. Extensive research was needed o establish where each had come from, and why, and all suitable personal documents were confiscated and used to create new identities for illegals.

These were added to the ever-growing body at work in East Germany. There, in the 1940s and 1950s, KGB officers had perfected the practice of forging entries in the *Standesamtbucher* (citizens' registers) by borrowing or stealing the huge volumes and, whenever they found a gap between lines, adding an extra name to create a new person, perhaps a child of real parents who were dead.

The head of the Second Department was Pavel Gromushkin, a man from a humble background who had been carried to the top of his profession by sheer energy and enthusiasm (he was a member of the All-Union Volleyball Federation, and active in the leadership of the Dynamo sports club). Never having had a proper education, he spoke in the vernacular, and often became lost for words — as on the famous occasion when, presenting an award to some girl on International Women's Day (8 March), he meant to say 'Give her a clap', or 'Give her a big hand', but came out with, 'It's not enough just saying it — congratulate her with your hands!' — a remark whose unintentional ambiguity caused great delight around the corridors.

Always full of anecdotes, he often spoke of the British traitors Burgess and Maclean, and of how he had helped prepare their flight to the Soviet Union, personally supervising the preparation of their documents and schedules. He also spoke of Helen and Peter Kroger, who had to flee from America when the authorities there started to arrest atomic spies. 'They're very good comrades,' he said. 'We must do everything we can to get them out.' When Konon Molody, alias Gordon Lonsdale, was released from gaol in Britain in 1964, he again became active. Later, in 1971, as we were chatting one day, he grew emotional with pride. 'Oleg,' he said confidentially, 'I must show you something. Look at this!' He opened a drawer and brought out a perfectly forged American passport. 'The first one!' He beamed. 'So many years of work! We had a hell of a job to make paper with the right fibre content but now we've done it.'

You never knew who you might meet in the corridors of Directorate S, for illegals who had been exposed and brought back to Moscow were liable to appear there, as if the place were their club. Among them was Molody — a splendid man, full of fun, always laughing, bubbling with sarcastic anecdotes about the bosses. He told me that when he was released after four years in gaol, and returned to Moscow, he got a telephone call from the financial section of the First Chief Directorate. 'Comrade Molody,' said the clerk, 'will you please come down and collect your wretched money? We're holding so much that it's become a burden.' Molody promptly went out, bought a small grip and took it to the cashier, who handed over a colossal heap of notes. At the savings bank down the road, Molody took his turn in a queue, and when he opened his bag at one of the hatches, the young woman nearly fainted. Controlling herself, she counted in the largest sum she had ever seen — perhaps 20,000 roubles, and a terrific amount in Russian terms. Within minutes, the bank contacted the police, checking that this immense deposit was in order.

Another time I was acting as *Kultorg*, or organizer of cultural activities, a post that entailed selling tickets for Moscow theatres. One day when I offered some to Molody, he riffled through my selection, rejecting everything until he came to the Romany gypsy theatre, for which he bought two tickets. A couple of days later he ran into me, full of indignation. 'What were you up to, making me buy those bloody seats?' he demanded.

'What was wrong? Weren't they any good?'

'The seats were fine. It was the gypsies — it turned out they were all bloody Jews!'

Another survivor with whom I often talked was Rudolph Abel, the KGB man caught by the Americans and sentenced to thirty years in 1957, but released in exchange for the U-2 pilot Gary Powers in February 1962. He was entirely different from Molody, being embittered and disillusioned. After his rescue, he was attached to the Fifth Department, but without any function, or even a desk: he had a room, with only a chair in one corner, and he would come and sit there. One day on Dzerzhinsky Square he ran into Ernst Krenkel, a hero of the 1930s with whom he had served in a machine-gun unit in 1929. They had since lost touch. When Krenkel asked, 'Where are you working now?' Abel said, 'Don't you read your newspapers?'

'Well, I must have missed something.'

'Ah, I work here.' Abel pointed at the KGB main building.

'Really!' said Krenkel. 'And what do you do there?'

'I'm a museum exhibit.'

The remark was bitterly ironic — and Abel's cynicism was by no means misplaced. Years later I heard that Anatoli Lazarev, who succeeded General Tsymbal as head of Directorate S, remained suspicious to the last that Abel had been an American agent. As the former illegal lay dying, Lazarev ordered a man to surround his bed with a consignment of the newest listening equipment, in the hope that during his final delirium he might say something which would give him away.

After their return to Moscow, both Lonsdale and Abel acted as lecturers and consultants to latter-day illegals, and they travelled a good deal to provincial KGB departments. For people outside Moscow it was quite a thrill to see such heroes of the intelligence service in the flesh, and to hear their stories at first hand. Wherever they went, they were wined and dined, and they had at least two months' holiday every year.

Molody was exceptional in his high spirits: few senior KGB officers had any sense of humour, and juniors made jokes at their peril. One day in my second year I was approached by a pleasantly intellectual-looking man who introduced himself as the editor of the Directorate S magazine, and asked if I would contribute a funny article. Humour was not really my line, but I did my best and wrote a piece about hobbies and collecting, casually mentioning that in our Directorate people collected many different things. Some, I wrote, collected bottles of drink, but the contents had a curious tendency to disappear, so that the collection became one of empty bottles.

When the magazine came out and was going its rounds, I was summoned to see General Tsymbal. He asked if I had written the article about hobbies, and when I agreed, said, 'That was rather ambiguous, what you wrote about drink having a tendency to disappear.'

'Isn't that what happens?'

'Well,' he blustered, 'we aren't supposed to say such things. It suggests that our officers drink. In fact' — he lowered his voice to a heavily confidential tone — 'I myself don't see anything wrong with what you wrote. But, you know, people from the Party committee asked me to have a word with you about it…'

It was an open secret that many KGB officers drank to excess. Early in my time with the Second Department Mr Podgornov, one of the deputy department heads and a friendly fellow, disappeared for three or four months, but then was reinstated. Later it emerged that he had rarely been sober in the office, and a secret search had revealed bottles hidden in the safe and filing cabinets. He had been persuaded to go into hospital for a spell of drying-out. That he had been allowed to resume his job was an indication of how widespread alcoholism had become: the authorities who let him come back were reluctant to throw the first stone.

Another year I noticed that a certain officer always took a bottle of whisky out of his safe and poured himself a tumbler just before he went home in the evening. In due course I reported him to the deputy department head, who listened with keen attention and a peculiar look in his eye, but without making any comment. Suddenly I realized that the boss was doing exactly the same, and I rapidly backed off. Even though such blatant cases often came to light, people in the KGB drank less than those in the rest of Soviet society, who tried to drown their sorrows and frustrations in alcohol. Yet it was typical that the men who sought to control the minds of the entire nation could not tolerate even such a feeble joke. Later my brother told me how he, too, was reprimanded for trying to be funny, and his wife became alarmed that he was going to lose his job for having been frivolous.

What I never managed to find out, and still do not know, was the number of people with whom we were dealing: how many illegals were in service, how many were recruited each year, how many failed in training. Foreign signal organizations, listening to radio traffic, produce a figure, but it is certainly inaccurate since some of the communications are fake, made only to confuse hostile monitoring agencies.

Another tantalizing question was why I had not been taken on for training as an illegal, while others with languages less fluent than my German secured places. Years later I discovered that one of the men who interviewed me was a psychologist: he had detected an oddity in my speech — a slight jerkiness or irregularity of rhythm which he thought would surface in any language I spoke and might be dangerously distinctive. My mother used to talk in the way he described, so it was possible that I did too, but when I mentioned it to another senior officer, he dismissed it as ridiculous. 'That had nothing to do with it,' he insisted. 'The problem was your brother.'

It seemed that the KGB had an obsession about the dangers of two brothers working in the same organization, and especially in the same

181

country: the risk of them defecting was deemed too great. Yet I was never convinced about this, and to this day I remain uncertain about why I was rejected. Why should proximity undermine two brothers' loyalty to the State?

During the 1970s the majority of people in the KGB were still heavily indoctrinated, and regarded defection as an act of treason so outrageous as to be almost incomprehensible. When Oleg Lyalin went over to the West in London during September 1971, he became a universal hate-figure. Another shocking defection was that of Stanislav Levchenko, who fled the KGB in Tokyo and went to the United States in 1979. When Viktor Grushko, the department head, addressed his staff on the subject, he described the defection as 'an unnatural, perverted action'.

*

By 1963, when I was twenty-four, I began to feel it was time I got married, and I started searching in earnest for the right girl. I hoped to find one who could speak German, so I began to frequent colleges in which girls were learning foreign languages. Once I went so far as to pretend that I was an inspector, sent by the Young Communist League, and sat in on a lesson in the philological faculty of Moscow University. Some of the girls there were highly attractive but, as I sat at the back, listening and watching, I could see no way of approaching them.

Then one evening, I went to a dance evening at the Lenin Pedagogical Institute, a vast teacher-training establishment with many departments, like a university. There I was much taken with a beautiful half-Armenian girl, Yelena Akopian, who was training to be a teacher. Like all Armenian women she had beautiful eyes and hers were especially striking, a fine shape and a bright green colour, set off by her dark hair.

Cautious inquiries revealed that she was twenty-one, and about to finish her course in German. She told me that her father, Sergei Akopian, had been killed in a plane crash in June 1941, two months before she was born. He had worked for a firm testing new military aircraft, and had the bad luck to be flying as navigator when a prototype Tupolev 31 crashed during a test flight, a few days after the Germans had invaded Russia.[1] Her mother, a Russian woman, had married again, and her second husband, an engineer, was a good man; but there was a suspicion that he carried a faulty gene, and indeed their son, Yelena's half-brother, was diagnosed as schizophrenic at the age of twenty-four. I wanted to get married because I thought it would be good for my career, and help me if I were sent abroad. Yelena was also keen because there was still a shortage of the right kind of men in Moscow, and girls were afraid that if they passed the critical moment they might find themselves left on the shelf. So, without much real thought or self-examination on either side, we hurried into marriage.

I found Moscow's wedding palaces thoroughly unappealing, with their tinsel decoration and pompous rigmaroles, so we went to a register office and had a simple ceremony, with a few friends as witnesses. Yelena, being even poorer than I was, had nothing to wear but a modest dark green dress, and she was very nervous. Then we went back to my parents' flat, where my mother had arranged dinner for a group of friends. The occasion went off all right but was not a great success, because my mother did not approve of my decision to get married without consulting her:

---

1   Later in Denmark I bought a book called Tupolev's Camp (banned in the Soviet Union), which told how in 1938 the celebrated aircraft designer and his associates had all been declared Enemies of the People, and fenced into a kind of camp, where they continued to work as prisoners. The book, by one of the inmates, described how Pilot Ivanov and Navigator Akopian were killed in the crash of Tupolev 31.

she felt we should have talked things through much more — and maybe she was right. I think she was jealous of Yelena: certainly she and my sister Marina were jealous of Vasilko's wife Ella (short for Elvira), even though they concealed their feelings fairly well. My mother and Marina were never unkind to Yelena, just rather cold.

Ella, by the way, was good-looking, being slim and long-legged, which was unusual for Russian women. I thought her rather sophisticated, but later I saw that her polish was only skin deep. Her father was a clerk in an ammunition factory, who confided that in the 1930s and 1940s he had been an interrogator in the NKVD. It was he who spoke about 'achieving concrete results', by which he meant capital punishment, and because he used the phrase without regret, I realized that he was a real, old-fashioned KGB man, without university education, compassion or mercy, who had been happy to send people to another world, just to achieve concrete results. When I heard that, I liked him a good deal less.

In any case, Yelena and I had got married. We could not afford either the time or the money for a honeymoon, so we went straight to live in a flat that was normally occupied by an illegal but was luckily empty. It was close to the Ostankino, the television tower, which was then under construction, with work proceeding twenty-four hours a day, and lights blazing all night. The flat contained little furniture, but it was good enough for beginners.

Graduating from college, Yelena got a job as a German teacher in a school but soon she found she hated both the place and the work as she was not a natural teacher, and had only moderate German. Neither did she like doing overtime, nor taking on extra-curricular activities.

Much more serious was the coolness which, all too soon, began to develop between us. I started to wonder whether or not she was a good partner for me. Our characters were very different: whereas I was outgoing, energetic and always thinking about politics, she tended to be rather inert, both mentally and physically. Looking back, I suspect there was never any real love on her side and mine never had a chance to develop, so that our relationship never became close.

It would have been better if I had known in the first place that she had no intention of having children. As it was, she got pregnant, and had an abortion without my consent. When she found she had conceived, she became hysterical: she developed an absolute horror of having a baby, of giving birth. She lacked the maturity to manage a child, and she sensed this instinctively. Everything connected with the idea appalled her. Her instability had a bad effect on me, making me confused. My attitude to Yelena (and to all women) was naturally respectful. Her wishes were important to me. If she did not want to have a baby, I did not see how I could force her to. Did I want a child? I was not sure, but I felt that, by nature, I was a family man, and that I would like to become a father. I discussed the matter with her endlessly. I pointed out that her doctor had found everything normal, and had said that it would be good for her to have the baby. 'Surely the doctor's right?' I said. 'Why don't we go ahead and have it?' But she became so hysterical, so violently opposed to the idea, that I did not feel I could insist. But if she did not want children, how could we ever become a proper family? A feeling of emptiness plagued me for years, gradually growing stronger and, although we continued to live together, the bond between us was one more of convention than of love.

Then, towards the end of 1965, a slice of luck gave us both new hope. One day Mr Podgornov, he of the hidden bottles, summoned me to say that the department had been offered a slot in Copenhagen. We had several people in Finland, he said, but had never had anybody in Scandinavia. Then he made some flattering overtures. 'I've been watching you,' he said. 'You're an able young man. It would be an

185

awful waste if you only went to East Germany. You ought to work in a proper operational environment, cultivating targets in a Western country.' He went on to say that he had served only in Zaire, which was beset by many of the shortages suffered in Moscow, but that even Africa was better than the Soviet Union. Denmark, he insisted, would be paradise: 'You'd really love it there. So if you don't mind, I'll lobby for you to go.'

When I pointed out that I spoke only Swedish, and that none too fluently, he brushed aside my protestations. 'Don't worry, you'll soon adapt and learn Danish — and if you don't take the chance, there are plenty of others who'll snap it up.'

I left the interview with my heart pounding. The prospect of living abroad was intoxicating. Yelena was equally thrilled, and we set about making preparations to go to Copenhagen.

A few days before we were due to travel, the owner of our flat suddenly returned and we had to leave in a hurry. We stayed with my parents for the short time that remained. My last few days in the office were hectic. We had little information about Scandinavia, and no chance of learning Danish, because there was no teacher, no textbook and no time. It was all I could do to wind down my other duties before leaving in the first days of 1966.

Chapter Seven – Copenhagen

Most Soviet diplomats travelled to European destinations by train, usually in special carriages which went right through from Moscow to their destination, but we were told to fly so we packed as many of our meagre household belongings as we could into suitcases, and took off by Aeroflot jet. In the plane I suddenly noticed that the cuffs of my shirt were badly frayed, the people in the seats alongside could see them and I spent some time squirming awkwardly as I tried to turn them under and hide the ragged ends, reflecting on how poor and inexperienced we were.

We arrived in Copenhagen on a brilliant winter day of frost and diamond-bright sunshine, early in January 1966. At once I was struck by the beauty of the city, its cleanliness, its prosperity. After the drab austerity of the Soviet Union, it was a new world — a wonderland of handsome buildings, gleaming cars, shops packed with goods — especially stylish modern furniture — such as we had only dreamed of.

We were met by Ninel Tarnavsky (who liked to be known as Nikolai), officially head of the Consular Department at the Embassy, but also Deputy Resident, or second in command of the KGB station, with responsibility for the KR (or counterintelligence) Line. He turned out to be a kind man, stationed in Copenhagen with his wife and daughter, but he never brought off the slightest operational success or penetration. The summit of his achievement was to establish a relationship with a senior figure in the Danish security service, and even this he managed only by domestic means: as his wife was a skilled cook, he got her to lay on a stylish dinner for this important officer, and regarded it as a triumph that he accepted the invitation.

The Soviet Embassy was in Christianiagade, an attractive quarter just north of the city centre. Other countries also had their bases close by, and it was a standing joke that we were separated from the American Embassy only by a graveyard. Our premises consisted of three large, white-stuccoed villas — an establishment that had once been some rich man's home. The biggest building had elegant, high-ceilinged rooms on the ground floor, ideal for receptions, with big oil paintings on the walls, vases in the corners, and a large, central hall which went right up to the roof, with a balustraded landing round it on the first floor. The main KGB station was in the loft, just under the roof, although later, when we needed more space, we built new offices in the basement. Across a courtyard stood a second villa, with the Consular Department on the ground floor. The third building contained a small leisure centre and club, with a school for the children. All around was an attractive garden, and there was also a mews, with garages — once stables — on the ground floor, and small flats for staff above.

Quite by chance I had met Leonid Zaitsev, the Resident, or head of the KGB station, once before, when I was at School 101 and he had come on a course. On that occasion he had suggested that I should go to work in his department, but I had already been earmarked by Directorate S for service with the illegals, so I had to refuse his overtures. By KGB standards he was a thoroughly nice character, and prepared to defend his friends: a man of enormous industry, dark haired and round faced, whose ruddy cheeks and sparkling black eyes accurately reflected his zest for life. He had few weaknesses, for he did not pursue women or drink anything except the odd glass of dry white wine; yet he was a powerful trencherman, and, in due course, his love of food markedly filled out his tall figure.

There was also a harmless, if slightly ridiculous, streak of vanity about him: after a trip to Britain, where he saw smartly dressed City types sporting folded handkerchiefs in the breast pockets of their suits, he bought simulated handkerchiefs by the dozen, sheets of cardboard, with a frieze of white cloth triangles along one side, cut them up, and went about with his breast pocket permanently adorned. He also adopted a number of British customs, such as insisting on taking flowers whenever he was invited to a party, and writing to thank his hosts afterwards.

His main problem was that just because he was meticulous, disciplined and conscientious, he believed erroneously that everyone else in the KGB must be the same. Also if he decided that colleagues or subordinates were doing something wrong, he had an irritating way of nagging at them, as if repeated criticism would cure them of their bad habits. He had an insatiable appetite for work, and kept a huge ledger in which he registered his multiple activities: the overall plan of action for the station, meetings with targets of cultivation, development of counter-surveillance routes, all in minute detail. He also tended to overestimate the knowledge and abilities of young officers, delegating too much responsibility to them. However, when he became personally involved in a case, he took immense pains —as when he and a junior colleague, Nikolai Korotkikh, were trying to recruit a black American, and he spent hours rehearsing every move, as if for a stage production.

One of Zaitsev's first actions on my behalf was to arrange for me to learn Danish. When I tried to watch television in the Embassy on my first evening, I was terrified to find that I couldn't understand a single word, so different was it from Swedish in both vocabulary and pronunciation. Soon, however, I joined the Berlitz school in Stroget, the main pedestrian street in the centre of Copenhagen, where I was allocated two teachers, one a student, the other a man in his sixties.

It was an excellent idea to confront me with two such different influences simultaneously and my instructors' questions kept me on my toes. When the young man asked what I thought of the Danish welfare state, I could not tell if he was fishing for a compliment, or wanted a critical assessment. Deciding the second was more likely, I said something not entirely complimentary, only to see him look disappointed, and to realize that I had made a mistake. The old man, in contrast, opened with a slow question about furniture: did I prefer old or new? 'I expect you prefer old furniture,' I replied, 'but to someone like me, coming from poor Russia, which is full of hideous old furniture, I find modern Danish designs very exciting.' It turned out that he considered modern furniture hideous, but the good-natured argument that followed was ideal for learning.

I did two lessons a week at Berlitz, and then joined adult education classes for a 'Danish for Foreigners' course at a ridiculously low fee — the equivalent of £2 for six months. I found the challenge of a new language fascinating, particularly when it was presented in such a lively and imaginative way. In eight months I could carry on a normal conversation, but when I returned to Copenhagen on my second posting in the 1970s I became fluent.

I was surprised to find how high a proportion of the people working in our Embassy were spies. Ostensibly there were twenty civilian and four military diplomats; but of the twenty only six were genuine, from the Ministry of Foreign Affairs. Of the remaining fourteen, nine or ten were KGB, and the rest GRU. (This proportion remained about the same in all the Soviet Union's Western embassies, including London, until the great scandal of 1971 when the British expelled 105 Soviet officers in a single purge.)

The nerve centre of the Embassy in Copenhagen — as in every such Soviet establishment — was the *referentura*, a specially protected suite of rooms in which the cipher clerks worked, receiving and despatching coded messages from and to the Centre. The rooms of the KGB and GRU Residents were defended against eavesdropping to a high degree by mechanical and electronic devices; they were lined entirely with metal, like ovens, with all the windows bricked up, so that the inmates had to work in horribly claustrophobic conditions. Yet the *referentura* was still more heavily protected. As elsewhere, it was on the first floor, to keep it away from tunnels — with which the KGB were obsessed — and the single door leading to it had no handle or keyhole on the outside, no aperture but one tiny fisheye peephole for those inside to scrutinize visitors. A bell was concealed in a recess beside the door, and those who knew about it rang to alert the clerk on duty. Inside were four small rooms, one each for the cipher clerks of the KGB, GRU, Embassy and Trade Delegation, all with their own ciphers and equipment. There was also a larger room, a kind of air-lock, in which people other than the cipher clerks were allowed to read telegrams. Once on duty, the senior cipher clerk was not allowed to leave the *referentura* under any circumstances.

One of the cipher clerks, Leonid, was the first person with whom I made friends. A man of about thirty-five, he had a wife a couple of years younger and a small child. Because of his job, which made him a high security risk, he was not supposed to go anywhere alone, and when he began to make friendly overtures, asking Yelena and myself round to supper, I suspected that he might be doing it with the ulterior motive of trying to secure lifts, for I had been allocated a car (first a big, heavy old Soviet Pobeda, and then, joy of joys, a new Volkswagen Beetle). Because they were an amusing couple, I did not mind driving them about, and I took them on several excursions, to the beaches and into the woods to pick mushrooms.[1] Later, when I had been ill, the wife made a half pass at me, which I did not feel like reciprocating, but we remained on good terms. We were all devastated when, in December 1968, Leonid made a dreadful mistake.

One of his duties as cipher clerk was to receive and send the KGB part of the diplomatic bag. Letters and documents arrived as film, but in the package there was sometimes an enclosure wrapped in brown paper. One morning Leonid tore off the wrapping and threw it straight into the stove which he used for destroying documents, not noticing that the parcel had included a thousand dollars in clean (that is, old but untraceable) notes, destined for one of our agents. An appalling loss, considering the low level of salaries. The rest of us rallied round, contributing large numbers of kroners to help him reduce the debt, and to pay it off, Zaitsev got the Centre to extend his tour of duty from two years to three.

My own cover was that I was working in the Consular Department of the Embassy. I presented myself as a member of the diplomatic staff, but in that guise I was really no more than a clerk, dealing with inquiries

---

1   At School 101 all the students had learnt to drive and had passed a test; but neither training nor test offered any real challenge, as we simply cruised about the clear, open roads near the school and never had to contend with traffic. The result was that most of us were far from safe in the early stages of our motoring careers.

about visas, wills and inheritances, and sometimes transferring funds to heirs in Russia. Each day began with a general conference presided over by the Ambassador, during which relevant items of news were read out for the benefit of the company by those who knew Danish. For the next couple of hours after that I was supposed to help Tarnavsky and his wife handle visa applications. Because we received no help from the Ministry of Foreign Affairs, we were busy and it was valuable experience to talk to so many ordinary Danish citizens. In those easy days before international terrorism had become widespread, procedures were delightfully relaxed. I worked at a desk in one corner of a large reception room, and people waiting for attention sat on sofas round the edge. Feeling that it was my duty to be nice to everyone, I would take each applicant and sit with him or her at a coffee table to conduct our business.

For most members of the Embassy and KGB staff, the high spot of the day was the lunch hour: then we sallied forth in droves to our operational meetings, all out to cultivate local contacts. It was then that the KGB practice of handing out unlimited funds to its members poured money into the pockets of restaurateurs all over Copenhagen.

The form was that at the beginning of the month every officer would draw an advance of about two hundred and fifty pounds against his expenses for entertaining contacts, and if he ran out of cash prematurely, he could draw more with no questions asked. The system was an invitation to corruption, for accounting was slack, the principal weakness being that we were encouraged not to ask for receipts in restaurants. This rule derived from the KGB's archaic belief that to ask for a copy of the bill was somehow infra dig; that it was more polished and cosmopolitan simply to wave away the invoice with the tip. Stylish this may have been yet it also spelt fiscal disaster, for it meant that nobody had to produce any accurate account of where his money had gone.

We were supposed to write reports of our activities: the Centre kept demanding information, and calling for as many names as possible to be included. But in fact we reported on only our most significant meetings: if the contact was classed as an agent, a confidential contact or a target of cultivation, we were obliged to put in every last detail — name of restaurant, address, map reference, date, time, arrangements for meeting, personal facts about the contact, and presents or money given.

Needless to say, because the system was so deeply flawed, people constantly took advantage of it, inventing meetings and creating ficti- tious contacts while they pocketed the money. Years later in England I saw how an officer called Viktor Muzalyov perfectly exemplified this trend. One day in London our lady cashier said to me, 'Oleg Antonovich, did you know? Muzalyov draws two hundred pounds against expenses every month, and always puts in an account showing he has spent precisely that amount.' When I challenged him, Muzalyov claimed that he thought it was his duty to make his accounts tally precisely but we discovered that he was pocketing the cash, not just because he wanted it, but to cover that he had no contacts. Such reports as he produced were sheer fantasy, including those about his alleged meetings with the trade union leader Rodney Bickerstaffe. For months Muzalyov graphi- cally described how he had been cultivating this important target, but in fact he never met him.

In Copenhagen, under Zaitsev, who was strict and upright, corrup- tion remained more or less under control, but under his successor it ran riot. Oddly enough, one thing that KGB officers did not do was take their wives out to meals under the pretence of entertaining Danes: first, they did not dare to for fear of being spotted, and second, the wives would never have condoned any such practice. They had no idea of the scale of the abuse that was going on, and they would have been horrified by the idea of spending a fortune on lunch when they had so little cash for everyday needs.

Apart from the constant effort to find and cultivate targets, my principal task was to gather information about documentation and to look for Scandinavian identities, Danish ones above all. Until then the KGB had never done this kind of work in the region, so at least I was breaking new ground, the first man to explore local systems of registration and describe them to the Centre. The work proved a relaxed form of research, which I enjoyed, and it was not long before I found out that the foundation of the registration system lay in the ledgers of the official established Protestant Church, or Folkekirke. If we could gain access to the ledgers — as our predecessors had to the *Standesamtbücher* in East Germany a generation earlier — we would be able to create any number of Danish identities. First, though, we had to find priests or their attendants who would respond to cultivation.

Then the question arose as to how we should proceed if we found a cleric who was prepared to lend us a ledger for a couple of nights. The answer was that we would ask Moscow to send out a team of forger-artists. I, or a fellow-officer, would draft the entry we wanted — name, place and date of birth, names of parents. Then, if there was space at the end of a page or the close of a year, the visiting experts would enter the new person's details there; failing that, they would take the whole book apart and rebind it with a new page inserted.

My most regular task was to meet couriers on their way from or to Moscow and escort them between the airport or the main railway station and the Embassy. All of them arrived carrying a briefcase fitted inside with a metal box made up in compartments which held containers of film. If it suddenly became necessary to destroy the briefcase's most secret contents, the courier could press a button, which would release acid and melt the film in seconds.

There was a tradition that the couriers who came to Scandinavia once a fortnight travelled by train as far as Helsinki, Oslo or Copenhagen, and then flew on to Reykjavik, where the KGB and GRU stations were being refurbished, and new listening equipment was being installed for eavesdropping on US radio traffic from the air-base at Keflavik, in the far west of Iceland. For my first couple of years in Denmark I was constantly receiving these couriers and posting them onwards, together with bulky items of equipment being transported as diplomatic baggage. Four days later, they would pass back through, minus their loads.[2]

Most of the couriers were former professional sportsmen from the Dynamo club, burly chaps who had retired in their late thirties and joined the service. For them the job held many attractions: they travelled widely at no cost to themselves, ate free, and had various cosy contacts in the embassies, where single women secretaries were often waiting for them. Moving regularly through eight or more countries, they were on a non-stop sexual odyssey, and it was always refreshing to hear travellers' tales from such jolly, straightforward people.

Another of my tasks was to speed the transit of illegals who passed through Denmark on their way home for holidays in Russia. Our method was to infiltrate them on to Soviet passenger ships, several of which maintained a regular service between Le Havre and Leningrad, and every transit operation was thoroughly planned. The captain of the ship would be interviewed, or even recruited as a KGB agent; then, at my first special meeting with the illegal I would brief him on exactly

---

2 Once as a courier was waiting for a train in Stockholm with an immense package, a passing Swede asked him in Russian what it was. 'Diplomatic baggage, obviously,' he replied, to which the Swede retorted: 'Oh, I thought it was a royal — a grand piano!'

what he had to do, and take over all his documents. At a second meeting I would give him a Soviet seaman's passport made out in the name of one of the crew members. Even if the Danish authorities carried out a fairly thorough check, the details would tally with the crew list and it would not be apparent that there were two men with the same name on board: naval discipline did not apply, and the captain never lined up his whole crew together on deck so that they could be counted.

Because everyone was nervous that the illegals might be exposed, we took a lot of trouble over handling them. We considered it dangerous, for instance, to let them go on board carrying large pieces of luggage because that made it obvious that they were just joining the ship. Instead, we made them leave their heavy bags in lockers or at the left-luggage depot at the main railway station and then hand me the keys or receipts at a clandestine meeting. There was a small risk that when I went to recover something from the left-luggage depot, and handed in a ticket, the attendant would ask me what my suitcase looked like but that was a minor problem. Again, whenever an illegal came off a ship, the KGB did not consider it safe for him to walk down the gangway on his own in case the Danish surveillance should pick him up. Rather, we arranged for the captain to come down with him and put him into my car, as though we were going off on a sightseeing trip. Often I had a second car behind me, and as we were leaving the dock area the driver would slow down to a walking pace in a narrow street, where he could not be overtaken, so as to balk any surveillance team trying to stay with me.

Towards the end of March Zaitsev summoned me to his room one morning and said, 'Why are we getting so few meets?'

'What meets?' I said. The technical term was barely familiar.

'You don't seem to understand. Every member of the Residency, whatever his job, is supposed to cultivate Danes and recruit them as agents. That's the main purpose of our life here. The rest of your job you can do in your spare time. The essential thing is to cultivate people.'

I was so naïve, after two years' immersion in paperwork in Moscow, that I had not started to think operationally. I was used to burrowing among files, certificates, statistics and legal documents but not to tackling strangers, especially in a foreign language. The idea terrified me — but Zaitsev helped a bit by giving me specific examples of what I might do: recruit a Dane who might become an illegal agent, like the Krogers, or someone who would act as a live letterbox, or someone in the Consular Department of another embassy, who could supply us with foreign passports.

In fact, my only solid recruiting achievement in all those four years was the acquisition of one live letterbox and his wife, who agreed to pass letters to and from illegals. The man was a schoolteacher, son of a former KGB agent, and after I had held some preliminary conversations with him, Zaitsev helped me sketch out the crucial meeting which would lead to recruitment. As always, the Resident's attention to detail was impressive: he planned every course of the menu, insisting that we had champagne, fillet steaks and *crêpes flambées*. His main point was that everything must look seductive: it was essential that we had a flaming spirit lamp brought to the table for cooking the pancakes. His tactics succeeded, to the extent that the man and his wife — a pretty young girl — agreed to work for us, although in the end it was she who proved the tougher and more committed of the two.

In Church affairs, my luck improved when I got a specific request from Moscow to acquire a birth and baptism certificate for a man fighting to win an inheritance suit. The person concerned had been born in Horsens, a small town in Jutland, and here was an official request for information from a legal authority in the Soviet Union. Rather than write or telephone, I decided to visit the place, which was two and a half hours' journey away by road and ferry. I was rewarded by finding that the Catholic priest was a charming man in his sixties with the German-sounding name of Niels Oppermann. I got on so well with him that I started making regular visits, taking him boxes of cigarettes and the odd bottle of whisky, which he much appreciated in spite of twinges of guilt about drinking and smoking.

His elderly housekeeper would lay out a cold lunch for us in his house across the courtyard from the church, and often I would bring the conversation round to his registers of parishioners. He brought the books over and left me to make notes from them, obviously willing to help. If I had gone one stage further, and offered him money to let me borrow them — what then? I kept hoping that he would co-operate, because the Catholic Church, unlike the Protestant, was exceedingly poor and received no funds from the State, but our negotiations never reached that delicate point: I saw that his books were far too thin, and contained so few names that it would have been impossible to hide new ones among the old.

*

On the domestic front things went reasonably well at first, but later deteriorated. Yelena and I had been allocated a brand-new flat, which Zaitsev had somehow managed to acquire in anticipation of our arrival. But before we even reached Copenhagen the accommodation had been purloined by Nikolai Korotkikh, the KGB officer celebrated for his skill at recruiting agents. The reason for his abrupt arrival was that the Embassy had identified a soft target in the form of a communications clerk in the American Embassy, a man who drank heavily, liked company, chased girls and frequented nightclubs, and was short of money. Having found out where he lived, they decided to take an apartment in the same building and install Korotkikh in it; then, at a later date, they would set up an 'accidental' meeting, which would lead to cultivation and recruitment.[3]

So much for the plan. What happened was that Korotkikh arrived before his flat was ready, and moved into the one designated for me. Being a good colleague, he apologized handsomely, but for the time being Yelena and I were put into the guest room in the basement of the Consular building, which was not as bad as it sounds. Its windows were rather high, but the room itself was enormous, and we had all the necessities, including a cooker, shower and lavatory. Being young and unspoilt, we accepted it happily enough for a couple of months. The shortness of the journey to work, up one flight of stairs, was a major asset.

When at last we moved, the spaciousness of our new apartment seemed incredible: admittedly the place was almost empty, but we had three rooms and a kitchen, all to ourselves. And what rooms they were, with fine wooden floors, a fitted kitchen, a small balcony, and everywhere workmanship of the highest quality. Gradually, with help from the KGB station, we managed to buy curtains and a few pieces of furniture, all modest but adequate. One day a visiting Dane amused us by spotting a tiny crack between wall and floor, and exclaiming in horror. 'If you knew what we were used to in Moscow,' I told him, 'you wouldn't worry.'

---

3   The Ambassador's early-morning meetings were a great strain for Korotkikh, who had usually been drinking all night in his attempts to turn the American. 'Oleg, Oleg,' he would groan in my ear, almost anaesthetizing me with alcohol fumes, 'I'm totally smashed!' Yet Zaitzev insisted that he should attend, for the sake of appearances, even if he was allowed to disappear soon afterwards to catch up on his sleep. One of nature's great boozers, Korotkikh made several recruitments, and once at a conference in Moscow confided the secret of his success: 'I make it a rule never to speak to my target about anything except booze and women!'

We were short of money because my pay was pitifully low, and in Denmark inflation was rampant. Later, salaries were raised substantially, but then we had the tantalizing experience of seeing the shops bursting with things we longed to buy, but were unable to afford. Yet that was a relatively minor problem: much worse, Yelena began to exhibit what I can only call anti-domestic tendencies. Becoming an ever-more ardent feminist, she lost interest in cooking or cleaning, and behaved in what was to me a most peculiar way. Her own room, for instance, was chaotic, with clothes strewn all over the floor, and she made no effort to keep the rest of the flat in order. If I sought to remonstrate, she was always ready with some fashionable feminist phrase, to the effect that there were better things for women to do than housework. There was a kind of exaggerated vanity in the way she tried to save money by never spending anything on the flat, yet every now and then she would recklessly lash out on an expensive suede coat or pair of shoes. (Because she thought her legs were too short, she went in for immensely high heels.) This became even worse during our second tour, in the 1970s.

As a mild form of retaliation, I took a course in cookery, which I found useful, although most of my fellow-students already knew a good deal and I was permanently labouring to catch up. Goaded by the memory of how many of my precious books in Moscow were falling apart, I also enrolled for a course in book-binding, which my father had always told me was a most enjoyable craft (he was right).

We had not been in the new flat for long when we were invited out to supper one evening by a Danish couple, a policeman and his wife, a gifted amateur artist who specialized in high-class copies of famous paintings. I had been cultivating him, partly because he had some duties in the harbour, and partly because I thought he might lead me to other useful contacts. Now, I sensed, *he* was starting to cultivate *me*, and something made me feel that the main purpose of the invitation was to keep us under control for the evening, so that the Danish counter-intelligence service could bug the apartment with microphones. Before we left, therefore, I squeezed a small blob of glue into the crack between one of the bedroom doors and its frame.

When we came home, not only had the glue been dislodged but the door was standing wide open. Clearly we had had visitors, and I assumed — rightly, as it turned out — that the Danes could now listen to our conversations. What I did not find out until years later was that when they came in that night, they accidentally let out Yelena's black cat, which ran along the balcony and gained access to the communal stairs. After a sharp chase they managed to drive it back into our flat, but the incident threw them off balance and made them careless about closing the inner doors.[4]

At least Yelena was working, and in a job she enjoyed. This was in the KGB listening station, which eavesdropped on the radio networks of the Danish security service. Her task was to listen to recordings made earlier in the day, and transcribe significant details or passages for further analysis. Generally she would start in the afternoon, so that she could work on the tapes made of the Danes following Soviet diplomats, KGB and GRU officers on their way out to operational lunches. If the surveillance thought they were undetected, they would talk freely, not knowing that we were picking up every word. Part of Yelena's job was to evaluate the levels of surveillance used, and to decide how many cars had been behind whom. For easy reference the Danes gave us all nicknames. The Ambassador's deputy, for instance, was

---

4   While I went jogging, Yelena used to take the cat for walks on a lead; but one day it ran off and disappeared. All we found were its bloodstained collar and lead, and we could only conclude that it had been eaten by a fox.

called Bondar, and the Danes christened him 'Bonde', a neat nickname, because the word means 'peasant', and he looked just like one, albeit a fairly sophisticated specimen. I was known as 'Gormsen', or 'Uncle Gormsen'. Many an afternoon and evening Yelena heard the Danes give out, 'Uncle Gormsen's proceeding westwards on So-and-So,' and afterwards I would be able to analyse the tactics they had been using, whether they had been driving on parallel roads, and so on.

Sometimes she listened live, and occasionally events became dramatic — as on the day when an agent was driving up from Holland to meet one of our officers, Boris, for supper in the harbour at Dragor, a little town on Amager Island, some twenty kilometres from the city centre. Just before 7 p.m. Yelena suddenly heard the signs of active pursuit: it sounded as if the Danes had either picked up the incoming agent and were behind him, or were on the tail of our own man.

At once she called the duty officer and reported alarming signals. Listening in with her to the Danes talking between their cars and to headquarters, he deduced that it was the agent who was being followed. It looked as if the Danes must have been given a tip-off by the Germans or Dutch.

Urgent action was needed. The plan was that after the meal the agent would go out to his car, fetch whatever he had brought to the meeting, hand it over, and receive a payment in exchange. This had to be prevented at all costs. The duty officer, Anatoli Seryogin, consulted Zaitsev, who took an instant decision: within minutes Seryogin was on his way, with an assortment of fishing tackle in the back of the car as cover, alongside Sasha, our operational driver, to break up the meeting and snatch Boris out of danger.

Twenty minutes later they reached the harbour, and to demonstrate their innocence to the surveillance team, presumed to be in another car somewhere close, they started fishing. Then, as soon as he dared, Seryogin sent the driver into the restaurant, with orders to show his face, in the hope that Boris, who knew him well, would realize that something was amiss and leave at once. Boris saw him, and was surprised, but concealed any reaction, so that the manoeuvre had to be repeated a few minutes later. This time the driver went up to him and said in mid-conversation, 'Borya, I'm sorry, but you must leave immediately. Your son's dangerously ill.'

This had the required effect. Boris stood up, apologized to his companion, insisted on paying for the meal, put money on the table, and left, driving quickly away to the trade delegation's block of flats. The agent, an experienced operator, understood that all was not well and when, on glancing casually round, he saw a single man sitting in a corner, he too made a swift getaway.

But for our quick reaction, the meeting could have had serious consequences. The Danes might have arrested either or both of the parties, and held Boris until he could be collected by a representative of the Embassy. They might also have confiscated whatever was being passed — probably a part or documents connected with high technology — and photographed the handover. Any of these actions would have been awkward for us. As for the agent — bad luck. But it would have been difficult for the Danes to prosecute him.

It was this incident which, unfortunately for us, led the Danes to tighten up their radio procedures. Going over what had happened, they drew their own conclusions, and later started to disguise their communications, so that although we continued to pick up a good deal, intercepts became harder to interpret. My search for identities proved laborious, and my chances of success became even smaller when the Danes began to transfer their population register from the old church books into a central, computerized system. Nevertheless, I discovered the mechanics of how passports, birth and baptismal certificates were issued, and I was able to put this knowledge to good use when the Centre got leads on two German soldiers who had married Danish women and had children by them during the Second World War. Those children had full rights as Danish citizens, and my task was to acquire copies of their birth certificates without revealing that I was a Soviet citizen. This I managed by claiming to be a distant relative: I got copies of the documents and forwarded them to Moscow, where they helped put two illegals in business.[5]

Another minor but useful discovery was that of a small town on the German border where marriages could be registered easily. Procedures had been made so simple that any couple, even foreigners, could come along and get married in a few minutes. When I visited the office, I pretended I was writing a paper for the Soviet authorities about various aspects of Danish law, but I forwarded details to the Centre in the hope that they might prove useful.

Life was full of curious incidents, many of which would have been ridiculous had they been less nerve-racking. In one operation we dropped money for an illegal in a deadletter box, and as a signal to him we left a large bent nail on a windowsill in a public lavatory. The answering signal, showing that the money had been collected, was supposed to be the top of a beer bottle, placed on another windowsill in the same building. Imagine our consternation when we found a bottle-top in the right place, but from a bottle of *ginger* beer. Was this the same thing?

---

5   One of these, Vitaly Nyukin, had been at the Institute with me. Later, in the 1970s, I taught him Danish, and later still he was posted to Singapore. In 1985, on the day after my secret interrogation by the KGB, all the other illegals were abruptly recalled to Moscow, but he was somehow overlooked and left in the Far East until 12 September, when the British announced that I was alive and well in England.

Was the signal adequate? Or did it mean something different? Even though it was past midnight, we brought Zaitsev into the discussion, and there we sat in the small hours of the morning, a gaggle of KGB officers anxiously debating whether or not ginger beer counted as beer. None of us knew what the stuff was. I remembered it only from the autobiography of Karl Marx, who described how he bought ginger beer for children in Highgate. It certainly did not sound alcoholic. Nevertheless, in the end we decided that the signal was good — and we were right, for the illegal had got his money.

Panic set in again when I sent an officer called Cherny to check another signal — a piece of fruit left lying on some grass. Back he came saying, 'Yes, it's there. There's half an orange on that bit of lawn.'

'Did you stop to make sure?'

'No, I just drove past. But it's there all right.'

When I consulted that illegal's list of signals, I became alarmed. An orange meant that the man was in danger. Maybe he was on the point of being arrested. Catastrophe could be threatening: immediate action was needed. Busy as I was, I decided to check the signal for myself. I got out my car and drove past the site. There lay the object, quite clearly an apple, which meant, 'Am leaving the country tomorrow,' and so, far from needing any action, gave us respite from looking after our colleague. Back in the Residency I said, 'Mr Cherny, it's only an apple. Why did you lie to me?'

'I told you, I thought it was an orange.'

'You should have stopped to make sure.'

He shrugged, as if he considered the matter of no importance, but he had given himself away. Either he had not been to the site at all, or he had driven past at speed, too scared to slow down in case he should be spotted by some alien observer.

The episode demonstrated the fallibility of the signals system. On another occasion soon afterwards I went to check a site in central Copenhagen where the illegal, having collected a cache of money and letters from a deadletter box on the outskirts of the city, was supposed to have written a figure 5 on a water-pipe which ran down the outside of a block of flats. Reaching the place at the preordained time, I found no figure 5. Ten minutes later I made another pass to check every possibility, that I had the right block of flats, the right pipe, and had come at the right time. Everything was in order, yet still there was no signal. It was already 9.30 p.m., and, knowing how meticulous Zaitsev was in such matters, I went straight to him and explained what had happened. As a recent recruit, not yet fully trusted with responsibility, I had only been used to look for the receipt signal. The drop had been carried out by an older officer, who had already gone home. 'All right,' said Zaitsev immediately, 'we'll go and check both sites in your car.' So off we went, on an icy winter's night.

The deadletter box was in a classic site, in a hole beneath the trunk of a living tree, in a half-wild park on the north-eastern outskirts of Copenhagen. As I drew up and parked a few yards away under the firs, Zaitsev said, 'OK, see if the package is still there.'

I walked warily forward, my mind spinning as if in a nightmare. Just as I reach into the hole, I kept telling myself, floodlights will blaze up and cameras will start whirring: we shall both be totally compromised. Yet my groping fingers closed on cold air, and nothing disturbed the stillness. The package had gone. We still did not know whether to feel relieved or alarmed: someone else might have got the money and letters. The only thing to do was to visit the signal site yet again — and when we did, there was a nice neat 5 on the water-pipe, just where it should be.

'Do you believe me — that I came twice before and found nothing?' I asked anxiously.

'Oh, yes,' said Zaitsev. 'Obviously the fellow was late, that was all.' But he sent the Centre a long telegram reprimanding the illegal, which proved a bad idea, as people in Moscow took offence, feeling that his criticism rubbed off on them.

*

One evening in 1967 I was suddenly sick, and smitten by a severe pain in the stomach. It was 8 p.m., and Yelena was still at work in the Residency. Because the attack was so violent, I rang for a mobile doctor, and one soon arrived, but he turned out to be useless — young, pompous and over-confident. 'It's nothing but stomach catarrh,' he said. 'Take this, and you'll be fine.'

He handed me a pill, which I dutifully swallowed. But stomach catarrh? I had never heard of any such complaint. Soon, far from feeling better, I grew worse: fingers and toes began to go numb, and I was in such pain that I feared I would faint. In desperation I rang the Embassy and asked Sasha, the operational driver, to take me immediately to the casualty department of the nearest hospital.

There I queued for half an hour before somebody noticed that I was in a bad way. Then suddenly people flew into action: inside another half-hour, after various tests, I was on the operating table. A mask was placed over my face, and that was the last I knew.[6]

Next morning, though weak, I was recovering, and when the house doctor came, he said, '*Deres appendix var meget betendt*. Your appendix

---

6   In submitting to the operation on my own, I broke a fundamental KGB rule: that no officer may be anaesthetized without a colleague being present, for fear that he may give away secrets while unconscious.

was very inflamed. You got here just in time.' Silently I cursed the pompous young doctor and his stomach catarrh and I vowed there and then not to pay his bill. Later, when he telephoned to protest, I said, 'What makes you think I owe you anything? You nearly killed me.' Still he insisted on payment, but, armed with advice from a Danish friend, I threatened to report him to the Society of General Practitioners: this worked like magic, and I never heard from him again.

One episode of trouble seemed to lead to another. While I was still at home recuperating, Nikolai Tarnavsky rang in a state of agitation saying, 'Oleg, I need your help!'

'Don't be silly. I'm flat on my back.'

'No, it's urgent. Yura has hanged himself.'

'Yura!'

'Yes, we've got to identify the body.'

Yura was not a member of our station, but an officer from the Estonian KGB, who had gained a place at Copenhagen University in an exchange of students between Denmark and the Soviet Union. A man of about twenty-eight, he was a victim of Zaitsev's blind enthusiasm for work: the Resident had not been perceptive enough to see that Yura lacked ability and was poor at languages. Instead of letting him carry on gently, Zaitsev had pressed him frequently to write more reports, cultivate more fellow students, produce a plan of operations. Now it turned out that the poor fellow had hanged himself in a shower cubicle, worn down by the strain and loneliness of living among strangers, especially in the dark of the Scandinavian winter.

Our immediate necessity was to identify his body. Tarnavsky's problem was that he spoke poor Danish, and also that he was deaf in one ear. The result was that when a policeman telephoned to tell him that a Soviet citizen was dead, he had failed to identify the hospital to which the body had been taken. Ill as I was, I struggled up, and Tarnavsky drove me back and forth all over Copenhagen in search of a phantom hospital with 'Frederik' in its name. After following several false trails and startling various receptionists with our inquiries — 'Have you got a dead Russian here?' — I belatedly discovered that Frederik was the name of the street, and realized that the hospital was only half a mile from my flat, between there and the Embassy. Eventually we found several policemen on duty, and went with them to the morgue, where they uncovered a body, asking, 'Well, is it him?'

The hanging had distorted the features so much that the face hardly resembled Yura's, as I remembered it. Nevertheless, I said, 'Yes, it's him.' Then, glancing at Tarnavsky, I saw that he was as shocked and uncertain as I was. Yet he, too, confirmed the body's identity. Although we went through a period of uncertainty, Yura never surfaced again.

Back in the station, we urgently discussed the disaster. The police had ruled out any suggestion of foul play, and the death looked like suicide. Talking to his fellow students later, I found that Yura had struck them as not a very sociable person: he had joined in their discussion groups, but not with any enjoyment, and it seemed that the stress of trying to operate in a foreign environment had become too much for him. No doubt this was true; but later we discovered that another factor had played a part in the tragedy. Two years earlier Yura had got married to a girl who was said to be highly attractive but, because the slot in Copenhagen University was for one person only, he had had to leave her behind in Tallinn. Then a friend had told him that she had started an affair.

*

With all these varied activities, my time was well occupied yet, inevitably, my mental development was proceeding fast towards enlightenment and rejection of the whole Communist system. The physical and intellectual attractions of Copenhagen were in themselves highly seductive: there was so much beauty, such lovely music, such excellent schools, such openness and liveliness and cheerfulness among ordinary people, and — trivial as it may sound — such wonderful libraries, that I could only look back on the vast, sterile concentration camp of the Soviet Union as a form of hell. It was only a tiny detail, but in the libraries they issued you with all the books you wanted and gave you free plastic bags so that you could take out as many as you could carry. This impressed me enormously.

In purely material terms, I saw more and more clearly that political freedom and economic prosperity are closely connected, and that combination of the two produces spiritual and cultural freedom as well — the opposite of what Communist dogma was trying to make Soviet citizens believe. At that time one of the most prominent slogans in Moscow was 'CAPITALISM IS ROTTING AWAY'. When people returned from countries like Denmark, and their friends asked, 'Well, *is* it rotting?' they would answer, 'Yes, but the smell of decay is wonderful!'

Above all, I revelled in Copenhagen's music. I went to concerts in halls and churches, and constantly listened to the radio, or to records at home. I was fascinated by the works of composers with a religious connotation — Bach, Handel, Haydn, Buxtehude, Schutz and Telemann. Such music was never played in the Soviet Union, but here life was full of it, especially at Christmas and Easter.

In this atmosphere of freedom, I blossomed as a human being, starting to play badminton, joining clubs, and, whenever I was away from my Soviet colleagues, talking to people like a normal man. What I did not know was that the Danes learnt a good deal about my state of mind by eavesdropping on my conversations with Yelena through the microphones in our flat. I had still not rejected the Communist system entirely, but in private I had become openly critical of the purges, of the routine violation of law, and of the totalitarian control which prevailed in the Soviet Union. Yelena, who was easily influenced, listened to my sceptical views, and began to share and echo them, often becoming even more outspoken than I was. I kept a good deal to myself, while she was inclined to chatter away.

One event in particular increased my disillusionment: the trial, in 1966, of the writers Andrei Sinyaysky and Yuli Daniel. That shook liberal-minded Russians everywhere, but especially those working abroad. We could hardly believe that at home things were going in the retrogressive, Stalinist direction, and we tried to shut our eyes to what was happening.

Then in the spring and summer of 1968 fresh, radical intellectual forces began to surge through Europe. In Czechoslovakia a well-intentioned but weak new head of the Party, Alexander Dubček, was swept forward by his country's movement towards liberalization, and started to relax Stalinist controls, ushering in what became known as the Prague Spring. All over Western Europe students began to stage riots, first in West Germany, then most notably in Paris, where May became the 'month of the barricades' and thousands of people were injured in running fights with the police. For the young people concerned, all this was immensely exciting, and I admired their spirit — as well as their predilection for psychedelic art. But from a standard Russian point of view the youth revolution looked like dangerous folly. I saw that there was a great confusion of minds in Western Europe, and that the main threat was not from the relatively benign regimes against which young people were protesting, but from the tyrannical, military, secret-police power in the Kremlin, which, with its 400,000 troops in East Germany, was keeping the Baltic and East European countries suppressed beneath its iron fist.

In Copenhagen we talked constantly of the youth revolution, but the subject of most intensive debate was Czechoslovakia, where Dubček's reforms had seriously alarmed the Kremlin. In July, as a thousand Soviet tanks and 75,000 troops massed on the Czech border, we found ourselves dividing into two camps, those in favour of the Czechs, and the hard-liners, who wanted order restored. The pro-Czech faction included my friend and colleague Mikhail Lyubimov, then deputy head of station, and we felt desperately involved. 'No,' we kept saying, 'they *can't* invade! They won't *dare* to!' — for we saw Czechoslovakia as our one hope for a liberal future, not only of that country but of Russia as well. It was wishful thinking, and we were foolishly supposing we could influence events by exerting moral pressure and righteous indignation from long range. At the same time the hard-liners, who included Anatoli Seryogin, an incorrigible Stalinist, were demanding firm action by Soviet forces. In the end one of them said, 'OK, let's have a bet on it. A case of champagne on the fact that the invasion goes ahead.' It was a measure of our desperation that, in the face of all the evidence, we took the bet.

As the world knows, the invasion went ahead on the morning of 21 August; and it was that dreadful event, that awful day, which determined irrevocably the course of my own life. Over the past two years I had become increasingly alienated from the Communist system, and now this brutal attack on innocent people made me hate it with a burning, passionate hatred. 'Never again will I support it,' I told myself. 'On the contrary, from now on I must do everything I can to fight it.' Even as the tanks were smashing their way into Prague, I rang Yelena from the booth in the main hall of the Embassy, on a line which I knew was bugged by the Danes, and cried, 'They've done it! It's unbelievable. I just don't know what to do.'

This was my first, deliberate signal to the West. I knew it would be heard and taken note of. To say that I was asking the West to approach me would be an exaggeration. All I meant to say was, 'I hate this. I can't stand it. I feel bitter about it. I protest. Please realize that I am a decent person, not like the rest of my colleagues.' My outburst did not produce any immediate reaction, but there is no doubt that it led, in due course, to my co-operation with the West.

I was by no means the only person in Copenhagen who felt outraged. Throughout the morning Czechs living in Denmark kept arriving at the Embassy, not so much to protest as to try to find out what was happening: they were in shock, desperate to know if the news was true, and if so why. In the afternoon things turned ugly when a crowd assembled outside and people began to pelt the building with missiles, some of them incendiary devices. Several smashed through the windows and landed on the floor, luckily without causing any serious fires; throughout the attack the Consul kept walking round his department cynically making a list of replacements he would claim in compensation from the Danish Ministry of Foreign Affairs: 'Ah, good. We could do with a new sofa — and a new table.'

As for my own future course of action, I could not immediately see what to do. When I went back to Moscow, I thought, I would write and circulate truthful reports which would reveal the facts about NATO: that the West had no aggressive intentions against the Soviet Union, and that on the Soviet side propaganda was affecting even those who were supposed to be making realistic political assessments. Then I saw how childish any such idea was: to try to organize underground cells in Russia would be futile, for the domestic KGB would penetrate them at once.

Nevertheless, I was determined not to remain one of those many thousands of Russians who restricted their contempt for the regime to the odd indecent gesture, and that made with the hand in the pocket. In due course I would do something constructive. I realized that the first thing I needed to do was to switch from working with the illegals and go into political intelligence, which would put me much closer to the front, in a position to obtain intelligence myself. This, then, became my next objective.

For the time being, life had to go on. One day in the autumn of 1968 I mentioned to Zaitsev that, although I was enjoying life in Denmark, I was really a German specialist and that I would love to go to Germany as a tourist, to see some of the places about which I had only read. Normally such a trip would have been difficult to arrange, for all Soviet officials living abroad were doing so on the basis of individual permission, specially granted, for the country in which they were working, and nowhere else. Yet Zaitsev found a way round this by sending a telegram to the Centre which claimed that, 'led by operational considerations', he had decided that it would improve the security of operations with the illegals if 'Mr Gornov' (my mother's patronymic) were to visit West Germany twice, once by rail and once by road, so that he could make a thorough study of border procedures on both sides of the Danish—German frontier. So well did he phrase his recommendation that the Centre forgot its normal obsession with special permissions, and simply said, 'All right.'

We had no trouble obtaining a German visa, but my request for one alerted the German security service, who set up elaborate surveillance measures on their side of the border. Already I was under heavy surveillance by the Danes, who were still trying to determine which of us alleged Soviet diplomats were KGB men, and who (we calculated) had spent more than three hundred days tailing me.

For once Zaitsev decided that we would deliberately give my followers the slip. The door of my flat opened on to a balcony, which led to the staircase, so that if I walked out normally, anyone watching from below would see me go — the outer wall along the balcony was only waist-high. This time, under Zaitsev's instructions, I opened the door carefully, crawled out on to the balcony, pulled the door to behind me, proceeded invisibly on all fours to the staircase, ran down one flight and took the lift to the basement garage. There Sasha was waiting, and we drove out with me lying on the back seat of the car.

As usual, a Danish surveillance team in a car was waiting for me to appear, but they did not grasp what was happening, and we reached a suburban railway station without being followed. There I caught a train back to the central terminus, and an hour later, that same evening, I was on the express to Hamburg. To the considerable rage of the BfV, the German security service, I visited Hamburg, took a train to Jutland, inspected another crossing-point there, and on the next day caught the train back to Copenhagen, all without being picked up.

Perhaps it was foolish of Zaitsev to have suggested that I should make two trips in quick succession. For myself, all I had wanted was to visit Germany on a quick tour paid for by the KGB, but now, by sending Intelligence Officer Gornov on two missions within a few days of each other, the Embassy stirred up a hornets' nest of activity in the Danish and German security services. This time there was no question of shaking off the surveillance: I drove southwards to the ferry hotly pursued by two carloads of Danes, and on the far side was immediately picked up by three carloads of Germans from the BfV. Leading my hefty tail, I drove down to Bonn, where I visited a friend in the Soviet Embassy, and went on up the Rhine, enjoying the prospect of steep vineyards and castles perched on crags, to see some of the towns which I knew from my history studies, Koblenz, Mainz and finally Frankfurt.

There, on Friday evening, I parked the car in the central square outside the main railway station, and went off to do some shopping, one particular target being an ammonia pistol, for warding off attackers, which a colleague had asked me to buy him. Back in the car, I set off again, and quite by chance as I crossed the square a huge wave of cross-traffic cut off my pursuers and bogged them down. They suffered a double blow: on my first trip to Germany they never picked me up at all, and on my second, in spite of intensive efforts, they lost me for the second half of the journey. In a few days I had acquired a reputation as a slippery and dangerous customer.

In terms of useful intelligence, the trip yielded practically nothing, but it did give me vivid confirmation of how strongly West Germany had recovered from the ravages of the Second World War. I knew that by 1945 much of the country's industry, and thousands of homes, had been destroyed yet now I saw no sign of a ruin anywhere, only beautiful new roads and houses, and, in the Ruhr especially, new factories of imaginative design. The air of prosperity and dynamism impressed me greatly: here again was proof that the combination of freedom and democracy works wonders, and the contrast with East Germany — dark, primitive, poor and depressed — was overwhelming.

*

My manoeuvres in Germany made the Centre nervous, and they began trying to recall me on the grounds that I was under threat, having attracted an unhealthy amount of attention. By then, however, Zaitsev had conceived a plan that, on his behalf, I should ghost a book about Denmark, which he proposed to pass off as his own work, and he persuaded Moscow to let me stay on. A telegram came saying, CEASE OPERATIONAL ACTIVITIES. STAY TO MAKE ANALYSIS, BUT

NO MORE OPERATIONS, and I was free to launch into a year of leisurely research and writing, which I much enjoyed. It became possible for me to finish work at 6 p.m., and to take advantage of the long, light summer evenings. I stepped up my badminton, and began to run again, both activities enhanced by the beautiful surroundings, whether new sports halls or ancient woods, in which they took place.

One Saturday in February 1969 the Ambassador suddenly asked if I would help him by driving immediately to the airport and entertaining an important visitor until he was ready to take over. The traveller turned out to be Galina Brezhnev, daughter of the Chairman, changing planes on her way to Stockholm. She was then a tall, slim but rather masculine figure, clad in an expensive-looking astrakhan fur coat, and accompanied by her son, a poisonously spoilt brat of seven.

I had bought a newspaper, and the headline — of course —was HOW LONG CAN BREZHNEV HANG ON? When I showed it to her, she insisted that I should translate the story, so I began to read it out, word by word. It was a ridiculous article, in which the author totted up the number of times that Brezhnev's name had been mentioned in speeches on the Day of the Red Army (23 February), and claimed to detect from his analysis that a plot was being hatched against him. Naturally Galina did not like this, and kept saying, 'No, no — it's all wrong.' When the Ambassador eventually arrived, we all went off for a drive through the city, and lunch in the Embassy.

Towards the end of 1969 I had one last burst of operational activity when I set off with Zaitsev for what I hoped would be the decisive meeting with Oppermann, the priest I had been cultivating in Horsens. All went well until, on our way up through Jutland, Zaitsev inadvertently drove up to the gates of a military base. At once he turned round and went on, but someone must have noticed our diplomatic number plate and passed a report up the line to the security service, for a little while later, as he was motoring on, Zaitsev suddenly said, '*Za nami khvost*' — There's a tail behind us.

As I have mentioned, the KGB maintained a strict rule about never showing the surveillance that you have seen them. When something like that happened, you were supposed to keep going and bring your cover story into play, visiting some objective other than your real one and then returning to base. But on this occasion Zaitsev was rather put out, because it seemed unprofessional that the Resident should have made life difficult for one of his subordinates. He carried on in the hope that we would shake off the tail, not by any violent manoeuvres but through some stroke of good fortune, for instance at a traffic light, as had happened to me in Frankfurt.

Luck deserted us, however, and when we reached our hotel in Horsens, the surveillance was still behind us. 'I'm sorry,' said Zaitsev. 'I'm afraid you'll have to ring him and say that the meeting's off.' Clearly he was right — but how to call? With typical paranoia, we assumed that the telephones in the hotel were bugged. After some reflection we decided to go for a walk along the harbour, close by. On the quay stood several terminal buildings, for passengers travelling to and from the islands, with telephone cabins beside them, and as we passed one of these, Zaitsev kept walking while I nipped in and made a quick, untraceable call, apologizing that we could not keep the rendezvous. A couple of weeks later I again made the trip — on my own, this time — to say goodbye to Oppermann and thank him for his help.

Over Christmas we had time on our hands. For us atheists there was no holiday, but with all Danes taking time off and offices closed, none of our normal contacts was available. The result was a good deal of drinking and celebration, and at one party our political discussion became heated, in a clash of intellects between myself and Seryogin. With several drinks inside me, I was provoked to make derogatory remarks about the Communist system, and suddenly realized that I had gone too far. But Seryogin, instead of losing his temper, took me in his arms like a great bear, and said, 'Oleg Antonovich, if you feel like this, why do you stay in the system [which meant in the KGB]?' 'Oh, well,' I answered, 'between friends we can say anything we like.' I was left with the unpleasant feeling that I had done something silly but Seryogin, reactionary though he was, never denounced me.

I had hoped to stay in Denmark for a few months longer, but the man nominated to succeed me was anxious to start the good life of the West, and began manoeuvring to take over. So it was that in January 1970 Yelena and I regretfully packed and set off for Moscow.

Chapter Eight – Marking Time in Moscow

The poison of European life had entered my system. Back in Moscow I was shocked to find how shabby everything seemed: it was impossible to forget that Over There another life was going on, better than ours in every respect — not just more colourful and attractive in material terms, but full of intellectual vigour, and fired by the twin flames of freedom and democracy. When, once again, I saw the queues, the shortages, the filthiness of public lavatories, the bureaucracy, the corruption, the red tape, the rudeness of officials, the impossibility of obtaining redress when one had a complaint — when I saw all this, I felt physically ill. I now found the relentless propaganda actively offensive, and I came particularly to dislike the official music which blared out from radios and loudspeakers in public places, all the most patriotic and least interesting pieces, written according to Communist formulas. That ghastly totalitarian cacophony, itself a form of propaganda, made life hideous until I trained myself to close my ears to it.

By no means everyone returning from abroad felt the contrast as sharply as I did. To those who had been in Algeria or Mozambique, for instance, Moscow seemed wonderful. Yet even people who had been in East Germany had to admit that the DDR was better off than we were — even if they were careful not to speak freely about the miracles they had seen across the border in places like West Berlin. The official line was that a spell in a normal, wholesome Soviet environment would cure anyone of the poison of abroad — but for me there was no antidote except to return.

I found some compensation in that I was able to buy a new flat. While abroad I had joined a housing co-operative, put my name on a list, deposited some money and now we had a brand-new flat in the area on the edge of the city known as Belyayevo, where eight-storey blocks were going up in green fields. Because local furniture and fittings were so poor, I had brought back some Scandinavian wall units, and I spent many hours happily drilling holes, until one wall was almost entirely covered with shelves from floor to ceiling.

Although our partnership was no easier — it had become a working relationship rather than a romantic one — Yelena and I had decided to stick together for the time being as there seemed no sensible alternative. Fortunately she again got a well-paid job, this time in the Twelfth Department, which listened to embassies, flats and hotel rooms. On the English side of the department there were dozens of transcribers, eavesdropping on the American and British embassies, on other English-speaking embassies, and on visitors; but on the Scandinavian side there were only three slots, and luckily one of them came vacant at the right moment. Yelena's Danish was already good, particularly for listening, and she had picked up a good deal of Swedish and Norwegian from television programmes in Copenhagen. Now she prepared to learn both languages properly, and she was taken on with the rank of senior lieutenant.

The clandestine listeners were regarded as highly important, and people who excelled themselves received decorations: for example, the woman who eavesdropped on Henry Kissinger, the American National Security Adviser and later Defense Secretary, during negotiations for the Strategic Arms Limitation Treaty (SALT), won a special award. Generally they monitored tapes, rather than live conversations, using a foot control to stop the tape or run it back, and writing out long-hand notes which secretaries later typed. As in Denmark, they were sometimes required to transcribe entire conversations, and sometimes given the freedom to make selections. Different technical devices were known to the KGB by various letters: 'A' stood for telephone, 'B' for microphone, 'C' for observation through keyhole, 'D' for one-way mirror. The term 'letter operation' was thus a euphemism for one of the most widespread of KGB activities, the use of a technical device against a specific target. The transcribers were also furnished with standard abbreviations to account for time-lapses or passages of silence during which nothing was being said, among them 'PA', which stood for *polovoi akt*, or sexual intercourse.

I made it a rule never to ask Yelena about her targets: it was better for both of us that I should know nothing. Nevertheless, I was well aware that her work demanded not only concentration but also considerable skill. The easiest part of it was listening to bugged telephones: people who did that were known as 'the lucky ones', because the sound was usually clear, and the meaning of what had been said unambiguous. Sound picked up by microphones planted in walls tended to be poor, and needed acute interpretation. In spite of the difficulty, people who specialized in this line became brilliant at it, and regarded themselves as the real professionals, while the easier work could be done by amateurs.

Back at work in Directorate S, I applied to join an English course at the Dzerzhinsky High School; but my department head, Pavel Gromushkin

— ever the peasant — boomed out, 'What's the use of learning English? You can never work in England, you're blown!'

At the time I thought he was referring to the enormous number of days I had spent under surveillance in Denmark, and to my unfortunate trips to West Germany. Only some time later did I hear that the authorities had another reason to be anxious about me. It turned out that two KGB officers in Buenos Aires, on their way to empty a deadletter box, had walked into a trap: as lights snapped on, they found themselves surrounded by police, got into a fight, started to run, shed incriminating material as they went, were caught, searched and interrogated before they were released and expelled from Argentina.

At much the same time, the Argentinian secret service also arrested a couple of Soviet illegals called Martinov, who I, quite by chance, had put on to a Russian ship in Copenhagen, on their way to Leningrad. After questioning, the Argentinians sent them on to Washington for further debriefing, and Gromushkin was convinced that there they would give everything away: they would relate how a man from the Soviet Embassy, with a diplomatic passport, had put them on the boat, and they would give a physical description of me, so that by now all the Western services would know that Mr Gordievsky, alias Gornov, was an intelligence officer.

How much of this reasoning was realistic I could not tell. The Martinovs had never known my real name but the Danes could easily follow the trail back to me. (Two years later another senior officer described all this talk of being blown as nonsense. 'Most of our officers can be regarded as blown after a couple of months in a foreign country,' he said. 'What does it matter? Even if you aren't blown already, you will be in a few weeks so it makes no difference.') In any case, Gromushkin decided to send me to a country not under the influence of the Western services, and aimed me towards Morocco. That meant I had to learn French, and for the next two years I went to French courses.

Those two years proved an in-between, inconsequential time. I was put into an analytical group, where the work tended to be boring and uneventful — although I inevitably learnt a good deal more about how documents were created, and came across some choice examples of KGB behaviour. For example, we had two or three people planted in international hotels where their job was to photocopy foreign passports. Sometimes we urgently needed an up-to-the-minute passport stamp, and whenever this happened we would send somebody speeding round to one of the hotels. On just such an errand to the Intourist Hotel at the lower end of Gorky Street, I spotted our man in the foyer, and a group of thuggish-looking fellows loitering near the entrance. My man spoke to them, then came over and gave me an envelope, whispering, 'Do you know who they are?'

'Well, they look like KGB to me.'

'That's right. They're the surveillance unit attached to the hotel. And d'you know what? They've got a couple of rooms fitted up with hidden cameras, and that stunning girl at the reception desk has just been making love with her boyfriend! Doing everything!'

'That's too bad,' I said coldly. 'Don't you realize? She's not a target of cultivation. Nor is her boyfriend. All you're doing is filming innocent people for your own amusement.'

Immediately the man became worried, thinking that I was about to denounce him. Of course I had no such intention, but the episode represented the KGB at its normal low ebb.

In technical terms we were starting to fall behind some of our allies, particularly the East German Stasi (secret police), whose document-manufacture had become very sophisticated, using fine colour photography rather than the old catalogue of colours on which they had relied earlier. During my time we, too, went over to the new system, which was much more accurate and objective.

Occasionally the department was augmented by the arrival of illegals who, after service outside the Soviet Union, had not been sent abroad again. In a class of her own was Nora, an extraordinarily forceful, energetic and aggressive woman, full of life and ideas, who had worked as an illegal in several countries, leaving behind her a trail of cast-off husbands, none of whom had been tough enough to stand up to her for long. In her strength and vigour she was admirable, but she had one disastrous idiosyncrasy: body odour, such as none of us had ever experienced or even imagined. Her immediate boss christened her 'The Ginger Lady', believing (wrongly) that ginger has a powerful smell.

One day she was put to sit in our room, and we were all terrified, because her stink was intolerable: even when she went out, it remained overpowering, and we spent hours discussing what we could do about it. So intimidating was she that at first no one would tackle her, but then a man who sat in the middle of the room, who we knew as Colonel Petropavlovsky, agreed to have a go.

Some days later he reported quietly that he had had a word. At first she had been enraged, he told us, and had cried, 'The comrades can put up with it!' But he had gone on to suggest that it was better to keep body and clothes clean with frequent washing, rather than resorting to deodorants, and in the end she had calmed down. Then she disappeared for a few days, and, when she came back, to our unbounded relief we found that the smell had gone. Yet still she had a secret up her sleeve. 'You know,' she said casually, 'I've got a new interest in life. I bought a season ticket to the swimming pool, and I go there every morning on my way to work.' Poor pool! Poor fellow swimmers! But at least the problem had been shifted off our own territory.

*

The great event of 1971 was the expulsion from Britain of 105 KGB officers. This was a bombshell, an earthquake of an expulsion, without precedent, an event that shocked the Centre profoundly. It was triggered by the defection of Oleg Lyalin, a member of the KGB station in London, and in particular of the Thirteenth Department, the unit responsible for gathering information about strategic targets, sabotaging key facilities, and providing safe houses for the teams which would be sent into enemy territory during the first few days of all-out East—West conflict. Even before Lyalin's defection, the British security service, MI5, had a pretty good idea of who was who among the serried ranks of alleged diplomats in the Soviet Embassy, but with his help their knowledge became precise and, out of a total of 120 KGB and GRU, they sent 105 packing.

This unprecedented event led to a violent shake-up in Moscow, and especially in the First Chief Directorate's British—Scandinavian Department, which dealt with political intelligence and was the most important arm of the intelligence service. The head of the department was demoted, and his place was taken by Dmitri Yakushkin, a formidably outspoken man.

Unlike most of his KGB colleagues, Yakushkin came from a noble family, but from one of those clans which never suffered after the revolution. He was the great-grandson of one of the Decembrists, the group of officers, mostly aristocrats, who clubbed together early in the nineteenth century and tried to engineer an uprising against the Tsar. Other members of his family had joined the Bolsheviks early in the 1920s. He grew up with the commanding height, the patrician looks and the aquiline nose of a nobleman, and expectations to match: he had no doubt he would become a senior figure in one organization or another. His first attempt, however, was a failure: he joined the Ministry of Agriculture, only to realize that this was not the place for him. When he switched somehow to the KGB, his career prospered, and he was sent as a senior official to the United Nations headquarters in New York. Then he returned to Moscow, where he became deputy head of the American Department, and in the autumn of 1971 was promoted to head of the British—Scandinavian Department.

By the time I met him his hair had turned silver-grey, and, as I soon found out, his baritone voice boomed out *fortissimo* when he became annoyed. Our first brush took place almost at once. In the flat one morning I happened to hear on the BBC World Service that the Danish government had decided to expel three Soviet spies, alleged to be diplomats, from the Embassy in Copenhagen. As soon as I reached my office, at 9 a.m., I telephoned a colleague who looked after Danish affairs on the political side and told him the news.

'Have you heard that?' I asked.

'No,' he replied. 'We've had telegrams saying that the issue hasn't been settled yet. We're hoping for the best.'

Five minutes later my telephone rang, and a terribly loud voice, audible not only at arm's length, but all round the room, began to roar out of it. 'COMRADE GORDIEVSKY!' it bellowed. 'If you INSIST on spreading rumours round the KGB about alleged expulsions from Denmark, YOU WILL BE PUNISHED!' So thunderous was the threat that several colleagues glanced at me fearfully.

This was Yakushkin, sounding off in characteristic style. Obviously the man to whom I had spoken had gone straight to him and obviously he was infuriated by the idea of beginning work in a new department with yet another expulsion. Within hours telegrams from Copenhagen landed on his desk confirming what I had heard. Other men — Westerners, certainly — would have rung briefly to apologize. Not Yakushkin. His method of making things up was rather different. Ten days later he called again, and said in a perfectly normal, polite voice, 'Comrade Gordievsky, would you be so kind as to pop up and see me?'

Up I went, into his office. Having taken a good look at me, he set me back by asking, 'How would you fancy working in my department?'

'Well!' I hesitated, but recovered quickly. 'I've always dreamt about working in political intelligence. And of course, I would love to go abroad again, particularly to Oslo or Stockholm.'

'No, no!' said Yakushkin quickly. 'It's Copenhagen where I need someone. We have to rebuild our team there. You speak Danish. I've been asking about you all over the First Chief Directorate, and it seems that, of all the people available, you're the only one with the right language qualifications. Besides, I understand that your work with contacts is good, and that you know how to deal with people.'

My heart and mind were racing. Much as I wanted to see another Western country, I knew that any foreign posting would be infinitely better than Moscow. Also, at the back of my mind, the enormous, reckless idea was already smouldering that I might make contact with someone in the West, British or American.

Concealing my excitement, I said, 'But how will you get me out of Directorate S? Will General Lazarev let me go?'

In his big-boss way Yakushkin blustered, 'Leave it to me!' and away I went, full of sudden hope. Then, of course, nothing happened. The weeks dragged by — two, four, six — until one day I met Yakushkin in the corridor and said, 'By the way, what happened about your offer?' He looked uncomfortable, because it went against his pride to have failed, and said, 'I couldn't get you out. That bloody General Lazarev won't release you.'

We decided that the only thing to do was for me to make a personal appeal. Normally any such tactic was regarded as self-defeating for if a man comes along and says, in effect, 'I'm sorry, but I don't like working in your Directorate,' the boss takes it as an insult. In my case, however, it seemed the last resort — and then, as if to endorse my decision, there came a cruel yet beneficial twist of fate, in the form of the death of my brother.

Vasilko had been ill for some time. On his travels in South-East Asia he had contracted hepatitis B, and he had been brought back to Moscow to work from there as one of the Nagayev group of roving illegals. Although told to stop drinking alcohol, he had foolishly carried on, and whenever I had seen him, he had looked worse and worse. All the same, it was a severe shock when he died, aged only thirty-nine, in May 1972.

Having been a serving officer, he received a full military funeral: a cremation, during which his coffin was lowered through the floor of the building, as if into the earth. As the service began, I suddenly found myself thinking of Misha, a blind musician who had married the daughter of the woman from whom we rented a dacha in the 1950s. Having lost his sight in the war, Misha never realized how ugly his wife was; but they had one child, and I think were reasonably content. Then he died, still fairly young, and as we were approaching the crematorium for his funeral, Vasilko had said to me, 'Poor Misha suffered a lot in this life, but now his troubles are at an end.'

How clearly those words came back to me as we said goodbye to Vasilko. The main speech was made by the Party boss from Directorate S, who played a larger role in the service than normal because he was a kind of tutor and educator for the illegals working from Moscow, half priest, half personnel officer. His address was poor, and at the end of it he made a bad mistake, announcing, 'Now let us say farewell to Oleg Antonovich...*ahem!*...Vassily Antonovich Gordievsky.' At that moment, as the floor opened and the coffin began to go down, soldiers with automatic weapons fired three single blank shots, and as the floor closed again, the national anthem was played over loudspeakers. I was left reflecting on the speaker's slip of the tongue. It did not worry me unduly: for one thing, it suggested that in the KGB I was better known than my brother, even though he had served with distinction and won a decoration. For another, there is a Russian proverb which says that anyone who is buried by mistake can look forward to a long life. So the error, though irritating, seemed a good omen.

After the funeral we all went round to Vasilko's parents-in-law where there was much eating and drinking — too much — and further speeches. Some relations had not even known that he was in the KGB, and were astonished when they heard the three shots. What his award had been for nobody seemed certain, but I believe it was for his rescue of the illegal who developed a persecution mania in Sweden, a difficult assignment which he managed with considerable skill. Much about him remained mysterious to the end, not least the name under which he had lived and worked. I knew that he had assumed an Austrian identity — which accounted to some extent for the accent with which he spoke German — but, true to his training, he had never told me what he was called.

Sad as it was, his death turned to my advantage, for I was able to use it as a moral lever in putting pressure on Lazarev. A few days after the funeral I went to see him, thinking that the moment was psychologically in my favour: now that my brother had died as a result of his work for Directorate S, it would be hard for the boss to refuse my request. Sure enough, Lazarev said, 'All right. If you don't want to work here, I can't keep you. I'll let you go.' But then he turned nasty and began to talk in a most unpleasant way: 'You think that we here are black-bone, and that in the political department you'll be a white-bone man,' and so on. The illegals were surrounded by a romantic aura, and, according to official mythology, his Directorate was the most important in the KGB; but, of course, it annoyed him greatly that a man who had proved himself able and a good linguist should want to move on to the political side.

Typically, Gromushkin, my department head, now made a protest and tried to keep me. It was not as if I had ever done much good work for him. My German was excellent, my Danish serviceable, but I had found the work in Moscow deadly dull, and in Denmark I had failed to recruit anyone of significance, either in a foreign consular department, or in a register office. In other words, my service to Directorate S had been entirely undistinguished — and yet Gromushkin tried to hold on to me, out of sheer spite.

While I was waiting for release, my department-to-be began moving out to Yasenevo, the fantastic new headquarters just being completed in the woods outside the Moscow orbital road. There, a magnificent Finnish building of ultra-modern design had been cleverly fitted into the sloping terrain, with access-ways and car parks beautifully set into the trees. No expense had been spared. There were three futuristic conference halls, one to seat a hundred, another for three hundred, and the third for eight hundred, this last cast in the form of a stage and amphitheatre, all in white marble. The building had full air-conditioning, with blinds between the twin panes of double-glazing, and the windows commanded wonderful views of birch forest and meadow. The canteen and cafeteria were excellent, and there were several first-class libraries, and a vast archive department, all close-carpeted, spacious and quiet. The *banya* (sauna) was reserved for use by the bosses, but the swimming pool, football pitch, gym and tennis courts were open to all.

Directorate S had no desire to head for this new Mecca. In their view it was much too far away. All their personnel, the illegals' residential flats and safe apartments were in the city centre, together with their support services such as photography, ciphers and surveillance. How could all these people move out? They remained in the main building, the Lubyanka, which they later regretted.

My own order to move came through at last in August — and highly convenient my new workplace proved, for it was no more than twenty minutes' journey from our flat. One evening I happened to be in the building as part of a team of extra duty officers, who did a twenty-four-hour stint to help the regular professionals. As not much was happening the general in charge took three of us to sample the bosses' sauna, attached to the sports centre. This was spectacularly fitted out, with plenty of space, beautiful Finnish wood, excellent showers, and the fluffiest towels imaginable. We enjoyed ourselves hugely, trying it out. Then our guide asked if we would also like a glimpse of the private sauna reserved for the head of the First Chief Directorate and his guests. We said, 'Of course!' and a moment later he slipped us through a locked door into a truly palatial suite, where everything was on a still larger scale: an enormous sauna, a room in which to lie down and relax, and a dining room with an elegant whitewood table, chairs all round, and a refrigerator full of drinks. Such was the style to which the real bosses were accustomed.

I worked at Yasenevo for only a few weeks, and in the first days of October we left again for Copenhagen. By then Yelena had become well established in her listening job: she had been promoted to captain, and was earning a good salary. Naturally her employers did not want to lose her, but again Yakushkin came to our rescue and prised her out by sheer force of rank and personality.

Chapter Nine – Changing Sides

Arriving in Copenhagen for the second time on 11 October 1972, I found myself in a dilemma. For years I had been wavering, but now I was anxious to make contact with someone from the West, and to help the Western powers. I had, however, to press on with my KGB work, which was aimed first at acquiring intelligence, and second at subverting Western policy and institutions. I consoled myself with the thought that much, if not most, of what I was doing was completely harmless.

Officially I was a second secretary in the Embassy, and later I moved up to first secretary, becoming the official press attaché, an excellent cover, which required me to be in frequent contact with Danish newspapers, television and radio, and to cultivate good relationships with the media, politicians and civil servants. I had time to read a lot, listened for hours to the radio, wrote reports and generally prepared to take over from my predecessor, Leonid Makarov, a poorly educated but methodical man from whom I learned a good deal.

In my two-year absence, an extraordinary change had come over the city: with censorship thrown to the winds, the permissive society was rampant. Bookshops and cinemas peddled hard pornography in the most blatant displays, and the beaches were dotted with naked men and women. Within the city limits women were supposed to remove only the tops of their swimsuits, but further out total nudity prevailed.

In the KGB station I was now a political intelligence officer, an interesting job that involved much more overt activity than my earlier role. My task was to acquire contacts in places like the Danish Ministry of Foreign Affairs and other government departments, as well as in the political parties, the trade unions and the media — any organization through which the KGB might be able to influence public opinion. I might, for example, cultivate the head of an organization opposed to the European Common Market, because the policy of the Kremlin and the KGB was to split Europe and prevent its consolidation.

This kind of manoeuvring could be quite stimulating and yet, perhaps because I was older and more experienced, I saw how ineffective the bulk of KGB work was. Most of it was what we called 'active measures', and amounted to no more than attempts at manipulating public opinion through speeches, newspaper articles and brochures. There was practically no real intelligence work, in the form of recruiting agents: although we continued to hunt for contacts, the Danes proved exceptionally resistant to our overtures. Prosperous, fired by patriotism, a sense of duty and integrity, they did not want to be recruited.

Another reason for our lack of success was the weakness of the Resident, Anatoli Danilov, who had succeeded Zaitsev. In England, on an earlier posting, Danilov had brought off a memorable coup by recruiting an agent who had high value in KGB eyes; but after that he had been content to rest on his glory. 'I've done my bit,' he would say. 'I'm not bothering any more.' By the time I arrived, he was drinking a great deal, particularly at lunch, and doing little work. I found him an uninspiring leader — and he once did something that made me positively despise him.

We were both on leave in Moscow at the same time, and Danilov was about to go on holiday in the south, leaving in the early hours of the morning. Because he was afraid he would not be able to get a taxi, he asked me to pick him up and drive him to the airport at 2.30 a.m. I cannot remember whether or not I managed to get in a nap first, but when I set out at two o'clock to collect him the whole of Moscow was alive with empty taxis, cruising hopefully with their green lights on. My entire night was destroyed, and I reflected bitterly that if a man treats his subordinates like that, they will never have the slightest respect for him.

In Copenhagen, the apathy of the Danes notwithstanding, one or two men were prepared to help us, and among these was Gerd Petersen, who had been declared a confidential contact by the Centre long before I arrived. An unprepossessing little man, with long, greasy hair and the sagging pot-belly of a beer-drinker, Petersen was a dedicated left-wing politician. For years he had been an out-and-out Communist, but then he shifted his ground to become deputy leader and later leader of the Socialist People's Party. Since he was also a Member of the European Parliament, and an official observer at the arms-control negotiations, he was a valuable source of news and gossip for us: not a witty man, but an intelligent one, full of interesting information. In 1973 it fell to me to take him over, and I ran him until the end of my time in Denmark. An exhausting business it was, too, for he loved his food and drink, and lunches with him often lasted four hours: after innumerable shots of schnapps, washed down by tall, foaming glasses of beer, it needed intense concentration to remember everything that had come up in conversation.

Not that Petersen was popular with all the Soviet officials in Copenhagen. One day Danilov made the mistake of boasting to the Ambassador of how well the KGB was getting on with him whereupon the Ambassador exclaimed, 'I hate that nasty little fox. How can you possibly be in touch with him?'

Things looked up when Danilov was replaced by a far more interesting and sparky new Resident, Alfred Mogilevchik. In his late thirties, dynamic, he had worked in Britain, spoke excellent English and German, and was determined to liven up the station. I got on well with him from the start, but even so was surprised when, within a few months of arriving, he said he wanted to make me his deputy.

'I've only been on the political side for two years,' I said. 'All the rest of my time has been spent on the illegals.'

'That doesn't matter,' he replied. 'You've got the brain, the energy and the ability to deal with people. Also you know Denmark and speak the language. What else do I need?'

And so, with the approval of the Centre, I became Deputy Resident, a success in terms of prestige, but not one that made any difference to my rank (which remained that of major) or salary. To this day I am haunted by a scene that took place a few months after my promotion. Arriving at the Embassy one morning to start work, I found the hall half full of people standing about in rigid attitudes as if paralysed. In the middle was Mogilevchik, looking stricken, his eyes swollen as if he had been crying. Somebody whispered that his wife had died suddenly in the night: he had come back from a reception to find her suffering severe pains caused by a blood-clot in the arm. He had called in a doctor from a Russian ship but the man arrived too late to save her.

The disaster had a devastating effect on the Embassy, for everyone had liked the wife, a good-looking woman with two handsome children. Mogilevchik was recalled to Moscow, as it was the practice of the Centre to bring back people who lost their families. Not until later did the truth begin to come out. I heard from a Danish journalist with good police contacts that the wife had committed suicide, and later still it emerged that Mogilevchik had been a bully at home, treating her like a peasant (although his own father was only a humble Byelorussian). Probably he was also having affairs, and I suspect that he spent part of that fatal night with some other woman. The private lives of the Embassy staff sometimes proved more dramatic than their work.

Later in 1976 a man arrived who was to have a profound influence on my career: Nikolai Gribin came to the Copenhagen Residency to serve under me. A complex character, very much a child of his time, he had the advantage of being slim, dark and handsome, and wore a neat moustache, which became him well. Although on the one hand a typical toady and careerist, he had many attractive features: apart from his looks, he had a pleasant, easy voice, and sang romances or modern Russian ballads, accompanying himself on the guitar. This, coupled with his wife's being an outstanding cook and gifted at producing a beautifully decorated table — by which Russians set great store — made him a natural entertainer, and the parties the couple gave actively boosted his career. Gribin was abstemious, took care of his health, and drank only moderate amounts of white wine.

His career went off to a flying start when he recruited, as agent, the bearded left-wing Danish photographer Jacob Holdt, who had worked in the United States and specialized in taking pictures of slums and drug-addicts, presenting them as the true face of America. Holdt's work had already appeared in exhibitions and in books, but Gribin cultivated him assiduously. He then had the nerve to inform the Centre that all Holdt's photographs derived from active measures of the KGB, which had been carrying on its normal task of running down America. The Centre swallowed this, and gave Gribin high credit.

Thereafter he withdrew from operational work, and concentrated exclusively on administration, taking infinite pains to please his bosses in Moscow. He studied their habits and preferences minutely, and, whenever he went home on leave, took them presents of things that they particularly coveted, something optical for one, something electronic for another, books for a third, medicine for a fourth, pornographic videos for a fifth. Also, he put much effort into writing letters, which were serious, neither too long nor too short, and showed consideration for people, as well as strong interest in work.

In due course he became Resident in Copenhagen, and in this role also he shone, running the station efficiently, and entertaining on a lavish scale at home. His bosses thought him a splendid fellow, and he achieved rapid promotion, leapfrogging over me to become head of the Third Department of the First Chief Directorate in 1984.

*

Meanwhile my own mental evolution had been continuing. For months I had been seeking some means of making contact with the West, and I had started to look on my KGB activities as a kind of hobby rather than as work: I was improving my reputation in Moscow by sending back cleverly written reports, but I was doing nothing that could damage the West. I had discovered how easy it was to manipulate the KGB.

Twenty years on, it is difficult to remember what a dreadful place the Soviet Union had become in the 1970s. From the vantage point of the 1990s, President Gorbachev called that time the 'era of stagnation' — and that was a classic understatement. Everything was deteriorating, standards of behaviour as much as physical conditions. The optimism of the early 1960s under Khrushchev had died away; then, at least, there had been a feeling that although the regime was still Communist, it was going forward. In the 1970s under Brezhnev the feeling was not merely of no progress, but of retrogression.

Although President Nixon and Henry Kissinger went to Moscow to negotiate the SALT treaty, it was clear that the Soviet Union had reached nuclear parity with the United States, or even overtaken it, and was deliberately extending its intercontinental missile superiority. It had also become aggressively imperialistic all over Africa — in Mozambique, Angola, Ethiopia and Algeria — and was growing ever more hostile towards China, hysterically inflating the threat represented by the Chinese. At home, the KGB had grown to a grotesque size, the First Chief Directorate alone increasing from 5000-odd to 16,000 personnel.

This expansion was financed with proceeds from the sale of oil, for when the international oil crisis led to a temporary global shortage, Moscow found that it could profitably dispose of a useful proportion of its own oil abroad. In the Soviet Union the centralized economy was still functioning as inefficiently as ever, but injections of foreign currency from the sale of oil encouraged the government to believe that it could easily continue its operations abroad, giving money to Communist parties and financing the KGB. This largesse provoked a curious reaction on the part of the intelligence services, which felt that, to justify their own expansion, they had to provide ammunition for the Soviet leaders: hence the paranoia about hostile Western intentions, fed by fanciful intelligence reports, which developed during the 1980s.

Until the early 1970s I clung to the hope that the Soviet Union might still reject the Communist yoke and progress to freedom and democracy. Until then I had continued to meet people who had grown up before the revolution or during the 1920s, when the Soviet system was still not omnipotent. They were nice, normal Russians — like some distant relatives of my father who were engineers: not intellectuals or ideologues, but practical, decent people, embodying many of the old Russian engineer characteristics so well described by Solzhenitsyn. But then the last of these types died out, and the nation that emerged was composed purely of *Homo sovieticus*: a new type had been created, of inadequate people, lacking initiative or the will to work, formed by Communist society.

My belief at the time was that the nation would never recover, but that at least something ought to be done to protect democracy in the West against the huge concentration of military power and the deluge of propaganda. In practical terms, this meant that I must try to help Western Europe and North America to protect their security, their independence and their freedom, by whatever means I could devise.

Those means were limited. All I could do was to pass information, to show what the KGB and the leadership in the Kremlin were doing. Of course, in the sum of things, I knew little, but I reckoned that even fragments of knowledge would be better than nothing. I was naïve enough to suppose that, since in the KGB every fact and statistic was secret, or at least classified, any disclosure would be potentially valuable; later I realized that although a report might be classified, it did not necessarily mean that it had any interest or importance.

Looking back now, I find it extraordinary that I was driven so hard by ideological compulsion. Yet my feelings were immensely strong because I was living and working on the frontier between the totalitarian world and the West, seeing both sides, and constantly angered by the contrast between the two. The totalitarian world was blinded by prejudice, poisoned by hatred, riddled by lies. It was ugly, yet pretending to be beautiful; it was stupid, without vision, and yet claiming to be fit to lead the way and pioneer a path into the future for the rest of mankind. Anything I could do to damage this monster, I gladly would.

*

Often at diplomatic parties I saw diplomats (or were they intelligence officers?) from the British and American embassies, yet I did not know how to bridge the huge gap between us in a way that would not embarrass or prejudice either side. Also, I was inhibited by a serious inferiority complex, caused by my inability to speak English. In the end, it was the other camp that made the first move.

At about eight o'clock on the evening of 2 November 1973 there came a knock on the door of our flat. When I opened it, there to my astonishment stood Lazlo Barany, a Hungarian who had been one of the best triple-jumpers in the Track and Field Club at our Institute in Moscow.

'*Bog ty moi!*' I exclaimed. 'My God! Lazlo! What the hell are you doing here?'

Even as he grinned and shook hands, a sixth sense told me that he had not come of his own accord, but had been sent by one of the services. The immediate question in my mind was, British or American?

He began to tell some elaborate story of how he had come over on business from America, where he was living, and was staying with a Danish girl he had met in London. By chance he had heard I was working in Copenhagen, and longed to see me again after all those years…I stopped him, brought him in, introduced him to Yelena and gave him a whisky. He looked much as I remembered him: a good European face, blue eyes, short brown hair neatly cut and parted. Yet my mind was a whirl of conflicting ideas and emotions. I was delighted to see him, because he had been a good friend, but I was also apprehensive, and did not believe a word of what he was saying. At the same time, I was troubled by a foolish but inescapable embarrassment about the smallness of the flat: although new, it was rather primitive, and I felt ashamed to have been discovered living in such drab surroundings.

'I wish you'd come to see me in my Moscow flat,' I said. 'That's much nicer.'

'Never!' he replied. 'There's no chance of my going back there.'

He told me that he had defected from Hungary in 1970, and for a few minutes we carried on a desultory conversation, but he remained tense. He finished his drink, stood up, and said, 'Look, I'm disturbing you. Let's meet for lunch tomorrow, and we can have a proper talk then.' He gave me the name of a restaurant in the city centre, and I agreed to meet him at one o'clock.

His visit left me feeling profoundly disturbed. That he had been sent, I had no doubt, but why to the flat, where Yelena was bound to see him? If our marriage had been sound, it would not have mattered, but as things were, I knew that it was doomed and would end as soon as we returned to Moscow — which made everything much more dangerous. In an attempt to reassure her, I explained that I had known Lazlo well at college, and said how strange it was that he should suddenly arrive like that, but I could see that she, too, was worried by his appearance. For years afterwards I feared that it might have been some inadvertent remark of hers that finally gave me away. At lunch next day Lazlo seemed more relaxed, more like his old self. We had a window table and sat comfortably, watching people pass back and forth in the pedestrian street outside. He told me that he had settled in North America, where he had become an insurance agent.

'What a waste!' I teased. 'Why didn't you find a more challenging job? You speak Russian, French, English. You'd make a brilliant expert on international relations.'

He shrugged off my suggestion, and began to defend the Western way of life. Again I was tense. In this, my first encounter with someone representing the Western services, I saw a need to be extremely careful. I was walking on the edge of an abyss, and must not go over the brink. Thus, although I longed to explain that I had been entirely pro-Western since the invasion of Czechoslovakia, I merely remarked that in the Embassy we had bet each other a case of champagne about what the outcome in Prague would be.

'Oh,' he said, with a touch of bitterness. 'So you had a *sportif* attitude to that event, did you? Well, the fate of a whole nation was at stake.'

I longed to say that I knew this perfectly well, that I felt great personal bitterness about it, and that I saw the invasion as the principal turning point of my own life. But I forced myself to remain noncommittal, to reveal only the tip of the iceberg of my real feelings. As I did not know who had sent Lazlo, or what his authority was, I thought it essential that although I should put out positive signals through him, I should not lose control of the situation or become easy prey to anybody. Neither did I want to call his bluff by telling him to come clean about his mission. Our meeting ended inconclusively, but I knew that I had given away enough for him to put in a positive report.

The period that followed was difficult. Every day I expected some further approach, but it was nearly three weeks before one came. When the British made a move, it caught me off-guard. Having become enthusiastic about badminton, I had taken to hiring a court at the ungodly hour of 7 a.m. I would pick up a girl student called Anna, drive her to the court, and have an hour's match. Evidently the British knew this — with the help of the Danish surveillance, who had seen my car parked outside the club — and one morning I was in the middle of a game when a man suddenly appeared beside the court, not in sports gear but dressed for the office, with an overcoat over his suit. It was an old-fashioned hall, built in the 1930s, with no accommodation for spectators beyond a few benches, and when the newcomer showed himself clearly, it was obvious that he wanted to speak to me.

I recognized Dick immediately, for he was one of the best-known diplomats on the Copenhagen circuit: in his early forties, tall, with dark-brown hair and a good-looking typically English face, he stood out in any gathering through the sheer force of his ebullient self-confidence. His voice was not loud, but his personality was so striking that he tended to dominate any conversation in which he took part; and if I sometimes wished that he might show a little more humility, I could not deny that he had a great gift for cheering people up. He gave the impression of enjoying his work, knowing everybody, and being in control of events. It was entirely in character that he would turn up at Embassy parties whether he had been invited or not, either scrounging an invitation from a colleague, or just coming along without one. In those days, before international terrorism forced the introduction of more stringent controls, it was difficult to check whether he was supposed to be there or not — but, in any case, everyone was glad to see him.

Now, though, in the early morning, I felt slightly annoyed: this seemed an unsuitable place in which to make contact, and it was rude to my partner to ask her to stop playing. I apologized to her and proposed a short break, then went over to ask Dick what he wanted. He simply said that it would be nice to meet in some place where we would not be over-heard. I agreed, and we made a rendezvous for lunch in three days' time.

This man, I felt certain, had an important message for me; but in contrast with his normally extrovert behaviour, he was stalking me slowly and carefully, taking every precaution.

Many Russians, knowing that the host was an intelligence officer, would not have accepted the invitation; and, as he afterwards let on, he was not sure that I would come. But I decided to go — and I decided, for the time being, to play the game straight from the Soviet end. Back at the Embassy I went to Danilov and asked, 'What do I do? This fellow from the British Embassy has invited me to lunch. Should I accept?'

Danilov cabled the Centre for guidance, and Yakushkin, who was broad-minded, promptly replied: 'Yes! You should be aggressive and not shy away from an intelligence officer. Why not meet him? Take an offensive position! Britain is a country of high interest to us.'

So I had official permission to go ahead, which in itself was a form of deception on my part; but because I had handled the matter in that way, I knew that I would have to write a report after the meeting. No matter, I thought, I can manage that.

We met in the restaurant, and our conversation was no more than a cautious sounding out. Dick was less ebullient, more considerate, than at diplomatic receptions, and I was surprised when he began to speak about the numbers of KGB officers employed under cover in Soviet embassies, and wondered why Moscow sent so many intelligence officers abroad. When I gave noncommittal answers, he skilfully steered off that subject, and, in spite of language difficulties, took trouble to talk about subjects of interest to me, including religion, philosophy and music. Towards the end of the meal he asked if I would have to put in a report on our meeting, and I said, 'Probably, yes, but I'll make it a very neutral one.' I wanted to give him the feeling, without expressing it, that I was keen to meet again. Both of us were careful not to speak about the future, and we parted without making any further arrangement.

My report to the Centre was as bland as I had promised. I deliberately made it long, to increase the apparent importance of my own initiative, but did not commit myself in any way. In sum, I said that our meeting had been of interest, but no more than that. (Later I heard that Yakushkin was delighted with my memorandum.)

After that, silence fell, and to my consternation no further contact took place for nearly a year. Then at last, on 1 October 1974, Dick appeared again outside the badminton court and invited me to a meal at his own house. I said I would prefer some public place, and we settled on the Skovshoved Hotel in the northern suburbs. After an agreeable and harmless dinner there, I felt it was time I took the initiative, and suggested that we should meet again in the bar on an upper floor of the new Scandinavian Air System's (SAS — the airline) Hotel on the way out to the airport.

This time, as soon as Dick arrived, the feeling between us was different. As we sat in the bar, in mid-conversation he said abruptly, 'This isn't a good place.'

'Why not?'

'We might be seen accidentally.'

'By whom accidentally?'

'Any of your colleagues.'

'Oh, no. This is an expensive hotel. I don't think any of them come here.'

But Dick was not happy, and for our next rendezvous he named an inconspicuous little restaurant a short distance north-west of the city centre, in a district definitely not frequented by Soviet personnel. All at once we were almost colleagues, speaking together of precautions. In inviting Dick to the SAS hotel I had known what I was doing, and I was alive with anticipation; he had sensed this, and felt the same. So at last we began to speak in plain language.

When we went to the restaurant three weeks later, ours was a perfect clandestine meeting: two intelligence officers coming together to do business. Without messing about, he said, 'You're KGB.'

'Of course.'

'Tell me, then. Who is the PR Line deputy in your station?'

For a second I stared at him in surprise. Then I could not help smiling as I said, '*I* am! You boasted that you knew who everybody was, but you don't even know who I am!'

'Really!' He seemed impressed. 'All right, then. I'd like you to meet someone special, a senior officer who will come from London.' He went on to explain that his own time in Copenhagen was running out, and that he would have to hand me over to a colleague. I was sorry to hear this, since he had always been so friendly and optimistic, but I saw that his move was inevitable. Our conversation was still difficult because of our lack of a common language, and Dick found it strange that, for all my desire to help the West, I could not speak English. I, too, was irritated with myself for never having learnt. Anyway, he indicated that the next time we met he would take me to a safe apartment and produce a man who could discuss things in a language properly understood by both sides. With these factors in our favour, we could put our relationship on sound foundations, and begin serious co-operation.

Both sides were still wary. The British, as I later discovered, could hardly believe that my reactions to their overtures were spontaneous. Rather, they suspected that I was deliberately setting up a major provocation. The deputy in the KGB station so keen to co-operate with the enemy? It looked like what the Americans call a dangle, a bait. At that stage the Americans had an obsession about dangle operations because they had been fed loads of rubbish on the subject by a KGB man called Galitzine, who had defected in Finland. They imagined that the KGB was able to dangle a senior officer such as myself, when any such move was out of the question because a man of my rank would never be risked or allowed to speak to a foreign service. If he did, official doctrine had it, he would be bound to reveal something, and in the KGB there is nothing that *can* be revealed because everything is a closely guarded secret. So there was absolutely no chance of my being a dangle but that the West did not appreciate this was a measure of the vast gulf of misunderstanding which separated the two sides in the Cold War. I conceived it as part of my mission to reduce this ignorance, which constituted no mean danger. Even as Dick was proposing our next meeting, the British were not sure whether I was under control. They thought it quite possible that I might lead KGB colleagues to the flat, which they would then attack, beating up anyone inside and declaring the whole exercise an anti-Soviet provocation.

However, Dick gave me a date and time and, at the appointed hour, I was outside the restaurant on a dark winter evening. He appeared punctually, and said, 'Come, I'll show you the way.' As we walked, turning a couple of corners, he was his usual friendly self, but I assumed that a secretary or colleague was sitting in a car close by, armed with a telephone, so that she or he could warn the people in the apartment if they saw anyone following us.

For the first time I was entering enemy territory. I was not afraid of being kidnapped, but I knew that things were now serious: this was the real start of operations. Biting my nails in agitation, I accidentally nipped one finger and made it bleed.

As I entered the flat, I was confronted by a big man, whom Dick introduced as Michael. He was tall and physically powerful, and I immediately felt ill-at-ease with him. Yet my most pressing need was to do something about my finger.

'I'm sorry,' I said. 'I need to patch myself up.' Things could hardly have been more awkward. My hosts seemed as nervous as I was — and now their guest had arrived injured! In some embarrassment Michael said, in German, 'The bathroom's upstairs. There's stuff in the cupboard.' I went up to the second floor — a rarity in Scandinavian flats — and stuck a plaster over my wound. Then I came down and our conversation began.

I was surprised, and not a little put out, to find the big man acting in a hostile, almost threatening manner. I expected our co-operation to begin in a spirit of friendliness and enthusiasm: I had hoped that the British would be grateful that I was offering help, and risking a good deal on their behalf. Far from it: Michael lit off into a barrage of abrupt questions — 'Who is your Resident? How many KGB officers are there in the station?' — as gruffly if he were interrogating a prisoner.

In his mind, that was close to what he was doing, for afterwards, when I tried to discover why he had behaved like that, I learnt that he had interrogated German prisoners after the Second World War and knew no other way of questioning a stranger. Someone else suggested that his aggressive attitude was his way of suppressing his nerves, which were probably as taut as mine. In any event, the inquisition continued for some time, and I did not like it.

Even as Michael was hectoring, I began to say to myself, 'Take it easy. This can't be the true spirit of the British intelligence service. Most of them must be nice, normal people. This fellow can't be representative. It's just his style. Whatever he says, I must suppress my anger, because it's the West, not him, with whom I want to co-operate.'

Eventually things began to go better. I could see that it was difficult for Michael to relax but at least his hostility lessened. When I felt that things were winding down, I said I wanted to work for the British with a clear conscience, and to that end I wished to lay down three conditions.

'First,' I said, 'I don't want to damage any of my colleagues in the KGB station, because there are some nice people among them. Second, I don't want to be secretly photographed or recorded. Third, no money. I want to work for the West out of ideological conviction, not for gain.'

There was a pause while Dick and Michael glanced at each other. Why I had come up with the second condition, I could not be sure: perhaps it was just instinctive shyness, or some inhibition caused by the fact that I was launching into a new career. Then Michael said, 'Your second and third points — absolutely all right. No problem. But as to your first, how can we damage your colleagues? For one thing, we don't want to, and for another, there's no operational need to harm them. On the contrary, if you do co-operate with us, we'll find ways of giving your colleagues extra protection. Now we know what your position in the station is, we'll think not twice but three times before we or our allies take a decision to expel anybody.'

I was glad to hear that. Then Michael said, 'Look, we can't continue talking in restaurants. Somebody's bound to see us, and everything will be destroyed. What we'll do is rent a safe flat, where we can meet in protected conditions.'

'Really!' I said. 'That'll be very expensive.'

'Worth it, though.'

'But if we're only meeting once a month…'

'Don't worry.'

To my disappointment, Michael said that it would be he who ran me — and the meeting was at an end.

I had one more brief encounter with Dick, who gave me details of the flat and a date for my first rendezvous there. He also supplied me with materials for invisible writing together with an address in London: if anything went wrong I could summon help. The new flat was way out in the suburbs but, because Copenhagen is quite small, I could reach it by car in only twenty minutes. I began going there in the spring of 1975, and visited the place regularly throughout 1976 and 1977, up to July 1978. Luckily I was under surveillance far less often than during my first tour: I was, in any case, of less interest to the Danes because I was operating so much above board, and now, although the surveillance teams had no inkling of my connection with the British, I expect that oblique pressure was applied on their superior officers to give priority to other targets. As far as I know, I was never followed as I drove out to the rendezvous.

One potential hazard was my diplomatic number plate, but fortunately I could leave my car tucked away in a good park between apartment blocks and walk the rest of the way. Only once in those three and a half years did the car pose a problem. As I was driving out one winter evening, dark had already fallen, and it began to snow — not the sort of conditions in which you would expect anything suspicious to happen. Quite by chance a member of the Danish security service, who probably lived close by, noticed the number plate of my parked car, and was able to follow my footsteps in the settling snow. He tracked me right to the top floor of the block of flats, and then, by careful observation, even deduced which flat I had gone into. In the morning he reported to a senior officer, and his operational section began to investigate. (At a high level the British were passing some of the information I gave them to the Danes but, of course, this was not known lower down the ladder.) It took a tremendous effort on the part of two senior bosses to call off the hunt. They had to cook up some excuse for not authorizing any action —and somehow they succeeded — but the mishap gave us a shock whose after-effects lingered.

*

At first I was disappointed by the British failure to appreciate the depth of my alienation from the Communist system. I repeatedly told my contacts that my ideological development had been completed on 21 August 1968, the day Soviet tanks rolled into Prague; I kept saying that I was 100 per cent aware of the political realities that prevailed — and yet the message did not seem to penetrate. At our early meetings, Dick — an intelligent man by any standards — insisted on bringing along cuttings from British newspapers that described some fresh Communist outrage, some appalling example of Soviet behaviour. He knew that I could not read the English reports, but perhaps he felt that they would bolster my resolve.

'Look, Dick,' I would say, 'I know it all ten times better than the hacks who wrote those articles. I *know* all about the crimes. I *know* about the millions who died in concentration camps. And here you are, trying to persuade me that Communism is bad! My mission is to show you that the system is even more ghastly and dangerous than you think. I come from the heart of it, so I know. And yet you bring me newspaper cuttings to turn me into a political dissident! Good God, I've been a fully fledged dissident for seven years and more.'

Gradually we progressed to more useful topics. During the first eighteen months I concentrated on one particular subject before I forgot the details — the immense and highly sophisticated operation the KGB ran to create false identities. Then, it was only three years since I had been involved in it. I remembered a great deal and, for meeting after meeting, I talked in German to Michael about it.

Then one day he came along with a paper, saying that he had made a detailed summary of my remarks. He asked me to read and check it. I found it excellent. When I reached the end, I said, 'First class. You must have very good analysts in your service.'

'Analysts?' he said. 'Where? Who? I did it all myself.' Whereupon this man, who was always so serious, laughed happily because I had paid him a compliment. Even at that moment, though, I was wondering whether anyone *could* have written so full a paper from notes alone, and later I realized that, of course, all my talks had been recorded.[1] In bugging me, the British had broken their word about one of the fundamental conditions I laid down at the outset. They also occasionally lied to me about the nature of our partnership: they claimed that they were running me without the knowledge or support of the Danes but, of course, I knew that this was nonsense. I resented their finding it necessary to tell these untruths but thought that the Danes may have asked them to: if I were arrested by the KGB, I would at least be able to claim that the Danes had never been involved.

Over the months, Michael gradually softened. He was Scottish, and, looking back, I see him as an austere Presbyterian priest, serious about his religion and ethics. He was not an easy man with whom to joke, but he was dedicated and hardworking, always making notes, preparing himself well and asking good questions. After living for years in England, I now see that he was rather less outgoing and relaxed than most British people, and his not-very-well-developed sense of humour occasionally made the going heavy. When, after about a year of discussions, I once again remarked that there were a number of good people in the KGB, he said, 'Oh, come on. That's absurd!' — quite unable to accept an idea which did not fit in with his own preconceptions.

Michael remained my man for two years. Then one day he announced that he was about to be moved, and that it was a blow for him to have to

---

1 I strongly suspected this at the time, and years later I got positive proof of it when, in a country with a larger British station than the one in Denmark, a specialist in operational technology casually remarked that it was he who had installed the wiring to bug the flat in Copenhagen where my meetings took place.

leave because his association with me had been fascinating and so useful for him. His successor, Andrew, whom he introduced, was inspiring in every way, always cheerful, always sincerely apologetic about any mistakes he made, and helpful in explaining to me how Whitehall and the British government functioned. This proved important for me, as I began to understand how a Western society worked, which gave me a tremendous advantage. This new man was about three years older than me, and spoke adequate Russian; but he was highly able, and also had German, as well as three other languages.

The question arose of how to convey secret KGB information to the British with maximum efficiency. At one stage they suggested lending me a camera, with which I could photograph documents in the Residency. The idea appalled me: just one glimpse through a half-open door, and everything would be finished. Then I began to wonder: were the British under the same pressure as our own people? The Operational Techniques Department in Moscow was constantly producing new technical devices — miniature cameras, secret writing materials, short-wave radios — which they forced on the officers in the field, and through them on the agents, because use of the gadgets at the front justified their own existence. In the stations we tried to make our contacts use all these devices, not because they were necessary or beneficial but merely to satisfy the Centre.

When the British started to suggest secret photography, I said, 'Look, is there some demand from London for this? Do you have a norm of the number of devices that have to be in use? Because if you do, I'll accept one, and we can pretend I'm using it just to make life easier for you.' When they saw what I was getting at, they burst out laughing, and I felt embarrassed at having revealed how ignorant I still was of Western mental attitudes.

A better alternative was for me to make notes and bring them out. I could not take away telegrams from Moscow because they were too well protected, but at least I could copy out relevant parts of them. Then we devised a more effective plan. As I have said, messages for the KGB were brought from Moscow by couriers as film, which the Resident cut into lengths and handed to each officer concerned with that section. When Andrew heard this, he asked if I could bring out my part of the film, the messages from my department, which might amount to a dozen or more letters and documents, and lend it to him so that he could copy it.

All I had to do was hand over the film at a rendezvous during the lunch break, and collect it half an hour later. But extracting the film from the Residency was not as simple as it sounds. The KGB station was still on the top floor of the Embassy building, under the roof, alongside the GRU. Strictly speaking, the Embassy cipher clerks were supposed to collect all sensitive material and lock it into the *referentura* during the lunch-hour; in practice, secret films and papers remained in our briefcases, which were on our desks or in steel lockers in our rooms, while we were out. Yet there was still a chance that one of the clerks, who were theoretically entitled to search briefcases during the lunch-hour, would come looking for a particular item while I was away, and not be able to find it. There was also a small risk that I would be caught entering or leaving the Embassy with incriminating, top-secret material in my pocket. Every excursion to meet Andrew was therefore highly charged.

Since I normally went out to lunch anyway, either home or to meet a contact, there was no need for elaborate cover stories. I usually went only a short distance and met Andrew in St Annae Platz, near the Royal Palace and the harbour, in the city centre. I would go into a telephone kiosk and apparently be making a call, when he would come past and stop, ostensibly to ask directions. In that brush-contact I would slip him the film. About thirty-five minutes later we would pass each other again at some other agreed place nearby and complete our handover.

Once, for a change, we met on the Island of Amager, and there he took me to his hotel room to show me what he was doing. Before unpacking my roll of film, he put on a pair of thin white cotton gloves and then used a simple but ingenious light device to copy it. So quick and efficient was his method that I was able to hand the British hundreds of classified KGB documents, some of them extremely illuminating. One coup was that we managed to copy the whole 150-page annual concerning the diplomatic side of the Soviet Embassy, a document which proved of high value to the Danes.

Now that I was actively working for the British, I was much easier in my mind. Far from having qualms of conscience about collaborating with them, I felt relief and euphoria that I was no longer a dishonest man working for a totalitarian state. My new role gave point to my existence. At the same time, of course, I had to conceal what I was doing from everyone in my life, Yelena included. Had we been close to each other, this would have made things awkward at home: for everyone's safety, a spy has to deceive even his nearest and dearest. Our relationship had degenerated so badly, however, that I felt no difficulty about keeping my activities to myself.

All the same, I began to be more careful in my political statements. In the past I had often been quite flippant, and more prepared than most of my KGB colleagues to criticize the regime. Now I stopped, so as not to attract attention: I had no wish to be sacked or punished for irresponsibility while I had more serious business in hand. It was easy enough to do this for the atmosphere both in the KGB and in Soviet society was deteriorating: openness and lightness disappeared and the regime headed into a neo-Stalinist age.

This trend was made clear to me by a visit of the well-known literary critic Vladimir Lakshin, who had become famous in the 1960s for his praise of Solzhenitsyn: a brilliant article about the novel *One Day in the Life of Ivan Denisovich* had made him the darling of the intelligentsia. But now, when he came to Copenhagen, and I rushed to greet him, full of 1960s' enthusiasm, he turned cold and dismissive, not wanting to talk. Later I realized that after Solzhenitsyn's expulsion from the Soviet Union Lakshin knew how vulnerable he himself had become — and since all embassies were full of spies, why should he open his heart to a stranger?

New officers coming from Moscow gave other indications of how things were going downhill. Nikolai Gribin, who arrived in 1976, was by no means a liberal: on the contrary, he was thoroughly conformist. Yet even he said that things were getting worse, which made it easy for me to keep quiet. Another distinguished visitor from Moscow was the composer Dmitri Shostakovich, who came with his young third wife and his son to give a lecture. At the end I asked the speaker which other contemporary composer he considered to be nearest to him in spirit. He answered, 'Benjamin Britten.' Next morning the son asked me to translate reports from the local press and, although I warned him that the Copenhagen newspapers tended to be disrespectful, he pressed me to go ahead. I had hardly started on an article by one exceptionally rude music critic, when he cried, 'Enough! Enough!'

*

During my second tour in Denmark badminton came to play an important part in my life. Having joined a club, I took an active part in its affairs, playing in matches and competitions, especially on Sundays. Badminton enabled me to live like a normal Western person, playing with Danes and relaxing afterwards over a beer in a cafe. Back in the Soviet Union after my first tour, I had found that the Soviet Badminton Federation was in a poor way: the sport received no subsidy from the State, and was supported only by the efforts of enthusiasts. Hoping that I might be able to improve things, I offered my services and was made a member of the board. In Denmark again, I wrote fictitious memoranda, allegedly emanating from important people, saying what a shame it was that the Soviet Federation was not a member of the World Badminton Federation or even of the European Badminton Federation. Our friends and sympathizers, I wrote, regarded our presence in those organizations as highly desirable, to counterbalance the influence of the Chinese. That did the trick: the Soviet Federation joined both major bodies, and later I arranged a visit of five Russian teams, accompanying them on a tour round the country.

In 1977 yet another complication entered my life in the form of Leila Aliyeva, a girl who was working in the typing pool at the World Health Organization's offices in Copenhagen. The daughter of a Russian mother and an Azeri father from Azerbaijan, she was tall and striking, with distinctly Oriental looks — very Turkish, in a nice way, except that she had a big nose. She was then twenty-eight, eleven years younger than me, and I fell in love at first sight.

The circumstances were awkward, to say the least. She was living in a flat, to which I never went because she was sharing with other girls and was surrounded by neighbours. Obviously we could not go to my flat. The result was that although our love flared up quickly, we only went twice to a hotel before the time came for me to return to Moscow. Nevertheless, we made plans to marry as soon as I could disentangle myself.

For different reasons, we were both eager to have a family. After a sterile and disappointing first marriage, I was approaching forty, and some animal instinct was telling me to look for a woman who could become the mother of my children. Leila also felt that her time was running out and, because Azeris are such warm, family people, the prospect of remaining childless was worse for her than for purely Russian women.

I found that as the daughter of a strict Muslim household she had been kept away from boys until it became impossible for her father to control her any longer. She had been isolated from outside acquaintances until she was almost twenty; and from sixteen to eighteen, when other girls were rushing from party to party, from one boyfriend to another, she had been kept in seclusion. Even at school her father had forbidden her to play volleyball, because he thought it unacceptable for a woman to show her legs by wearing shorts.

Unusually for a Moscow girl, she had started work straight from school. Most parents tried to get their daughters into university at any price, but Leila began as a typist in a designer bureau at the age of only eighteen. Then she switched to the youth newspaper *Moskovsky Komsomoletlz* — one of the better publications, which was still trying to be lively and interesting. There, too, she worked as a secretary, but because, like most of her family, she wrote well, she soon moved up to being a reporter. Her happiest memories were from her two years spent covering events in Moscow. Then someone told her that if she applied to the Ministry of Health she might get a job in the World Health Organization, and, after a kind of positive vetting, she did just that. Again she became a typist, but she was eager to work and live abroad, and also she earned a good salary — even if she had to pay the lion's share of it back to the Embassy, as did all Soviet citizens who worked in other organizations abroad.

In Moscow, as she told me rather sketchily, she had had a passionate affair, at last, with a completely unsuitable man. He was a heavy drinker and lacked direction in life but, because she was madly in love, she became almost a slave to him — a relationship that he enjoyed and exploited, treating her like dirt. After a while, this became unbearable for her, and they parted.

As far as I could tell, she had had no other lovers, and I got the impression that her experience of close relationships was limited. I put this down to the Muslim element in her background, and she agreed that her upbringing had been inhibiting. Yet she had great potential: she was sociable, interesting, original, witty and eager to be liked. The prospect of living with her one day was enormously appealing.

At first Yelena did not know that I had met her. Then slowly she realized that something was going on, and she made a couple of unpleasant scenes in the flat. The worst thing about this was that the Danes were listening, and passed word of our wrangling to the British; the next thing I knew, Andrew was anxiously inquiring if my work for him was causing me undue stress. I told him part of the truth — that my marriage was in a bad state — but I added, 'Don't blame yourself. This has been going on for ages, and is nothing to do with you.'

And yet in a way it was: my decision to help the West had introduced a new element into my life. I realized that — as usual — I had allowed my head to rule my heart. That I was now covertly fighting Communism, purely for ideological reasons, meant that half my existence and my thoughts had to remain secret: I could not open my heart to anyone. With Yelena this had hardly mattered, as our partnership had always remained superficial, but now, with Leila, what would happen? Could I establish the close, warm relationship I longed for? All I could do was follow my instincts and hope that things would work out.

For month after month my clandestine assignations had continued without any scares. But then vague rumours began to circulate that the KGB was leaking. The stories came from officers returning after leave in Moscow, where people gossiped and talked shop for hours on end. For me, there was nothing sinister about these rumours — until January 1977. Then a cold prickle went up my spine when I heard that in Oslo the Norwegians had arrested a woman called Gunvor Haltung Haavik, an elderly secretary in the Norwegian Foreign Ministry, who had been a KGB spy for nearly thirty years. Until then I had never known her name but in the previous year a new KGB officer posted to us from Moscow, Vadim Cherny, had begun talking to me about a woman agent in Norway known as 'Greta', and I, of course, warned my British contacts. When the arrest took place, I thought that it must be my information that had led to her exposure — and I have several times been credited with her downfall. Later I found out that the Norwegians had been on her track since at least 1975, so that whatever I said merely gave them additional ammunition.[2]

From Cherny I also learnt that the KGB had another, even more important agent in Norway, also in the Ministry of Foreign Affairs, and that it was someone with a journalistic background. These details I also passed on, and they were instrumental in the eventual unmasking of Arne Treholt, a flamboyant, fair-haired political activist who at the time of Haavik's arrest was thirty-five and a leading personality in the Norwegian Labour Party. (It took the Norwegians years of investigation

---

2   Haavik held more than 250 meetings with various case officers over twenty-seven years of espionage, and handed thousands of classified documents to the KGB. Six months after her arrest she died in prison of a heart-attack, before being brought to trial.

Cherny — a mediocre worker, typical of the KGB — later committed suicide in Moscow when he found he had cancer, shooting himself with a pistol which he kept in the office.

before they were able to pinpoint him. They were still searching when I arrived in England in 1982. I was then able to identify him positively, and he was finally arrested on 1 January 1984, as he was about to board a plane for Vienna with sixty-six classified documents from the Norwegian Ministry of Foreign Affairs in his briefcase.)

Also in 1978 I learnt by chance that the KGB or GRU (or possibly both) had acquired an agent in Sweden, a member of some security organization, either civil or military. My information was sparse but I warned the British that the Swedish intelligence community had been penetrated, and they passed on the message. It turned out that the Swedes already had other small indications that there might be a traitor in their ranks, but it was my tip that led them to Stig Bergling, who had worked in the civilian security service, then switched to the military service, and gone to Israel as a member of the United Nations' peacekeeping force. With the Israelis' co-operation, the Swedes arrested him out there, brought him home, and gaoled him. It turned out, as I had suspected, that he was a son of two Soviet services: he had been recruited by the KGB, but then had been passed to the GRU, who ran him in the Middle East.[3]

In Denmark the KGB had no agent comparable with Haavik or Treholt: the only threat of any consequence to the West was a fat policeman in the immigration department whom the KR Line had been running as an agent. He was useful, because he could tell the KGB about Danish policy towards foreigners, embassies and so on, and the police often picked up rumours from the security service, which was

---

3 In 1987 Bergling was released from gaol to spend the weekend with his mistress. He disappeared, and the Swedes rightly concluded he had defected to the Soviet Union. Taken to the Lebanon by the GRU, he worked there as an agent, but then in 1994 surrendered to the Swedish authorities, and was returned to prison.

only a specialized branch of their own organization. To stop that leak, I told the British about the policeman, who was soon moved away to some provincial town. It was easy enough for the authorities to shift him, because he had been drinking excessively and therefore they had a ready excuse.

*

At Easter 1978, because KGB business seemed slack, I took the opportunity of going into hospital for an operation on my nose. For several years I had suffered from nasal congestion, which had developed into asthma, and a small operation was needed to open up the air passages. The first time I presented myself, the doctor did some checks and said, 'I can't operate, your blood pressure's too high.' I said, 'All right. Let's try again tomorrow. I'll come back.' At the Embassy I found some pills, took them for twenty-four hours, and presented myself again. They seemed to have done the trick, and the operation went ahead — although afterwards the surgeon told me that it had produced a disgusting amount of blood.

I spent the next four days recuperating. Nobody came to see me: Yelena had no desire to, and Leila did not feel confident about visiting someone else's husband. I did not mind as I had a lively companion in the form of a lonely old Dane, a great drinker, who had come to grief after an evening in a pub. When he emerged, in the early hours of the morning, frost had set in, and he measured his length on some ice, breaking his nose. Because he lived in a cold little flat, he was delighted to have a few days in a luxurious hospital, with pretty nurses, excellent food, and a Russian for company. When I got someone from the Embassy to bring in a couple of bottles of vodka, the nurses were thrilled, and made a splendid Easter lunch, with lavish food, and fruit juice spiked with vodka.

As the time approached at which I would have to return to Moscow, Yelena and I were trying to make decisions about what we would do when we got home. She was ambivalent about her intentions: in any other society she would have divorced me promptly, but the KGB were immensely hypocritical and puritanical about such matters and would, we knew, make things as difficult as possible for us. For my part, I knew that a divorce would lead to acrimonious exchanges with my bosses in the office, and with executives of the Party. There was also the question of what position I might be appointed to next. As in all departments of the KGB, the more senior one became the fiercer grew the intrigues surrounding the promotion of candidates to particular jobs. I needed support, and here my superior in Copenhagen, Mikhail Lyubimov (who had succeeded Mogilvechik as Resident), proved good to me. 'They'll go for you,' he warned me. 'Not only will they condemn you for the divorce, which they don't like. They'll also accuse you of having had an affair *en poste*, which will be bad for you. Let's soften the blow by doing something positive.'

Lyubimov became a friend for life. A genial, relaxed fellow with a good brain, he had been posted to the London station in the 1960s, determined to subvert the whole of Britain, including the Royal Family. The result was that he fell in love with the place, and became an enthusiastic advocate of all things British, not least English literature and Scotch whisky.

Now, by sending a couple of favourable reports to the Centre, he gave the impression that my work in Denmark had been good, and persuaded the powers that I was the best candidate to become deputy head of the Third Department of the First Chief Directorate. In our terms this was a tremendously important post, in effect, the deputy head of the third most important department in the KGB. The idea was that I would become supervisor of the Scandinavian and Finnish sections, and that my next posting after that would probably be as head of station in Stockholm or Oslo, or even Copenhagen yet again.

Chapter Ten – Fresh Start

Back at the Centre in Moscow, I went in to see my department head, Viktor Grushko, an engaging character not at all typical of the KGB. As his name suggested, he was Ukrainian, and was short, rotund, with lively brown eyes and black hair. His colouring suggested the presence of some Balkan or Turkish blood, and he had a soft, smiling approach which accurately hinted at his strange combination of laziness and industry: although he liked to take things easy, he could work hard if he had to. Unlike Zaitsev, he realized at an early stage in his career that intelligent delegation was the way forward, and he did not try to do everything himself. Neither was he intimidating: his voice was soft, and free of any regional accent. Although he was not an intellectual, he had a good native wit which enabled him to hold his own in intelligent company. His first posting abroad, to Norway, had been as a clean diplomat.

As I came into his office, he was all smiles, and I could see that he was about to have the pleasure of offering me a magnificent promotion; but before he could do that I handed him a letter from Lyubimov, which explained my domestic problems. 'Viktor Feodorovich,' I warned him, 'before you say a word, you'd better read this.'

As he read, the merriment drained from his eyes. 'Yes,' he said wearily, 'I'm afraid this changes everything.' Suddenly he saw that instead of a simple promotion he had a scandal on his hands. He sighed and added, Now I'm afraid you'll have to stick to Partcom [a kind of second personnel department]. For the moment I'll keep you in the department, and you can be a senior officer running important errands. I have plenty of work for you — don't worry.'

He began to talk of other things. 'What about Otto?' he asked. 'Did that meeting take place?'

'Oh, yes,' I said, and I started to describe my final contact in Denmark. But even as I was speaking, I saw a look of terrible boredom come over Grushko's face: he simply did not want to bother with small-scale operations such as the one I was describing. He wanted nothing to do with the huge reports that people kept sending in from foreign stations: even though he was head of the department, he never read them, knowing that most of what they said was invented and that the contacts they described were utterly unimportant. What he wanted was news of real agents like Treholt but, of course, I had none to give. Failing that, he was eager for gossip about personal relationships in the stations: who was doing what, what feeling was like between the Ambassador and the Resident. After a while, he said, 'All right, then. Off you go and enjoy your holiday but you'd better be prepared for unpleasant conversations.'

I had plenty of those. As always, mean-minded people were keen to exploit the discomfort of my impending divorce and inflate its negative aspects. 'You've had an *affair*,' they said menacingly. 'While on assignment you became involved in an *affair*. Very unprofessional.' Their sole object was to create scandal and make my life difficult.

Humiliating scenes were most likely to take place at meetings of the Partcom, which regarded itself as a moral guardian of the staff. There the committee would go through the record of the person who had sinned, forcing him (or her) to repent in public, to grovel, to promise that he would cleanse himself and accept the judgement of his comrades. Neglected or beaten wives would complain about the behaviour of their husbands, asking for them to be denounced as scoundrels, or sometimes appealing for help in getting them back.

Attacks were all part of the normal back-biting and competition for places, but in my case they were exacerbated by jealousy. By then I had won a reputation as a thorough, politically right-thinking officer, strong in all aspects of my work: a good linguist, a competent writer of reports, a historian, a front-line operator who had proved himself skilled at making contacts and had run a couple of agents in Denmark. The KGB was full of people who, though good in some areas, were weak in others and it was these flawed characters who led the intrigues, inspired by envy of someone who could perform well across the board.

A month's convalescence in the hot, dry air and sea climate of the Crimea did much to restore my damaged nose, which was still sore and congested after the operation. I stayed at a sanatorium between Yalta and Gurzov, which brought back happy memories of that phenomenal holiday at Artek, not far along the coast, where the long-legged East German girls had run rings round their keepers.

In Moscow again, I tried to come to terms with the fact that, although now a senior officer, I had no definite function. I also found that I had to be constantly on my guard against unpleasant surprises, the worst of which occurred as the result of an exercise conducted by the British traitor Kim Philby. From time to time the KGB would present Philby with a case for analysis, and late in 1978 they turned him on to the Haavik affair, having sanitized the material by changing names so that he could not tell where the events described had taken place.

His conclusion, based on a careful study of events, was that the leak which betrayed the agent could only have come from inside the KGB.

One morning soon after that Grushko gathered his senior officers in his office — seven of us altogether, including himself —and said in his most serious voice: 'There are signs that the KGB is leaking, and that the adversary is getting information.' He explained how Philby had reported on the Haavik case, and told us the conclusion he had reached. Then he added: 'This is particularly worrying, because the pattern of events suggests that *the traitor may be in the room at this moment*. He could be sitting here among us.'

I needed every ounce of physical effort that I could muster to stop myself blushing. I pinched myself sharply in the thigh, through my trouser pocket, and the sudden pain distracted my attention for an instant, helping me to keep my face straight. But it was a close shave, and left me feeling sick.

I had another unpleasant moment with Aleksandr Tchebotok, a friend who had cultivated one particular Danish journalist so successfully that Lyubimov described him as fully recruited. One day Tchebotok came into my office and said querulously, 'The trouble with this man is that whenever I try to talk to him about co-operation, he says, "But what if there's a traitor in the KGB? He'll be bound to give me away, and the authorities will find out about me."'

The remark was so sudden that I made some inarticulate sound, which Tchebotok inevitably noticed. Good friend though he was, and none too bright, he was immediately worried, and asked, 'Are you all right?'

'Yes, thanks,' I said. 'It's just that I'm in such a mess at home. I can't stop thinking about family affairs. People are being very unfair about my divorce.'

By making him feel guilty, I managed to turn the conversation on to harmless territory — but it was a good lesson in the need to keep my composure better.[1]

Then again, a few months later, a specialist in Arctic affairs, Anatoli Semyonov, began talking about an apparent leak in his sphere. Sitting at his desk in his own little office, this highly intelligent man said, 'As you know, we've been paying special interest to Arctic affairs since 1973, and the KGB has been the main force in the drive to make the polar ocean and surrounding territories a major strategic asset to the Soviet Union. It's all been top secret — and yet, in recent years, we've started to feel that the West knows more than it should about our operations there. Odd, isn't it?'

I managed to make some noncommittal remark, but my stomach was churning. The number one Arctic power was Norway, and I knew that Arne Treholt had been supplying us with extremely useful information. The number two power was Canada, but Denmark was also important because Greenland was part of its territory, and over the years of my association with the British I had passed across much background material, some verbally, some in the form of documents. Probably Semyonov consulted me purely because he knew I was a Danish specialist — but I remained harried by the fear that he might somehow have been harbouring positive suspicions.

During this difficult period I made no attempt to contact the British. I had hidden my instructions for doing so in the most secret places I could devise, and I knew that contact sites were being watched regularly. If I appeared at one, my message would get through, but I did not intend to take any action unless I heard something new and dramatic about penetration of the West. Every now and then I learnt new details of KGB

---

1   Tchebotok fancied Yelena and, although I do not believe he ever had an affair with her, I knew that he once photographed her naked to the waist.

operations. which would certainly have interested the British service, and more facts about Treholt gradually surfaced: one day his identity was finally confirmed for me when I saw, upside down on someone's desk, a half-covered piece of paper bearing the letters OLT. But the risk of being spotted by the domestic KGB was so high that attempts at making contact would have been justified only by some exceptional development.[2]

Besides, I had another reason for biding my time: already I had started to feel that I might go abroad again, and I set my sights on being posted to Britain. The first step would be to obtain a transfer to the British section in my department, and with this aim in mind I began to cultivate the people there. This proved no easy task for they were a tight-knit little group, with their own habits and traditions, all speaking English and deliberately distancing themselves from other colleagues.

Luckily I got on well with the deputy department head in charge of British affairs, Dmitri Svetanko, who, although bossy, was essentially kind-hearted. With his bald head, protuberant eyes, sagging belly and choleric temper, he looked the heavy drinker he was (every few months he would go over the top and get into a fight, or threaten to break up a restaurant); but he was also industrious, and liked men of action, among whom he numbered me. We struck up a bit of a friendship.

If Svetanko was basically good-natured, the same could not be said of the head of the British section, Igor Titov, a truly evil man, profoundly anti-British. Much younger, barely thirty-five, but prematurely balding and with a dark-grey tinge to his skin, he gave the impression of being permanently dissatisfied. He rarely laughed or let his face soften into

---

2   The Directorate responsible for surveillance in Moscow, No. 7, and known as semyorka (figure seven), employed about 1000 men, and these were reinforced by another 500 or so from the Moscow Oblast Directorate, so that at least 1500 men were available for surveillance in the city.

any show of friendliness; rather, he maintained a cynical, disapproving look, which was reinforced by his habit of chain-smoking. Neither did knowledge of his private habits increase my respect for him: when cartons of duty-free cigarettes arrived for him in the diplomatic bag from London he could hardly wait to snatch them up and lock them away in a steel cabinet. He also received through the diplomatic bag a steady supply of pornographic magazines, bought for him in Soho, carefully wrapped, and addressed to him personally. These rags he would pass round to cronies, before handing them on as small bribes or payments to anyone who had done something for him.

Much as I disliked ingratiating myself with such a creature, I steeled myself to cultivate him, knowing that he was a key figure. We began to have lunch in the canteen, and I struck up a working relationship. At the same time, I belatedly set about learning English by enrolling on a course run by the First Chief Directorate.

The teaching department there was the nicest part of the entire KGB organization. It was staffed almost entirely by women, all of whom were friendly, intelligent and dedicated to the study of English language and literature. Those who had been to England were the envy of their less fortunate colleagues but they all seemed far more human than other KGB personnel because they had absorbed some of the cultural and spiritual essence of England.

One of them — a woman in her thirties, whose wonderful green eyes redeemed her rather dumpy figure — touched me deeply by consulting me about a moral problem which was troubling her. Should she tell her daughter the truth about how life should be, she asked, in a fair, free democratic society like that of the West? Or should she avoid worrying the girl, and let her be brought up in the fog of propaganda, with all its attendant lies, that prevailed in the Soviet Union? 'If I once tell her about real values, it will make her unhappy,' she said miserably. 'What am I to do?'

I found it moving that someone who did not know me well should trust me enough to ask such a question. I said, 'Whatever the future, you should bring the child up with the proper values: tell her about justice and honesty, and give her an understanding of good and evil. Then slowly explain about the existing system.' I could see how difficult this was for the teacher, who looked at me full of doubt, but it was the only answer I could give.

When she and her colleagues discovered that I had a background of other languages and was genuinely keen to learn, they made special efforts to help me. Yet they showed a curious lack of interest in the history of language, a subject that fascinated me. One day in a break between lessons I drew a chart on the blackboard which showed how various words had mutated from German to Danish, from Danish to Swedish and Swedish to English; my teacher seemed impressed, but I suddenly realized that it had never occurred to her to explore the historical background of her subject.

The full English course lasted eight terms, spread over four years, and for most people there was a strong incentive to pass it because any officer with a certificate of competence in a new language could claim a 10 per cent rise in salary. (The maximum increment was 20 per cent, for two languages and, as I already had German and Danish, I did not stand to gain any more.) At first I found the going hard: for homework each of us was given a tape of the BBC World Service's morning news bulletin and told to make a full transcript. Study periods were held in the morning one week, in the evening the next, and I found it hard to fit them in with my job, but I was determined to work at an accelerated pace, and I managed to cram four years' study into two. I am sure I was helped by all my earlier linguistic training, in German, Swedish, French (to some extent) and Danish, but I was particularly pleased that I, by far the oldest man on the course (forty-one when I began it), outpaced the younger students.

On a beautiful day in the summer of 1981 I took my final exam — and passed. This did not mean that I could speak English fluently: my knowledge was still superficial. But what a language this was! For a foreigner, English is like a huge building which one has to get to know and, as somebody remarked, the closer you come to it, the taller and more daunting it appears. (One sign of its sheer size was that my best two-volume English—Russian dictionary contained 160,000 entries, compared with only 60,000 in a French—Russian dictionary of similar scope.)

Although my speech was still faltering, I could read quite well, and I became fascinated by the short stories of Somerset Maugham, whose style I found exceptionally clear. Also, in the political section of the KGB library, I was amazed to discover all six volumes of Sir Winston Churchill's *History of the Second World War*, translated into Russian and published by the Military Publications House in 1955, during the Khrushchev thaw. The edition was a handsome one, in the same hardback format as the originals, and I was riveted by the discovery of so much information about the war, especially as it was presented by a leading Western statesman. Reading away, I began to understand how the British civil service functioned, how cables were composed and sent, and so on, so that the experience became highly educational for me.

Sitting in the coach on the way home from the office every evening, I would have a volume on my lap, and whenever I came across something of special interest, I would read it aloud. My fellow officers were so bored by the familiar journey that they could hardly help but listen.

One episode I gave them was the one in which, during 1942, Churchill visited Stalin in his inner Moscow dacha, styled 'State Villa No. 7', and described how, in the most difficult year of the war, the little wooden building was full of fresh fruit, fine French wines and servants. In the garden Churchill found 'a large glass tank filled with many kinds of goldfish which were all so tame that they would eat out of your hand', and he made a point of feeding them every day. He was also shown a new air-raid shelter 'of the most luxurious type', with lifts descending around 30 metres into the earth, and fully furnished accommodation at the bottom. 'The lights were brilliant,' he wrote. 'The furniture was stylish "Utility", sumptuous and brightly coloured. I was more attracted by the goldfish.'

'Isn't that marvellous?' I cried, but my colleagues did not know what to say. No KGB officer could possibly make any positive comment about a British statesman…and eventually one mumbled, 'What a great humanist! He liked the fish best.' How feverishly those same people must have discussed me after my escape in 1985: 'Remember how he was always reading those wretched books and praising Winston Churchill!'

An early chance to practise my English came in the task of translating reports by Kim Philby. To my disappointment I never met him, but Svetanko had established a routine of sending four or five young English-speaking officers to seminars which he conducted in a safe flat, a spacious apartment in Gorky Street. There, once a year, Philby would address the young hopefuls on various aspects of British life, explaining how different types of people would speak to each other. Then he would create little scenarios: 'Imagine I'm your contact, and I'm a lawyer. Let's have a conversation, and you ask the questions.' Then he would act as businessman, journalist, intelligence officer, and afterwards he would write secret reports on his pupils' performance.

One day Svetanko asked me to translate a batch of reports —and a tough task I found it. Philby had written them in elaborate, complicated English. There was a certain irony in this, for in spite of his lifelong profession of admiration for Soviet Communism, his spoken Russian remained poor, and he never learnt to write a word of the language. Why had he used such stylized English for his reports? Was he trying to impress someone? Or was he sending out a signal of contempt, challenging us poor simpletons to understand him?

Whatever the reason, I rose to the task and worked my hardest to render his long, convoluted sentences into Russian, including all their nuances. Since I have always loved translating difficult texts, I found it an enjoyable exercise, and in the course of it I saw that, for all his pretension, Philby was a shrewd judge of character, with a perceptive understanding of other people.

A naturally idle man, he did not want much work, so he conducted these seminars between October and December but every year Albert Kozlov, the link between him and our department, bought him a birthday present to keep him happy. Occasionally Kozlov asked me to help him find something suitable, and, since there was nothing of quality in any normal shop, we always went to one of the antique shops (of which there were then four in the whole of Moscow). One year we had a particular triumph when we found an elaborate writing-set, dating from the turn of the century, which fitted the bill exactly. On another occasion I asked Kozlov to take Philby a book about him written by a Dane, so that he could sign it for me. Back it came a few days later bearing the inscription, 'To My Good Friend Oleg — Don't believe anything you see in print! Kim Philby.'

The first book in English that I read straight through from start to finish, understanding everything, was Frederick Forsyth's *The Day of the*

Jackal, brought to me by Kozlov one evening when I was detained for a few days in the KGB medical centre, suffering from some bronchial infection. While there I also read the whole of Fielding's huge novel *Tom Jones*, although this was in Russian.

*

On the domestic front I had to make a completely fresh start. While in Denmark I had acquired a new flat in Moscow by putting down a 40 per cent deposit, out of a total cost of fourteen thousand roubles — although the law on property was so poorly defined that I was never sure what my rights of ownership were. I paid the money to a group of KGB officers who had organized themselves into a co-operative: each of us put down a deposit, and the group raised the rest by borrowing from banks. As far as I could tell, I had bought the freehold of the apartment, and would be able to occupy it in perpetuity, or until the block fell down.

Yelena and I decided that, once we were divorced, I would live in this new flat, and she would retain our old one. She did well out of the arrangement, keeping not only all the new clothes she had bought in Denmark but also our china and a good deal of the furniture, including the wall units which I had so painstakingly put up for my books. In Copenhagen she had continued to work for the KGB, so that she held her seniority and returned to Moscow as a captain, earning a good salary. She resumed her old listening job, and continued to earn substantial amounts. (When I discussed our affairs with the head of the Partcom, he said, 'Whatever you do, don't mention Yelena's money.')

For the time being she camped in the new flat and I stayed in the old, which temporary set-up led to considerable irritation. I did not mind that Yelena broke open the packing case of my own possessions, which had arrived from Copenhagen, and began to use them. That was hardly important. But one day when I happened to be free in the morning and went to the new flat to collect some things I needed urgently, to my consternation, I could not open the door. The lock seemed to have jammed, and I was forced to go down to a call-box at ground level and telephone Yelena in her office.

'What on earth have you done to the locks?' I demanded. 'I need some stuff urgently.'

'Oh…ah!' She sounded unusually flustered. Then she said, 'I'll see to it. Wait a few minutes and try again.'

I hung around outside the building, and a couple of minutes later out scuttled a man in his thirties, who disappeared rapidly round the corner. I did not feel jealous, exactly: there was nothing like that left between us. But I could not help feeling annoyed that she had invited a man into my flat and left him there with all my nice new things from abroad.

Our divorce, presided over in court by a female judge, was brutally straightforward. Yelena displeased this powerful lady by chewing gum (a sign of nerves). 'Stop doing that!' said the judge sharply. 'You're in court. Now, your husband is divorcing you because you don't want to have children, and he does. Is that right?'

'Not at all!' said Yelena. 'He fell in love with a pretty girl. Nothing else.'

In a way I admired her for being so cynical and honest; but the judge did not find her convincing. 'I accept the husband's reasons, and grant a divorce,' she said. 'But he, the plaintiff, will have to pay the legal costs.' During her preliminary discussions she had warned me that costs might amount to four hundred roubles, but in the event she made me pay only a hundred and fifty. I felt I was lucky to have a female judge, because she discerned that Yelena was self-centred and egoistic, and saw how little she cared about husband or family.

In October Leila came back from Copenhagen on holiday. She was staying with me in the old flat when, one morning, the doorbell rang: it was my brother-in-law, Valentin, Marina's husband, calling to announce, 'Anton Lavrentiyevich died in the night.' My father was eighty-two, and, although he smoked excessively, had been in reasonable health. I am glad to say that he and I were on good terms during his old age. To the end of his life he remained what he had always been, a dedicated Communist, but we had long since ceased to have ideological arguments. He knew that I was working in foreign intelligence but was too professional to ask questions about what I was doing. Many of his friends and contemporaries had already died, so that few people came along three days later when we said goodbye to him at the crematorium. For the wake, more than thirty relations crowded into my parents' tiny flat, and I made what I think was the speech of my life, extolling the high ability of this son of a railway ganger, who had established himself as a leading first-generation member of the intelligentsia, and then had brought up his children to do equally well in the second generation. To some extent his death was a liberation for my mother, who was eleven years younger and still active, and had been irritated at having to spend so much of her time looking after a man of his advanced age.

*

Yelena and I duly switched flats, but that winter of 1978-79 proved one of the coldest in living memory. From December to January the temperature remained incredibly low, even by Moscow standards (-28°C by day, and down to -36°C at night), and my new apartment, which still had no curtains or proper lights, was far from homely. In the middle of the cold spell I went down with influenza, and felt so ill that I called a doctor. The young woman who answered my call prescribed some antibiotics, and then, looking round at the chaos, said severely, 'Really! You should look after yourself better. Why doesn't your wife take better care of you?' To which I replied, 'I'm not married.' The doctor glared at me and said, 'By your age, you're *supposed* to be married,' with which she swept out.

In January Leila returned from Denmark for good, and we were married in a simple ceremony. I felt that at my age it would not be appropriate to make a great occasion of it, so we went to a register office, and invited only my sister Marina, and Leila's brother Arif and his wife Katya, an exceptionally nice couple, who became good friends. Afterwards we all went to Leila's parents for dinner.

That she was eleven years younger had worried us both at first, but by now we had grown used to it. I reassured myself by thinking that this was exactly the age gap between my parents, so that I was merely repeating a family pattern. Also, I consoled myself with the thought that my father, too, had been married twice. Thinking back, I remembered how my grandmother had once let slip in my presence, 'Anton's first wife…' but how she had stopped short, looked at me in fear and added quickly, 'You didn't hear me say that. If your father finds out, he'll kill me.' Other generations, I reflected, had their problems, just as we did.

Setting up our flat was enormous fun. Our relationship was warm and close, everything I had always longed for, and we enjoyed launching ourselves into the battle of getting things done in Moscow. We had some beautiful modern furniture from Denmark — lovely chairs, a leather-covered sofa and a marble-topped coffee table, all chosen by Leila — but I wanted extensive bookshelves once again, and for these we went to a local firm that made furnishings to order. Dealing with this company was an experience in itself, and a revelation of how Moscow really functioned. The firm was half public, half private, and its craftsmen, though skilled, were grossly overworked. Our two carpenters would arrive with shelves which they had already roughed-out in their workshops, but they would begin to drink at 11 a.m., and were so dependent on alcohol that they kept making pathetic appeals to be topped up. 'We need a shot of dope,' they would say shamelessly, knowing that I would pour out tumblers of neat vodka. 'Time for a shot.' By the afternoon, they had had so many shots that they hardly knew where they were or what they were doing. Because they had an official job, I paid a fee to their firm, but I also paid them privately, and in the end they succeeded in covering two walls with good-looking shelves.

Leila also wanted wall units for the kitchen, and when she heard that a large furniture store was about to take delivery of some, she joined an all-night queue. That proved a fascinating sociological experience, and in the morning she was immensely proud of having achieved her objective. 'Western people don't know what real happiness is!' she cried in triumph. 'Real happiness is to queue all night, and then get what you want.'

Once the flat was fully furnished, running it was cheap since most things were heavily subsidized by the State. Our central heating cost the equivalent of six pounds a month, electricity about eight pounds, and the telephone about four pounds. (The heating was ferociously powerful, and since our radiators had no thermostats, the only way we could cool the flat was by opening the windows, even when the outside temperature was -30°C.)

Our only problem was that we could not find Leila a good job. For the moment, though, this did not matter, since we wanted to start a family, and she soon became pregnant: our first daughter, Maria, was born in April 1980, followed by Anna in September 1981. Both births took place in maternity homes, and these I can only describe as torture factories in which the most brutal methods were used and anaesthetics were unknown. The idea of a father being present at the birth of his child was unheard of: no visitors were allowed, and it would not have occurred to the authorities to admit anyone except professional medical staff.

Thus, when our first child was due, I had to take Leila in and leave her. I knew she was in a lot of pain, but that was the last I heard until, next day, a member of the staff rang and said that a baby girl had been born without complications. After another three days I was given a time at which I might come and collect her, and I joined the usual throng of fathers and other relatives gathered outside the home and waving to their loved ones in the windows. Protocol demanded that I should bring a bunch of flowers for the young mother, and five roubles for the nurse who carried the baby out, a ritual with which I was delighted to go along.

Leila proved a first-class mother — a role she mastered particularly well. During her first year back in Moscow she also finished a correspondence course in journalism under the auspices of Moscow University, aiming to win the Certificate of Higher Education which was vital to success in Soviet life. She had started this before her stay in Denmark, and now had to write a diploma report, or final paper — a modest version of a Ph.D. When she asked me for ideas about a subject, I had an inspiration. 'I know!' I said. 'The Communist press in Denmark. It'll be a first because nobody has ever done it.' I began to dictate to her and found it dead easy since I had been studying the subject at first hand for years, and knew it inside out. Between us we produced a long paper, full of interest, and the head of her department — a well-known journalist and teacher at Moscow University — made a special request to be her sponsor. So Leila won her certificate — which, sadly, she has never used.

She was marvellous in the home, putting to good use experience gained when she was a child. As a young girl she had helped look after her baby brother, born when she was eight or nine, when life was difficult; working with her mother had given her an ideal practical grounding in most domestic practices.

*

In the KGB there was an unwritten rule that if someone got divorced and then married again, time must pass before he could be professionally forgiven: events must demonstrate that the new relationship was in good order and the new family doing well. After the birth of Anna, things became easier for me but from time to time intrigues would flare up. Now, working at high level in the Centre for the first time, I saw how vicious and bitter these internecine squabbles could be, especially when Gennady Titov (no relation of Igor) succeeded Grushko as head of the Third Department.

This Titov, nicknamed 'The Crocodile', was one of the most unpleasant and unpopular officers in the whole of the KGB. Undoubtedly he had a certain glamour, being quick-witted, well informed, and full of vulgar jokes and anecdotes. He had an astonishing ability to talk *mat* — the alternative language used by Russian men among themselves, in which every other word is an obscenity — and, if the door of the room opened or a woman appeared, to switch back to normal speech in mid-phrase, without the slightest hesitation.[3] He was also a good listener but he was totally unprincipled and prepared to do anything to secure his own advancement. His career was made when, as KGB Resident in Norway from 1972 to 1977, he ran Arne Treholt; and although he was expelled from Oslo when Haavik was unmasked, he continued to handle Treholt,

---

3   Russians claim, but have never proved historically, that it was the brutal savages of the Tatar-Mongolian horde who brought mat with them and foisted it on the natives.

meeting him in Helsinki and Vienna. His most powerful single weapon was his ability to flatter: he shamelessly flattered not only Treholt but also his own boss, Vladimir Kryuchkov, head of the First Chief Directorate.

At least Grushko, a former diplomat, was able to put a façade of decency over his actions. Gennady Titov, in contrast, was cynical and boorish. Titov and Grushko spent countless hours scheming and playing office politics, chasing what were known as *apparatniye igry*, or departmental gains, trying to advance their own careers, secure in the knowledge that, if they failed to get what they wanted at a particular point, they would stay where they were, but that if they won, they would be promoted.[4]

Of course, not everyone in the KGB was as unpleasant as these two: as I had told the British, the organization included some truly first-class people, among them Albert Akulov, who was appointed deputy department head in succession to me. A real intellectual, and broadly educated, he had a wide knowledge of history and a phenomenal memory. Also, he spoke Finnish, Swedish, German and English. I never met anyone else in the KGB with such ability and natural good manners: he was never rude to anybody, and he could speak eloquently, without notes, on a variety of subjects. Grushko, though probably jealous, treated him decently, but the loutish Titov hated him, seeing such a cultured man as an irritation, a potential threat and a daily reproach to boorishness.

There was one particularly unpleasant scene when Titov and Svetanko, the deputy head, between them lost a secret document — in KGB

---

4 They succeeded so well that in the end Kryuchkov became chairman of the KGB, Grushko his number two and Titov his number three. Then, to my boundless satisfaction, all three went down in flames after the attempted coup against Gorbachev in 1991. Kryuchkov and Grushko were both arrested on suspicion of plotting, and Titov, though claiming to have had nothing to do with them, was removed from the KGB.

terms, a serious crime. After a desperate hunt, Titov began to make mendacious accusations in the hope that he could blame some junior member of his department; just in time, his secretary found the missing document, a thin sheet of paper which had stuck to another by static electricity. By then, however, Titov had shown his true face — and a horrible sight it was.

Every now and then I had to act as duty officer and go through the elaborate ritual of opening and closing the department. In the evenings, as each officer left, he would put the keys of his safes and his room into a little wooden box, close it, and press his own individual stamp into a lump of plasticine, to make a seal. I would then collect all the boxes and put them in the safe in the room occupied by the secretary to the boss. Having locked the safe, and put the key into another wooden box, I would get out a spare set of keys and open up all the rooms again for the cleaning lady, who made her round during the next hour and a half. When she had finished, I would again lock all the rooms, and hang a wooden tag on each door, with my own stamp on a Plasticine seal. Finally I would lock the door of the secretary's room, seal it with the same device, put the key into a wooden box, seal that also and take it to the secretariat of the First Chief Directorate, which was manned twenty-four hours a day.

In the morning I would arrive at 7 a.m., before anyone else, fetch my box, unlock the secretary's door, take out the individual officers' boxes and arrange them on the desk. When each man came in soon after eight, he would take his box, break the seal, take out his keys, open his own door and finally open his safe. When the boss arrived, between eight and nine, I would make a little formal report: 'Comrade Colonel, in the time of my duty nothing extraordinary has happened...'

This was one of the few military elements in the KGB, which for 99

287

per cent of the time behaved like a civilian organization. Nobody ever wore uniform: suits were the order of the day —and sober ones at that. Anyone who dressed in a loud or ostentatious fashion attracted widespread criticism, both overt and otherwise. Especially in the First Chief Directorate, people were expected to be courteous and well mannered. Shouting and stamping were out, and orders were supposed to be given in the form of requests. Some people would go to ridiculous lengths in this respect: a big boss would purr, 'My dear Lyonya, please have the kindness to go to the fifth floor on my behalf and fetch that book.' But any such request was an order, and even if many officers sounded as mild as sheep, they were wolves at heart.

A new shadow was cast over me when my friend and supporter Mikhail Lyubimov returned from his position as head of station in Copenhagen and found himself swept up in a scandal worse than mine. He, too, was having matrimonial problems, but he had the misfortune to fall in love with the wife of a KGB agent. This man, an informer, wrote a letter of complaint to the Central Committee of the Communist Party, saying that 'The local head of the KGB used his position of power to take my wife away from me. As a KGB agent, I was powerless to defend myself...'

The authorities were outraged, not least because Lyubimov did not come clean until after his next promotion had been announced: he had just been appointed head of a think-tank attached to the First Chief Directorate when the news of his infidelity broke. This was altogether too much for the puritanical bosses: in not declaring it before his appointment, he had deceived the KGB, they trumpeted, and now he was dismissed outright. Whatever their real feelings on love and marriage, the truth was that Titov and Grushko saw him as a potential threat, and orchestrated the campaign against him.

Lyubimov's departure not only meant the loss of a talented man: it also made my own life more difficult, because everyone started to say, 'What the hell's going on in Denmark? The place is full of scandals breaking out everywhere.' Merely to have served in Copenhagen was to invite suspicion. I also felt a sense of personal loss as Lyubimov had proved a good friend and would have helped me still more in future.

The result of all this was that my position continued to deteriorate. I still went to important meetings, and twice I wrote the department's annual report, which showed that great trust was placed in me. Yet I was not sure that I had any future in the KGB, and this uncertainty gave me the idea of joining the Andropov Institute.

Officially the Red Banner Order Andropov Institute of the KGB, but generally known by the name of the KGB chairman, the Institute was the overblown modern successor of School 101, a huge, pompous intelligence centre. At that time it was developing what it called academic activities. The aim was to create a faculty of scholarly people writing theses or studying to become lecturers and teachers: recruits were being sought, and because I seemed to be in a *cul-de-sac*, as far as my career was concerned, I decided to join for a year or two.

I had reckoned without the malice of senior colleagues, who again brought up the matter of my divorce and made entry difficult for me. I therefore switched to the idea of remaining in the department but becoming a postgraduate student, writing a thesis on the psychology of the Scandinavian nations. Thus I spent several months at the Institute, in two separate periods, but when I saw the other people in my group, I realized that I had joined a bunch of freaks. One was a secret alcoholic, and one had been working in East Germany but was tormented by violent family rows. Another was a sex maniac who kept telling us how, in the middle of some open space, he had made love to a woman so vastly fat that he had had to adopt some special position to achieve entry. I kept thinking: In some ways I'm just as odd as any of them. I never finished my thesis because word began to go round the department that the authorities were looking for someone to work in Britain.

For me it was a major stroke of good fortune that, in the autumn of 1981, a slot became available at the Soviet Embassy in London. Not only that, the post was an attractive one, that of Counsellor. The department needed a senior man with wide experience, someone whose career had been under the umbrella of the Ministry of Foreign Affairs. For various reasons, nobody else was suitable. After the mass expulsion of 1971, few cover positions were available in Britain, especially on the diplomatic front. The result was that fewer KGB had tended to work under cover of the Embassy, and more had used the media: the authorities had taken to recruiting people from the journalism faculty of Moscow University, and a number of journalist-KGB were available but no diplomats and certainly no one suitable for the position of Counsellor.

Gennady Titov had a number of cronies, and he began to invite them into his office so that they could deliver lectures on their own specialities, for officials of the department to assess them. After each had performed, Titov would ask, 'What did you think of that? Did you like him?' But the cronies were so uniformly awful that Titov's officials — much as they wanted to flatter him — all came to the same conclusion: that they could not stand any of his candidates, who were simply not up to the job.

Only one other candidate seemed possible: Viktor Kubeykin, who had served in Britain during the 1970s and had worked actively with the British Labour Party and the trade unions. Among the many people he had sought to cultivate had been Ray Buckton, general secretary of ASLEF, the rail drivers' union, who had been given the code-name

Bartok, because Kubeykin's wife was a musician. He had managed to get closer to Richard Briginshaw, general secretary of the print union NATSOPA, a man who he regarded as someone who might possibly be willing to co-operate with the Soviets. But when the Ministry applied for a visa for Kubeykin, it was categorically refused by the Foreign Office in London, where the security service knew too much about him.

That left only myself. Luckily for me, Nikolai Gribin was appointed head of the department — and, slowly, the idea started to prevail that Gordievsky might be the solution to the problem. I supported the idea as hard as I could, while remaining humble about my qualifications and not saying too much. For Titov and Grushko, it was deeply galling to know that, if I got the job, they would not benefit. Had they been able to shoehorn some protégé of theirs into the slot, they would have gained influence in London but if I went it would not advance their cause in the slightest because I had no other powerful friends, inside or outside the KGB, who would be gratified by my appointment.

In January 1982 Titov announced that he was going to test the water. The British had just applied for a visa for a new Counsellor whom they wanted to appoint to their Embassy in Moscow, and the KGB decided to do a little horse-trading: in their reply to the British application, they implied, without saying as much, that they would grant the British their visa if they in turn granted mine. Little did they realize that the British needed no persuasion. On the contrary, Titov half expected the ploy to fail. 'Gordievsky's well known in the West,' he said. 'They may easily reject him. But let's try it anyway.'

For me, of course, the prospect of going to London was electrifying; and Leila, who had no inkling of my connection with the British, also became tremendously excited. Yet the process of getting all our papers in order proved agonizingly slow.

By then, after numerous defections, the pile of paperwork needed by a person leaving for abroad had risen to monstrous proportions. The more defections that took place, the greater became the number of forms that had to be filled in: everybody concerned wanted to transfer responsibility to someone else, so that if a man did go absent, so many people would have been involved in putting his dossier together that it would be difficult to blame any individual.

My new diplomatic passport came through from the Ministry of Foreign Affairs in record time, and application forms for my visa, together with photographs, went off to the British Embassy in Moscow. (We also needed photographs of Leila and the girls, and had to take them to a studio on a freezing day when all the buses were jammed in the traffic, with snow lying on the ground — Anna was only four months old.) The normal delay at the British Embassy was thirty days, and when my visa was granted in only twenty-two days, I was both annoyed and alarmed: the British had been too quick off the mark for comfort. The sheer speed of their reaction aroused the suspicions of an experienced man in the personnel section of the Foreign Ministry. 'It's very strange they granted you the visa so quickly,' he said. 'They *must* know who you are — you've been abroad so much. When your application went in, I felt sure they'd turn it down. They've rejected so many requests lately. You can count yourself *very* fortunate.'

I did. But my positive vetting was far from over, and for months I remained uncertain about whether I would reach London or not. Two main files were going the rounds, one on my personality, containing financial and medical documents, and one on my career to date. In March these were requested by the Fifth Department of Directorate K, which investigated all suspicious cases, and there they remained for weeks. So long did they keep them, far longer than usual, that Svetanko became indignant and exclaimed, 'Oh, these wretched secret policemen! Endlessly checking up on us! What right do they have to do that? We can perfectly well check up on ourselves.'

As I waited, I began to study British affairs, about which I knew little. Margaret Thatcher, already denounced by the Soviet Union as 'the Iron Lady' and 'the Wicked Cold War Witch', was half-way through her first term as prime minister, and the KGB had eagerly watched her confrontation with the miners, who came out on strike in February 1981. In terms of Soviet propaganda, Mrs Thatcher was a typical, reactionary, right-wing Western leader, a close ally of President Reagan, bound, by virtue of her Conservative nature, to be hostile to the Soviet Union. The KGB had a clearer view of her, as an extremely intelligent prime minister and a clever manipulator: some people even felt sorry for Edward Heath, whom she had forced out of the Conservative leadership. We also discussed, with no little amusement, the totally fanciful claims by British authors that Sir Roger Hollis, former head of MI5, had been a KGB mole.

But there was far more interesting material than this close at hand, in the form of files kept in the British section, which I began to read for background information. These were not the most secret documents, which were stored in the department head's archive, or in separate personal files, but I saw several files on Britons regarded by the KGB as agents and confidential contacts, and these were highly revealing.

A Briton who figured prominently in the files was Jack Jones, the trade union leader. In the 1960s he also had attracted the KGB's interest, especially when he became executive officer at the Transport and General Workers' Union in 1963, and then General Secretary in 1969. Attempts to contact him had been temporarily frozen after the débâcle of 1971, but occasional contacts had begun again afterwards, and there were clear indications in the file that the KGB wished to revive its association with him (this task fell to me when I reached London).

My own documentation was still not complete when Argentina invaded the Falkland Islands on 2 April 1982. The despatch of a combined task force from England, and the ensuing war, brought out a great surge of animosity against Britain. If the hostility of the Soviet Union was strong, that of the KGB was almost hysterical. I was amazed by its virulence, and I could see only two reasons for it: one, that the majority of the KGB were influenced by official propaganda, and two, that the mass-expulsion of 1971 still rankled. Even then, more than a decade after the event, there was a feeling that for Soviet intelligence officers life in Britain had never again been the same, and that operations there were hampered to an irritating degree by restrictions on personnel. All in all, people were keen to see Argentina, regarded as a friendly Third World country, give the arrogant Britons a bloody nose. Besides, many of my colleagues thought Britain was going to lose: they started counting ships and casualties. My view was that Britain, a major NATO power with so much modern technology behind her, must prevail.

Yet the KGB had a far more worrying foreign preoccupation than a scrap in the South Atlantic. This was Operation RYAN (the initials standing for *Raketno-Yadernoye Napadenie*, or Nuclear Missile Attack), the largest peacetime intelligence operation ever launched by the Soviet Union: it assumed that the United States and NATO were preparing a pre-emptive first nuclear strike, and its aim was to gather information on the hostile intentions of the West. The idea of a sudden attack, which had no foundation in reality, had been floated by Andropov at a major KGB conference in Moscow during May 1981. Almost certainly it had derived from the Soviet high command and the KGB and GRU had been ordered to work together on global intelligence-gathering. Clearly, the Residency in London would be a key source of information.

Eventually my personal files were released, but still the build-up of documentation ground on, and it was not until 28 June — five months after my visa had come through — that I was able to book air tickets to London. As the day of our departure approached, excitement rose to fever pitch: the girls — Maria at two, Anna at nine months — were too young to appreciate what was about to happen, but for their parents it was almost like being put in orbit and sent to the moon.

On the day of departure I felt acutely nervous, fearing that some last-minute snag would bring all my plans to nothing. As I was preparing sandwiches for relatives who were coming round to say goodbye, I managed to stab myself: I had left a pat of butter in the refrigerator until the last moment, to stop it melting and, as I tried to cut it the knife slipped and the point drove deep into my hand. Luckily it did not hit a bone or cut a sinew, and I was able to patch myself up and continue with the party —but the accident was a little sign of how taut I had become.

Chapter Eleven – London

My Status as Counsellor entitled us to first-class seats on the Aeroflot jet, so that the three-and-a-half-hour journey passed comfortably enough. But Heathrow was a shock: never in my life had I seen so many aircraft; never had I smelt such a stink of aviation fuel. After the modest proportions and cleanliness of Copenhagen, London seemed a colossal mess. A car from the Soviet Embassy met us, and our drive into the West End of the city was itself a revelation. I had frequently read that London was one of the richest cities in the world — but here was a vast, undistinguished urban sprawl, with street after street of grimy old houses, litter in the gutters, and appalling traffic. To some extent the squalor was redeemed by the little gardens in front of the houses, and by the immaculately kept public parks but, on the whole, I had imagined that everything would be much tidier and more attractive.

Our flat, in Kensington High Street, was also a disappointment — small, dark, poorly equipped, and in every respect inferior to the one we had left in Moscow. Yet soon we found compensations in our immediate neighbourhood, not least in the form of Edwardes Square. This magnificent private garden, the largest of its kind in London, big enough to jog round, and frequent winner of a competition for the best-kept garden square in London, was open to people from the Embassy, and was a great luxury.

Our plane came in at about six in the evening, so that by the time we reached the flat, our priorities were to put the girls to bed and settle in. Much as I wanted to ring the secret number I had carried in my head for the past four years, I had no chance to do so. I knew nothing about our surroundings, and had no idea who might be watching us, or from where. Even if I went to a public kiosk and put in a call from there, I might easily be seen, and arouse somebody's suspicions. My only course was to be patient. I did not mind — I felt elated to have reached Britain. I felt that simply to be in London, with my head full of KGB and Kremlin secrets that I could pass on, was a mighty victory for British intelligence and for me.

Next morning was cool and cloudy, and I went round early to the Soviet Embassy at No. 13 Kensington Palace Gardens, a large, impressive house standing back from a private, tree-lined road, only a few yards off the busy thoroughfare of Bayswater Road. There I met up with Lev Parshin, another new Counsellor, who had been on the aircraft with me. Before we could take stock of our surroundings, we were swept into the daily conference presided over by the Ambassador, Viktor Popov.

I did not like the look of Popov, and soon my intuition proved correct. A cantankerous little man, short and weedy, he had a round, half-Tatar face and a permanently sour expression. That first morning he led off in typically sarcastic fashion, clearly irked that nobody had told him that Parshin and I were coming. 'Comrades,' he began portentously, 'two new Counsellors of the Embassy arrived yesterday. This is their first morning in London. A simple question: if we get two new Counsellors every day, how many will we have by the end of the year?'

My relationship with Popov remained difficult from then until

I departed for Moscow three years later — and the elation I had felt the previous night evaporated during the course of the morning. The London Embassy, I realized, was dramatically different from the one in Copenhagen. There I had been lucky enough to have two reasonable bosses — Mogilevchik and Lyubimov — and as the station had not been regarded as particularly important, the people staffing it had been more or less normal. London, a place of high importance, was full of the nastiest people imaginable, both in the Embassy and in the KGB station. The envy, the vicious thinking, the underhand attacks, the intrigues, the denunciations, all these were on a scale that made the Centre in Moscow seem like a girls' school, and turned life into a nightmare.

The Ambassador himself was the subject of scandalous gossip for he had married a second wife twenty-eight years younger than himself. What particularly annoyed Popov's enemies were his intellectual pretensions. He had once been head of the Moscow Diplomatic Academy, which ran special courses for people joining the diplomatic corps from outside, and because he had presided over some research, with a few teachers under him, he regarded himself as an academic.

Both Popov's deputies were hostile to me, for various reasons. One, Dolgov, was an able and hard-working diplomat, but the other, Bykov, had been appointed purely because of the status of his father-in-law, Pyotr Abrasimov, the Soviet Ambassador in East Berlin and an influential Party *apparatchik*. When the Polish Pope John Paul II was elected in October 1978, Bykov happened to be in temporary charge of the Embassy, and made a complete fool of himself by sending the Centre a long telegram in which he made the point that a Slavonic Pope would be a tremendous advantage to the Communist bloc, as he would give us stronger influence over the Vatican, the Catholic

Church and the West. Unfortunately for Bykov, the official conclusion was precisely the opposite: that a Polish Pope was a dangerous threat to Communism.

Head of the PR (political) Line, and my immediate superior, was Igor Titov, who had preceded me to London, but had become no more civilized in transit. The only thing to recommend him was that he had reintroduced a practice, much enjoyed in the 1970s, whereby on a Friday evening all the KGB political intelligence officers would gather in the garden of a pub in Notting Hill Gate, and sit talking shop for hours. The pub was reputed to be the place in which Oleg Penkovsky had been debriefed by the British during his short trips to London during the 1960s and, of course, it was against all KGB rules for the staff to collect there.

The greatest ogre in the station was the Resident, Arkady Guk, a huge, bloated lump of a man, with a mediocre brain but a large reserve of low cunning. Just as Stalin hated the Jews in the Politburo, and could not sleep until he had destroyed them all, so Guk loathed intellectuals and in particular the Ambassador, against whom he waged a continuous private war. Unable to forgive Popov for his intellectual superiority, he dedicated most of his mental energy to the campaign.

In this his principal toady was Leonid Nikitenko, the KR (counter-intelligence) Line deputy, a tall man, good-looking in a way, who could be charming if he wanted, and was not a bad counter-intelligence officer. I found that Guk's predecessor as Resident, a Latvian called Lukasevicz, had hated Nikitenko, and had tried to humiliate him, and that Nikitenko had returned his loathing with interest. The result was that when Guk took over, Nikitenko did everything possible to please his new boss, suppressing his own personality and ideas in his attempts to flatter. He and Guk spent most of their working day locked in the

Resident's office, smoking and drinking neat vodka out of tumblers while they dreamt up ever-wilder and more malicious gossip, principally about the Ambassador.

The animosity within the building was so strong that I felt it immediately, on my first day. Many of the hints that Guk and his sycophants dropped were outrageous: 'I think the Ambassador could be a British agent…There are signs of a leakage…Maybe he's working for them… What I wonder is how he manages to satisfy her…No wonder she drinks…' Nikitenko did not necessarily share Guk's opinions, but, determined to keep in with him, played his tune all the time.

Guk disliked me from the start. Although not clever, he was well served by instinct, and seemed to feel that there was something different about me. He cannot have had any inkling that I was working for the British: rather, he saw a man entirely different from himself, a man with intellectual interests, who read books as well as magazines and newspapers, the only one in the station whose radio was tuned to play classical music.

Occasionally, after a few large vodkas, he would mellow and offer advice. I once confided to him that I was nervous of the responsibility of running the station on my own — which I would have to do if both he and Nikitenko were away — and he said, 'Don't worry: it's easy. Whatever the problem, whatever the dilemma, *ask the Centre.* They love giving advice and instructions. The second thing is, *do whatever you can to prevent defections.* The worst thing that can possibly happen is the defection of a KGB officer. Do absolutely anything to stop one of your own men taking off. A KGB officer knows everything a diplomat knows, and a lot of specialist stuff besides.'

Guk went on to boast how he had once prevented the defection of a KGB reservist, one of the men called up in the 1970s to work in organizations outside the KGB but attached to it. This man was stationed in London, and married to a Russian, but he fell in love with an Englishwoman. Although a good worker, he was overwhelmed by the experience, came to Guk, said he was infatuated, and confessed that he did not know what to do. Guk pretended to listen sympathetically, and then made soothing noises. 'All right,' he said. 'There's no hurry. Let's see what we can sort out.' But this was pure deception: at once Guk opened up a correspondence by telegram with Moscow, preparing an operation to evacuate the man as quickly as possible. The moment the documents were in order, and an air ticket had been bought, he went round to the man's flat at 5 a.m. and woke him up, crying, 'Quick! Get dressed! Something urgent's come up.' With the poor fellow still only half awake, he bundled him into a car, drove him to the Embassy, thence to the airport, and frogmarched him on to a plane for Moscow.

Alcohol always brought out Guk's tendency to brag about his achievements. He enjoyed relating how, while stationed in New York, he had discovered the hiding place of the KGB defector Nikolai Khokhlov, and had proposed to the Centre that he should be liquidated. Permission was refused, on the ground that more important targets had precedence; and the same thing happened when Guk proposed the assassination of Stalin's daughter Svetlana Alliluyeva, who by then was living in America. The truth was that although Guk liked the idea of throwing his weight about, he was a major liability to the KGB: with his low intelligence and poor judgement further impaired by a combination of alcohol and bigotry, he made it impossible for the Centre to gain any clear picture of the true state of affairs in Britain. One Russian word summed up his character perfectly: he was a *samodur*, or petty tyrant, prone to attacks of *folie de grandeur*, and always liable to behave irrationally.

One of his obsessions was the Underground. He urged all members of his staff to use it as little as possible, and to go by surface transport whenever they could. The reason, he said, was that many of the advertisement panels along the walls of Underground stations were in reality glass-fronted booths, in which sat members of the British security service, spying on the KGB as they went about their business.

Guk's animosity against me spread to those others in the station who licked his and Nikitenko's boots, principally the analyst and writer of political reports, Valery Yegoshin. Narrow-faced, with close-set eyes and thin lips, and light brown hair which turned even fairer in summer, Yegoshin had a rather austere and even intellectual appearance, appropriate enough for someone who was a historian by training. Not only did he carry a useful store of dates and facts in his head: he was also skilful at concocting plausible political reports out of odds and ends culled from newspapers, magazines and press conferences. Able to read English easily, he ploughed through a large amount of raw material, and could regularly turn out one or even two substantial reports a day.

This facility was invaluable to Guk, for political reports were the station's showcase, and whatever happened — even if people were on holiday or ill — the news must keep flowing. Guk himself was incapable of writing a report: so limited was his ability that he often did not even understand what papers were about. But he was happy enough to sign, and take the credit for, whatever Yegoshin wrote, so it was not surprising that he valued his analyst above all other officers. Yegoshin, for his part, was a dedicated internal spy, always whispering in Guk's ear private details about his colleagues which might be used to discredit them. Before my arrival he had heard that I, too, was a political analyst, which, of course, turned him against me: he considered himself *the* analyst, the only one who knew what to report and how to present his material. So, to protect his own position, he adopted a hostile attitude, which, since my main work in the KGB was political reporting, made things difficult. Thus, almost immediately, I found myself besieged on all fronts.

I soon saw that relations between the Embassy and the station were none too cordial, and that the station itself was split into cliques. Igor Titov was working under the awkward cover of correspondent for the *New Times*, a semi-official foreign affairs weekly, published in English and other languages. As this meant he had to be away from the station for much of the day he decided that he, too, needed to be on good terms with Guk and Nikitenko, and he also started to support them.

Another despicable toady was Slava Mishustin, picked personally by Guk, who put him in charge of Line I (information). His principal task was to collect and systematize the information coming into the station, including all available facts about the restaurants and meeting places that officers were using for their rendezvous with contacts (no restaurant was supposed to be used more often than once every six months, and we were supposed to check a list before booking). This work gave Mishustin the perfect excuse for keeping a close eye on everyone else's movements. Had he been a cheerful fellow, things would not have been too bad but he had a carping nature, and was never happy. Neither was his wife, who was employed in the Embassy as an accountant. Both of them watched every move, reported frequently to Guk, and tried to scrape up discreditable information about anyone they disliked.

On my second evening in London it was a relief to escape from this hotbed of intrigue and make the telephone call that had been on my mind for years. Still not knowing who was who in the street, or where the observation posts were sited, I slipped out to a call-box and dialled my personal number. Imagine my relief and delight when I heard Andrew's voice at the other end: only a tape, but undoubtedly a tape of Andrew. 'Hello, Oleg!' it said. 'Welcome to London! Thank you so much for calling. We look forward to seeing you. Meanwhile, take a few days to relax and settle in. Let's be in touch at the beginning of July.' Disappointing as it was not to have immediate live contact, the sound of that voice was immensely reassuring.

On the day suggested, I rang the same number again, and this time Andrew was there in person. 'Come to the Holiday Inn in Sloane Street at 3 p.m. tomorrow,' he said. He explained that he would be in the lobby, together with a female companion, and that when I saw him, I was to continue walking straight through, out of the far doorway into the street behind the hotel, where his car would be in a multi-storey park.

It was a simple but effective plan. Following his instructions, I saw him sitting on a chair, with a fine-looking, middle-aged woman beside him. As I approached, they rose to their feet and began walking to the far door. I went after them, across the street and up to the first floor of the car park, where he greeted me and introduced his assistant as Joan. We then drove to a safe flat in a new block in Bayswater, and got down to talking.

Andrew explained that he was already working in a different country, and had come to London specially to greet me, as he was the only available British officer who knew me personally. At our next meeting he introduced me to my new mentor, Jack, who was brilliant, the best minder I have ever had. Young, of medium height, with dark hair already receding, he was married, with four children, and besides being highly intelligent had all the warmth of a true family man. He was a first-class intelligence officer, but also truly kind, full of emotion and sensitivity, honest both personally and in his ethical principles. As the expression goes in Russian, he had a fine structure of soul. Tremendously quick to take the point and to understand my problems, he was forever analysing things and looking for new solutions.

Joan was older, about fifty-five, with ash-blonde hair, and a face that seemed to embody all the traditional British qualities of decency and honour. Over the next few months she became another wonderful confidante. Not the least of her virtues was her skill as a listener: she imparted confidence by the speed and sympathy with which she absorbed ideas. No mere assistant, she turned out to have been the architect of my escape plan: beginning as early as 1978, she had done a great deal of thorough research work to produce it, and in due course she set about creating a streamlined version.

One of Jack's first actions was to hand me the key of a safe house, between Kensington High Street and Holland Park, in which I could instantly go to ground, with or without my family if I ever had to disappear. It was a terraced house, normally occupied by one of the British staff, and a good, anonymous retreat. (Whenever I went on leave, I would hand back the key, and leave it with my friends until I returned.)

The initial plan was that I should meet the British once a month, but I soon found that I had so much to tell them, so many complicated matters to discuss, that we met far more often. Copenhagen had been shallow water in comparison with London: here we were in mid-ocean.

*

Luckily for me, the Centre did not seem to realize that ever since the big expulsion of 1971 the London station of the KGB had been relatively small (we had only twenty-three officers, and the GRU fifteen). The result was that Moscow, regarding Britain as a country of leading importance, kept up a hail of information. Different departments, competing with each other and seeking to justify their existence, poured out briefing papers, instructions, background information and requests of all kinds. To write and generate correspondence was, for them, a bureaucratic imperative, since the greater the volume of paper they sent out, and the more responses they elicited from foreign stations, the more real work they seemed to be doing. The consequence was that the Centre churned out an immense volume of information, any of which I was at liberty to pass on.

One disadvantage was that documents travelling by diplomatic bag no longer came as film, so that we could not copy them as we had in Copenhagen. But the British were equipped with efficient cameras, and there was always a girl secretary, ready to snap whatever papers I brought with me to lunchtime meetings in a safe flat. I never had any problem explaining where I was going: always it was 'to meet a contact'. But because it was safest for me to leave the station last, after everyone else had gone out, and be back before the cipher clerks returned from lunch, our meetings were necessarily short. Every day there was a potential danger that one of the clerks might stay in and exercise his right to search rooms and satchels — but that was a risk I had to take. Whenever I got back to my room in good time, before anyone else was around, I would close the door while I removed whatever documents I had taken with me from my pockets. But I could not do that if other people were back, as we were supposed to keep our doors open all the time, and I had to wait for a moment at which I could safely unload.

At the Embassy, each day began with the Ambassador's conference, which often degenerated into farce, especially if Popov tried to be funny, or simply made so many critical remarks that he irritated everyone else. Then Guk would give a pep talk, telling people to be vigilant, but he was a poor speaker, and often gave his listeners the giggles. The meeting generally lasted so long — up to two hours — and was such a waste of time that people tended to make appointments so that they could miss it. The GRU, considering themselves an organization apart, would detail a couple of representatives to attend but let it be known that the majority of them had better things to do than sit there for the first two hours of the morning.

Although most of the KGB strength was concentrated in the Embassy, we also had between six and eight officers attached to the Soviet Trade Delegation, which, for thirty years, had had a building of its own in Highgate. There, modern offices had been built for the KGB and GRU sub-stations, together with separate rooms for a listening post. Besides these, we had four officers working under the cover of journalism, one of them, Yuri Kobaladze, easily the nicest man on the London staff, and three officers attached to international organizations: a completely useless man in the International Wheat Organization, a slightly better one in the International Cocoa Organization, and another in ship repair. Yet the strength of Soviet intelligence in England was considerably greater than these figures suggest. I knew, for instance, that Line X (science and technology) were running several agents, but I never discovered who they were. Also, Nikitenko was running one confidential contact in the circle of Denis Howell, the Labour Party's Shadow Sports Minister, and another buried in the Jewish community. Again, the GRU, a smaller but more highly disciplined organization than the KGB, was also active but I never had any idea who its contacts were.

One of my own first tasks was to re-establish contact with Bengt Carlsson, general secretary of the Socialist International, which he ran from an office in North London. This organization was weak, but the

Centre had always been fascinated by it, and was determined to keep a close grip on it. Carlsson, still in his thirties, was a leading member of the Social Democratic Party in Sweden. He had been included in the KGB network as a special unofficial contact, a category introduced during the 1970s for prominent politicians close to the KGB, and met its representatives occasionally to share information and ideas.

I was still in the first months of my stay in England, and everything seemed alien and unfamiliar. Besides, my English was poor. It was thus with some trepidation that I sought out the Socialist International office, which turned out to be modest, on two floors of a little house. I need not have worried: Carlsson proved much more sympathetic than I had expected, and I soon saw how highly he valued his relationship with the Russians. Obviously he was under great pressure from his own organization, for he could not work easily with Willi Brandt, the chairman and German Chancellor, and he was also being chivvied by the socialist parties of Spain, France and Italy, who wanted to break the northern Europeans' domination of the Labour movement. Caught between several fires, he spoke to me quite emotionally, in English, and I was able to put in a most positive report, stressing the warmth of his feelings towards Moscow.[1]

Inside the Embassy, life was dominated by a terrible paranoia about bugging: often the staff appeared able to think of nothing else. To appreciate the extent of their obsession, it is necessary to know the layout of the various Embassy buildings and their neighbours. The building on the corner, nearest Bayswater Road, was the Consulate, No. 5 Kensington Palace Gardens. No. 10, next to it, contained flats,

---

1   Carlsson later returned to Sweden, where he rose to become an important official in the Ministry of Foreign Affairs, and then the United Nations envoy to Namibia. The KGB kept in touch with him, but he was killed in the Lockerbie air disaster of 1988.

a sauna bath and a small Embassy shop, in which, among other things, one could buy duty-free drink and cigarettes: vodka cost a pound a bottle, whisky two pounds fifty. (In the Embassy itself there was also a small 'operational' store of drink, cigarettes and other small presents designed for contacts, so that there was never any fear that big-time boozers like Guk might run out.) The next building, No. 12, was the Nepalese Embassy, and presumed by us to be used as a listening post by MI5. Next to that stood No. 13, the main Soviet Embassy building, which housed the *referentura* (on the first floor), the KGB and GRU stations, in loft and basement respectively, the Ambassador's offices and apartment. (The Ambassador's bedroom was on the floor below the Residency and he was plagued by fears that the KGB was spying on him through the ceiling. Once when Guk pointedly invited him to inspect the KGB's accommodation, he spent much time glaring at the floors, trying to spot hidden cameras or peepholes.)

No. 16, across the road, contained offices for Soviet military personnel, and the radio station; and we believed that another building was occupied by MI5, who sat there watching every arrival and departure through telephoto lenses as well as by direct observation. This made it impossible for any of us to come or go without being seen, and made us feel very exposed. Part of No. 18 also belonged to the Embassy, and contained a library, a club and a couple of diplomats' offices (in one of which I was supposed to spend some of my time). The other half was the Egyptian Embassy, which we also suspected of being an MI5 listening post.

Our ideas about the Nepalese and Egyptian buildings being used by the British were, of course, ridiculous. But the central supposition, which governed the existence of everyone in the Embassy, was that the British secret services were making colossal efforts, and using every means, to eavesdrop on our communications and conversations — as, indeed, the KGB was doing to the British Embassy in Moscow. Thus people claimed that the British had dug a special tunnel under Kensington Palace Gardens, wide enough to admit the passage of small vehicles, for the purposes of espionage. Branches were supposed to lead off underneath various embassies, and the Soviet headquarters particularly, for facilitating the installation and exchange of listening equipment. Because it was assumed that bugging devices had been installed in the Nepalese and Egyptian embassies, no conversations were allowed in the rooms along the walls facing or adjoining those buildings.

The contrast with Copenhagen was painful. There, we had taken certain precautions, but in summer we used to have the skylights in the roof open all the time. In the London Embassy almost all the windows had been bricked up. The only man still able to enjoy daylight was the Resident, and his room was protected on three levels. First there was a general jamming device, which produced a buzzing noise and was supposed to frustrate listening microphones. Then, in the windows, separate electronic protection produced special sound-waves; and Guk had radio loudspeakers fitted into the space between the two layers of double glazing, which automatically came on whenever he entered the room so that a faint burbling was always audible.

Electric typewriters were banned because it was thought that they could be bugged. We were not even allowed to use manual machines (although we did), because it was feared that the rhythm of keys being struck could be picked up and decoded. No computer was allowed in the building because that, too, could be easily penetrated. When I played music through a portable radio on my desk, the operational techniques Line officer would come up and say, 'You really shouldn't have that thing on, you know. It may automatically transmit anything you say to the opposition. They're listening through radios all the time.'

People were constantly talking about strange wires which ran down the core of the building, and saying that it was high time for the entire system to be renewed. (This was idiotic because for generations no British person had been allowed to enter the building except under close supervision.) There were notices on every wall reminding us 'DON'T SAY NAMES OR DATES OUT LOUD.' Yegoshin, who had a flat in our building in Kensington High Street, once cut me off when I began to say something innocuous on the stairs and whispered histrionically, 'Stop! The walls are listening!'

Even with all these layers of protection, the risks were still considered unacceptable, and in the middle of my time a special development team of workmen from the KGB was flown in to rebuild our offices. They removed all our possessions, stripped the walls back to bare brick, put in a kind of mattress foundation, and then lined the room with a box of metal sheeting, like an oven. With that in position, they fixed up lights, pasted up new wallpaper, put down carpets and replaced the furniture. Even then, with the metal boxes more or less hanging within the brick walls, they were deemed to need individual electronic protection, which one switched on with a button whenever one went in.

The safe room in the basement, used for conferences, received the same treatment: it was stripped, lined with metal, and fitted with electronic protection. All this made it incredibly claustrophobic, and even more so during major conferences, when a room designed for about forty people had to accommodate sixty or seventy. In spite of air-conditioning, the atmosphere grew desperately hot and foetid and any long meeting became a major test of stamina.

The phobia about being constantly spied on extended into the city. My predecessor as Counsellor, Ravil Pozdnyakov, once warned me in all seriousness never to carry out any operation in Edwardes Square.

I told him it would not have occurred to me to do so because the place was so close to home — but I asked him why he had mentioned it.

'Because the whole square is covered by television cameras.'

'Really! Where are they, then?'

'On the roofs of the surrounding buildings.'

'Have you ever seen them?'

'No, but they're bound to be there, because in Moscow we'd certainly put them round any square used by the British.'

People also assured me that the gardener who looked after the square was an agent of the security service. So convinced were they of this that, in the end, I asked the British point blank whether they did indeed have television cameras there, and whether they retained the services of the gardener. Their response was uproarious laughter at the absurdity of the suggestion.

Members of the Embassy and KGB were hypochondriacs and, because medical facilities in the West were so much better than those at home, making visits to doctors became a prime sport. I myself — no hypochondriac, I hope — had a narrow escape when having a dental crown repaired by a specialist to whom the British had recommended me. By ill luck my car was spotted by MI5 surveillance near the Royal Hospital in Chelsea, and an investigation was launched into why a Soviet official had been in that area of London: fortunately, before much progress had been made, my own contacts managed to have the hunt called off.

It was the deliberate policy of the Centre and the Party to make Soviet communities abroad feel as isolated as possible, and to inflate the threat supposedly presented by foreign security services. Thus in London every small accident or setback — a flat tyre, a broken window — was interpreted as an attack or provocation by opposing forces, and, once again, paranoia fed on itself. If anything, the sense of isolation was probably increased by the existence of the Soviet dacha, a lovely castle set in woods near Hastings, which some crazed millionaire had left to the Embassy sixty years earlier. Here, too, expatriates lived in a closed circle of their own: although supposedly for the use of the whole Soviet community, the luxurious accommodation was reserved for the Ambassador and the most senior members of his staff. Once a year, in April, a huge party was held there, the occasion being *subbotnik*, the day of cleansing, on which the whole of the Soviet Union turned out for major spring cleaning. In Kent this became the excuse for a huge barbecue. After a couple of hours' gardening, and a token tidy-up of the forest, everyone made merry at a great feast.

The Residency's obsession with security was matched by that of the Centre with Operation RYAN, the attempt launched in 1981 to gain early warning of the pre-emptive nuclear strike allegedly being planned by the West against the Soviet Union. I quickly discovered that my colleagues in the PR Line regarded RYAN with some scepticism: they were not seriously worried by the risk of nuclear war yet none wanted to lose face and credit at the Centre by contradicting the First Chief Directorate's assessment. The result was that RYAN created a vicious spiral of intelligence-gathering and evaluation, with foreign stations feeling obliged to report alarming information even if they did not believe it.

The continuous demands for RYAN intelligence threw an enormous strain on our resources. We were supposed, for instance, to make a regular count of the number of lighted windows in all government buildings and military installations thought to be involved in preparations for nuclear war, both in and out of working hours, and to report immediately any deviations from the norm. We were also required to identify the methods of evacuation which would be used by government officials and their families, to find out which routes they would use and where they would go. I think even Guk found this ridiculous and, although he paid lip service to the Centre's demands, he delegated the task of maintaining detailed observations to a junior officer who had no car and was not allowed to travel outside London without special permission from the Foreign Office. The unrealistic nature of these instructions — the yawning gap between the perceptions of the Centre and conditions at the front — perfectly summed up the futility and danger of much KGB activity.

When I began passing details of RYAN to Jack, he was astonished and could scarcely believe them, so crass were the Centre's demands, so out of touch with the real world. Yet I believe that in revealing the depth of the Soviet leaders' paranoia to the British, I made one of my most vital contributions to international safety. By the beginning of 1983 tough speeches by President Reagan and his secretary of state, George Schultz, had put the Soviet leaders into a state of acute apprehension; and their fears were reinforced when they learnt about the United States' Strategic Defense Initiative (SDI), commonly known as Star Wars — the plan for using anti-missile missiles to create a nation-wide shield against intercontinental attack. Because the Americans had landed a man on the moon, the Kremlin reasoned, they had the capability to create the Star Wars system, and were most probably preparing for all-out nuclear war in a few years' time. By explaining this to the West, I believe I played some small part in keeping international tension to tolerable levels.

*

Once clear of the Embassy, we KGB were free to move around as we liked, without restrictions: we were operational officers, expected to initiate our own contacts. With the departure of Pozdnyakov, who had preceded me as head of the PR Line, I was left in control of a European diplomat whom the Centre had classed as an agent and I began to meet him, usually for lunch. To my considerable frustration, I found that, although he was fully prepared to eat large meals, he never told me anything of the slightest interest and our meetings were a waste of time. The trouble was that I could not admit this to the Centre, where Pozdnyakov had become a department head: I therefore had to descend to normal KGB practice and concoct reports which grossly inflated the value of the agent's contribution.

As for my British contacts, my seniority made things easier for me, as I did not have to account for my movements too closely. However, I began to find myself in difficulties, for my English was still poor, and I was bringing in so little information that Yegoshin and Titov began to complain to Guk behind my back. My response was to ask my English friends for help: I pointed out that much of my time and mental energy were being spent on feeding them classified or secret information rather than on finding and consolidating KGB contacts, and I asked if they could supply me with some titbit of useful fact each time I saw them.

This they began to do. Of course, there was nothing sensational: they could not pass me anything classified but, if they used their imagination, they could always come up with something worthwhile. One young officer typed out very good little summaries about, for instance, current problems in South Africa, or the state of the Anglo-American relationship: each was about three-quarters of a page, which I would take back with me, translate into KGB language, embellish with a few extra details, and hand in as my contribution. By this means, I slowly pushed up my rating.

My meetings with the British soon took on a regular pattern. I would drive into the underground garage and pull a plastic cover over my car to conceal the diplomatic numberplate. Upstairs, I would find the team waiting for me. At first, because it was lunch-time and I was always hungry, they laid on a full-scale meal, but time was so precious that I soon suggested they should reduce this to sandwiches and a can of beer, so that we could talk more easily while we ate.

At the beginning I hoped that these sessions would rapidly improve my English but Jack, whose Russian was adequate, asked me to talk in my own language, since that was quicker and more accurate with a tape-recorder running. (Later I learnt that Jack had to spend very long and tiring hours transcribing the tapes.) Joan would sit in a corner, not understanding much, but whenever we had a break I would speak to her in English. For ease of reference, I was known as Feliks, the cover-name which I had suggested to Michael in Copenhagen: I had taken it from Feliks Mainer, my Estonian friend at school, and at that stage did not realize that the word meant 'happy' or 'fortunate' in Latin.

There was no chance of being followed by the KGB on my way to the safe flat, but once on my way back to the Embassy, just after I had left the apartment block and was crossing Connaught Street, a couple of blocks in from the Bayswater Road, I saw Guk go past driving his ivory Mercedes. As I was about to step out of the road on to the pavement, I assumed that he must have seen me, and I got back in a state of some agitation, wondering what story I should invent. In the event, none was needed, for when I met him later in the afternoon he did not mention the incident, and I realized that he had not seen me: he was such a poor driver that he had had all his attention focused on the road and other traffic.

Later, in 1984, we deliberately used Connaught Street as the scene of an experiment. One of the Line N officers, in charge of illegals, claimed that he always had the most enormous surveillance behind him, five cars at a time. I thought he was imagining it: I supposed that because the British knew quite a lot about the KGB, through me, they would hardly bother to put five cars behind a single officer. When I challenged him, however, he became indignant and produced a piece of paper with five registration numbers written on it.[2]

'Well,' I said, 'this is fascinating. Let's set a trap. You drive along Connaught Street at lunch-time one day, and I'll be watching from the window of the Duke of Kendal pub on the corner to see who's behind you.'

Our plan worked perfectly. Instead of going home for lunch, I drove up the Bayswater Road, turned left and right, parked, and went into the pub, where I bought a pint and stationed myself in a window. At 1.25 p.m. my man drove slowly past and, sure enough, there behind him were three of the cars whose numbers he had taken. The first crew looked tense, no doubt because in that heavy traffic it would have been easy to lose the target, but the other two seemed relaxed. Where cars four and five were it was impossible to say: maybe on parallel streets. But, in any event, my man was vindicated.

Soon after that Prokopchik, the acting head of Line X, told me that he had seen even more cars behind him; and when I remonstrated about this with Jack, saying that it was a great waste of British resources, he told me that they suspected Prokopchik of running two agents but that they could not find out who they were. In this I was unable to help

---

2   In due course I discovered that the middle-rank MI5 officers organizing the surveillance knew nothing about my involvement with MI6 and were operating normally.

him, for it was fundamental practice in the KGB that one line never told another about what it was doing.

*

With all this activity, time passed at an extraordinary speed: Leila and the family settled down well, and we found that, although our flat was not very comfortable, life in Kensington had many advantages. There were little Turkish, Arab and Iranian restaurants, which gave out wonderfully Oriental smells all afternoon and evening, and excellent food shops, many run by Indians and Pakistanis, which stayed open until midnight, to say nothing of the unlimited shopping facilities in High Street Kensington, Knightsbridge and places further afield. The High Street was full of life until late at night, which delighted Leila. As for me, I could run in Holland Park, which was beautifully kept. In due course the girls began going to a local school, and they picked up English at an incredible speed — so fast that they began to use it as their first language when talking to each other and to their dolls.

*

Almost before I had got my breath, twelve months had flown: it was June 1983, and the time was approaching for me to go home on leave. For several weeks I had been aware that something unusual was brewing in the station. Guk and Nikitenko were constantly discussing some subject that was evidently of greater importance than their normal preoccupations.

Then one day Guk, unable to contain himself any longer, said, 'Would you like to see something exceptional?' Whereupon he showed me photocopies of two highly classified documents, produced in English by MI5, giving the full order of battle in the KGB and GRU stations.

'*Bozhe!*' I said softly. 'My God! Where did these come from?'

Without giving details, Guk said that an envelope had been pushed through the letterbox of his flat in Holland Park late one night. The messenger had claimed in a letter to be a security service officer and, clearly, he knew that the surveillance on the block of flats stood down at midnight because he had come after that.

Of course I was immediately on fire with curiosity to know how accurate the documents were and, above all, to find out what they said about me. But I feigned nonchalance as I glanced first down the list of GRU. Then I said, 'Oh, I don't really know what they all do anyway. But what about us?' I saw at once that almost all the twenty-three KGB officers had been correctly identified, and that they had been listed under three grades. Grade One was entitled 'fully identified', Grade Two 'more or less identified', and Grade Three 'under suspicion of belonging to the KGB station'. To my immense relief, I saw my own name under Grade Two. That meant, obviously, that the compiler of the list knew nothing of my British connection; it also gave some explanation of why I had been granted a visa so swiftly the year before. But the list also assigned KGB officers to their various lines — PR, KR, X and N — and represented a considerable achievement.

'It's pretty accurate,' I said, as I handed back the document.

'Yes,' Guk agreed. 'They've done well.'

Who was the messenger, and what lay behind his overtures? Our immediate feeling was that the initiative was the beginning of what the KGB called a game, and the Americans a dangle. Certainly Guk got this impression, and he never changed his mind. Nikitenko, I believe, considered the approach genuine, but by then he had become so used to buttering up Guk that he suppressed his instincts and sided with his boss.

Also on Guk's desk I saw a letter from the mysterious messenger, asking the Resident to come to a meeting. Later I caught sight of another of his missives, which had been left in Nikitenko's briefcase; this one was addressed to 'Comrade Guk', and even used his patronymic with his first name: Arkady Vassilyevich. It suggested exceptionally complicated procedures for dry-cleaning on the way to the rendezvous and for the posting of signals — the writer was a man of some imagination, fascinated by the paraphernalia of espionage. The letter was signed 'Koba', the name used secretly by Stalin before the revolution and openly thereafter.

Of course his overtures caused some excitement in the Residency; but Guk and Nikitenko decided to reject them, for two reasons. First, the writer never offered any additional facts beyond his first lists. His order of battle, though accurate, was no news to the KGB men, who hoped for more definite information about how their ranks had been penetrated. Second, his proposed method of setting up a meeting was so complicated that it made them wary of committing themselves to any follow-up.

They therefore ignored the approaches, and never answered. But then another letter arrived, and somehow I learnt that the writer was proposing to communicate yet again in the first days of July. As I was about to go on holiday, I thought I had better act fast. At the first opportunity I slipped out to a telephone kiosk and rang the emergency number which I carried in case I needed to make immediate contact with the British. I said I would be at the flat at 1 p.m. I felt excited, and not a little nervous, because the situation was one of high drama: almost certainly a traitor was at large, and if he knew about my involvement with the British services, my own life was in danger.

I found that Jack was temporarily away, and in his absence it was Joan who met me. By then I had total confidence in her, and was delighted to see her, but at the same time I felt that this meeting was a huge responsibility for a general service officer not used to conducting complicated intelligence debriefings. Nevertheless, there was nothing to be done except tell her what I knew.

'I'm sure this is some sort of operational game that the security services are playing with the KGB station,' I began in English, 'but we'd better make sure.' I told her the outline of what had happened, and she came out with a classically calm, British reaction. 'As far as I know,' she said, 'there is no operational game in progress.'

Tense as I was, I loved that phlegmatic response, and I went on with the rest of the story. She made thorough notes, then hurried away. A couple of days later I met Jack, back on duty, and gave him a fuller version of events. Then I left with the family for our holiday in Moscow, with the affair very much in the air.

*

At least the journey home was enjoyable. We took the train—one of those long-distance carriages beloved of Russian travellers, which went the whole way from the Hook of Holland to Moscow. After a short night on a ferry, we found the carriage waiting for us in the Dutch port and knocked up the two Russian guards, who were asleep in their compartment; the attendants were expecting us, knew our places, carried our luggage aboard and stowed it, to earn their little bribes. Then we took an electric commuter train into Rotterdam, where we went sightseeing and thoroughly enjoyed ourselves. Back in the Hook of Holland, we felt ravenous, so we found a Chinese restaurant: the meal was delicious, but so huge that mountains of food were left over at the end. When Leila, with her characteristic lack of inhibition, asked the waiters if we could take it with us, they said 'Sure!' and packed it into neat little boxes. We ate the rest *en route*.

On holiday, I was worried about what was happening in London. Back at the station on 18 August, I tried not to show any curiosity, and avoided asking questions unless they were absolutely necessary. But in my other incarnation I found that the British had caught their man, even though the hunt for him had proved exceptionally difficult. A senior officer in MI5 had said to MI6, 'Not in our organization, look in yours.' So the search was concentrated there for a while, only to switch back to MI5, where about fifty people had had access to the documents of which Guk had received copies. In the end three suspects were identified, and a decision was taken to put them under surveillance. But the question was, who could do the job? They knew all the surveillance people like old acquaintances. Their faces were entirely familiar. Normal methods were out, and *ad hoc* surveillance teams were formed from officers and secretaries in MI6, not professionals, but people with at least some training in the work.

It was a combination of surveillance outdoors and close observation in the office that led the investigators to Michael Bettaney, an officer in his thirties, working in MI5's counter-espionage department. Like many people doing something outrageous, he eventually went on to a high, becoming overexcited and saying strange things: 'If I were a Soviet agent...If I'd been in touch with Guk, the KGB Resident...' Further suspicion derived from the discovery that he was preparing for a trip to Vienna, home of the biggest KGB station in Europe and the one with the easiest access, since the Austrians used no surveillance.

The service decided that it was too dangerous to let him go there. He was in possession of secrets from many theatres of operation, including Northern Ireland where he had once worked. The authorities therefore made a secret search of his flat and found hundreds of classified documents hidden beneath the floorboards. With his guilt no longer in doubt, he was arrested.

It was vital for the British — and for me — that his trial was managed in such a way that my lead to him was covered, and word was put about that he had given himself away by making a fundamental error. When the arrest was announced on 16 September, Nikitenko seemed to make a connection, and told Guk that this was probably the man who had been trying to approach him. Guk, however, was so immersed in conspiracy theories, and understood the West so poorly, that he preferred to go on believing that no real man existed. He still maintained that the British had been playing some sophisticated game against us, and that the announcement of an arrest was merely their way of ending it. He remained convinced that there would be no man and no trial. When Bettaney stood trial the following spring, and was sentenced to twenty-three years' imprisonment, the British declared Guk *persona non grata*, which was ironic, considering that he had done nothing to help Bettaney, and expelled him from the country.

I do not think Guk or Nikitenko ever connected me with 'Koba', alias Bettaney. They may have thought that his exposure was their own fault, that the leak derived from their excessive discussion of the affair. The other people who knew too much about it were Yegoshin, Titov and Mishustin, as well as the cipher clerks and radio operators. Titov had known about it from the moment the first letter arrived but he was expelled in the spring of 1984, when the British discovered that he had been targeting an American student, with the aim of recruiting him.

On the eve of his departure Guk had a leaving party in the common room, which took the usual form — but the food and drink were exceptionally good: beer, wine and vodka flowed in abundance, and

the buffet was laden with sandwiches, *piroshki*, meatballs and salads.
A rota of speeches had been organized. First Guk's friend Nikitenko
held forth, and then it was my turn. Out of necessity and practice I had
developed a knack of saying the right thing at such events, and I felt
I did quite well, including a good many facts and some compliments
about Guk. Yet I must have sounded just a touch too smooth, and very
slightly insincere, because all Guk said, immediately, was, 'You've learnt
a lot from the Ambassador.' In the art of making insincere speeches,
Popov was undisputed champion. He never spoke from the heart, and
Guk correctly sensed that I had not done so either.

With the departure of Guk, his circle of cronies broke up. Yegoshin,
the analyst, had already started going downhill, drinking heavily,
smashing cars, and being cautioned by the police. Because of his position, he had been allowed to operate freely anywhere in London; he
gave his contacts lunch in the most expensive restaurants and also added
twenty or thirty pounds to every bill. His abuse of the system was blatant:
he made no attempt to conceal it, but regarded it as a reward for the
brilliant work he was doing. In the end he was shot down by Nikolai
Gribin, by now head of the department, who found out what had been
going on. In June 1984, when Yegoshin was on holiday in Moscow,
Gribin summoned him to an interview. Yegoshin arrived drunk, as
usual, and tried to take a flippant line, whereupon Gribin remarked,
'You don't seem very interested in your job.'

'Oh, well,' said Yegoshin airily, 'if I'm not needed any more, I'm
quite prepared not to go back.'

'All right, then,' said Gribin. 'You can stay here.'

That was an immense blow but stay he did, and it fell to me to empty
his desk in London. In one of the drawers I found a note saying, 'Please
be very careful about my savings', and there was a large brown envelope

stuffed with notes, amounting to a couple of thousand pounds. This, I knew, was merely his pocket money because he had been passing his salary to his wife: he had made a small fortune by brazenly deceiving the State. Honesty compelled me to parcel up the envelope and send it to him through the diplomatic bag.

Yegoshin's behaviour had often driven me to distraction yet now I saw that we were going to miss his ability. When I asked Gribin how we would do without him, he replied, 'Oh, you'll manage. And we in the Centre will manage too.' But I insisted that he should send us a replacement. He did — a man called Shilov (code-named Shatov), less talented, but adequate, who saw us through a difficult time. In Moscow, where drink was much more expensive and difficult to come by, Yegoshin pulled himself together and did useful work.

*

All through 1983 the Centre had continued to bombard us with farcical RYAN instructions. We were told, for instance, to look out for 'increased purchases of blood and a rise in the price paid for it' at donor centres, and ordered to report any changes immediately. Any surge of activity in this sphere would be a sure sign — the Centre had no doubt — of impending hostilities. What they failed to realize was that in Britain no payments are made for blood donations. Frantic efforts were made to discredit President Reagan, and frequent telegrams from Moscow repeated that his administration was actively preparing for war. In the autumn East—West tension rose to a dangerous pitch after the shooting down of a Korean airliner, KAL 007, over the Sea of Japan on 1 September. Within a few days it became obvious to the world that the Soviet fighter pilot, who fired two missiles and then announced on his radio, 'The target is destroyed,' had made a terrible mistake, but the Kremlin and the KGB made all-out efforts to demonstrate that 'the intrusion of the plane into Soviet airspace' had been 'a deliberate, thoroughly planned intelligence operation', directed from 'certain centres in the territory of the United States and Japan'. So manifestly absurd was this lie that many of my colleagues in the Residency were dismayed by the damage done to the Soviet Union's international reputation.

Chairman Andropov, by then mortally ill, denounced the United States in apocalyptic terms with vague but strident claims that hinted that President Reagan was secretly preparing a nuclear strike, but Soviet paranoia reached its zenith during the Nato command-post exercise Able Archer, held in Europe from 2 to 11 November. The aim of this was indeed to practise nuclear release procedures, and because some details differed from those of previous exercises, they struck Soviet surveillance teams deployed round American bases as particularly sinister. When the teams detected changed patterns of officer-movement and an hour's radio silence one evening, the KGB decided that American forces had been placed on alert. In the middle of the exercise flash telegrams sent by the Centre both to our Residency and to the GRU station told us of this stand-to, and implied that it might represent the first stage of preparation for nuclear war.

When the exercise ended peacefully, the paranoia in Moscow became slightly less acute and, without wishing to seem boastful, I think I can say that the information which I was passing weekly to the British may have helped lower tension, since the West began to make reassuring noises on the nuclear theme. But then in November, when Cruise missiles were deployed in Britain and Pershing missiles in West Germany, anxiety climbed again in Moscow and the demands for RYAN intelligence remained as pressing as ever. In his annual review at the end of 1983, Guk had had to admit 'shortcomings' in the Residency's quest for intelligence about 'specific American and NATO plans for the preparation of surprise nuclear missile attack on the USSR'. The Centre had answered angrily, blinded by its own prejudices to the fact that no such plans existed.

In London the Soviet persecution complex surfaced in a quite different form, over two unfortunate suicides. One man, a senior official connected with Soviet—British trade, hanged himself in his lavatory, for no clear reason but probably the result of personal problems, alcohol and pills. The other death was that of the wife of an official in one of the international organizations, who had been working as a receptionist in the Embassy. Perhaps because of some medical problem — she may have thought she had cancer — she threw herself out of the window of their fifth-floor flat and was killed. Both bodies were sent to Moscow and examined in the KGB hospital where doctors claimed to have found traces of some chemical substance which they said must have been administered by the British special services to upset the victims' mental balance and induce them to commit suicide.

This was nonsense. Neither victim was a target nor of any interest to the British. The man had worked in a commercial organization, and the woman was merely a receptionist, but the diagnosis was yet another sign of how Soviet paranoia was feeding on its own neuroses. Guk expected some positive verdict on the bodies; everybody concerned wanted one. The KGB medical personnel who carried out the autopsies were only too ready to provide one: they did what was expected of them, and produced the right answer.

However, with the death of Andropov in February 1984, and the decision by Mrs Thatcher, Vice-President Bush and other Western leaders to attend his funeral, tension eased still further; and under Andropov's dim successor, Konstantin Chernenko, the atmosphere never again grew so dangerously volatile. In London, Nikitenko, who became Acting Resident after Guk's departure, found it hard to take RYAN seriously. Yet for me personally the stress of that year never slackened, since I was constantly switching between two totally different worlds.

Chapter Twelve – British Targets

The principal objective of the KGB in Britain, as elsewhere, was to recruit agents who would be able to steal classified information of military or political value. In this, during my own time in London, the KGB was markedly unsuccessful; yet the KGB was also steadily pursuing its parallel activity of creating favourable propaganda, and in this field its success was noticeable. It categorized anyone of interest it came across as a potential 'target', and those targets, after a substantial period of cultivation, would be declared by the KGB as either 'agents' or 'confidential contacts'. Agents were supposed to be more or less conscious assistants to the Soviet state; in their relationship with their case officer there was some degree of discipline and the Centre insisted that contact between them took place in secret. A 'confidential contact' was a person who, in the KGB's eyes, was or might be prepared to be helpful to the Soviets, but the pattern of the relationship was dictated by the contact themselves. There was no discipline and Moscow rarely insisted on secrecy. In cases where 'agents' and 'confidential contacts' were not able to obtain valuable information and were to be used mostly for forming a favourable public opinion to Moscow, they were called 'agents of influence' or 'confidential contacts of influence'. These were likely to be people whose political inclinations might make them sympathetic to some aspect of the Soviet view of the world; many were idealists and most 'gave' their 'help' unwittingly. They would be fed selected information, given the Soviet view on whatever was happening and encouraged to develop their views along the lines the KGB wanted. Every target of cultivation would be given a code-name by the KGB to keep their true identity secret in case the correspondence was intercepted.

'Contacts' did not usually know they were being pursued, or that the 'press attaché' or Soviet correspondent buying them a drink or a meal was, in fact, a KGB officer. Many would have been horrified if anyone had suggested they were actively 'helping' the adversary. But no KGB officer could disclose to his targets that he was a member of the intelligence services; so we posed as diplomats, trade attaches, journalists and the like; that was the 'cover' we had been given in order to get into the UK in the first place, and to operate there.

It must be made very clear that what I am disclosing in this book is what appeared to the KGB or what was noted in the KGB's records. The fact that someone was regarded as an agent of influence or a confidential contact meant no more than that it was how the KGB regarded them. These were in any event largely passive roles: contact was cultivated by us often over long periods of time; and was received by the targets with differing degrees of welcome. And in most cases, because we were operating under cover, the targets would have been justified in assuming that we were what we said we were: diplomats, journalists or trade attachés.

On the intelligence front, our highest aim was to penetrate the administration of the day, whether Conservative or Labour, and discover government secrets. In my time the KGB in Britain was living largely in the past, and still sticking too often to socialist politicians, a hangover from the 1960s and 1970s, when Labour had been in power. In the 1980s my colleagues were, of course, eager to penetrate the Conservative Party, but, except in a few cases, we lacked the resources and skill to do so.

If I put names to all the people I could mention in this chapter, it would cause uproar. Unfortunately I have to be circumspect: I am constrained by the stringent and archaic libel laws of the country. Although everything I could write here would be absolutely correct, some of the proof that would stand up in a court of law is locked away in KGB files in Moscow, which are not accessible to me. Nevertheless, I hope I can show how the KGB sought to manipulate some public figures in the cause of Soviet propaganda.

Considering the tenor of the Labour Party's manifesto for 1983, it is hardly surprising that Moscow, its front organization, the Soviet Embassy, in London and the KGB cultivated the British Left so assiduously. The socialists were calling for unilateral nuclear disarmament, cancellation of the Trident missile system, refusal to deploy Cruise missiles, and the removal of American nuclear bases from Britain, all objectives warmly welcomed by Moscow.

In Soviet eyes, the KGB's most valuable confidential contact in London was the veteran Labour MP Fenner Brockway. No matter that, by the 1980s, he was more than ninety years old: his left-wing sympathies and his incurable naivety made him a perfect subject for cultivation, and for years he was run by Mikhail Bogdanov, the most polished and sophisticated member of the KGB station.

The son of a musician in Leningrad, Bogdanov was then in his early thirties, handsome, well dressed and personable. His cover job was that of London correspondent of the Moscow newspaper *Socialist Industry*, and he worked from his flat near the western end of Kensington High Street. Since his journal had no means of servicing foreign correspondents, the position was entirely bogus and left him plenty of time for cultivating likely targets.

Bogdanov drove Brockway everywhere in London — to the restaurant, from the restaurant, to the House of Lords, to his home — buying him whisky, sweaters, gloves and anything else that took his fancy. In those days Moscow placed tremendous importance on peace movements such as the Campaign for Nuclear Disarmament, and did all it could to manipulate them. Most people in the West thought CND and similar bodies harmless enough: arms control, committees in Geneva...everyone wanted the nations to disarm, and it all sounded so innocent. Moscow, though, was making a deliberate and purposeful attempt to throw a smokescreen over its own ever-expanding production and deployment of nuclear weapons. 'It's the *West* who is developing its nuclear arsenal,' said Soviet sources. 'It's the *West* who is testing them, the *West* who is installing all these bloody Pershing-2 and Cruise missiles in the heart of Europe.'

With typically cold-blooded cynicism, Moscow exploited anyone naïve enough to sing its own tune. No British public figure did this more effectively than Brockway, whose World Disarmament Campaign, a relatively small organization which he founded with Philip Noel-Baker in 1979, continually played into KGB hands. So often in his speeches did Brockway spout ideas fed to him by Bogdanov that in our reports to the Centre he featured more than any other politician. He was always doing good work on the KGB's behalf, in London, East Berlin, Prague, Brussels and elsewhere, not least in his advocacy of nuclear-free zones, which the Kremlin wanted to create so as to corral Western fire-power in the event of global war. He was little more than a puppet in KGB hands.

Curiously, in his last book, *98 Not Out*, published in 1986, Brockway did not mention Bogdanov or the KGB. This suggests that he probably realized the true provenance of his faithful chauffeur and amanuensis, but even so was unable to discern that his own activities posed a considerable threat to the West. It was, in a way, an oblique tribute to the success of the KGB's operation that a statue to Brockway was unveiled in Red Lion Square, London, during his lifetime, in 1985.

Two others seen as helpful by the Soviets were the Labour MPs Frank Allaun and James Lamond. Both were deeply involved in the pro-Moscow peace movement, and both seemed to the Soviet Embassy to behave as if they were agents not of the KGB but of the International Department, always doing exactly what the official Soviet peace committee wanted of them. Their trips abroad, their statements, their behaviour, their votes — all appeared to Moscow to be nicely in line with Soviet propaganda. No doubt they would not view their association in such a way, but I can only relate what was recorded in KGB files and the Soviet Embassy memos.

Soviet attempts to manipulate Western peace movements took many forms. Visitors to the Embassy came from all walks of life and included such obvious targets as Bruce Kent and Joan Ruddock, for instance, general secretary and chairman of CND. They did not like receptions but along with many others came openly for private conversations with the Ambassador, his deputy or Lev Parshin; they also travelled widely, to Moscow and the East European countries, and wherever they went, people from the official peace committees sought to influence them. In London Bogdanov tried to make contact with Joan Ruddock, and invited her to drinks; whether she was nervous that someone might compromise her or try to photograph her in the company of a Soviet official, I do not know, but she stayed away. Her anxiety was, no doubt, increased by the rumours that CND was receiving Soviet money although I have no evidence that this was true.

For sheer naivety, we all agreed that no one could touch Tam Dalyell, the Old Etonian left-winger with a castle in Scotland. Although never classed as a confidential contact, he became useful to the KGB's propaganda initiative because of his obsession about the sinking of the Argentinian cruiser *Belgrano* during the Falklands War. As I have said, the KGB and the Soviet establishment were strongly on the Argentinian side in the conflict, so that anyone who criticized Britain's handling of the war and the Conservative government found a warm interest in Moscow.

Again, it was Bogdanov who courted Dalyell: he met him frequently in London, and stayed at his castle — and, indeed, in the acknowledgements in his book *Thatcher's Torpedo* Dalyell mentioned Bogdanov as a sympathetic Soviet diplomat from whom he had received help. Whether or not Dalyell realized he had been dealing with a secret intelligence officer is another matter: I doubt it. Bogdanov, for his part, reckoned that he had contributed a number of good ideas to the book, and reported enthusiastically on his dealings with the author. In the London station's annual report to the Centre for 1983 (which I compiled), there was a section on Tam Dalyell, saying how helpful to us Dalyell's obsession had been. Unfortunately when I submitted the report to Guk for clearance, he in his ignorance changed 'Tam' to 'Tom' without asking me so that the document went off to Moscow with a glaring mistake in it, much to Bogdanov's disgust. This highlights another problem we faced; not only the ignorance of the likes of Guk but the insatiable demand for information from the Centre. Meeting this demand meant that KGB officers had to keep up a steady flow of reports; such a flood of information meant that no one was capable of sorting out the good from the bad and so officers often exaggerated their successes and up-rated the importance of their contacts.

However, some politicians appeared to support the Soviet line so freely that the KGB saw no need to influence them. One such was Tony Benn, whose views seemed to the Russians almost indistinguishable from those of the Communist Party, and whom the Embassy could rely on without any promoting to make pro-Soviet, anti-American statements in the House of Commons and on other prominent platforms. With a typical lack of acumen, Popov failed to notice that large sections of the British public regarded Benn as an eccentric and did not take him seriously. One day, at the ghastly morning conference in the basement of the Embassy, the Ambassador made the following pronouncement in a rather pained voice: 'Comrades, reading my memoranda over the past twelve months, I find that some of the information which I put into the mouths of contacts and sent back to Moscow has proved entirely misleading. One important politician made a number of public predictions, which I put over with great enthusiasm. Looking back, I see that all his assessments were wrong, and that none of his predictions has come true. So please in future, when *you* write *your* memos, be very careful. And please re-read your memos for the past year to find out who's been consistently off-beam.'

I was sitting next to Lev Parshin, and whispered in his ear, 'Who's he talking about?'

'Who d'you think?' Parshin answered. 'Tony Benn.'

Another day Popov canvassed our opinion on how he should initiate a conversation with David Steel, the Liberal leader, who was coming to a reception. The Ambassador asked, 'What if I said, "Mr Steel, do you realize you have the same name as our great leader Stalin?" [*Stalin* is Russian for steel.] What do you think? Would that be a good line to open with?' We all looked at each other in agony but no one dared speak.

One man highly regarded by the KGB was the red-bearded *Guardian* journalist Richard Gott, who had been recruited as a prominent left-winger during the 1970s, but who had then lost touch. Gott resigned from the *Guardian* at the end of 1994 following revelations about his 'connections' with the KGB. Another person, who must remain unnamed, became the object of KGB interest and during my time in London the Centre issued instructions to make contact. It was decided that a suitable inducement would be a payment of six hundred pounds in cash.

The job of handing it over fell to Bogdanov, and we had an intense discussion about how the money should be passed. Bogdanov and I decided the best thing would be to put the cash in an envelope and hand it over during or after a lunch meeting, but when we suggested this to Guk he shot the idea down, saying that it was far too risky: money in an envelope was obviously incriminating if the carrier was searched.

Guk's preferred method was one he had used in New York: to stuff the bundle of notes into the pocket of the recipient as he walked past in the street. We pointed out that, although this might work in winter, when people were wearing heavy over-coats, it was a non-starter in summer. Eventually I had the idea that we should buy a cheap plastic wallet, put the money in that, and hand it over. Guk agreed. 'Not in the restaurant,' he said. 'After you have left. Walk round a corner, and then quickly, before the surveillance can catch up to see what you're doing, pass it.' So that was what Bogdanov did — and later he had several meetings with the person, none of them very productive.

An embarrassing episode took place in the winter of 1982-83, when Igor Titov decided to see if there were more journalists in addition to Gott worth targeting on the staff of the *Guardian*. With some difficulty he persuaded the Central Committee to authorize a tour of the Soviet Union, and off went a group from the newspaper. In Russia they were dispersed and sent on various assignments; then they returned and published a special issue devoted to different aspects of Soviet life. Needless to say, even though they were basically sympathetic, they could find little that was positive to write about, and dogmatic members of the Central Committee soon accused Titov of having involved them in an exercise which had produced an unfavourable result. Defending himself, he sent Moscow a long telegram analysing the special issue, and pointing out that about 60 per cent of it was in favour, so that on balance the enterprise had been worthwhile. Nevertheless, it left a bad taste in many mouths.

When it came to handing out money, I did my fair share. In Copenhagen I had watched Lyubimov giving cash to the Communist Party of Denmark, and in London I handed over four-figure amounts in dollar bills to the Communist Party in the Philippines and in South Africa, as well as to the African National Congress. Representatives of these organizations would come to the Soviet Embassy twice a year; one such was a pensioner then living in London, who had taken part in what he called the 'class struggle against American imperialism' before and after the Second World War, and, forty years later, was still authorized to receive money on his old friends' behalf.

Yet although Moscow was prepared to support such people financially, the KGB was not allowed to recruit Westerners who were avowed Communists. Thus a man like Ken Gill, general secretary of the white-collar union TASS, was never cultivated by us because he was a leading member of the Communist Party of Great Britain, and often mentioned as a possible leader of it. All the same, I got to know him well because I often had to take delegations from Moscow to meet him.

Through all vicissitudes Moscow preserved an extraordinarily reverential attitude towards Communists in the West, an attitude exemplified in their treatment of Andrew Rothstein, one of the founder-members of the Party in England. By the time I came to England Rothstein was already in his eighties, yet the Embassy conceived it their duty not only to look after him but also to use him as a consultant on difficult policy questions. Supposedly Communists themselves, the Soviet diplomats of the 1980s often found it necessary to discover what a real Communist thought about a particular issue, and frequently drove out to his home in North London to take his advice. I went once, and came away depressed that this shabby old man, immutably dogmatic, reactionary and narrow-minded, should remain an authority, and that the Embassy should want to preserve him. (It was fitting that he should live close to the cemetery in which Karl Marx is buried. As late as 1989 he was still proclaiming 'Communism will come', and he died, unrepentant, in 1994, aged ninety-five.)

Among my own contacts, none gave me more trouble than Ron Brown, Labour MP for Edinburgh Leith and former trade union organizer, famous for such scandals as smashing the mace in the House of Commons, and being caught stealing his mistress's knickers. By the time I arrived in London, contact had already been made with him, and it fell to me to continue whatever relationship there was. The trouble was that Brown had a Scottish accent so thick that I, still struggling with my English, could scarcely understand a word he said. KGB rules laid down that meetings with contacts must be clandestine, and should not take place in the centre of London. But because Brown was a working MP, tied to the House of Commons, he could not be expected to take more than a couple of hours off for lunch; he did not have time to drive out to the suburbs, and would not have wanted to anyway. I had to meet him in places like Queensway and Kensington High Street. This meant that when I wrote my reports I was obliged to invent a spurious rendezvous somewhere further out, as well as the dry-cleaning route I had taken to this non-existent place.

Then, since I could scarcely understand him, I also had to invent our conversation. I used to sit there listening to him and making intelligent faces, wondering what the hell I was going to write in my report. I am not sure who he thought I was, certainly not a KGB agent — and he may well have been giving me an interesting run-down on events in Parliament. Equally, he could have been describing the weather in Scotland. For all I understood, he could have been talking Arabic or Japanese. Thus every detail of my summary — the place, the route, the conversation — was false: a circumstance as I have already indicated by no means uncommon in KGB annals.

After my escape from Moscow in 1985, and the announcement that I was safe in England, Brown wrote to Mrs Thatcher accusing her of having sent me, a British agent, to spy on him. The sad fact was that, even if I had been acting as he claimed, I still would not have picked up one word in ten of what he uttered.

Nevertheless, the KGB felt that Brown could be of use, even if only passive use — as when he made a trip to Afghanistan in 1981, accompanied by his parliamentary colleague Robert Litherland. The two made statements supporting the Communist regime in Kabul against the Mujahideen so, to Moscow's way of thinking, backing up official Soviet propaganda. During their tour they posed for a newspaper photograph in front of a monument in the form of a tank mounted on a plinth, and later the Young Conservatives pirated the picture for a poster. In a speech balloon one of the intrepid travellers was made to say, 'We've never seen a single tank in the whole of our time in Afghanistan,' and the headline above the picture warned, 'Socialism is bad for your eyes.'

I had learned a good deal from Mikhail Lyubimov about how, in the 1960s, the KGB had recruited left-wingers and dealt with them as proper agents, using all the paraphernalia of espionage, including deadletter boxes, signal sites and so on. 'Why did you bother with all that covert stuff?' I once asked. 'Why didn't you just have overt relationships with them?' To which Lyubimov had replied that, on the one hand, the Centre expected the KGB to handle agents like that, and on the other the use of those methods had the effect of disciplining the man, and making him feel that he was in a proper relationship with his case officer. As for the British, they probably thought that if the money was there, why not take it? I do not know whether they believed the information they handed over was useless or whether they didn't really care. Few, however, would have regarded themselves as spies; many may have been caught up in the romance of it all.

One day, instructions came to renew our efforts with one particular potential 'confidential contact': Jack Jones, the veteran trade union leader, who was then over seventy and retired. I tracked him down with the help of Anatoli Chernyayev, a Line X officer working in the Embassy who had a huge knowledge of the British trade union movement, and arranged to be introduced to him in his flat — a typical council flat, and a typically philistine environment, with few books, and everything in an exaggerated state of tidiness. After I had twice visited the apartment, we started to meet in restaurants but, grateful as the former union official was, he was also absolutely useless. By then he was a pensioner — and what good was that to the KGB? In his memoirs, *Union Man*, published in 1986, he followed Fenner Brockway in giving no mention of his involvement with Soviet intelligence but in his case it would have been because he really was not aware of who we were.

Jack Jones did, however, inadvertently do me a considerable favour. One day I took with me a brochure from the Trades Union Congress which gave a long list of union leaders, and asked him to comment on them. This he did to such effect that I was later able to write a three-page summary, which I added to my report of our meeting. 'Our agent's information on trade union personalities was so extensive', I wrote, 'that I am attaching it as an appendix.' The combined document made it appear that he had been outstandingly helpful and volunteered many facts of the greatest value. You can see from this what the facts really were and how, by careful reporting, success can be created out of very little.

That telegram produced an extraordinary reaction in Moscow, when I was there on holiday a few months later. Ravil Pozdnyakov, the departmental head responsible for Britain, joined a lunch given to Suslov, head of the British and Scandinavian department of the Ministry of Foreign Affairs. Suslov, a powerful imbiber, arrived already drunk. Pozdnyakov, a Tatar from a Muslim family, was not used to alcohol, but he began drinking to keep Suslov company. When he arrived back in the office a good deal the worse for wear, the alcohol seemed to have changed his personality, making him excessively open and sincere. 'Do you realize what you did with your report, old boy?' he burbled genially. 'You showed what an idiot I am, what a lousy intelligence officer! Your appendix proved that you could extract good information even from a hopeless contact. It was incredible! I was very impressed.'

I looked at Pozdnyakov with close interest, thinking what an extraordinary difference a couple of glasses of wine can make.

Because Jack Jones produced so little I met him only five or six times in all, and mostly we exchanged harmless talk about the unions and the Labour Party. But we also discussed Neil Kinnock a good deal, because he was leader of the opposition. Curiously enough, Dmitri Svetanko had shown a flash of intuition in Moscow back in 1981, when I was in the process of joining the British desk. A report from the London Residency had named Kinnock as the Labour politician to watch, and Svetanko had endorsed the suggestion, cabling back that he was regarded as the man of the future, and should be carefully observed. For all the KGB's interest, Kinnock remained ignorant of the organization's attempts to make connections with his party. I had a feeling that Kinnock was much more alarmed about the Trotskyist penetration of the Labour Party than that of the KGB — and probably he was right.

Kinnock's successor, John Smith, struck me as easily the most impressive man in the Labour Party. I met him only once, at an Embassy reception, but I saw that he had a quick, strong intellect, and that, besides being well in control on the domestic front, he understood foreign policy and technical aspects of arms control. He showed curiosity about everything, along with a willingness to meet Russians and discuss things with them, and I felt sure that he was Labour's man for the future. Like thousands of other people, I was shocked by his sudden death in 1994.

An agent with a long record was the veteran politician and trade unionist Bob Edwards, MP successively for Bilston and Wolverhampton, who had fought for the Republicans during the Spanish Civil War, and had led delegations to the Soviet Union in 1926 and 1934. His recruitment had taken place so long ago that it was lost in the mists of antiquity, but for many years he had been personally run by Leonid Zaitsev. This was easy when Zaitsev was posted to Britain, during the 1960s, but later, when he had become head of Directorate T, and a major-general, he insisted on continuing to run Edwards, partly because he liked keeping in touch with an old friend, partly because he wanted to go on being an operational officer, and partly because the connection gave him the excuse for making occasional trips to Europe. Since Edwards was an enthusiastic European, a Member of the European Parliament from 1977 to 1979, and also involved with the Western

European Union (a paper military alliance), they often met in Brussels, where Edwards had excellent contacts and access to useful military and political information. So highly did the KGB value him that he was awarded the Order of the People's Friendship, the country's third highest decoration. The medal was kept in his file at the Centre, but Zaitsev once took it with him to Brussels, so that the recipient could at least see and touch what he had won.

On holiday in Moscow I had met Mikhail Lyubimov, and told him how I had started to work again with various of his old contacts. 'Good,' he said. 'But what about Mikardo? In the fifties and sixties he was regarded as an agent, and a very good one. But then after Czechoslovakia he faded away.'

Ian Mikardo, as far as I know, never worked with the KGB again, but once when I was back in London I saw him with Clive Ponting, the civil servant — never one of ours, so far as I was aware — sitting in one of the window seats at the Gay Hussar, the Hungarian restaurant in Soho much favoured by Labour politicians and trade union leaders. In another corner, armed with a bumper of cognac and a foot-long Havana cigar, was a man regarded by the KGB as one of our most important and active confidential contacts, general secretary of a major union. Studying the scene, I thought: That figures. Mikardo is no longer getting KGB support, but this fellow is. That cigar started life in Cuba, and came here via Moscow and the diplomatic bag. I also used the Gay Hussar to target another trade unionist, Alan Tuffin, general secretary of the post workers' union, in whom the Centre had expressed an interest. I soon saw that he was a solid, middle-of-the road man with no interest in foreign policy, and I decided that there was no prospect of developing him.

Some Labour MPs, far from wanting to co-operate with Soviet

interests, stood out robustly against them, none more so than Edward Leadbitter, member for the Hartlepools, who seized every chance of asking questions in the House of Commons about Soviet espionage. To the KGB he became a hate-figure, and our telegrams to the Centre often rang with the refrain: 'Mr Leadbitter, the person notorious for trying to inflate anti-Soviet spy-mania in Britain, has done it again.' Another hate-figure was Stefan Terlezki, the Ukrainian-born Conservative MP for Cardiff West, who was always vociferously opposed to Soviet ideas, and appeared to Moscow to be rooting for Ukrainian nationalist movements.

The KGB's interest in trade union leaders was a hangover from the 1960s, when the unions had been all-powerful; and in the 1980s, in spite of Mrs Thatcher's reforms, we continued to cultivate them enthusiastically. Yet the Soviet ace in this sphere was not a member of the KGB. Boris Averyanov was often mistaken for a KGB colonel, but he was merely an exceptionally clever official of the Central Committee's International Department. From his base at the World Federation of Trade Unions in Prague, he travelled all over Europe, visiting British and Irish unions at least once a year, usually twice, and always appearing in Britain for the Trades Union Congress. His knowledge of union affairs was prodigious. He knew the history of every union backwards. He knew the officials and every detail of their backgrounds: he knew the names of their wives and children, where they lived, what their recreations were. Also, in talking to them he was cordiality itself and was always welcome at a meeting.

Besides Averyanov in Prague and the KGB in London, yet another organization was busy courting British trade union officials: the department in Moscow known as Directorate RT (standing for 'work on the territory'), which was independently cultivating targets through various Soviet facilities. Officials in this department knew full well how easy it is to recruit people when they are abroad: since they tend to behave less responsibly than at home, and drink too much, it is relatively simple to put them under pressure by surrounding them with agents or listening devices and creating some incriminating circumstance. Staff from Directorate RT would arrange holidays for Western trade unionists, and encourage them to attend conferences abroad.

One leading recipient of their bounty was Jim Slater, second-in-command of the Seamen's Union. By the time I arrived in London, Slater was already listed as a confidential contact, and a man from RT who came to Britain gave me an enthusiastic account of his cultivation — how Slater had visited Russia, how impressed he had been by the Soviet struggle against Fascism, how he liked the country and the people. It was strictly against the rules for the RT people to give us, in the KGB, any feedback about their own contacts, but in this case they were delighted with their achievement.

Among specialists, one man considered helpful, although unwittingly, was Fred Halliday, a specialist in Arab affairs, and at that time a Fellow of a policy studies institute. During the Iran-Iraq war he emerged as a leading expert, and often appeared as a commentator on television. As an independent left-winger, he spoke out against American and Soviet policies but was perceived by Moscow as being likely to follow the Soviet propaganda line. Yuri Kobaladze kept in touch with him, and reported that they got on well. Although Halliday was critical of Soviet policy the friendship was seen as advantageous by the KGB, which profited from receiving good analysis on Arab affairs.

Kobaladze was half Georgian, an intelligent man free from the chauvinism which beset most pure Russians, but even he was thoroughly naïve in some matters. One day he asked Halliday if there was such a thing as a global Jewish conspiracy. 'Yuri!' said Halliday reproachfully.

'How can you ask such a ridiculous question? Of course there's no such thing.' Yet when Kobaladze mentioned the conversation to me he was still not sure that Halliday had given him a true answer.

Relationships like that between him and Halliday could not be kept secret by the KGB but were conducted in the open. Yet the PR Line officers, knowing that Moscow did not like such overt contacts, told lies in every report and pretended that their meetings were clandestine. In this respect Guk was regarded as part of Moscow, rather than head of the London station: because he had such poor knowledge and understanding of Britain, his officers told the same lies to him as they did to the Centre — and I was part of the conspiracy.

One day Kobaladze came to me in some distress. He and his wife had been invited to dinner by Halliday, but he had told Guk that he was going to see a man whom he hoped to appoint a confidential contact. Guk, driven by his ridiculous ideas about some recent 'deterioration of the operational climate', and quoting recent information that a provocation had been planned, forbade him to go. Yuri appealed to me for help. I agreed that it would be rude to refuse an invitation at such short notice. 'All Guk's ideas are based on KGB paranoia,' I said. 'We can't deceive ourselves that this is an operation. Of course it's nothing of the kind. It's just a dinner. Go, of course. Don't tell Guk, and I'll cover for you.' Kobaladze was hugely relieved and grateful, and duly kept his appointment. Halliday never gave away anything but, because of his views, the KGB continued to present its relationship with him as an operational involvement.

There were, of course, many public figures whom the KGB would have liked to cultivate, but for whom they had neither the time nor the resources. One such was Stuart Holland, the high-profile Labour MP who specialized in foreign affairs. Moscow told me I should get hold of him as it was hoped that he might become an asset to the KGB, but although I once had a long talk with him, nothing came of it, and it was clear that the Centre had been wrong. Moscow was also eager that I should make contact with Dick Clements, the author and journalist who had been editor of *Tribune* from 1961 to 1982, and then became a senior adviser to Neil Kinnock. After years of attempts at cultivation by others, he was taken over by Kobaladze but the KGB decided to abandon him.

Yet another public figure in whom Moscow showed interest was the author and broadcaster Melvyn Bragg. One day in London we received a long letter about him from the Centre, saying that the KGB had monitored him while he was visiting East European countries: they had not yet tried to contact him but, after studying his record, they had come to the conclusion that he was good material for cultivation, as he was progressive (that is, in Moscow's eyes, friendly to the Soviets), and also influential in the British media. Like many such suggestions, this one was killed at birth by lack of resources: if we in the KGB did not have sources even in the most important places — the Foreign Office, the Prime Minister's office, the Home Office —how could we afford to chase after individual media men? But I never received the slightest indication that Bragg would have played our game.

One curious episode concerned Lady Olga Maitland, who at that time was not an MP but an energetic and noisy right-wing campaigner against peace organizations such as CND. We often discussed her in the Residency but never did anything about her until we acquired a new recruit from Moscow, Sergei Sayenko. Young, slim and handsome, once a champion middle-distance runner, Sergei became distinctly interested in Lady Olga, not just as a target but as a person. Because I did not think that she had any information of strategic or political importance,

I told him several times to lay off, but he persisted in meeting her, and I assumed that he just enjoyed her company. I have no evidence that she ever made any ideological or, indeed, any other concessions to him but all the same I found their relationship strange, from both the intelligence and the human point of view.

On the Embassy side, as opposed to the KGB, the clean diplomats carried on a good deal of cultivation under their own steam, openly inviting politicians to lunches and receptions and not being put out if their guests stuck up for Western ideas and methods. Julian Amery, who had been Conservative Minister of State at the Foreign and Commonwealth Office from 1972 to 1974, was particularly strong in this respect: he frequently came to the Embassy, and enjoyed himself there, but always upheld the British line with vigour. So, too, did John Biggs-Davidson, another Conservative MP, a friendly man, who explained many things to me. A Catholic, and much in favour of the Establishment, he once hit back briskly at someone who asked him about the possibility of withdrawing troops from Northern Ireland. Now, look,' he said, 'if I asked you about withdrawing Soviet troops from some province in Central Russia, what would your reaction be? Our troops are in Ireland because it's part of the United Kingdom — and that's it.' Another frequent and friendly guest was Norman Atkinson, the Labour MP for Tottenham, who was popular with the Soviet diplomats, and on all invitation lists — as was Sir Anthony Buck, then chairman of the Conservative Parliamentary Defence Committee. Anthony Marlow, Conservative MP for Northampton, was also busily cultivated by the Embassy: then as now he was strongly pro-Arab, an alignment useful to the Russians, whose aim was always to damage Israel by supporting the Arabs, and so to undermine American interests in the Middle East.

A few MPs were considered too extraordinary for the KGB to bother about them. One such maverick was Frank Cook, who struck the KGB as always being eager to demonstrate his anti-British attitudes. However, during one reception at No. 18 Kensington Palace Gardens his behaviour became so uncouth that nobody in the KGB showed any further enthusiasm for cultivating him.

Equally left-wing, and often found at Soviet receptions, was Denzil Davies, who at that time was shadow defence secretary. I kept thinking how extraordinary it would be if Labour came to power, and the defence secretary — a notoriously keen imbiber —proved to be fundamentally pro-Soviet and anti-American. Well, we never found out on either account!

Sometimes the Embassy's manoeuvring was blocked by instructions from Moscow. For instance, Kenneth Warren, MP for Hastings, an aeronautical expert and a member of many select committees in the House of Commons, seemed eager to become a guest of the Soviets, he had a genuine interest in Russia, but telegrams from the Centre said, 'Stay away from him, because he may be connected with special services', a very usual expression of KGB paranoia. I never discovered any confirmation of this but I found Warren, who, of course, didn't know who I was, sympathetic, and was grateful for his interest. With Peter Temple-Morris, Conservative MP for Leominster, things were the other way round. A telegram from the Centre advised us (wrongly, as it turned out) that he was sympathetic: he was certainly outspoken, and had an Iranian wife: it might be useful if we got in touch with him. When I met him at Embassy receptions, I found him knowledgeable, friendly and curious, in the best sense of the word, but I never detected any evidence that he would be prepared to help. If I had spoken better English, and been less busy, I should have liked to cultivate him but, as things stood, I had no chance.

Perhaps the most enigmatic of all our contacts was Robert Maxwell, the millionaire tycoon who was lost overboard from his yacht off the Canary Islands in 1991, and later found to have embezzled millions of pounds from his companies' pension funds. Ten years before that, in Moscow, I happened to see a copy of a telegram sent by Popov from London, which described a meeting with Maxwell. The message itself was of no interest, but on it Svetanko, the deputy department head responsible for British affairs, had scrawled, 'Look at this arch-spy.

I glanced at it and said, 'Dmitri Andreyevich, what do you mean?'

'Maxwell's a British spy,' Svetanko answered. 'He's been in British intelligence ever since the end of the war, and the Embassy's playing stupid games with him. They're idiots to have anything to do with him.'

That seemed strange to me. When I reached London I found that Maxwell — originally a Czech — had once been an MP, but had long since given up politics in favour of full-time business, and had become the epitome of a bloated, old-fashioned capitalist, rude to his staff and widely hated. Yet, as I watched him talking to Popov at Soviet Embassy receptions, I saw that the Ambassador held him in high regard. I also learnt that he had earned himself considerable influence with the Central Committee in Moscow by publishing the collected works of Andropov, Chernenko and Brezhnev in English — a move that powerfully flattered the latter-day Soviet leaders.

What particularly irritated the KGB was that, although they regarded Maxwell as a spy, the Central Committee ignored their warnings and continued to develop their relationship with him. Then, at the end of 1984, a request came from the Centre asking us in the KGB station to provide a detailed assessment of the man. It fell to me to write this, and I produced what I thought was a realistic sketch. I said that Maxwell was a former politician who had become a leading businessman, and that he liked having influence with important people in Eastern Europe. In Britain, I wrote, his standing was not good: he was unpopular with the trade unions, who regarded him as the worst kind of boss, arrogant and pompous. I mentioned that in earlier years he had been connected in some way with intelligence.

By then Guk had left, and Nikitenko was Acting Resident. When he read my draft, he said, 'We can't send it like this because we've always maintained that Maxwell is definitely a British spy.'

'Now, look,' I said, 'he's getting on. Whatever he may have done once, he's obviously not still running errands for any of the services. It's typical KGB nonsense about him being a spy.'

'Well...' said Nikitenko doubtfully, 'we aren't revolutionaries. We can't change our line just because Guk's gone. Let's add a paragraph on these lines: "We do not rule out the possibility that after meeting important persons in the East European countries, Maxwell, being on good terms with the British intelligence services, may write detailed reports of his impressions..."'

'All right,' I agreed. 'If you insist.' So we added something on those lines. But I got the impression that Moscow's sudden interest indicated some change of attitude towards Maxwell. It seemed that they planned to make even more use of him — and later rumours certainly indicated that the KGB had begun to manipulate him as a publicity agent.

*

My conclusion from all this is that if the Labour Party had been returned to power in the general election of June 1983, the KGB would have been in a strong position. Even if we had no fully fledged agents in the party, we did have some good confidential contacts and helpful friends, all ready to talk. With Labour in power, the KGB would have been able to pick up a great deal of information about what was going on within the British government. On the other hand, when Margaret Thatcher and the Conservatives came back in a landslide, our prospects, not surprisingly, were much poorer.

Chapter Thirteen – Acting Resident

With Guk gone, Nikitenko hoped to take over as Resident, and he schemed relentlessly to that end. But until the Centre made up its mind, he merely acted as a stand-in.

One minor sensation of the summer of 1984 was the return to Moscow of Oleg Bitov, a former senior editor on the Moscow *Literary Gazette* who had defected during a film festival in Venice the previous year. After extensive debriefing by MI5, Bitov had sold his story to the *Sunday Telegraph* for forty thousand pounds, and appeared to have settled down well in London, living in a flat in East Sheen. He had begun to travel in the United States and Europe, and was hoping to make a literary career for himself in the West: apart from producing articles, he had recently signed a contract to write a book about his life. A reasonably intelligent man, who specialized in translation work, he was also self-important, impractical, and had a weakness for alcohol, whisky particularly.

On Thursday 16 August he disappeared. His car, a red Toyota Tercel, was later found abandoned in Emperor's Gate, Kensington. Friends were puzzled, especially as he had just started on a course of dental treatment to replace several unsightly metal false teeth: after the first appointment, in a series of six, his gums were full of gaps from which the old teeth had been removed, and it seemed an odd moment for anyone to abscond. Word went round that he had been snatched by the KGB and smuggled out to Moscow; some people even said that he had been a KGB agent all along. The mystery remained unsolved when, a month later, he appeared in Moscow at a staged Press conference, claiming, among other ridiculous and transparent lies, that he had not defected voluntarily, but had been drugged and kidnapped by the British, then forced at gun point to write his newspaper series.

The truth was simpler. Missing his teenage daughter Xenia, and worried that he could not fulfil his literary obligations, Bitov gave himself up. After lunch that Thursday in August, when everything was quiet during the holiday period, he walked up to the gate of the main Soviet Embassy building at No. 13 Kensington Palace Gardens and rang the bell. The duty guard asked what he wanted, whereupon he said, 'I'm Oleg Bitov. Let me in.' The guard, never having heard of him, told him to go away. Bitov then said, 'I've got something important here,' and threw his briefcase over the gate, so that it landed in the drive.

This galvanized the guard into telephoning the duty diplomat, who did know who Bitov was and let him in. Nikitenko, hastily called in, proceeded to interview him. Bitov said that he wanted to return to Moscow, and that, in return for safe passage, would give the authorities a great deal of information about the operational methods of the British services. His briefcase, he said, contained a series of cassette tapes on which he had recorded details of his experiences in Britain.

Against all the rules, whether on their own decision, or with special permission from the Centre, they took him into the Embassy and let him spend the night in a room in the basement normally used by the chef for laying out food before big receptions. Presently instructions came from the Centre to issue him with a temporary Soviet passport, and to smuggle him on to an aircraft for Sofia, the Bulgarian capital, where a representative of the Soviet Embassy would meet him and put him on a plane for Moscow. This the Embassy staff did: he was driven out of Kensington Palace Gardens lying on the back seat of a car, with a blanket thrown over him. Our people were astonished that the British surveillance had not seen him when he presented himself at the gates — normally, routine observation immediately picked up anyone who did that. But somehow Bitov was missed, and his disappearance created a sensation, not only in the press, but also within MI5.

Unfortunately I was on leave when all this happened but I returned to London at the end of August, to find everyone in the Residency talking about it: even though they had done nothing but hide Bitov for a couple of days, they thought they had brought off the most tremendous success, and Nikitenko was given an official commendation. At my next meeting with the British, Jack said, 'Oh, by the way, Oleg, do you know anything about a man in whom our sister service has an interest — Bitov? You may have heard, he's disappeared.'

I sat there, keeping a straight face. 'Bitov?' I said casually. 'Ah, yes, I did hear about him.'

'You *did*! What happened to him?'

'He's in Moscow.' So I told them the whole story.

*

In the autumn of 1984 we were told to expect an important agent from France. His code-name was Paul; he had a beard, and spoke only French. We were told that he would be run impersonally, as far as possible, through deadletter boxes, with an occasional visual contact, which would take place outside the cinema near Putney Bridge.

Nikitenko was instructed to study the place and start going there each Thursday at 8 p.m.

This he began to do, but then came another instruction telling him to stop for a while. Soon after that he went on holiday, leaving me in charge for the first time. While he was away we received a telegram asking us to find two deadletter boxes, for the same French agent, each big enough to contain a small briefcase. I asked the KR Line officer based at the trade delegation to find one deadletter box, and offered to look for the other myself. Because I was so busy, I approached one of my English contacts for ideas, and he came up with Brompton Cemetery, in the Fulham Road. That, he said, was a good wild and woolly place, and he even drew my attention to a particular grave. 'Look for a big holly tree,' he said, and he named that kind of tree in Russian: *kamenniy dub*, literally a stone oak.

One Saturday, I took Leila and the children out to the cemetery, and we walked along the central path. As we strolled, I noticed that most of the other visitors were men, in couples, and that several of them were wearing shorts, which struck me as rather odd. Not until later did I learn that the place was a favourite rendezvous for gays. Towards the end of the graveyard we came to a patch of dense undergrowth and shrubs: I could not find the tombstone my colleague had suggested, but I came on another which would do perfectly, with a stone standing almost vertically, and an ideal hollow behind it, screened by long grass. Having made some careful notes, I went home.

Alas, all these preparations proved fruitless. For weeks we watched the pub and the deadletter box, but nobody appeared, and in the end we learnt that this famous agent was not coming after all: a cipher clerk in the French military intelligence service, called Abrivard, he had died of cancer. Not that his identity emerged quickly: it took the French DST

(Direction de la Surveillance du Territoire) over two years to discover it. Wanting to assess the damage he had caused, they were determined to seize his notes and, after a long struggle, managed to steal them from Abrivard's former mistress.

*

On holiday in Moscow in August, I was summoned to the Centre for high-level discussions about my future, and there I again met Gribin, now head of the British—Scandinavian department. With his neat moustache and slim face, he looked much the same as ever and, even though I knew that at heart he was a toady and a careerist, I had to admit that his attitude to me was friendliness itself.

'Oleg,' he said, 'you're the ideal person to become my deputy here. I'd love to have you — hypothetically, that is. Of course it's impossible. The trouble is, you're abroad. You're only in your third year of service in London. On the other hand, the job of Resident there…'

He went on to describe how, since Guk's expulsion from Britain, he had been besieged by different lobbies and factions within the First Chief Directorate, all trying to put forward candidates for the post of Resident in the London station. He told me that for months he had been lobbying on my behalf, and that he had ridden off numerous attempts by various pressure groups to force their own men into the slot. Telephone calls, threats, pledges, begging requests — every approach had been tried. And who was the strongest other candidate, of all those thrust forward? None other than Vitali Yurchenko, a man with a primitive, military mind who had completed one tour in America from 1975 to 1980 but only as a security officer in the Soviet Embassy in Washington, and had never done any operational work abroad.

'How could I put up with such a man in London?' asked Gribin angrily. 'He wouldn't work. He would only play at being an important man in an important place. I couldn't have him. It's you I want.' Yet he went on to say that he would have to proceed with the utmost caution. 'The closer anyone moves to the position of head of station,' he said, 'the greater the danger, the more intense the intrigues, the more vicious the attempts to undermine and discredit him.' He told me he would keep in touch by letter to let me know how our joint campaign was going.

Then, in a fascinating aside, he said that everyone at the Centre had been thinking about the future of the KGB and of the nation, and he spoke with warmth of a new, up-and-coming politician called Mikhail Gorbachev, who was planning a visit to Britain for the end of the year. The KGB, said Gribin, had come to the conclusion that Gorbachev was the best bet for the future, and that it would do all it could to help him — though in the subtlest way, without revealing its allegiance. 'That's why, when he goes to London, we shall ask you to send us the best possible briefing,' Gribin confided. 'That way, it will look as though he has a superior intellect.'

One evening Gribin invited me home for supper with his wife Irina and their daughter Yelena, known as Alyonka. It was more than six years since I had last seen the girl, in Denmark, and then she had only been ten or eleven years old. I felt that it would be a good move to take her a token present, and I selected from my bookshelves a nice little edition of the work of Konstantin Balmont, a poet, like Lermontov, of Scottish extraction, who wrote at the turn of the century, and during the Communist era was regarded as thoroughly decadent. (His poems were not available in Russia, but I had bought that copy abroad.) I was aware, of course, that Alyonka must have grown up, but even so I was hardly prepared for the sight that greeted me when I rang the bell of the Gribins' flat. Both parents were dark — Nikolai black-haired and narrow faced, Irina half-Jewish, with a hint of the Oriental in the shape of her cheekbones — yet here stood a glorious blonde Russian beauty, with a lovely, interesting face, and generous hips well set on long legs, as if she had sprung from a traditional painting done a hundred years ago. Behind her hovered Gribin, proud and delighted that I showed such appreciation, and from that moment the evening went well, the book proving a particular success.

*

Back in London, just as Nikitenko had claimed credit for his success with Bitov, I too was keen to bring off some easy little coup, which would promote my image at the Centre without damaging the West. Almost at once, as if in answer to my prayers, just such a chance presented itself.

One day Mr Tokar — in Nikitenko's absence the senior counter-surveillance officer — came to my office in some excitement and said that a fascinating visitor had arrived at the Embassy: none other than Svetlana Alliluyeva, otherwise Mrs Peters, Stalin's daughter. Dressed in a headscarf and dark glasses, she had simply walked in, unrecognized by our own people or, as we found out later, by the MI5 surveillance, and said that she wanted to return to Russia, together with her daughter, Olga, who was then thirteen. Mr Tokar handed me an unsealed letter she had brought with her: ostensibly written to her son by her first marriage, but in fact addressed to the Soviet leaders, it was an outburst of rage and frustration against all the worst features of Western life.

I read it with a mixture of admiration and pity: admiration because it was well written and powerfully expressed, pity because its author was so deluded. It was the typical reaction of a Russian with Oriental blood in her veins, still influenced by her family's traditional, patriarchal way of life, against what she saw as the pernicious freedoms of the

West — pornography, drugs, alcohol, tobacco, and girls starting their sex lives at thirteen. Here was a woman — I saw as I read — who had defected in the belief that the West represented freedom, democracy, light and civilization, and now, twenty years later, had come to the conclusion that Western life was nothing but corruption, dirt, immodesty and degradation. Clearly, she was appalled by the prospect facing her daughter, and terrified that in another year or so she would lose control of her: that Olga would start to defy her mother, sleep with boys, experiment with drugs and stay out all night.

The burden of Svetlana's complaint was that she wanted to return to the more modest and dignified life of Russia. The trouble was, she had entirely forgotten what Russian life was like. In the two decades since she had defected in India, she had begun to idealize conditions in the Soviet Union, and did not know that life was worse than when she had left. In the sixties there had been fewer severe food shortages, less corruption, fewer bribes, and still a basic foundation of honesty; traditional Russian life had not been entirely destroyed then by Communism, and memories of Stalin's Terror had tended to enforce law and order. What Svetlana did not appreciate was that by 1984 everything had become a great deal less civilized.

Against the hopes and expectations of Russians serving abroad, the situation at home had been deteriorating steadily. Elementary public services like health and education had declined; food shortages were often acute; the range of goods on sale in shops was wretched; and people found it increasingly difficult to get their cars mended or their property maintained. Corruption was rife, not least in large sections of the Party apparatus, and although the KGB were aware of this, they could do nothing to stamp it out. The technological gap between the Soviet Union and the West was widening, and economic growth had all but stopped: the small percentage officially quoted was nothing but the result of manipulating statistics. Moreover, Soviet people perceived their plight more clearly than ever before because international communications had improved so much, and censorship could no longer keep out news of the world's progress.

Svetlana seemed blind to all this. But our task in the Embassy was to smuggle her back. First I asked a secretary to type out the letter, which was handwritten and difficult to decipher. Then, together with Tokar, I composed a telegram describing what had happened, and including part of the letter. The trouble was that Tokar — a Ukrainian from a humble background — had extremely poor written Russian, deficient in spelling, grammar and style: he spent hours laboriously compiling a draft, and then, because I did not want to compromise myself by sending a poor telegram, I had to sit down and rewrite it in longhand (typewritten telegrams being specifically forbidden on security grounds). This took me until 12.30 a.m., whereupon I handed it to the wretched cipher clerk on night duty, and waited to make sure that he could read and understand it.

Since Gribin had insisted that all important telegrams should go to him as well as to the KR Line, I addressed one copy to 'Severov', his code-name, and next day back came a positive answer: 'Continue debriefing and prepare for evacuation.' Under Chernenko — an old man, already sick — the administration was taking a reactionary, Stalinist line, and warmly welcomed the idea of Svetlana rejoining the faithful: the return of the prodigal daughter would represent one small yet definite ideological victory over the West.

We therefore prepared a simple evacuation plan, while giving her advice on how to sell her house, what to do with the money, and how to create the right arrangements so that if she needed her savings she could draw them from a bank in Moscow. Over the next couple of weeks she came to the Embassy four more times, and spent hours chatting with Mr Tokar over cups of tea and little glasses of brandy. Of course I told the British service what was happening, but they saw no advantage in keeping Svetlana against her will, and were happy to let her go.

When the time came, her exit presented no problems. Since she was officially Mrs Peters, an American citizen, we simply bought her an air ticket to Sofia. The affair earned me some credit — even though it had been child's play to set up — and in November the Centre sent a telegram commending Mr Tokar and myself.[1]

In the middle of the Svetlana negotiations a dramatic event occurred in British politics: the IRA bomb attack on the Grand Hotel in Brighton, during the Conservative Party Conference. On the morning of 12 October radio and television bulletins were full of the terrorist outrage: several people had been killed, Mrs Thatcher had had a miraculous escape, and millions of television watchers were haunted by the pictures of her Secretary of State for Trade and Industry, Norman Tebbit, being lifted, badly injured, out of the ruined building by firemen.

For me the question was, what should the KGB do about it? It did not seem to be any concern of ours. News of the bomb had been well reported by all the international agencies, and there seemed little more that we could say. Besides, the station was functioning well in its normal mode, and I enjoyed the feeling of being in charge. The officer responsible for technical gadgets, the cipher clerk, the man responsible for gathering reference material on restaurants and dry-cleaning routes, the operational driver: all were working efficiently, and the nucleus of the station was showing good discipline. In the morning I read the

---

1   Three years later Svetlana bitterly regretted her decision, and had to write a special letter to President Gorbachev, begging for permission to return to the West.

telegrams from the Centre, and answered those which needed replies. The afternoon passed smoothly, and at six o'clock I thought, Well, this has been a lovely day. Now I'm free, with no boss to detain me. I can go home and enjoy myself — play with the girls, take a drive, have a beer in the pub. So I locked the door of my office, went downstairs, crossed to the gate and reached my car. Suddenly I was hit by a flash of lightning.

What the hell was I doing, going home without having given the Centre a single line about the great event of the day? For them, of course, it was of exceptional interest, since the bulk of the domestic KGB in the Soviet Union work on State security and anti-terrorist operations. A major terrorist attack on the British government, and not a word from the KGB in London? Had the Acting Resident no ideas on the matter? No, it was impossible.

I ran back upstairs, shouting to the cipher clerk to hold on, and sat down to write a short telegram in which I took care to rub salt into the Centre's wounds by pointing out that the consequences of the attack would be favourable to the Conservative Party. The terrorists' operation had outraged all normal British citizens, and would diminish whatever support the Irish nationalists might have. It would strengthen backing for the government, partly out of human sympathy for people who had suffered, and partly because Mrs Thatcher had shown outstanding courage, remaining calm and decisive throughout the nightmare. Another factor likely to increase support was the fortitude displayed by those injured, Mr Tebbit particularly.

It took me about three-quarters of an hour to draft a concise telegram expressing these ideas, and I enjoyed every minute of it, feeling that for once the Centre was getting an accurate account of public reaction in Britain. Then, once again, I locked up and left for home.

*

It was not long before we had the first official news about the up-and-coming figure in the Soviet hierarchy. Gorbachev had once been in charge of agriculture, but in May had been appointed Ideological Secretary under the ailing Chernenko — an important step up for anyone manoeuvring to become General Secretary: Andropov had taken it, and now it looked as though this new man was on his way to the top. He was coming to Britain as head of a delegation from the Supreme Soviet, that pathetic body which called itself a parliament but which had never been elected, all its members being appointed. But what was the point of this visit? His trip to Britain was regarded as his first important overseas mission, and a stream of telegrams from the Centre revealed that — as Gribin had confided to me — the KGB had a special interest in the visit. One request after another demanded information: on Britain's position over arms-control questions, Britain's military role in NATO, Britain's economic and technological potential, Britain's role in the European Community, her relations with the United States, China, Eastern Europe. The Centre was supposed to be well briefed on such matters already, but clearly they felt a need for fresh facts and ideas. At the same time, the Embassy was bombarded with similar requests from the Ministry of Foreign Affairs, so that the two organizations were filing on parallel channels, and a kind of competition developed.

At the end of October Nikitenko returned from holiday, confirming from talks with senior officers at the Centre that the KGB was indeed behind Gorbachev, who had a friendly understanding with it, and that the trip was designed to give him a boost in his struggle for power. The KGB was backing him because he was a new man, a man for the future, an honest man who would fight corruption and all the other negative features of Soviet society.

Now we really began to miss Yegoshin, our brilliant but drunken analyst: the rest of us were not professional report writers and, anyway, we were busy with operational work. We therefore lobbied for a temporary replacement and it was now that we were sent the middle-aged Shilov, or Shatov, who at least knew what to do, even if he lacked Yegoshin's speed and sharpness.

It was at this stage that Gribin began to write me letters which I found disturbing. They contained no personal threat: rather, it was their peculiar brevity which gave me cause for concern. Each was short and factual, and couched in short, bald sentences, as if the author was inhibited from expressing any feeling by fear that somebody might be making up a file on him. The style was quite uncharacteristic of Gribin, and I felt that it must be a reflection of his new status: he seemed to sense that even private letters could be used against him if someone turned hostile.

By early December we had put over a mass of information to the Centre, but suddenly a request came that floored us: the Centre wanted specific facts on the miners' strike, which had been running since March. What benefits were the miners getting? What were they living on? Were they getting anything from the State? What were their prospects? Strikes and unemployment benefits were unknown in the Soviet Union: clearly, this bright new Mr Gorbachev had read something about the strike and had asked for basic information, which we were asked to supply before the end of the day.

Our trouble was that we could not find it. None of our normal journalistic or political contacts had any answers, and in the end I was obliged to ring Sally, a well-known Communist sympathizer who taught English in the basement of the Consular Department, the only English person allowed on Embassy territory.

A slim, good-looking woman in her mid-thirties, Sally worked in the offices of Novosti, the press-agency-cum-propaganda bureau, and over the past couple of years I had got to know her well. I was keen to improve my English and had gone as often as possible to the classes she gave. Many times, because no one else had come along, we had spent ninety minutes just chatting to each other. During one of these sessions she had suddenly said, in an offhand voice, 'I believe it's now fashionable for a woman of my age to acquire a lover.' Obviously it was some kind of invitation, but at the time I was so happily married, and so preoccupied with my double life, that I made no move to take it up; and when, on a couple of occasions, I asked her out to lunch, purely to extract information from her about the British Communist Party, she was clearly disappointed that I kept off personal matters.

Anyway, now that we urgently needed information about the miners, our relationship stood me in good stead. Because it was my instinct, as a KGB officer, not to reveal to any low-level member of staff that I was using a special source, I went out to a call-box and telephoned her from there. She was glad to give us the information we needed, and we were able to concoct a telegram that evening.

The Centre responded by asking both the Embassy and the KGB, separately, whether it should send money to the miners. After long debate the Embassy said 'No', on the grounds that the strike was being orchestrated by left-wingers, the Labour Party was uneasy about it, and a contribution from Moscow might damage the Labour leadership. The KGB also decided that it was not in Moscow's interest to support extreme radical movements in British politics. But the militant element in the Central Committee overruled both these recommendations, called us cowards, and allocated a million currency roubles (about nine hundred thousand pounds) to the miners. The question then was how to pass the money, and it was never clear to me whether or not the funds reached their intended destination.

*

Gorbachev's tour began on 15 December. By the time his car pulled up outside the Embassy gate in the middle of the day, the entire staff had gathered on the drive, together with their wives, to greet him. He shook hands with everyone individually, but when a group photograph was taken, I had a curious feeling that I should conceal myself behind someone else and not appear in the picture, for fear that one of my colleagues might later be branded with having had a traitor at his shoulder. The feeling was not well defined, but it made me uneasy.

First impressions of our distinguished visitor were not favourable. I know that people in the West found his face attractive: they considered his expression open and lively. For us, however, it was spoilt by obvious Turkic or Mongolian features. Many Russians have a slightly racialist suspicion of Asians, believing them to be corrupt and dishonest; and my colleagues, when they saw the Oriental features of Mr Gorbachev, felt instinctive distrust.

We got a better chance to form an opinion that evening, when he returned to the Embassy to speak to the diplomats and intelligence officers in one of the main reception halls. Again he shook hands with each of us — without any introductions being made — and then began to speak. We had understood that he would be in a hurry, as the time was already 7.30 p.m., and he had to change before being driven to a formal dinner, which was due to begin at 8.45. We expected the normal, five-minute pep-talk: 'Greetings to you from the Leadership of the Communist Party of the Soviet Union. You diplomats are in the leading ranks of the foreign policy front...' and so on. That was not what we got at all. Instead, Gorbachev held forth for forty minutes, clearly carried away by the sound of his own voice.

This, too, was a grave disappointment. His accent and vocabulary were those of a man from the south of Russia, the North Caucasus, an area whose speech had been heavily influenced by the arrival of Ukrainians during the nineteenth century. The argot was no longer Ukrainian, but merely South Russian, regarded in Moscow and St Petersburg as unpleasant and ugly, particularly displeasing as regards the letter G, which came out almost as H, so that Gogol, for instance, emerged as 'Hohol'. Brezhnev had spoken like that, and Gorbachev was the same. Also, with some words, he persistently put the stress on the wrong syllable: instead of *nachát*, he always said *náchat* — an awful solecism.

Not only that: his speech was neither polished nor grammatical, and contained enough elementary mistakes to annoy educated Russians. He also displayed a dismaying lack of self-awareness, going on for far longer than the occasion warranted. He made one or two interesting points — among them that American foreign policy was not shaped by some secret, imperialist, capitalist force which was somehow driving the government (as Soviet leaders and analysts had always believed), but was the product of several power-houses competing with one another, the White House, Congress, the State Department, the National Security Council, the CIA, the Defense Department and academic centres. This, at least was realistic and refreshing. But on the home front he was disappointing: he made no revelations, and gave no hint of *glasnost* (openness) or increased democracy, but spoke at length of the terrible winter which was damaging railways and powerlines in Siberia.

When it was over, I went in search of poor old Shatov, our temporary analyst, who had not been allowed to attend the meeting (to have caught a glimpse of Gorbachev would have been his dream). 'Well,' he said enviously, 'what was he like?'

'Just another Soviet *apparatchik*,' I sighed. 'Far too pleased with himself. He couldn't stop talking — went on for forty minutes.'

Shatov stared at me and said, 'Old boy, you don't understand. A member of the Politburo who can speak for forty minutes without notes — he must be a genius!'

The tour went off well, due largely to the excellence of the interpreters, who greatly improved Gorbachev's speeches in translation, and to the skill of Mikhail Bogdanov, who spoke first-rate English and knew the country well, and now helped me prepare the fact sheets with which we briefed Gorbachev every morning.[2] Yet there was another ingredient in the briefings about which no one else in the Embassy had any clue: the input from my friends in the British service. Every evening we were under pressure to produce a forecast of the line the next day's meetings would take, and this of course was impossible to discover from normal channels. I therefore went to the British and asked urgently for help: could they give me an idea of the subjects Mrs Thatcher would raise? They produced a few possibilities, from which I managed to concoct a useful-looking memorandum; but the next day's meeting was much more fruitful. When I asked for a steer on Geoffrey Howe, they let me see the brief which the Foreign Secretary would be using in his talks with Mr Gorbachev. My English was still poor, and my ignorance was compounded by nervousness and lack of time, so that I had to concentrate hard to remember all the points.

---

2   Bogdanov had been one of Kim Philby's brightest pupils in his little seminars, and by 1984 was cultivating some useful contacts at the Economist magazine. He established such a cordial relationship with Brian Beedham, one of the journalists there, that he persuaded the Centre to list him as a confidential contact.

Back at the station, full of excitement at my little coup, I sat down at a typewriter (illegally) and hacked out a rough draft, allegedly based on my general sources and what I had gleaned from newspapers. Then I gave it to Shatov, who laboriously rewrote it in such vague and general terms that Nikitenko, when he saw it, exploded with vexation. 'I can't show this to Gorbachev!' he cried. 'It's far too woolly.' I agreed, and said slyly, 'Leonid Yefremovich, I don't want to argue with Shatov because he's a very conscientious fellow, but maybe you'd like to have a look at my own version.' Nikitenko quickly read it and said, 'Yes! This is just what we need.' Instinctively, he noticed the Foreign Office briefing shining through my text — and in it went, verbatim.

Every evening Nikitenko would stand on the landing of the Embassy, holding our three or four typed sheets and talking to the guards until he got the opportunity to go in and lay the briefs on Gorbachev's desk. When they came out, sometimes with passages underlined to show gratitude or satisfaction, we took them back to the Residency and sent them as KGB analytical telegrams to the Centre, so that they would know what Gorbachev had seen. This system proved a great success — and we knew that Gorbachev was reading what we wrote with close attention, because one morning, after we had included a flattering paragraph about his wife, Raisa, which recorded how people had admired her, he made his first and only correction, crossing out five lines, to leave only two lines of modest, matter-of-fact tribute, and adding a note: 'It is very dangerous to make other members' wives jealous.'

Like her husband, Raisa went down well with the British — but to us she was a disaster, bigoted, arrogant and self-important. She refused to have our first choice of interpreter, Mikhail Bogdanov's wife, who spoke beautiful English, on the grounds that she was used to being surrounded by men. Instead, we had to give her Yuri Mazur, a former sailor from a humble background, but a man with a formidable intellect, who had known Britain for twenty-five years.[3]

In the event the tour was cut short, from five days to four, by the death of Marshal Ustinov, a leading member of the Politburo. Gorbachev could have finished his programme — the telegram from Moscow was one of information, not instruction — but he chose to go home, making only the briefest of visits to Scotland. A few weeks later in Moscow I heard that Nikitenko had received an order for handling the visit so well, but, in fact, the people who had made Gorbachev's trip a success were Bogdanov, Shatov, the SIS and myself. All the security had been organized by the British. I protested to Gribin that justice had not been done but, of course, there was no redress, and we could never find out what had happened — whether Nikitenko had ingratiated himself with someone in the entourage, or whether the decoration was simply given to the nominal boss.

In the longer term, Gorbachev's career continued to demonstrate the huge gulf between the viewpoints of East and West. In the West he became a hero, the first leader with the courage to pronounce that Communism was dead; but in the Soviet Union he was deeply unpopular and continued to be regarded as typical provincial Party *apparatchik*, with a provincial brain and education, who brought about a monumental political change more or less by mistake.

3   When Raisa went to Reykjavik for Gorbachev's meeting with Reagan, she cold-shouldered the Soviet Ambassador and his wife (a popular couple), and a few days later had them dismissed from their posts, because they had not shown sufficient awe in their attitude towards her. She also told Nancy Reagan that Communism was a superior scientific doctrine, and would triumph over capital-ism, which was doomed. The Russian people never regarded Raisa as a true First Lady, because her husband had manipulated the Party apparatus, rather than being elected. When Boris Yeltsin came to power, his wife was regarded as a genuine First Lady.

I feel that he is due some credit, but not much, because what happened was not what he wanted or what he was aiming at. He created a movement towards change, but the movement gathered such momentum that it ran away from him, out of control. He began with the idea of *uskoreniye*, or acceleration, the speeding-up of industrial and technological progress, because he realized that the gap between the Soviet Union and the West had widened so much that, if nothing were done, Russia would in the end be so far behind that she would have to surrender. His method was to divert resources into areas where we were not doing well, and his aim at that stage was not to abolish socialism so much as to discover ways of making it work better.

But the more he found out about the old system, the more he understood that it deserved the sharpest criticism. That was why, at the Plenum of the Central Committee in 1987, he launched the concept of *glasnost* and fiercely criticized the Brezhnev era as one of stagnation. All the crimes and shortcomings of Soviet society were like a colossal ulcer, covered by a thin skin, but not healed, suppurating beneath the surface: people started to write and talk about it more and more. Gorbachev himself was nervous about the momentum glasnost started to acquire — and it simply ran away from him.

*

Although no longer directly concerned with Line N, I had to deal several times with illegals. When I arrived at the Residency, an industrious man called Grachev had been controlling them from a slot in the Consular Department; but at the end of my first year he had left, and only two Line N officers remained in London, one working in the International Cocoa Organization, and the other in a boat-repair firm. The latter had an outstandingly beautiful wife, a stunning woman in her mid-thirties who had herself received a commendation — I think for going to Somerset House and procuring valuable documents on some pretext.

Both men were responsible for finding signal sites and reading signals, and one day the man from Cocoa announced that he had discovered an excellent new site, right in the middle of London. In Curzon Street, Mayfair, he reported, there was a wooden noticeboard, which would be ideal for chalk-marks. When I told Jack about this, he nearly fell off his chair in excitement, for the site was right across the street from one of MI5's main offices, and it seemed to offer an exceptional chance of spotting one of the elusive creatures who surfaced so rarely.

All I could tell them was that the woman, code-named Inge, was due to leave a signal any day. The head of the Russian counter-espionage section found a window which commanded a good view of the board, and set up a rota of watchers. By sheer bad luck, at the critical moment, someone offered the man on watch a cup of tea: lowering his binoculars, he turned to take it, and when he looked again, the signal had appeared. The woman had come and gone without him catching a glimpse of her.

Soon after that, a request came from the Centre to carry out a visual control on another of Grachev's illegals, and the task fell to me. I learnt that the man would be standing outside the window of a toyshop, with a copy of *Der Spiegel* sticking out of his pocket, at a particular time on a particular day: my job was simply to pass by on the other side of the street and make sure that he was alive and well. Having co-ordinated matters with the British security service, in the hope that they could photograph and identify the man, I took the tube to Morden, the southernmost station on the Northern Line, and arrived early to give myself plenty of time. My friends were there somewhere, I knew, but they were discreet, and I never spotted them.

As the time for the rendezvous approached, I took off my watch and held it in the palm of my hand, so as to make my timing absolutely precise. When I walked round the corner of the block, there he was, unmistakably, a fairly tall fellow of about thirty, with dark hair, wearing an anorak. He was obviously on the alert, eager to spot the observer sent to cast an eye over him. What he did not know was that two parties were watching him simultaneously. After a minute or so I went back to the Underground, and later discovered from my friends that they had followed him into it as well. When he took a train towards the centre of London, they did the same, and he led them unwittingly to a parked car, whose number they took. The details enabled them to identify him as an alleged German, working as a mechanic in some repair shops. (On the day of my escape from Moscow — 20 July 1985 — a team went straight there to arrest him, only to find that he had disappeared suddenly on 25 May, the day after I was interrogated by the KGB. Later we learnt that telegrams and radio messages recalling all illegals immediately had been sent out on 25 or 26 May.)

Another successful operation — successful on several fronts — took place in Coram's Fields, in Bloomsbury. This time my task was to deposit a special brick, made up by the operational technology department and containing eight thousand pounds in untraceable banknotes, for collection by another illegal. The site had been chosen by the boat-repair man with the beautiful wife: a footpath alongside a high wire fence, on one edge of the gardens. As it was a fine Saturday evening, I took the girls along with me — Maria was then five, Anna four — and my driver made a brilliant job of dry-cleaning our route around Central London, avoiding the centre.

Once again I had made sure that the security service was present. This time a cyclist appeared to be having problems with his machine, and a woman was pushing what looked like a baby, but was in fact a camera, in a perambulator. Soon after I had deposited the brick inside a plastic bag, a man appeared, picked it up, was secretly photographed, and set off northwards on foot, presumably towards the signal site at which he would make a mark to let us know that he had collected his money. On the way there the security service lost him, through being ultra-careful not to show themselves; but my driver, checking the site, found what looked like a poorly executed signal. As I knew for sure that the deadletter box had been emptied, I sent Moscow a message to this effect. A senior MI5 officer, meanwhile, suggested that the illegal's photograph should be exhibited on the television programme *Crimewatch*. He meant it as a joke, but it seemed to me a brilliant idea, and I was sorry that the service was too shy of publicity to go through with it.

Occasionally an illegal precipitated a minor crisis — as on a Sunday when I was acting head of station, and was also the duty diplomat in charge over the weekend. I was sitting comfortably in the Resident's office, formerly occupied by Guk, when there came a knock on the door, and in burst the operational driver, saying excitedly, 'The signal's there!' After checking a site for several days, he had seen a cross appear. Immediately I rang the cipher clerk, who had schemes of signals for every illegal. It turned out that the cross meant 'Need meeting urgently'. Another line in his entry gave the place for meetings (in Barnet) and the time, 1600.

Already it was 10.30 a.m. As I was on duty, I was not supposed to leave the Embassy, but when I rang the guard to see who else was around I found that there was no other KGB man who could sit in for me, even for a couple of hours. One clean diplomat who might have done it had just left for home. The situation looked desperate. There seemed only one thing to do. Asking the guard to hold the fort for a few minutes, I drove myself quickly to Holland Park and sought out the first secretary, Aleksei Nikiforov. I had no right to order him in: all I could do was beg for his help in a crisis. Luckily he was a nice man and agreed to stand in for me.[4]

Away we went to Barnet. As usual, the operational driver made a thorough job of his dry-cleaning, and we reached our destination with no problems. Having agreed with him that he would return to the rendezvous in half an hour, I walked the last five minutes of the route to the high street. The illegal was due to be standing outside a shop, looking into the window — and there he was: a young man, in his late twenties, strongly built, with short black hair. In a way he looked quite Russian, but he could equally have been a New Zealander or an Australian.

As I came up to him, I brought out the key phrase: 'Didn't I meet you on the *Majestic* in June '81?'

He smiled and said, 'Not June '81. It was August '82.' His English sounded excellent, but he said, 'Shall we speak English or Russian?'

'Oh, nonsense!' I exclaimed. 'Russian, of course.'

Then he said, 'I've finished the operation. Here's what I've got to send to the Centre. Please get it to them as soon as possible. I'm leaving the country soon.'

Part of the prearranged drill was that we should walk some way together, like friends chatting, so we headed out into some playing fields, which were good and open, with few people about, and no one close to us. But the young man was not at ease. Soon he said, 'Well, that's it,' and walked off, as if he barely trusted me.

Back at the Embassy, I thanked Nikiforov profusely for his help,

---

4   In 1994 he did an excellent job in Bosnia as Moscow's representative in the negotiations for a peace settlement.

delivered the package to the cipher clerk, and immediately sent the Centre a telegram. I told my English friends about the incident but we never identified the man, even though we returned to the case and studied it again after my escape. Almost certainly his operation was a documentary one: probably he had come to England to get a passport, but although we went through all the applications made during that period by applicants between the ages of twenty and thirty, we could not pinpoint him. Like the coelacanth, the prehistoric fish, the illegals normally swam at such a depth in the ocean that it was almost impossible to spot them from the surface.

*

For months Nikitenko clung to the hope that he might be officially appointed Resident, lobbying friends in the First Chief Directorate with subtle letters. But then in January 1985 I was summoned to Moscow for a high-level briefing, and this made it clear that I had been chosen as the best candidate to succeed Guk. I found Gribin the same as ever, friendly and resolute on my behalf. What was more, he appeared to have won the latest power struggle.

But then an unfortunate incident took place at the department's annual conference, at which I, among several others, was detailed to make a speech. Gribin told me it was important that I should make a good impression, so I worked hard at my address, and it turned out well, if slightly longer than it should have been; what upset things was that the chairman of the meeting, Pozdnyakov, introduced me as 'the Resident Designate in London, Comrade Gordievsky'. Gribin was furious, because this sort of premature announcement, before things had been properly decided, was exactly what he wanted to avoid. Immediately after the meeting the man who ran the personnel department stormed back to his office and rang Gribin, demanding to know who had appointed me, so that Gribin had to distance himself from Pozdnyakov's statement — typical KGB politics.

In spite of this setback, I went to see all the department heads concerned, including the head of Directorate S, Yuri Drozdov, a tall, lean general on whom Frederick Forsyth based his character Yevgeni Karpov in his novel *The Fourth Protocol*. He, also, offered me a job, saying that he would be pleased to see me back in my old Directorate; but he alarmed me by asking me to keep close track of Nicholas Barrington, a senior British diplomat, 'because we need to settle a score with him.' The KGB suspected Barrington of having helped Vladimir Kuzichkin to defect from Iran to Britain in 1982. When I reached London I warned my people, who took immediate precautions. Then I visited the cipher department, where I received some instruction in the use of codes and cipher equipment. Finally, in my last hour in the building, I happened to read a circular which said that a KGB officer, Lieutenant Colonel Vetrov, had been accused of spying for France, tried, sentenced to capital punishment and executed. The news sent a shiver down my spine — but at least I was soon able to pass it to the British, who told the French.

Back in London in early February, I found Nikitenko by no means reconciled to the news that I was about to leapfrog him. He had begun writing letters which aimed to undermine me, and had also started to withhold telegrams which I should have seen. Apart from that, all seemed well, and I continued to receive encouraging letters from Gribin.

Then, in the middle of March, his communications ceased. I did not know what to make of this. The work of the Residency carried on normally, and the silence from Moscow was only faintly ominous. On 24 April Nikitenko's replacement arrived, a sinister fellow called Korchagin, who should have run Abrivard. I took over formally from

Nikitenko on 28 April, and he finally left for Moscow on 2 May.

At last I was on my own, in full command of the Residency. Yet I sensed that things were not as they should be. First, no telegram had come from the Centre permitting me access to the cipher communication codes; and second, Nikitenko had left behind his official briefcase. On opening it, I found it contained nothing but one small brown envelope, in which there were two photocopies of the letters from Michael Bettaney. Why had he, normally such a careful man, left behind papers that no longer had any relevance? Was it because he did not trust me, and felt he could not leave anything that was still secret?

These puzzles gave me a feeling of unease but for a couple of weeks life proceeded normally. In spite of all my efforts to improve East—West understanding, a vast gulf remained unbridged — as witness an event that occurred at the end of April. The British decided to expel five GRU officers, two uniformed and three who had been working under civilian cover. The dismissals had nothing to do with me, but both the Ambassador and Nikitenko, thinking on the same traditional lines, sent identical telegrams to the Centre claiming that the expulsions had been deliberately timed as a special provocation to spoil Soviet celebrations of Victory Day, which would fall on 9 May, commemorating the fortieth anniversary of the end of the Second World War. When I told the British of this reaction, they were dumbfounded by the absurdity of such an idiotic accusation: nobody in London had given the anniversary a thought.

Then, on the afternoon of Thursday, 16 May, the thunderbolt struck. I was sitting at my desk in the Resident's office when the cipher clerk brought in a telegram. As I read the handwritten message, I felt sweat break out on my back, and for a second or two my vision clouded. Fighting to control myself, I was dreadfully afraid that the clerk must notice how badly shocked I was.

'In order to confirm your appointment as Resident,' said the cable, 'please come to Moscow urgently in two days' time for important discussions with Comrades Mikhailov and Alyoshin.' Instantly I sensed that something was badly wrong. Mikhailov was the pseudonym of Chebrikov, chairman of the KGB; Alyoshin was Kryuchkov, head of the First Chief Directorate. This was a summons from the highest possible level. And yet I had been through everything during my visit to Moscow in January. I had seen everyone I needed to see, and had been fully briefed. This new instruction made no sense.

I felt slightly better next morning when another telegram arrived saying, 'As to your Moscow trip, please remember that you will have to speak about Britain and British problems, so prepare well for specific discussions, with plenty of facts.' In retrospect, I am sure Moscow realized that their first telegram might have sounded alarming, and were trying to create a more solid impression with their second. This certainly sounded more genuine, and for a while I dared hope that everything was all right. But I also sensed that I might be in mortal danger, and I considered disappearing then and there, something about which I had often spoken with my British contacts.

My latest case officer, Stephen, seemed more impressed than puzzled by the telegrams. So did Joan. Both said they would be fascinated to learn Chebrikov's master plan for Britain. To me this was almost the final straw: were possible words of wisdom from Chebrikov more important than my life? I was longing to hear them say, 'Oleg, we don't like this. Why not just stay here and vanish, to start another life?' But they said nothing of the sort, and when I asked whether there were any signs, either from their own analysis or from other stations, that I might be in danger, their answers were reassuring. As far as they could tell, nothing had gone wrong. Only one man advised against my returning, and that was purely on intuitive grounds.

So I decided to obey the summons. But first I went through my modified escape plan yet again, and Joan showed me photographs of the forest rendezvous at which, in the last resort, I would be picked up. The only snag was that the pictures had been taken in April and October, when there were few leaves on the trees, and I might need to activate the plan in the middle of summer when the area would look quite different.

Once again, I could not share my problems with Leila. All I could say was that I had been summoned for top-level discussions, and when I caught the plane for Moscow, I went off fervently hoping this was true.

Chapter Fourteen – Sentence of Death

Flying over the Baltic, I had a wonderful view of Denmark, which lay basking in the sun, cradled in the arms of a blue, blue sea. Then suddenly I was in Moscow, and the difference was like that between day and night. Everything was grey and unpleasant, with people in uniforms all round, and long queues at the passport check. I found myself in the middle of a line, among a lot of foreigners. When I reached the hatch, there were only four or five people behind me, but the passport officer took such an age to deal with me that by the time he had finished, another flight had come in, and another immense queue had built up.

As a Soviet national, I should have passed straight through but the Borderguard officer, a simple-looking fellow, studied my passport for an inordinate length of time. Next he consulted some notes, repeatedly looking back and forth between them and my document. Then he made a telephone call. Watching him through the glass, I could practically see his mind working: he had discovered something wrong.

Later I found out that the passport officers had been told to inform the KGB the moment I crossed the border on to Soviet soil. In the arrival hall I was still on neutral, international territory, but at the control point I crossed the frontier into the Soviet Union. At that instant, I assume, an urgent telegram was sent to the Residency in London: what it said, I do not know, for the people in Britain were not aware of the plot to detain me.

Once through the checkpoint, I negotiated Customs without difficulty — but then something else unexpected happened. I had been told that Igor Titov, head of the British section, would be there to meet me, but there was no sign of him. Again, something seemed to have gone wrong. Outside, there was a shortage of taxis, but I saw that one driver who had already loaded two passengers was looking for a third. When he offered me his front seat, I took it. When I asked where he was going, he said, 'To the West German Embassy.' Here was yet another snag. In Moscow I was not supposed to consort with foreigners but I thought, What the hell! There was a chance that I would be noticed by the surveillance outside the Embassy, but I had to get home somehow, and it was worth the risk.

As we drove, I turned round, purely to be sociable, and said something in German to the couple in the back. They were not diplomats — only technical personnel — but immediately they were terrified. To have a stranger address them in German in the middle of Moscow — obviously they had been swept up into a KGB plot the moment they landed, and they sat there in silence, rigid with apprehension. I was thinking, What a reversal of roles! Normally it is *Homo sovieticus* who behaves like that in the presence of foreigners: now it's the other way round.

At my own flat, I sustained another shock, the worst yet. When I undid two locks as usual, and pushed the door, it would not move. Someone had turned the third lock as well, the lock for which I had long since lost the key. The discovery made me feel cold. No burglar would ever have done that: only someone with a set of skeleton keys... only the KGB.

Full of foreboding, I went down to the concierge, and from her desk rang Gribin, with whom I was supposed to make contact. During my two recent visits to Moscow he had been very sweet to me, but now he sounded cold. There was no warmth or enthusiasm in his voice. In a very off-hand way he just said, 'How are things?'

I launched into a litany of complaints. 'The first thing', I said, 'is that Igor never met me. I don't know why.'

'Oh, really?' said Gribin. 'That's strange. He was supposed to.

'The second thing is that I can't get into my flat…' Because I was so wound up, I went on for some time, and this irritated Gribin. He must have realized immediately that a silly mistake had been made by the people who carried out the secret search. He was irritated by everything — by me, by my flat, by the locks, by the people who had made the blunder, by the whole tedious difficulty which I, a suspected person, was causing him.

Presently I rang off and went in search of assistance from a family a few storeys higher: a young man whom I had helped to join the KGB, and his father-in-law, a former surveillance man, now retired but still active, doing plumbing and electrical repair jobs. He came down with some tools, but found he could not pick the third lock. 'I'll have to force the door,' he said. 'Then I'll patch it up as best I can.' He, too, thought it strange that the lock had been turned.

In the short time since I had landed, my mind had become schizo-phrenic. One part of it wanted to comfort me, saying, 'This is paranoia. Calm down. Things can't be that bad.' But the other part was working overtime: the long passport check, no Igor Titov, Gribin so cool, the third lock…This second voice told me to have a good hunt round. I went straight into the bedroom and looked under the bed where I kept two boxes of books that the KGB would regard as seditious — books on politics, art, which I had bought in Denmark. They were still there. Then I thought, No — stupid. If they did make a secret search, they wouldn't have taken the books anyway. What they were looking for was evidence of my collaboration with the British.

Presumably they had bugged the flat in my absence. I prowled the rooms looking for signs of microphones. In the lavatory I examined everything in the cupboard, and came on a little box of wet tissues which I had bought long ago in Denmark. Inside the lid was a covering of thick foil, and now, in the middle of it, there was a hole where someone had pushed a finger through. At once the suspicious half of my brain said, 'That proves it!' But the other half said, 'It could have been anyone. It could have been Leila, or some curious guest. The hole could have been there for years.'

It was difficult to settle down or sleep. My mind was whirling with the vital question: who had betrayed me? How much did the KGB know? What should I do?

On Monday morning I was due in the office. The man who drove me was Vladimir Chernov, expelled from Britain as a spy in the autumn of 1982, one of the nicest members of the London station. Since then he had become a personal aide of Viktor Grushko, now a deputy head of the First Chief Directorate. On the way in I said, 'Volodya, is everything all right? When I left for London at the beginning of February, the talk was all about me being appointed Resident. Now it's 21 May, and I still haven't heard anything.'

'It must be all right,' said Volodya stoutly. 'I was still taking papers about you to the Secretariat at the end of April. Everything was in progress then.'

At the department Gribin met me. He seemed nearly normal, but not quite. 'You'd better start preparing', he told me, 'because the two big bosses are going to summon you for a discussion.' He gave me some questions to think about; but instead of just saying, 'OK, be yourself. Talk naturally,' he launched into a complicated explanation of how I should conduct myself in the presence of Chebrikov and Kryuchkov. He pointed out that they represented the summit, the royal court, of the Soviet Empire, and warned me of their personal preferences and special tricks. Later, I realized that he was acting out a charade, which accounted for his slightly odd manner.

Again I said how surprised I was about the lock on the door of my flat, but again he did not want to talk about it so I stopped. Next Titov started to apologize for failing to meet me: he claimed that there had been a misunderstanding, and that he had been looking for me in the other wing of the terminal. Then I was summoned to Grushko's office. I felt as if I was going into an audience with a monarch, and found him a different man from the one I had known in January: cool, hard and relentlessly inquisitive. 'What about Michael Bettaney?' he asked. 'It looks as though he was a real man, after all, and seriously wanted to co-operate with us. That means he could have become a second Philby.'

Wanting to rub salt into the KGB's wounds, I said, 'Of course he was real. And he would have been far, far better than Philby, from our point of view.'

'How's that?'

'Because Philby was working for us mainly at a time when we and Britain were allies, during the Second World War and up to the time of the Cold War, so that he was not all that important. Bettaney would have been an agent in the era of confrontation, when we are in a state of cold war with the West. He would have been *much* more valuable.'

'But how did we make such a mistake? Was he genuine from the start?'

'I thought so. I can't imagine why Comrade Guk didn't agree.'

Grushko thought for a moment, then said, 'Guk was expelled. But he hadn't done anything about Bettaney. He hadn't even made contact. So why did they sack him?'

I could not be sure what Grushko was hinting at. Did he think that the British had expelled Guk to make way for me? I merely said, 'That's right. He never contacted Bettaney. I think his mistake was to behave too much like a KGB man. You know what a big, pompous fellow he looks — always driving around in his expensive Mercedes, boasting about the KGB, playing the general. The Brits didn't like that.'

Grushko gave me a sceptical look, but said no more about it. Yet the atmosphere remained febrile. Later, a scene developed in front of my eyes when he met Titov in the corridor and tore into him for making such a blunder at the airport. Part of my brain was saying, 'There's something unnatural about this. Why is Grushko making such a fuss and humiliating Titov in my presence?' Either he was supposed to have met me and had made a mistake — the most natural explanation, for if Titov had been there, I should have felt more relaxed, which was what they wanted — or the KGB had deliberately not met me, so that they could see where I went if I left the airport on my own.

It was not long before another small but sinister event occurred. On Tuesday morning the diplomatic bag arrived from London: it should have been closed on Friday evening, while I was still in charge of the Residency, and sent off on Monday morning. Normally the cipher clerks were sticklers for protocol, and did everything precisely by the book. Yet this bag now contained a box bearing a peculiar inscription — 'For Mr Grushko's eyes only' — which had not been there on Friday.

It should never have come into my hands but somehow it did:

another blunder. I felt it, shook it, tried to judge its weight. The sober part of my brain told me clearly, 'Oleg, this box contains your personal papers, the contents of your satchel, which you left in London.' Probably the Centre had sent London a telegram on Sunday, while there was still time to reopen the bag. But in Moscow, because the clerks were so inexperienced, they brought me the package and asked me how to register it so that eventually it was I who delivered it to Grushko's secretariat.

Apart from all these errors, practically nothing was happening. For day after day I fiddled with the notes I had brought with me about Britain's economy, her position in the world, her relations with America, her achievements in science and technology, all the time awaiting the summons from on high. On the evening of Thursday, my fourth blank day in the office, Gribin offered me a lift into central Moscow. 'What if a summons comes, and I've gone?' I asked. 'Oh no,' he replied. 'There's no chance of them sending for you tonight.'

It was an unpleasant evening. A heavy drizzle set in, and the traffic was bad. In the car I continued to express disappointment. I pointed out that in London important work was going undone, and that, if there was nothing to detain me in Moscow, I would rather go back and deal with it. There was plenty to get on with: the parliamentary year was ending, an important NATO meeting was imminent, people running contacts needed guidance, and so on. Gribin remained offhand, saying, 'Oh, nonsense! People are often away for months at a time. Nobody's indispensable.' Yet still I sensed something wrong. His remarks struck a false note.

Next morning Gribin put out a sustained effort to make me spend the weekend with him and his wife. Clearly he had instructions to keep me under control, if possible under his eye, and he spent half an hour trying to persuade me to join him at some dacha. But so far I had had no chance of seeing my mother and sister, and I insisted that I wanted to remain in Moscow, so that I could meet them. In the end he gave up, and on Saturday they both came to my flat, where we had a good chat about life in England, sitting round our marble-topped coffee table. I told them how the girls now spoke English as their first language, and how Maria had learned to recite the Lord's Prayer in English.

Monday brought matters to crisis-point. Luckily I had with me some pep-pills which the British had given me in London, and one of these, taken every morning, helped fight fatigue. Without it, I might easily not have survived.

I was sitting in the office when a call came through on the telephone without a dial which went only to the department head. It was Grushko himself. 'Can you please come over?' he said.

'At last!' I replied. 'Is it one of the bosses?'

'Not yet.'

'What is it, then?'

'There are two people who want to talk to you about high-level agent penetration of Britain.'

He said we would meet these men not in his office but somewhere outside the building. That seemed strange, as well — but there was no refusing the order. Thinking that I was just off for a chat, I left my keys and briefcase on my desk and went to meet Grushko.

Together we went down to the lobby and out through the revolving doors. Soon a car appeared, but instead of heading for the front gates of the compound, which gave on to the Moscow orbital road, the driver went out the back and proceeded less than two kilometres to a compound of comfortable cottages designed mainly for foreign guests of the First Chief Directorate. We did not enter the compound but drew up at a single bungalow outside it, a house surrounded by a low fence, but otherwise unprotected.

It was a hot, sticky day, with the oppressive feeling that thunderstorms might build up. Grushko said, 'We're early — let's walk around.' So we strolled up and down, with him asking apparently frivolous questions about my parents and their background. At the time I could not see what he was driving at, and only later did it dawn on me that he had been trying to dig up some Jewish elements in my family. A virulent anti-Semite, Grushko was thinking, If Gordievsky's a traitor, there must be something Jewish in his ancestry.

After a while we went into the little house, which was pleasantly cool inside. It was well equipped with furniture made of light-coloured wood — ash or pine. It had one long, central room, and smaller bedrooms leading off it, all with fairly low ceilings, but everything looked bare, with no curtains or pictures on the pale walls. It looked as though it had never been lived in. There were two servants: a man in his fifties, very deferential but clearly KGB, who must have had some other job besides that of lackey, and a good-looking woman in her early thirties. Grushko said we would have our talk over a sandwich, and then proposed a drink. As it was only a few days since Gorbachev had brought in restrictions on the sale and consumption of alcohol, I said, 'Are you sure that's all right?'

'Oh, yes,' said Grushko airily. 'Look, I've got some Armenian brandy.'

The servants brought out plates of sandwiches, and we each drank one small tot of brandy, which was good. (Armenians are proud of their spirits and, to this day, claim that Sir Winston Churchill drank only Armenian brandy.)

Then two men arrived. They were obviously KGB, but I had never seen either before, and I thought, How odd, they're supposed to be from my Directorate. But they looked more like counter-intelligence officers. The senior man, in a dark suit, must have been in his late fifties but looked older, with a lined face and the grey appearance that results from excessive smoking and drinking. His colleague, in a lighter suit, was perhaps ten years younger, tall, sinister and unsmiling, with a long face and rather prominent features. Grushko did not introduce them, except to say, 'Oh, Oleg, these are the people who want to talk about agent-penetration in Britain. Let's have lunch first, and then we can get down to it.'

It was all rather clumsily done, not nearly as smooth or subtle as it would have been in Britain. Grushko seemed excessively animated — no doubt because he was not used to taking part in a typically Chekist counter-intelligence operation.[1]

He began to play the role of a good host. 'Let's all have a drink together,' he said, and the servant poured brandies all round. Later, struggling to work out what had happened, I seemed to remember that the other three were served out of the first bottle, from which my initial tot had come. Then the servant had appeared with another bottle, indicating that the first one had run out.

In any case, I drank the tot straight down — and in a matter of seconds I was a different man. It was almost the same as when I had the anaesthetic for my nose operation in Denmark in 1978: there was no physical sensation, but instead of passing out, I was suddenly transformed into someone else.

---

1 The older man, I discovered later, was General Golubev, who had been promoted after claiming to recruit an agent in Egypt — even though, under Nasser, agents were two a penny. He became head of the Fifth Department of Directorate K, which investigates all abnormal developments, and later was promoted to be a deputy head of the Directorate, gaining the rank of General. His colleague, Colonel Budanov, succeeded him as head of the Fifth Department. Both, in other words, were highly trained investigators.

The next thing I knew for sure I woke up in bed in the room across the corridor, wearing only vest and underpants, unable to remember anything since drinking the brandy. It was early morning — the next morning. The bed was clean, the room fresh, but I felt sick, with a severe headache. I got up slowly, dressed, and went in search of the servant, asking for coffee. 'Certainly, certainly,' he said, and brought cup after cup, but the caffeine seemed to have no effect. I felt more depressed than ever before in my life. I kept thinking, '*They know*. I'm finished.' How they had found out, I could not tell. But there was not the slightest doubt that they knew I was a British agent.

Eventually the same two men reappeared, and their attitude was thoroughly ambivalent. They did not want to give away too much about the interrogation but on the other hand they did not try to conceal that an interrogation had taken place. For a while they watched me in silence. Then the younger one said that one of my remarks had upset him.

'Oh,' I said. 'What was that?'

'You accused us of reviving the spirit of 1937, the Great Terror.'

'Really!'

'Yes!' This came out aggressively, and the man went on in the same tone, 'Just remember one thing, Comrade Gordievsky, what you said wasn't true, and I'll prove it.'

Ambiguous as it was, that one remark gave me hope. I began to hope that things were not as bad as I had feared: perhaps I had panicked because I was a British agent. I told myself to keep calm and wait to see what developed. I felt too confused and embarrassed to ask what had happened to me. Had I been sick, or collapsed? Who had put me to bed?

'Another thing about you, Comrade Gordievsky,' said Golubev. 'You're a very self-confident man.'

'You think so?'

'Yes, you're over-confident.'

'You're implying I've been rude to you. If I have, I apologize. I don't remember. But it's the first time in my life anyone's told me I'm over-confident.' Then I asked, 'Anyway, what are we waiting for?'

One of them said, 'A man's coming to take you home.' For a few minutes we sat awkwardly, waiting. Then the younger man asked, 'Have you been around Britain much?'

'Not much, really,' I said. 'There's so much work at the Residency. Not much time to travel. There are only four places I've been — Blackpool, Brighton, Bournemouth and Harrogate.'

'Harrogate?' said the man sharply. 'Where's that?'[2]

'In Yorkshire. Some way north of London, near York. It's quite a nice town, and used a good deal for political conferences because they've built a very good new congress hall there.'

Eventually a strange man appeared wearing a dark suit, almost black, with a car and driver, and he took me back and dropped me outside my apartment block. There I was, unshaven, shaky and dishevelled, standing on the pavement at 11 a.m., a lovely summer morning. Once again, I could not get into my flat without help because I had left my keys on my desk. I had to go up to the family who had helped me before and borrow my spare set from them. Inside, I collapsed on the bed and tried to think. As the day wore on, my anguish and tension mounted until I was in a state of near panic. During the afternoon I felt an imperative need to speak to someone, and telephoned Grushko. It was a desperate move, but I needed to hear some word of comfort from him. At least he had been a member of my own department, and in political

---

2 It was this one question that later enabled the British services to identify Budanov.

intelligence, whereas the other two men were from somewhere else. I said, 'I'm sorry if I was rude to those fellows but they were very strange.'

'No, no,' he said, 'they're excellent chaps. There's nothing wrong with them.'

Grushko's unsympathetic attitude deepened my anxiety. I absolutely had to speak to somebody else. The only person I could think of was Katya, Leila's sister-in-law, an intelligent and analytical woman. I rang her, said I had a problem, and asked her to come round — so she did. She pressed a pair of trousers for me while we talked.

I felt a compulsion to run through what had happened. I said I had drunk a couple of glasses of brandy at lunch-time, and had collapsed. Katya did her best to comfort me, but when she had gone I realized that terror and panic were getting the better of me, and preventing me analysing events.

I rang Gribin and said, 'Something extraordinary has happened, and I'm very worried.'

'OK,' he said cheerfully. 'I'll come over with Irina, and we can go for a walk.' Gribin, still acting, as I worked out later, seemed nearly his old self, and Irina played her part even better. 'Don't worry, old chap,' said Gribin, after I had given him an outline of events. 'I'm sure it's nothing important. Let's talk about something more amusing. Tell me about your children, that story about Anna calling to you.'

I was glad of the diversion, and recounted the story of how little Anna, aged four, had looked up from the courtyard below, seen me in the window of our London flat, and shouted, 'Daddy, I love you!' The Gribins made much of the anecdote — but afterwards I felt sickened by their hypocrisy. Knowing that I was doomed to die, they deliberately brought up one of the tenderest episodes of my entire life, and exploited it to put me off my guard.

Next day in the office I recovered my keys. Titov — obviously still in the dark about my interrogation — made a great fuss about having found them, together with my briefcase, and not knowing what to do. Then the special telephone rang again, and Grushko asked me to go and see him.

I found him in his beautiful big office, sitting at a large table made up in the form of a T, with several chairs round it, as if for a conference. On one side of him sat Gribin, yesterday's friend, now looking glum; on the other was the No. 1 interrogator, General Golubev, whose name Gruskho had accidentally revealed while talking to me on the telephone the day before. Like a schoolboy, I stood at one side of the stalk of the table, in front of them.

Gribin did not utter a word, but Grushko began, 'Yesterday I spent the whole evening talking to Vladimir Aleksandrovich [Kryuchkov] about you. We know very well that you've been deceiving us for years. If only you knew what an unusual source we heard about you from! And yet we've decided that you may stay in the KGB. Your job in London is terminated, of course. There's no question of your remaining there. Your family will be brought back during the next few days. You'll have to move to a non-operational department. For the moment, you'd better take the holiday that's due to you, and after that we'll decide where to put you. Meanwhile, that anti-Soviet *maculatura* [mass of papers] which you keep at home — that you will deliver to the library of the First Chief Directorate. And remember, in the next few days, and for ever, *no telephone calls to London.*'

As these hammer-blows hit home, I began to feel sick with fear. But my only possible course seemed to be to feign innocence. 'I'm terribly sorry about what happened on Monday,' I said. 'I think there was something wrong with the drink or, more likely, with the food. I was in a very bad way. I felt awful.'

Suddenly Golubev seemed to wake up, and he said loudly, 'What nonsense! There was nothing whatever wrong with the food. It was delicious. We had very good cheese sandwiches. The ones with red salmon roe were excellent, and so were the ones with ham.'

In dire trouble though I was, I stood there thinking, What an incredible, surrealist experience! Here they are, more or less pronouncing on my life and death, and yet he's defending his bloody sandwiches.

'OK, OK,' I said. 'But obviously *something* was wrong. As to what you're saying about my deceiving you for a long time, Viktor Fyodorovich, I really don't know what you're talking about. But whatever your decision, I'll accept it like an officer and a gentleman.'

That seemed a pompous quotation, but in the heat of the moment it was all I could think of — and it had an electrifying effect on Grushko, who leapt from his chair, hurried round the table and shook my hand, suddenly looking far happier. I do not know what he had expected — perhaps that I would go to the General Secretary of the Communist Party and complain that some KGB officers had given me drugged brandy. Perhaps he had feared that I would make an hysterical scene in his office, which would have been embarrassing for everyone. But in any case he seemed immensely relieved.

As for me — I was anything but happy. I was thinking, This is total nonsense. How can I remain in the KGB if they know I have been working for a foreign country? Hundreds of men had been sacked from the KGB for the pettiest of crimes — losing an unimportant document, embezzling a small amount of money, or (like Lyubimov) becoming involved in scandals with women. How can they pretend that they will keep me on? Obviously they had some deeper long-term design.

I thought, The less I say, the better. The only thing to do is to use my holiday allowance, as they suggest. So I went back to my room, on one level devastated and on the other thinking, All the waiting and anticipation are over. They know what I've done. But for some reason they've decided to play with me, like a cat with a mouse. All I can do is get out and go home.

Before I could quit, the telephone rang: Gribin, from two doors along the passage. He called me in and said, '*Oformlai*', get your paperwork done for the holiday. That was all. Then he came in to say goodbye; with the need to act removed, he was cool and matter-of-fact. 'What can I say to you, old chap?' he began. Still wanting to fight my way out, I said, 'Kolya, I don't know exactly what this is all about, but I suspect that I've been overheard saying something critical about the Party leaders, and that now there's a big intrigue going on.'

'If only it was that,' he said, gazing at me. 'If only it was a question of some indiscretion recorded by the microphones. But I'm afraid it's far, far worse than that.'

I made a face to suggest that I had no idea what he was talking about, and muttered, 'What can I say?'

Gribin indicated that the meeting was over. 'Try to take it all philosophically,' he said — and with that I left, never to see him again.

Later, in Britain, my dearest wish was, of course, to dial his number and say, 'Kolya — do you remember? You told me to try to take it philosophically. Well — I did!' But I never rang him. He was immensely career-oriented and mendacious, like most Soviet men: he had furthered his career by petty bribery, by flattery, and by entertaining the bosses with his guitar and easy romances. That was his way. But also he was the most innocent of my colleagues in the KGB — and in the aftermath of my escape he was the only one to be demoted. Others should have been held responsible for my escape, but either they were outside the central apparatus of the KGB at the critical moment, or they were protected by their networks of personal connections. Oleg Kalugin, former head of counter-intelligence, was in exile in Leningrad. Gennady Titov and Viktor Grushko had made themselves such sycophants of Kryuchkov that he could not punish them for if he had done so, it would have implied that he himself was ultimately responsible, which he was.

So I left. But as I prepared to go on holiday, I was haunted day and night by memories of the interrogation. Clearly I was supposed to remember nothing, but, perhaps because of the pep-pill I had taken in the morning, one by one parts of it began to come back, and the burning question — which I could not answer — was: how much had I given away? Had I compromised myself entirely? Or had I managed to hold out?

It was as if flashes of light briefly lit up individual scenes. For instance, there had been a session about my books. 'Why do you have all those anti-Soviet volumes — Solzhenitsyn, Orwell, Maximov, and the rest?'

'But, of course,' I had said, 'as a PR Line officer I was supposed to read books like that. I needed to. They gave me essential background.'

Clearly the interrogators were trying to build a case against me. 'No,' they insisted. 'You deliberately deceived the authorities. You used your diplomatic status to import things you knew were illegal in this country. The number of books shows the extent to which you broke the law.'

Presently Grushko reappeared, walking round the table and again acting the host. 'Well done, Oleg!' he said heartily. 'You're having an excellent conversation. Carry on! Do please tell them everything. Educate them properly.' He went on like that for a while, then suddenly seemed to lose patience, and went out, leaving his henchmen to carry on.

As the argument ground on, the sound corner of my brain was saying, 'So they *did* make a secret search, after all.' Another give-away moment came when one of them asked unpleasantly, 'How can you be proud of your daughter Maria being able to say the Lord's Prayer? How can you, a Communist, speak like that about something connected with religion?' Again, the sound corner of my brain said, 'Microphones!' The only people to whom I had made that remark were my mother and my sister, and I had said it in the sitting room of my flat. That proved beyond all doubt that, in my absence, the apartment had been bugged.

It was clear that at intervals my brain, or part of it, had been making perfect sense, and had been able to draw these conclusions.

Then they began to say nastily, 'What about Spotty? What about Toad?' They were using the unflattering code-names which every KGB defector is assigned in the files. 'What about Rascal? What about Scruff?'

'I don't know what you're talking about,' I said, and I continued to profess ignorance until they were forced to name one traitor openly — Lieutenant Colonel Vladimir Vetrov, who had co-operated with the French intelligence and had been executed in 1984. They asked me what I thought of such people, watching my reaction and waiting to see what I said. Then suddenly the search came nearer home, and they started to talk about my own past.

'Ah yes, but we know who recruited you in Copenhagen,' said Golubev, chain-smoking as always. 'It was Dick Balfour.' 'Nonsense!' I said. 'That's not true.'

'But you wrote a report about him.'

'Of course. I met him once. Yakushkin told me to. And I wrote a report of the meeting. But he never focused on me particularly. He used to talk to everybody — and Lipasov especially.' Out of the mists the name came to my assistance.

'Lipasov!' said one of them. 'Why didn't *he* write reports, then?'

'Ask him,' I said. 'I've no idea. But he must have.'

Dimly I heard one of them keep repeating, 'Remember one thing. We've got irrefutable evidence of your guilt. We know you were a British agent. You'd better confess. *Priznaysya!* Confess!'

Then there was a pause. I remember Budanov sitting near me, while Golubev went out and then reappeared. His movements all seemed abrupt, but probably I was half asleep.

'*Priznaysya!*' he repeated hypnotically. 'Confess! You confessed very well a few minutes ago. Now please go through it again, and confirm what you said. Confess again!'

They were talking slowly and emphatically, as if to a child who forgets what he heard five minutes ago. I kept saying, 'No, I've nothing to confess. I've done nothing.' And so it went on.

Reconstructing events, I guessed that the interrogation lasted five hours, from 1.30 p.m. until nearly seven. At one stage I went to the bathroom, and I may have been sick. As I went, I saw the two servants staring at me in the most unpleasant way, the man especially. Later, I heard indirectly that I made several visits to the bathroom, and drank large quantities of water: the interrogators concluded that I had been trained by the British in techniques of combating drugs, and was trying to clear the poison out of my system.[3] In fact I just had a great thirst. On the other hand, it may well have been the single British pep-pill which I had taken that morning which helped me to hold out as well as I did. That was about all I could remember — and

---

3   This detail came from Vitali Yurchenko, who defected eight days after I had escaped.

still the key question went unanswered: had I or had I not given myself away irrevocably? For the moment I could not tell what the KGB had or had not found out; but it was clear that I was, in effect, under sentence of death, even if that sentence was suspended pending further investigations.

Every contact I had with officials deepened my sense of impending doom. My own doctor, a woman I knew quite well, looked worried when she gave me a check-up. 'What's wrong with you?' she demanded. 'Your heartbeat's irregular. You're frightened. What are you so scared of?' Whenever I met Boris Bocharov, who was in charge of the illegals in Britain, he kept asking, 'What went wrong?' Then one day he said, 'Now I *know* what happened. Your deputy defected.' I said, 'What nonsense! Nobody's defected. I can vouch for it.'

In the personnel department I had always got on well with the three women who worked in the secretariat, bringing them little presents whenever I came back from abroad. Now, when I told them I would not be returning to England, I saw in their faces that they knew something bad about me. Then, as I surrendered my diplomatic passport in the Ministry of Foreign Affairs, I found the same man who had done the paperwork to despatch me to England three years earlier. 'Are you sure you don't want to keep the passport?' he asked. 'If you give it up, do you realize I'll have to cross you off the list of the *nomenklatura*?' As I watched, he opened a big ledger and crossed out my name, so ending my life on the lowest rung of the Soviet élite.

Another distressing scene took place in my flat, when Aleksandr Fedotov, a radio-intercept specialist whom Guk had sacked from London, came to pay me a visit. Aware as ever of the listening microphones, I told him that I seemed to be the victim of a tremendous intrigue, that I had lost my job and my posting and, like him, would never return to London. As he was leaving, he expressed his warm sympathy, and said loudly, 'Oleg Antonovich, what can you expect in this dreadful totalitarian society?' I looked at him with agony in my eyes, unable to speak for fear of compromising myself still further. The listeners must have been on the alert: after my escape he was the one man dismissed from the KGB.

A few days later Leila and the children arrived back in Moscow. They had been made to leave London so suddenly that she had not even had time to buy the girls holiday clothes but, in spite of the haste, she reached Moscow in high spirits, and when I met them at the airport was full of enthusiasm about the special treatment they had received. In London an official of Aeroflot had met them and escorted them all the way to the aircraft, where they had first-class seats. When they landed, another Aeroflot man had escorted them off. Knowing that all this had been laid on by the KGB, my heart sank — and it was a bitter blow for me, in the car, to tell Leila what a disaster had befallen us.

'I'm afraid I'm in big trouble,' I began. 'We can't go back.'

'What d'you mean?'

'We can't ever go back to England.'

'Why on earth not?'

I pretended that my troubles were caused by KGB intrigues, which were worse than ever now that I was rising towards the apex of the command pyramid. At first Leila could scarcely comprehend our change of fortune, so suddenly had it hit her; but as she recovered from her initial shock she translated her immediate anxieties into worries about me, because she could see that I was depressed enough to be physically ill.

When she spoke about it to my mother, Mama, with her practical outlook, said, 'All right, let's get him interested in his car. Make him prepare it for its annual test.' So I spent some time at the garage in which the car was kept because without passing its test it was not allowed on the road; but the truth was that I hated all things mechanical, and did it only to fill in time and think about my predicament. Meanwhile, my stock of allegedly seditious books had been confiscated, and I had had to sign a list as they were being taken away. I knew my signature meant that even if the KGB managed to prove nothing else they could still give me a couple of years in gaol, for having the books.

In the flat it was almost unbearable to hear the girls talking English to each other, and saying, 'I don't like it here. Let's go back to London.' I tried to keep morale up by saying loudly for the benefit of the listening microphones, 'I shall complain to Mr Aliyev [like Leila, an Azeri, a leading member of the Politburo]. Let's write him a letter, because it's an outrage to treat a KGB colonel like this.'

Yet real life had to go on. Leila made plans to take the children for a long summer holiday in Azerbaijan, staying with relations of her father at a place on the Caspian where the girls would be able to swim. As for me, I was battling day and night with the problem of what I should do. Should I activate my escape plan before it was too late? I could only presume that the KGB were searching for further evidence which would seal my fate — and yet there was a chance that they might not find anything. With my wife and children around me, it was impossible to take such a harsh decision. My heart was aching so much that I could hardly bear to think about it. But slowly the conviction grew that my only real option was to flee the country.

Racked by uncertainty, I appealed to Gribin to give me a ticket for a holiday in some sanatorium and, after consultation with his bosses, he decided to send me to Semyonovskoye, a well-known KGB establishment

100 kilometres due south of Moscow. The statutory length of a stay in such a place was twenty-four days, and the KGB knew that, for that time, I would be effectively under control, although not physically restrained.

So, on 15 June, I set off by electric commuter train for Semyonovskoye, leaving the family in the flat, but planning to return and see them before they departed for the far south. I was not escorted — the KGB were pretending that they were not too worried about me — but almost certainly I was under surveillance. Arriving in the evening, I found the sanatorium attractively set in wooded hills, with a stream running through the grounds. I checked in with the duty doctor, who was expecting me, and told me I had been allocated a bed in a double room on the first floor, with a balcony facing the river.

The only disagreeable feature of the place was that an immensely deep nuclear shelter was being built almost in the grounds and construction work went on, with lights blazing, all through the night. I discovered that the shelter was a Category A model, designed for top-rank KGB officers and connected by underground tunnels both to the generals' block (part of the sanatorium) and to a luxurious dacha, once owned by Stalin but now used by KGB leaders.

Throughout my stay I was furnished with a room-mate, clearly put there to keep an eye on me. The first was a pensioner in his mid-sixties, very active and orthodox in his ideas, who for the first couple of days tried to follow me everywhere before he tired of this restless occupation. Probably he put in a bad report on me for sitting on the balcony and listening through headphones to foreign stations on my short-wave radio — but by that stage I was past caring. Little did he know that the BBC's World Service programme *Outlook* nearly made me cry with nostalgia: the good old English tunes they played represented a world I might never see again.

For the second half of my stay the pensioner was replaced by a lieutenant colonel of the Borderguard Troops: a typical Soviet officer whose aim in coming to the sanatorium was to drink and pick up a woman — in both of which he succeeded. In some ways he was an attractive character, and talked openly about his problems; he also told me a good deal about borders and frontier defences, a subject in which I had a rapidly growing interest. Although totally hidebound in some areas — believing, for instance, that Britain was crippled by shortages of material goods, and that life there was as bad a struggle as in Russia — he also had a streak of scepticism when it came to his own area of expertise.

He said he found it hard to believe Soviet propaganda's claims that spies and infiltrators were constantly trying to violate the country's borders and penetrate the frontiers from outside. 'That's obviously not true,' he said. 'All the border defences must be against something else. What do you reckon it is?' I said, 'Well, I think you're right. It's all to stop Soviet people trying to flee to the West.'

This relaxed minder spent much of his time with the woman he had picked up, and she, too, was an interesting character. She worked in the watching department of the KGB in Novosibirsk, spying on people through peepholes and hidden television cameras. When I asked if that wasn't rather amusing, she replied, 'Not at all. I spend my life watching wild, raw sex and violence — drunks beating up their mistresses, and so on. It's all incredibly depressing.'

Another of the residents was Leonid Makarov, who had arrived at the Residency in Copenhagen towards the end of my first tour there, and now held a senior position in the Ukrainian KGB. When he met me in the corridor, not having seen me for years, he did not appear in the least surprised or ask what I was doing. I felt sure that he had dropped into my Department in Moscow recently, and knew all about me. Yet he did show curiosity when he found that I had borrowed a book about the nineteenth-century Russo-Turkish wars from the library. 'For goodness' sake,' he said, 'what is there of interest in that old campaign?' I told him that one did not get a chance to study the Russo-Turkish wars every day — but it was a lucky encounter because it occurred to me that if I escaped from the Soviet Union, he would probably tell the department that he had caught me studying maps of Transcaucasia and the Turkish border. In fact I was privily studying maps of the border area between the Soviet Union and Finland, standing between the banks of bookshelves where no one could see me.

Outside, the weather remained perfect — warm without being too hot, sunny and dry. I swam in the river, and enjoyed jogging through the woods, where several times I spotted surveillance men hastily pretending to urinate into the undergrowth as I appeared; twice I walked the ten kilometres to the railway station, partly to increase my fitness, in case I had to make a long trek during my escape. On one glorious day the family came down to see me, and I found it incredibly poignant, not knowing when I should see the girls again. Their characters were developing clearly. Maria, or Masha, was active, bright, quick-moving, good at sports and interested in everything; Anna (who later slimmed down to become a good runner) was a bit plump, and inclined to be moody, but already devoted to animals and fascinated by insects. As I put them on the train to return to Moscow, we had only a few seconds, so I hopped on board and kissed them, just before the automatic doors closed.

By then my resolve was hardening, and soon after the family had gone, I took the decision to prepare for my escape. 'There's no alternative,'

I told myself. 'If I don't get out, I'm going to die. I'm as good as a dead man on holiday.'

So it was that I returned once more to Moscow, and began the sequence of moves described in Chapter One.

Chapter Fifteen – Free Agent

Awkwardly I scrambled out of the car and lurched to my feet, soaked in sweat, my trousers hanging down. All round stood the glorious, soaring, clean pines of a Finnish forest; close at hand I saw a ring of friendly, smiling faces, among them that of Stephen, my latest case officer from England, lit up with excitement. Nobody looked more triumphant than Joan, for the exfiltration plan had been hers alone, and it had worked like magic. It may sound as if bundling me into the boot of a car was a simple operation, but it had been preceded by an enormous, sustained effort. The British had watched the signal sites in Moscow for seven years: even when I was abroad, they had watched them once a week, and then, when I was back in the Soviet capital, every day.

Yet now the jubilation was shot through with anxiety about the circumstances of my betrayal. When Joan took me aside and asked urgently, 'What happened?', all I could answer was that I did not know. 'Obviously some information got into their hands — but how, I've no idea. You can see what trouble I was in — I've had to leave the family behind.'

For a few minutes I was borne up by the elation of success. The whole KGB had been after me, and yet we had outsmarted them.

What a victory for me, and for the British! I kept thinking, I'm safe! Not only that. Also safe was the huge store of knowledge accumulated in my head: now I could give it to the British government, and they, if they wished, could pass it on to the Americans. Looking at the happy, smiling, normal people round me, I again felt the tremendous contrast with the callousness and dirt and untidiness which had prevailed beyond the border. The faces round me were open and friendly and alive. I felt ashamed to think that in the KGB there were no such faces, only snouts, full of evil and vice and unpleasantness and hatred. I kept thinking of the book by Yevgeni Zamyatin, *Litsa i Khari*, 'Snouts and Faces'. Russians once had perfectly normal, nice faces, visible in pre-revolutionary photographs, but Communism had turned them into snouts, ugly mugs twisted by brutality and intrigue, which betrayed their owners' mental and physical degradation.

This was no time for lingering over philosophical reflections. Friendly Danes had brought me new clothes — trousers, a shirt and a sweater. None of them fitted but they were better than nothing. The rescue cars went on their way to Helsinki, and the rest of us piled into two Volvos for a marathon drive to the Norwegian border in the far north-west.

That trip took thirty hours, with only a few short pit-stops. The cars had food and drink on board, and, with the drivers taking turns — Joan and Jack alternating with two Danes — we just kept going. Every time we stopped to stretch our legs, the mosquitoes were hellish. On the way I learnt that when I sent out my emergency appeal for help most of my British friends had been on holiday but that they had been called in and had come at once to Finland. I also learnt that, against this very moment, the British had gone to the length of rehearsing the entire drive, not once but twice, so that they could judge conditions and timings in snow and ice as well as in summer.

Now in mid-summer we sped north along beautifully engineered roads, twisting and turning round huge lakes through a world of amazing greenness, on which darkness never fell. As we crossed the Arctic Circle into Lapland the forest gradually died out and gave way to meadows full of wild flowers. With my knowledge of the KGB and its vindictiveness, I became haunted by a vision of Chebrikov somehow organizing a blockade on the Finnish—Norwegian border: all cars, I felt certain, would be stopped and searched, Needless to say, when we reached the frontier, the road lay wide open: the guards were standing with their backs to it, and did not even turn round as we passed; but my apprehension must have affected the officers escorting me because, when we all got out and shook hands on Norwegian soil, I noticed that their palms were wet.

At Tromso we were met by a British officer and booked into a hotel. By then, with the immediate excitement worn off, stress and exhaustion were almost overcoming me, and I felt too ill to eat anything in the wonderful seafood restaurant where we had dinner. Even to dress in semi-respectable clothes seemed an immense effort, and I had to ask poor Joan, who was also dog-tired after our night on the road, to take up the bottoms of my new trousers, so that I did not look entirely ridiculous. In the morning I felt so bad that I suggested to Stephen that I should go into a nursing home for a couple of days to receive proper medical attention. His reaction was merely a nod: to him, all foreigners were hypochondriacs and he sensibly took no notice of my plea.

Next day we caught a local plane to Oslo. There a Norwegian officer led us through back corridors at the airport to put us on a British Airways flight for London. At Heathrow, Special Branch officers slipped us off the aircraft, avoided Customs, and took us straight to the car park of a hotel, where a high-powered reception committee had gathered to greet me. Among them was the head of British intelligence's Soviet section; another was one of the directors of the security service, John Deverell, a man of exceptional intelligence and charm, who became a staunch friend and ally.[1] Everyone was euphoric at scoring such a victory over the KGB: champagne flowed, and the atmosphere was one of celebration.

After a while my helpers drove me to the Midlands where a landowner had put his large country home at our disposal. It was a lovely old house, equipped with every comfort and full of servants, standing in splendid grounds; but I found I could not enjoy it. With the tension and excitement gone, reaction set in: I felt utterly worn out and wanted a room of my own and privacy — a place where I could read and be quiet and recover. Instead of that, the house was full of bustle, of people coming and going, and I could not concentrate on the one thought in my head, which was to find some means of making contact with my family and telling them what had happened.

On my second day in the country, Christopher Curwen, alias 'C', the head of MI6, arrived by helicopter. Obviously a man of high intelligence, he took up my point and worked at it like a terrier with a bone. How could we send a message to Leila, who was still in the far south of Russia? KGB surveillance men would probably be sitting on the staircase outside my own flat, waiting for me to reappear. What if I telephoned her parents, or Arif and Katya? Almost certainly those lines would be bugged by now. After chewing over every possibility, Curwen came to the reluctant conclusion that there was nothing whatever we could do. He was cold and objective, but clearly right.

---

1   He was tragically lost in the helicopter crash which killed twenty-five security officers on their way from Belfast to Scotland in June 1994.

His verdict left me even more depressed. I had imagined that the British services were omnipotent, that they could arrange anything; but now they were unable to manage even such an elementary manoeuvre as to send a message to my wife.

A retired security officer, spending time in the village beyond the grounds to pick up local gossip, soon found that people realized something strange was going on in the big house. 'This is no good,' he said as he returned. 'We've got to get out.'

Our destination was a nineteenth-century naval fortress on the south coast, now used by the intelligence community for training and seminars. I was offered a helicopter ride but, as a result of the recent stress, I had developed a foolish fear of flying, of being trapped inside an aircraft and unable to help myself if anything went wrong (this persisted for nearly eighteen months). I declined, and we went by car to the outskirts of London, where the all-but-complete M25 yawned smooth and empty but unusable, and on southwards.

At the fort we were met by a handsome, energetic-looking man in his early fifties, who introduced himself as the commandant. 'Of course I don't know who you are or why you're here,' he said cheerfully, 'but that doesn't matter. We're used to such things. Everyone loves it here. We're on the sea and it's a bit windy, but the fresh air is terrific.'

Of course he knew very well who I was, having been briefed the day before. Over the next few weeks we became good friends — and I shall always be grateful to his attractive young wife, with her striking dark-blue eyes: a specialist in flower-arranging, she always put beautiful vases in my room.

At first I lived in a wing of the fort overlooking the sea, where the accommodation was Spartan, but adequate. One morning as I went for a shower I saw a man who was new to me, bald on top of his head, but with curly short hair round the sides. He looked at me, not sure who I was, and an hour later we met officially. He turned out to be the main political analyst, and a brilliant one at that, among the most skilful in Whitehall. With him I began a marathon debriefing, which lasted almost without a break for eighty days.

Talking to this man, Gordon, with his huge knowledge and speed of assimilation, I discovered how much I had squandered in the past. In Denmark people had missed tremendous opportunities of extracting important information from me because they had tended to stick to mundane details about agents, names, leads, illegals, penetrations and all the other trivia, missing the larger political issues. Only a few of the names we had discussed in Copenhagen were of real significance: the rest were just material from the huge KGB correspondence, most of which, as I have said, was generated by people writing to justify their own existence.

Working together, Gordon and I produced a number of major reports, known to the service as CX Reports, which emanate from specially protected sources. As well as being enthusiastic and sharp, he wrote admirably, in short words and concise sentences, so that the reports were a delight to read. Being ambitious, and knowing his value, he could sometimes be difficult, but I relished working with him, and found life much more enjoyable now that it was filled with so much creative endeavour.

A few days after I had reached Britain, some hot news arrived from the United States: another senior KGB officer, Vitali Yurchenko, had defected to the Americans in Rome on 29 July, and had been taken to Washington. One of the first things he had told his hosts was that one Colonel Gordievsky —'probably your man' — was in big trouble in Moscow. The American services cabled Britain, 'We don't have any such man, do you?', and the Brits were able to reply with enthusiasm, 'Yes, we do! He's our man, and he's here in England.' I remembered Yurchenko: by training a counter-intelligence officer, who later switched to the American department of the First Chief Director-ate, by the end of 1984 he had become number one on Gribin's list of potential Residents in London. Although he had scarcely known me, he now did me a good turn: he had heard some details of my interrogation while he was still in Moscow, and confirmed to a sceptical British officer that the account I had given was true. But he could not throw light on the fundamental mystery of who it was who had betrayed me.

*

After a run on the beach or golf-course, a shower and then breakfast, I would start work at 9 or 9.30 a.m., and carry on right through until 6 p.m. There was no end to the people who wanted to talk to me and, although Gordon demanded the lion's share of my time, I generally switched to several different teams each day, doing two-hour stretches with each. The sheer variety of British people was a revelation. Until then I had got to know only three or four in Denmark and the same in London: now I was meeting brilliant officers every day, not least an Anglo-Indian lady bubbling over with fun and enthusiasm, and a deeply religious man called John, who was impressively thorough and meticulous and paid close attention to human problems. These new contacts made me realize how poorly organized the KGB was, both in its training and in its operations. For all its facilities — School 101 and the new Andropov Institute — its instruction and methods were crude compared with those of the British. The KGB was grossly overstaffed: its stations were too large, its officers were poorly controlled, and there was no focus on things that were important. But its greatest weakness, of course, was that all its operations were based on, and crippled by, Communist dogma.

At the fort I was admirably looked after, but I still felt tense and below par, suffering from the loss of the family. 'What have I done?' I kept asking myself. 'I was looking forward to life in the West — to all the freedom — and now I'm stuck here on my own. I've lost my children. I've lost my wife. I've lost my home. Everything's gone. Here I am, getting old, and what have I achieved? All I've done is ruin everything.' It was terrible to feel that, in spite of my escape, I had suffered a resounding defeat.

Bit by bit I heard what had happened in London and Moscow. About a week after I came to England, a message from the Centre reached the KGB station in London saying that Comrade Gornov had disappeared. The British watchers across the road got the impression that the Embassy went into a state of paralysis. (Weeks later they sent a team to remove all the possessions we had left behind in our flat in Kensington. These were packed up in boxes and sent to Moscow, but the next thing people saw was the furniture from the KGB station being brought out and moved to the workshop at No. 10 Kensington Palace Gardens, where it could be taken apart, piece by piece, to search for the secret transmitter-microphones which I was assumed to have planted in it.)

In Moscow the KGB waited in vain for me to reappear. They had no clue where I had gone, and after a while they began to think that I must have committed suicide. They therefore launched an All-Union Search, which meant that police and militia were looking for my body in ditches and under bridges the whole way from Brest-Litovsk to Vladivostok. Leila and the children were brought back to Moscow, where she was questioned endlessly but, of course, she had no more idea than anyone else about what had happened to me.

With a full briefing from me, the British now knew every detail of the KGB in London, and they had the ammunition to carry out a full-scale purge of spies. The Foreign and Home Offices started to discuss what to do about the heavy KGB and GRU presence. Most senior officials were in favour of a large-scale expulsion but I was afraid that another major blow to the KGB would diminish my family's chances still further, and I begged my contacts to exercise restraint, suggesting that some sort of deal might be worked out. Luckily a few senior officers were prepared to try for one, even though any such move was strongly against the instincts of the Prime Minister, Margaret Thatcher.

Eventually it was decided to approach a Soviet official secretly, and give him a verbal message saying, 'In case you're looking for Mr Gordievsky, he's here.' The message would make it clear that the British knew all about the Soviet intelligence presence in London, but that they would treat it leniently, allowing Moscow to withdraw people gradually, over a long period, provided the Gordievsky family was set free.

The difficulty was to find a contact to whom such a message could safely be passed. In the end the choice fell on a counsellor at the Soviet Embassy in Paris, not a KGB man but a clean diplomat whose name was familiar to me because Katya had once mentioned it in a thesis she was writing about centrist political parties in France. She had formed a high opinion of the man, who was Jewish and bright, and he seemed an ideal channel.

A meeting was arranged in Paris, and there, on the afternoon of 15 August, the message was passed. At my suggestion, it did not name me, but began, 'A former senior KGB officer, who until recently was head of station in London…' Our contact took the point immediately, and asked only one question: 'Why did you come to me?' Our messenger answered truthfully, 'Because we regard you as the most intelligent Soviet diplomat in Western Europe.' They agreed a procedure for meeting again in two weeks' time, and parted.

Thus, on the evening of 15 August, or the morning of the 16th, the KGB at last found out that I was safe and well in Britain. Their rage knew no bounds, and when their answer to our proposal came, on only the tenth day, it was pure vitriol. The officer who went to the second meeting in Paris returned full of gloom. The reply, he said, was one long tirade of abuse: according to the KGB, it was sheer impudence on our part to propose such an exchange, and outrageous to allow only two weeks in which to work out some arrangement. We were well aware that under the Soviet system such a matter could not possibly be decided in such a short time. In sum, the answer was a total rejection.

The KGB's anger infected Stephen. 'A reply like that demands a tough response!' he fumed. 'Now, Oleg, we've really got to throw all those damned spies out.' And so they did, drafting a list and preparing to make an announcement at the beginning of September. Yet now the Centre, sensing that retaliation was imminent, played a clever delaying card. On 29 August a senior official of the British department rang the Moscow Embassy and said, 'Mr Gorbachev wishes to see the British Ambassador, and may summon him at any time. Be prepared.' So for the next few days — from 4 to 7 September —the Ambassador, Sir Bryan Cartledge, stood by…and, of course, no summons came.

The British let off their bomb on the 12th, when they released a statement saying that I had defected. They made it sound not as if I had escaped from Moscow, but as if I had merely changed sides and stayed in Britain. At the same time, they declared twenty-five members of the Soviet Embassy staff *personae non gratae*.

In 1971, when the British expelled 105 Soviet personnel, Moscow's riposte had been weak: they had thrown out only sixteen or seventeen people from the Moscow Embassy, including several of no importance, thus demonstrating that they were anxious to remain on good terms with Britain. Now things were different. Having achieved the status of global superpower, the Soviet Union was in arrogant mood, and Gorbachev did not want to show himself a weakling. Besides, he regarded the KGB as his darling, and it was he who authorized a brutal response.

Moscow made an exact *quid pro quo*, also expelling twenty-five, but because the British official presence in the Soviet Union has always been far smaller than the Soviet presence in Britain, the number was, in proportion, high. In London the British security service had already prepared a second list of six names to put through if the Soviet response should be so foolish, and this they now did. Again Moscow retaliated with the same number. The loss of thirty-one people — even though twelve were businessmen — devastated the British community in Moscow, and effectively wrecked the Embassy. (Later, in the winter, the KGB leaked a totally invented story to the journalist Viktor Louis, saying that I had escaped by being picked up in a diplomatic car in Moscow, secretly taken into the Embassy, and smuggled out again in the hubbub after the reception.)

I felt bitter, because the atmosphere between the KGB and Britain had become highly poisonous, and I knew that my chances of extracting the family had diminished significantly. Life became difficult. I began having daydreams about Leila and the children arriving — I saw them coming through Customs at Heathrow — but I knew that it was all fantasy. For the moment, my only panacea was to bury myself in work. Gerry Warner, then deputy head of the intelligence service, was particularly sympathetic: seeing how important the family was to me, he launched a full-scale special initiative to get them out. The operation was given the code-name 'Hetman' — the title of leaders of the Ukrainian Cossacks — and soon the file on it grew to many volumes.

Several of my debriefing sessions were with Colin McColl, later head of MI6. I soon saw how sharp and eloquent he was but he once disconcerted me by remarking on how incredibly boring most KGB documents were. He was right, of course: the reports and messages were couched in utterly wooden and unimaginative language, but I, having risked my life to spirit them into Western hands, could not help feeling an element of personal criticism in his strictures.

On 16 September, who should come skimming into the fort by helicopter but Bill Casey, veteran head of the United States' Central Intelligence Agency (CIA), who wanted to brief President Reagan for his first meeting with Gorbachev, due in November. Being so fresh from Moscow, and having seen Gorbachev in action, I had plenty of ideas, and I spent the working day with Casey, while Christopher Curwen tactfully translated the American's questions for me (apart from his accent, he was having trouble with his teeth, which made him hard to understand). Over lunch we went on talking, and then Casey asked if he could use a tape recorder to catch some of my answers. I found it immensely flattering that such a senior figure should be taking notes like a schoolboy.

He was anxious to plan the meeting between Reagan and Gorbachev in Geneva, and he asked many questions about the Strategic Defense Initiative (SDI), commonly known as Star Wars. If America offered the Soviet Union a share in the technology of SDI, he wanted to know, would Gorbachev accept it? My answer was an emphatic, 'No.' I said that the Russians would think the offer was a trick, to involve them in colossal expense, and would not dream of accepting it. I suggested, on the contrary, that if the Americans were prepared to drop SDI, they might win important concessions on arms control. But Casey's reaction was as negative as mine: 'Never,' he said. 'SDI's the President's pet.'

'All right,' I said. 'But I think that in the long term SDI will ruin the Soviet leadership.'

Afterwards, Gerry Warner said that he considered it was this one meeting which, indirectly, set off the collapse and disintegration of the Soviet Union. The advice I gave Casey encouraged the Americans, at Geneva, to maintain their strong military position and take a tougher line with the Eastern bloc. This in turn made clear to Gorbachev what he was up against internationally, and at home forced him to take urgent measures to catch up with the West. So he began the reforms, which were swept up on the roller-coaster of political logic and ran away from him.

It was difficult for me to judge the value of my information to the West, but I believe I was able to contribute in four main areas.

The first was the political, military and strategic thinking of the Kremlin, especially Soviet arms control policy and attitudes to NATO. While still working in the KGB, I had smuggled out large numbers of secret reports on these subjects so that the West had direct sight of Soviet documents and methods. Later, during my first two years of debriefings, I was able to add a good deal more.

The second area was KGB operations. I was able to describe these at first hand: besides identifying individual officers, I gave details of methods used, the role of the illegals, with the result that several potentially dangerous agents and contacts were rendered harmless: Bettaney in Britain, Treholt in Norway, Bergling in Sweden, one man in France and others in Denmark.

The third area was the evaluation of Soviet threats — military, political, propagandist, and intelligence. In a few spheres the Soviet threat was greater than it appeared, but in almost all it was far smaller, and I was able to explain how the land lay. For instance, one British security officer told me that when he read the KGB's 'Plan of Work in Britain for 1984', which I had obtained for him, his hair stood on end; but when I told him how little of the plan was real, and how much was high-flown phraseology coined to please the Centre, he felt far more relaxed. Here, as elsewhere, I saved Western agencies huge amounts of money because I gave them the confidence to stop monitoring activities which did not merit their time or attention.

The fourth area was the explanation of Soviet psychology: how people thought, spoke and acted, both in the KGB stations in embassies abroad and in Moscow. By showing how the Communist bureaucracy worked, and how one department was connected with another, I was again able to save a good deal of work and expense.

*

In October I felt that I had spent long enough living in a barracks, and began looking for a flat of my own. My first searches brought disappointment: perhaps I had been spoiled by the high standards in Scandinavia, but here I saw one new flat after another flawed by poor workmanship or design. At last, however, Joan hit on a new development which was of superior quality: blocks of flats were set on wooded hills, and skilfully blended into the surroundings. There I bought an apartment.

On the night before I was to move in, and sleeping in a hotel, my case officer knocked on the door in the small hours and said, 'I've just heard some terrible news on the radio. Yurchenko's redefected.'

'I'm not surprised,' I muttered. 'He's just a *Homo sovieticus*, a piece of shit.' But Stephen, like other friends, was worried about my state of mind and feared that Yurchenko's action might give me ideas. There is a Russian proverb: 'Another man's soul is a dark place.' How could the British see or read what I was really thinking? They were afraid that, desperate to rejoin my family, I might vanish in the middle of the night and give myself up to the Soviet Embassy. I said, 'Don't worry, I'm not going to do that. And, anyway, I'm full of contempt for Yurchenko.' Later I wrote to Bill Casey, saying I was ashamed of the way Yurchenko had behaved, but that he was only a *Homo sovieticus*, and that no one should lose sleep over him. I wanted the letter to be one of sympathy for what had happened, but the CIA misinterpreted it as trying to console them for having made a mistake. In their answer they said that it had not been a mistake, but that, on the contrary, Yurchenko had been immensely useful to them while he lasted. Back in Moscow, he claimed that he had never defected voluntarily, but had been drugged and kidnapped — clearly basing his account on that of Oleg Bitov, who said exactly the same thing. The Americans retaliated by pointing out that the two worst tortures he had endured were learning to play golf and acquiring a tan on a sunbed.

*

Now that I had a home of my own, I began to enjoy an extraordinary sense of freedom. For the first time in my life I was free of inhibitions. For the first time I could trust people. I did not have to tell lies. I talked openly to many British friends, and the experience was exhilarating. I could open my heart, and, as we say in Russia, my soul. (The Russian for soul is *dusha*, and *dushevnost* means 'coming from the heart'.)

Now I understood how much my emotional life had been inhibited by intelligence work and the constant need to be secretive. All the time, while working with British intelligence officers, I had found them the epitome of friendliness, and I had longed to open my heart to them, but I could not because we were so busy that we simply had no time for emotional exchanges. Now everything had changed, and I was able to give rein to my natural conviviality. I began to entertain lavishly, organizing feasts at which I laid out mountains of smoked salmon, gravadlax, smoked eel, caviar and other delicacies, with vodka and wine flowing: I wanted both to relax, and to make as many friends as possible, so that more and more people would fight for the release of my family.

At the same time, my debriefing continued intensively, most often at the home of a new case officer, who happened to live quite close by. I would go round there to meet delegates from various departments, often by bicycle, and sometimes during the lunch break, while my contacts were relaxing over the meal that our hostess had laid on, I would go out for a run.

All through those months my most frequent request to the service was for help in contacting Leila. I did not even know where she was, and I had no idea what the KGB might have told her about me. One thing was certain, though: they would be putting heavy pressure on her, and coaching her minutely in what to say if I came through on the telephone. There was thus no point in my trying to ring her for even if I had got through she would only have been able to parrot out the lies forced upon her — that if I came home, I would be guaranteed a safe passage, that all would be forgiven. There was no point in writing as I knew letters would be confiscated by the KGB.

The best alternative, it seemed, was to send telegrams, and I arranged for one of these, containing powerful expressions of love for her and the children, to be despatched on my behalf from Paris every month. I thought it possible that Leila had taken the children to live with her parents, and considered sending the cables to their address; but then I thought that they, like most Russians, would be nervous of receiving any communication from a traitor, so I directed them to my sister Marina instead. I realized that she, too, might not like it, but at least the telegrams would be more likely to get through to her, and she would pass them on.

In this, unfortunately, I was mistaken: as Leila later told me, Marina turned out to be the most cowardly of the lot, and passed the telegrams straight to the KGB. Had she been braver, she could have made copies and delivered them to Leila but she did not have the guts even to do that. It was not until nearly a year later that Leila found out what was happening: by chance she was alone in Marina's flat when one of my cables arrived, and because I had had the wit to number them in sequence, and she saw that this was No. 9, she realized what I had been doing. That was the first communication she had received from me in twelve months.

Later I learnt that the KGB interrogated all the people who knew me, even those with the most tenuous links. Leila herself, Marina, Arif and Katya, all were taken, terrified, to the main interrogation centre in the Lefortovo Prison. Many members of the KGB were similarly questioned, including those who had been expelled from London: Mishustin, who had always felt that I was an alien element, was put through an inquisition, as was Lyubimov, even though he had long since been dismissed from the service. They were all innocent, of course, so they had nothing to be afraid of; but that did not lessen the stress of the experience.

At the same time, a parallel inquiry must have been in progress within the First Chief Directorate, but almost the only person to suffer demotion was my old friend and colleague Nikolai Gribin. Two key senior figures — Grushko and Gennady Titov — survived unscathed, and emerged as the most trusted allies of the Head of the First Chief Directorate, Kryuchkov.

In November 1985 a military tribunal passed a death sentence on me, *in absentia*, and ordered the confiscation of all my property. The best trophy was my car, it being the dream of every *Homo sovieticus* to own one, so some official of the court stole it and drove it away. A team arrived to strip the flat but, while they were at work the confiscation order was suddenly revoked. What happened, I think, was that the KGB became determined to recover me from enemy territory, and decided to use Leila and the children as bait. They reasoned, sensibly enough, that if they took away our home, the family would be unlikely to co-operate with them so all our property was returned, with the exception of the car, which the new owner/ thief had already smashed up. This infuriated Leila: she wanted that car so she went to court and started a case in an attempt to get it back. The case opened in 1987 and, at the time of writing (autumn 1994), is still running.

The KGB's attempts to lure me back were crude. At the end of my second year in England the Soviet Embassy demanded that I meet representatives so, after due consultation with my British friends, I agreed to see the Russians at the Foreign Office. I made it a condition of any meeting that they would deliver a letter from me to Leila.

One of the Soviet delegates was Aleksandr Smagin, an inexperienced man, whom I had known as the Embassy's lowly security officer, working in the room next to mine, and now, *faute de mieux* after the expulsions, the head of station. With him came the Counsellor, Givi Gventsadze, a clean diplomat, who later became Ambassador in Dublin.[2] All kinds of rumours had been flying — that I was mortally ill, that I had committed suicide. There had never been any proof, never a photograph, to confirm that I was in England, and many Russians still believed that my presence in London was a British fiction. The KGB had made strenuous efforts to discover more, even going to the length of persuading a Labour Member of Parliament to put down a written question in the House of Commons, but this had availed them nothing. When Smagin saw me far from dead, but fit and sharp in a well-cut suit, it was almost too much for him. He had brought me a letter from Leila, which he handed over. Of course it was a thrill to see her writing, and I opened the envelope with a flutter of excitement. But I only read two or three lines before I stopped. It was full of phrases like 'they've forgiven you everything', 'you can easily get another job'. I said, 'I see. It's been dictated by the KGB. There's no point.'

Gventsadze then asked a no-less-dictated question: 'Why aren't you telephoning your wife?'

'Givi Aleksandrovich,' I said sharply, 'do you realize what you're saying? In the presence of officials of the British Foreign Office you're admitting openly and loudly that the Soviet authorities have been violating international law by intercepting my letters and telegrams and now, at the dictation of the KGB, you're trying to make me talk, instead of using those other means of communication which you've been illegally interrupting.' That shook him, leaving him embarrassed and confused.

2 Having made the elementary mistake of recognizing the Emergency Committee which organized the coup against Gorbachev in August 1991, he was dismissed, and burst into tears at the press conference announcing his removal, so fervently had he dreamt of becoming Ambassador.

But Smagin said, 'Oleg Antonovich, *pochemou*? Why? Why don't you phone?'

'Because', I said coldly, 'I've no wish to speak to my wife when an operational officer is standing behind her, telling her what to say.'

'Oleg Antonovich, do you really think there's an operational officer living in your flat all the time?'

'No,' I told him. 'I don't suppose one is living there. But she's under continual pressure.'

In due course I found that my intuition had been not far wrong in that Leila was kept under close surveillance day and night for six years. The reason the KGB watched her so obsessively was never clear: most probably they feared that after I, a marked man, had been spirited out of the country under their noses, she, too, might disappear — and if she vanished with the children it would represent the ultimate humiliation.

I now realize that the letter I handed to Smagin was a serious mistake. Of course it told Leila how much I loved her and the children, and how I longed to be with them but I also gave her an entirely fictitious account of the reasons for my sudden disappearance, repeating the story of intolerable KGB intrigues which I had told her when she returned from London to Moscow. Looking back, I believe I was still off balance as a result of my interrogation. Somehow this had given me a profound shock. I knew full well that I was a traitor to the Communists' system so that they felt free to do whatever they wished — try me, poison me, torture me, execute me. Yet from a personal point of view I regarded it as an outrage that I had been drugged, and still, nearly two years later, I felt that I had been insulted. This led me to try to rub salt in the Centre's wounds by presenting the story of my downfall as if it had been the result of some terrible abuse of power by the KGB that had driven me out.

At the time I thought it clever to write such an account; I hoped that my version of events would protect Leila by confusing the KGB and delaying the official investigation so that the family could remain in the flat. It was far too late, however, for any such subterfuge. She knew as well as anyone that what I had written was nonsense and afterwards I strongly regretted it.

In all I had four meetings with the KGB in London. Their people were always courteous and careful but the pressure on me to return was unrelenting. On one occasion someone read out fine promises from a telegram allegedly emanating from the Centre: 'You'll be a free man… you'll get a job…you'll be happily reunited with your family.' I pointed out that there was no signature on the document, which was just a useless piece of paper. To the slight dismay of the British who were present, I retained a robust and aggressive stance throughout, rejecting all Smagin's overtures in peremptory fashion. He was particularly disconcerted when I told him that the letters he brought from Leila contained coded signals which showed that they had been dictated by the KGB.

'Signals?' he said angrily. 'What signals? How can there be signals if you haven't seen your wife for three years?'

In fact there were none, but I could tell from the length and style that the letters were not spontaneous. At that stage, of course, I could not know what an ordeal Leila had been going through. Frustrated in their attempts to recover me, the KGB had resorted to their usual dirty tricks, telling her that I was having an affair with a young English secretary, then that I had married her. Seeing that life would be easier for her and the children if she reverted to her maiden name, Leila went through the formal process of divorcing me. Even when we began to communicate again, her existence was tough. Not only was she watched night and day. Her mail was intercepted, her telephone tapped. Any friend who met her was immediately questioned by the KGB so that one by one her friends deserted her. In an attempt to secure some sort of anonymity, she reverted to her maiden name, Aliyev, but even so she could not find employment.

My only course was to build a life in the West and pray that one day she would be able to join me. At the fort many kind people had brought me books, and I had begun to assemble a library again: such was my interest in languages that in Moscow I had owned a hundred and fifty dictionaries, and soon I had brought my collection back to nearly a hundred.

After three years in the flat, I sold it at a good profit — my first real capitalist transaction — and bought a brand-new house. Never having owned a house before, I had had no idea of the quality of life it can provide. I loved the privacy and the space — the chance to put things like books and plants in their proper places, to spread bright rugs and runners over the floors and walk around barefoot. I rejoiced in being able to play music as loud as I liked, without disturbing anyone else, and in wearing as few clothes as I wanted. I also began to enjoy the garden, especially the smell of freshly cut grass: to a Russian, who always dreams about some warm place in the south towards the tropics, the scent of cypresses, in the sun or after rain, is highly evocative, and now it took me back to Gagra, Yalta and all the other resorts I knew on the Black Sea. Because there is so much wood in the house — in the roof, floors, windows and doors — it has a far better microclimate than the little concrete boxes of flats in Moscow. Going to bed at night, and hearing the house's noises — the clicking and creaking of wood — I imagine myself on a space-ship, speeding through space and time. But still I enjoy the sound of a train going by in the distance, because it gives me the feeling that I am not cut off from the human race, and can rejoin the rest of mankind whenever I want.

*

With my debriefing finished, I found that I was in strong demand from the political leaders and intelligence services of other countries, many of whom were eager to pick my brains. Apparently no other Soviet defector had ever been prepared to meet important political figures in this way, but it seemed to me essential that I, a witness from within, should explain to them directly how the Soviet system worked. Perhaps because I had already dealt with the West for so many years, and understood its methods, perhaps also because I had almost been caught by the KGB and had escaped with British help, I met a high level of trust wherever I went, particularly in America.

And so I began to travel on a scale of which I had never before dreamt. Before settling in England my knowledge of foreign countries was limited: I had spent time in East Germany as a student, served twice in Denmark, made two short trips to West Germany and one to Sweden — but that was all. Now I had wonderful opportunities, which took me repeatedly round the world.

My first trip was to France, where I was the guest of the intelligence service. What people I met there! Full of imagination, full of fantasy, full of good ideas and interesting observations, the officers were sharp and original: their excellence was exemplified in the person of Raymond Nart, head of the service dealing with Soviet espionage, a man of the widest experience, decorated for his work, and enormously stimulating. Yet for all their liveliness I never found the French in the least arrogant: sometimes they would ask me to dictate a political report on Soviet affairs, and they were always asking my advice on what to do and say. Also they entertained me royally, with splendid lunches and a trip to the opera. French food was a new experience, and on the whole an enjoyable one, though I found some of it rather rich.

The Germans also made much of me, particularly the officers of the external service, who struck me as more polished and cosmopolitan than their domestic counterparts. As I hadn't used it for ten years, my German had deteriorated so much that, although I could understand what was being said, I hardly dared speak for fear of bringing out a mixture of all the other languages I had learnt since. Apart from putting me up in style, my hosts presented me with a handsome set of German—Russian dictionaries, and also with a record of *Carmina Burana*, a neat reflection of an article by Andrew Knight in the British weekly *Economist* which had described how I once lectured the staff of the Soviet Embassy on Orff's little masterpiece. (I had felt cheerful when that story appeared in print, imagining KGB officers asking each other anxiously, 'What the hell is *Carmina Burana*?')

In all I made three trips to West Germany, and Otto Wieck, the outstanding head of the *Bundesnachrichtendienst* (BND), took care of me personally, organizing seminars at which the participants were encouraged to throw problems at me. At one point he gave a banquet, in which a dozen of us sat round a circular table, and he made a generous speech. When it came to speaking, I was only too glad to leave behind me the hypocritical and insincere outpourings that had been part of life at the Soviet Embassy. Now I could say what I felt about the West, and Western solidarity. It needed hard work to brush up my German for an address to the German service, and still more thorough preparation for a speech in Swedish, which I gave in Stockholm, and for which I practised with my bodyguard; but the reception I received always made such efforts worthwhile.

My third trip, predictably, was to the United States. In Washington I found myself working as never before: intensive briefing sessions began at 10 a.m. and lasted till 6 p.m., each of fifty-five minutes followed by a five-minute break, each with a different team. In the evening came a working dinner. At the CIA I addressed a seminar on the Soviet Union and Eastern Europe for three hours, with only a couple of short breaks. Small wonder that by the time I went on to Canada I was exhausted, and had to ask to be taken back to my hotel in the middle of dinner.

The level of protection I received varied a great deal. During my early days in England the services assumed that there was a significant threat from the KGB, who might try to assassinate me or snatch me back. I lived, therefore, under an assumed name, and when I began to appear before press or television cameras, I always wore a false beard and hairpiece. On my first trip to Washington I was heavily guarded, but in Israel a few months later the authorities laid on no security. In Norway I was protected day and night when I stayed with an intelligence chief in a bungalow only a hundred yards from the sea. The British seemed to think that a submarine might surface and the crew snatch me through the window, so they sent bodyguards to look after me. On my first trip to Stockholm the Swedish police, knowing that many Russian ships were in the harbour, did the same.

Some of my journeys were dictated by circumstances, and none more directly than my four trips to New Zealand, starting in 1986. I believe that the work I did there was particularly important, because for years the country had been under massive propaganda and ideological attack from the KGB and the Central Committee, and the ruling Labour Party had seemed unaware of the extent to which the fabric of their society was being damaged by subversion.

The Prime Minister, David Lange, and his Labour Party were anti-nuclear, and therefore anti-American, and Moscow had taken advantage of this. The Soviet aim was to have huge areas of the southern oceans declared nuclear-free, and deny them to nuclear-powered warships of the United States Navy: by reducing their sphere of operation as much as possible, Moscow would make it easier to keep them under control and destroy them in the first stage of any conflict that might develop. In its attempts to draw New Zealand into nuclear-free activities, the Soviet authorities had made tremendous efforts to penetrate and strengthen the Labour Party, partly through the local Party of Socialist Unity (in effect the Communist Party of New Zealand) and partly through the Trades Union Congress. When members of the ruling Labour Party were seen to be moving further and further to the left, alarm began to spread in intellectual circles as people saw that the country was losing its traditional balance.

This process had already started while I was still in the KGB but I warned specifically about it during my early debriefings at the fort. Notes of my conversations, together with an analytical paper by one of the British intelligence officers, soon found their way out to New Zealand. When I arrived on my first visit, in 1986, I found that my information had had a considerable impact. The security services had passed it to the Prime Minister, who, although the architect of the anti-nuclear proposals, was basically a solid Western man. Without abandoning his old policy, he became aware of its drawbacks, and strengthened his security organizations and monitoring activities. This brought him under attack from his own left wing, but he carried on the good work, took a more robust stance on Communism, and later expelled the Soviet diplomat who had been responsible for ideological penetration.

The New Zealanders also became fascinated by the illegals, about whom I told them a good deal, and eventually in 1991 they caught one, a young man in possession of a false British passport. Because a foreign spy working in New Zealand is not committing any criminal offence, they could only deport him, so they sent him to England, where he was detained for two days in case something incriminating could be found against him. My hope was that the British might use him as a bargaining counter to secure the release of my family but neither of these plans came to anything, and he was sent on to Moscow.

Other fruitful visits included two to Australia, and single journeys to Singapore, Malaysia, Thailand, South Africa, Kenya, Brazil, Saudi Arabia, Canada, The Netherlands, Spain, Portugal, Italy and Scandinavia. I was much struck that whereas in America, Britain, Canada, Australia and New Zealand I met top-level political leaders, the senior politicians of European countries avoided me — no doubt for fear of Soviet wrath. The difference greatly increased my respect for the Anglo-Saxon nations, and when I once mentioned this at a lecture in an Irish university, the hall exploded with applause.

In most countries I was immensely impressed by the level of the intelligence officers. The head of anti-Soviet espionage in Stockholm, for instance, was the most splendid eccentric I have ever met. He started his career as a merchant seaman, jumped ship in Spain, spent several months in the bullrings training as a *torrero*, came home, joined the police, and later moved to the security police. His department had invented an anthem of its own, in which the tune was that of a famous Soviet Air Force march, but the text was about fighting Soviet espionage and expelling intelligence officers on anniversaries dear to the Kremlin. A connoisseur of French wine, and a great lover of opera, which he played immensely loud in his house, the officer invented a theory that mental orgasms, which can be induced by opera, are more powerful than physical ones. This idea notwithstanding, in his late fifties he met a tall, beautiful woman — a police officer — and divorced his wife. Altogether I found him a most engaging character.

The Israelis were equally brilliant and original. During my first visit the head of the counter-intelligence service asked questions with incredible persistence. Whatever answer I gave, he would say, 'And why…? And why…?' never satisfied. At one point he took me into his office alone, leaving everyone else outside, including the curious British officers who were accompanying me, to tell me the story of a scientist who had turned out to be a KGB agent.

Of all my meetings with leading politicians, none was more stimulating than those with Margaret Thatcher. I already felt I knew her to some extent, for in 1983, while working in the KGB in London, I realized that the Soviet Embassy had never commissioned anyone to write a study of this outstanding leader. When I suggested that I should do so the Ambassador was delighted, so I sat down to compile a biographical-profile-cum-assessment, based on published sources but spiced with my own observations. Knowing that I must include something typically Soviet and propagandistic, I put in a paragraph or two about how she exploited class differences and promoted class warfare, but I also wrote that she had a fresh and imaginative mind. The Embassy liked the paper, and copies of it went back to Moscow, where it became useful on the eve of Gorbachev's visit to Britain.

One day in August 1985, when I was still living at the fort, and feeling depressed, my case officer rushed in all lit up. 'Look what I've got!' he cried. 'It's a letter to you from the Prime Minister!' Her message was that I should not give up hope of recovering my family: keep your spirits up, she wrote, and you'll get them in the end. Even if I felt that she was over-optimistic, I was grateful for her support and encouragement: I got the impression that she was trying to bolster my confidence.

Then in May 1986 she invited me to lunch at Chequers, the Prime Minister's official country residence. I drove to Buckinghamshire in the company of Christopher Curwen, still head of MI6, and when we arrived, our hostess herself was standing on the steps to greet us. I noticed that she wore little make up, and looked very simple: it was clear that she was not trying to impress anyone. Rather, she was warm and welcoming. I was feeling tense, knowing that my English was still only moderate but determined to do well.

When Mrs Thatcher asked what we would like to drink, both Chris and I opted for gin and tonic. Mrs Thatcher ordered something for herself, but then said how much she thought about dieting, and not eating too much, so that she did not put on weight. 'But surely,' I said, 'there are an awful lot of calories in any alcohol.' To which she replied, 'I know! But what a pity not to enjoy it!'

We were joined by Charles Powell, her press secretary, who seemed half-asleep after returning from a trip abroad. When our drinks came, served by girls in military uniforms, Chris and I sat at either end of a sofa, opposite her. As we both moved to put our glasses down on the sofa's arms, she said, without changing the tone of her voice, 'Use the side-tables, gentlemen.' Immediately I thought, What a typical English housewife! She is being very hospitable and nice and courteous to us, her guests, but she will not let us spoil the furniture. In the Orient, by contrast, and to some extent in Russia, a hostess's attitude would be quite different. She would see it as her duty to be unlimitedly hospitable and generous. 'You like that coffee-table? Do take it home with you. That chair as well…?' Here, we were merely cautioned not to damage the sofa.

After the drinks, I expected to start discussing important matters. But no, first she gave us a tour of the house, showing us many rooms, and telling us something of the place's history. My mind was concentrating so hard on what I wanted to tell her that I could hardly take in what she was saying. Then she led us into a room with a bow window, which looked out over the fields, and there we had a simple but good lunch. Again the talk was of trivialities, and afterwards, upstairs in the library, the servants offered us coffee in tiny cups, together with chocolates and cigars. I wondered if it was all right to smoke in such a splendid room. 'Of course!' she cried. 'Denis smokes like a chimney all the time.' So I took a cigar and lit it, still listening to her talking, talking, as I waited for the business of the day to begin.

At last she became serious and remembered her questions. They were tough and penetrating, about political strategies, arms control, chemical and biological weapons, Gorbachev's policies. All the big subjects of the day came up. At that time I was well versed in such matters, for it was only nine months since my escape. As I started to speak she listened intently, looking straight into my eyes, obviously taking in every word. Sometimes as she commented on my answers she was seduced by her own love of talking, and set off again, airing her knowledge. I saw that if I wanted to get through my list of points, I must make tactful inter-ruptions — and this I began to do. Our exchanges went on unabated until one of the servants appeared with a note. Mrs Thatcher looked at it and said, 'Oh, I'm terribly sorry. Someone else has come to see me. I'll have to stop.'

Was the interruption staged? We had no means of telling. But the Prime Minister took us downstairs, thanked us profusely for coming, saw us off from the steps, and stood waving as we drove away. She had been courtesy itself, in the best English tradition. Yet when I calculated how much time I had spent giving her information, I reckoned that of the three hours and forty minutes we had spent in her company, I had held forth for no more than one hour and twenty minutes.

My next meeting with her took place at No. 10 Downing Street in March 1987, a difficult period during which Anglo-Soviet relations had been at a low ebb for some time. But now Gorbachev had invited her to visit Moscow, and she wanted tips on how to deal with Soviet journalists. Points for speeches, discussions and press conferences were what she needed, and I started to reel off ideas. Knowing the weaknesses of the Soviet system, and the strengths of the West, I was able to speak fluently, with Charles Powell again taking notes — and before I knew what had happened, seventy minutes had gone by. Mrs Thatcher's time had run out, but still she was not satisfied and she asked me to go home and make a supplementary list of points, which I did.

Her trip to Moscow took place at the end of March and the beginning of April. A blazing success, it was dominated by the unforgettable interview she gave on Moscow television. Today, Russian journalists are as cheeky and aggressive as any in the West but in 1987 they were still respectful of authority, and they looked up to Mrs Thatcher as the Boss. Three leading commentators on foreign policy had been assigned to interview her and she cut them all to shreds. She argued, interrupted, bludgeoned and destroyed them, talking so fast and forcefully that often they could not even ask their next question. One of the ideas I had suggested made a particular impact. 'Tell them that 74 per cent of people in Britain have their own homes,' I had suggested. 'Not flats, but proper houses, with several bedrooms, all the facilities, and gardens.' She put this over straight, along with numerous other facts about Soviet SS-20 missiles in the heart of Europe, and the need for arms control. Her triumph was total, and Russians spoke about it for a month afterwards.

When she came home, she sent me a letter thanking me for my points, which had been so useful — and that touched me more than I could say. What Soviet official ever thanked a consultant for his help? I was delighted by the Prime Minister's modesty and gratitude, by her understanding of realities, and her acknowledgement of who it was coming up with ideas.

My third meeting with her, in September 1989, was not so successful. Again she invited me to 10 Downing Street, to discuss the rapid development of the Soviet Union, and all went well until she asked what I thought about the reunification of Germany, which then seemed only a possibility. 'Everybody's talking about it,' she said. 'What do you think it would mean?'

I told her I thought she need not worry. 'You, the British, made such a good job of de-Nazifying Germany in the forties that today the country has become one of the most liberal democratic countries in the world,' I said. 'If it comes to reunification, I'm sure West Germany will re-educate East Germany, and the whole thing will turn into a normal European state.'

I could see from her face that she did not like what I was saying. 'Bur surely the Soviet Union will object!' she exclaimed. 'They've always been against a strong, militarized Germany.'

I said I was not so sure. In the 1940s, when everyone was still in shock after the terrible casualties of the war, that was certainly true. But today, with nuclear weapons of all kinds available, the Kremlin no longer saw Germany as a threat. Second, and more important, the Soviet basic belief had always been that it would be wrong to object to the reunification of the nation. It was true that for a while the Kremlin had propped up East Germany — and, of course, Russia would prefer a Communist or socialist Germany to a right-wing one. 'But if it comes to the point of reunification,' I said, 'I don't think Moscow will raise any major objections. A united Germany has always been part of official Soviet ideology, and I think the Kremlin will remain true to that.'

Here Mrs Thatcher positively glared at me, intensely disliking everything she heard. I had not known that her ideas on the subject were precisely the opposite of mine, and that she was busy gathering allies to support her line. Just before I left, I quietly asked that when she next saw Gorbachev she would put in another plea for the release of my family — and she nodded. But it was a cool goodbye, and I knew that something was wrong. For a while I feared that my personal request had been out of place; but soon I learnt that it was not this which had upset her. What were out of place were my views on German reunification — and this was one of the few areas in which Mrs Thatcher proved wrong. Her role in bringing the Cold War to an end in the Soviet Union and Eastern Europe was tremendous, but over Germany she took the wrong line.

I am glad to say that our personal relations survived this setback. When we met again after she had left office, she was most friendly, and it was a pleasant surprise to find that she gave me a couple of positive mentions in her memoirs.

*

When I met President Ronald Reagan in 1987, there were two main objectives on our agenda. One was to impress and help the CIA, and the other to secure from Reagan a pledge that he would work for the reunion of my family. A few words would be enough. If the President said, 'We'll help you,' that would do: his word would be his command.

As I sat waiting in a pleasant antechamber of the White House, I felt unaccountably nervous. There was no need to feel like that, I knew, yet my anxiety persisted. Then General Colin Powell, deputy head of the National Security Council, came to fetch me, and we went into the Oval Office. Two chairs were set out facing the rest of the room, one for the President, the other for myself. It was an awkward arrangement: to look at Mr Reagan I had to twist round to my left, and the opposite if I wanted to face the audience out in front.

Somebody asked a question, and I began talking generally about Soviet espionage networks. I made a point about the illegals, saying that there were still a lot at large, and then spoke about Moscow's attempts to spread propaganda, create front organizations and influence public opinion. This subject was evidently close the President's heart, for he launched into a story — one of his favourites, I gathered afterwards — about how, as head of the cinema workers' trade union, he had tried to protect his people from Soviet influence and penetration. After that I felt less tense, and the atmosphere lightened. I was impressed by his warmth and cordiality, but as I was speaking I noticed that a look of bafflement occasionally came into his eyes, and I wondered if he understood what I was saying, or whether he had any real interest in matters of detail which lay beneath the most general facts.

In any case, I got twenty-two minutes of his time (the Labour politicians Neil Kinnock and Denis Healey got eighteen), and the all-important moment came at the end, when he put his arm round my shoulder and said, 'We know you. We appreciate what you've done for the West. Thank you. We remember your family, and we'll fight for them.' As he said goodbye, he repeated something similar, and the British head of station was delighted. 'You've got it!' he said. 'You've got it!'

When I met Mr Reagan's successor, George Bush, two years later, the format was exactly the same. The moment I was shown into the Oval Office, a photographer started to take pictures, and I was put into a chair in the same awkward position, with the President to my left and eight other people to my right, so that if I faced him I could not see anyone else. It struck me that he looked tired: even though he was only in the first year of his term, his face was drawn with exhaustion.

He led off in what I can only call typical Bush-speak: although I recognized a good many individual words, I simply could not understand a single sentence. What the hell was he saying? I felt petrified, and when he stopped, I hardly knew what to do. But when he asked, 'What do you say to that?' I had a minor inspiration, and deflected the question to the onlookers, by turning to them and saying, 'You know, I really didn't come here to deliver a lecture. That would be presumptuous of me. I'd prefer to answer simple questions about the current situation in the Soviet Union. Could you please ask about that?'

Very easily, without the slightest fuss, Mr Bush said, 'OK, then: will Gorbachev stay?'

That was exactly the lead I needed. I gave an answer, and immediately, like a university professor with a class of students, the President said, 'All right, and now let's have some questions from the floor.' Everybody tried to speak at once, and someone asked, 'If Gorbachev is demoted and replaced, what will Soviet policy be?' Without hesitation I replied, 'It's quite impossible to say. Whoever takes over, one fact is clear: that man's policy will have nothing to do with his previous speeches and articles. That is a rule of Soviet life. In the summer of 1917 Lenin wrote *Statement of Revolution* — and when the revolution came, his policy bore no relation to what he had said in the book. Stalin made endless statements in the 1920s, and his subsequent actions bore no relation to them. Khrushchev was allegedly a Stalinist, yet it was he who started de-Stalinization. Gorbachev was entirely a man of his own circle, and now look at his policy.'

At this Robert Gates, then deputy chairman of the National Security Council, nodded his head vigorously, so that I felt I had got my point across. Another member of the audience, Vice-President Dan Quayle, also showed strong interest, and when we finished, after a good stint of thirty minutes, President Bush tried to introduce him to me. As I had already met him on the way in, this created some confusion, but Quayle then asked me to go along to his own office so that we could have a private word.

In his big room we found two good-looking women of about forty, smartly dressed and got-up, sitting on a table swinging their legs. 'Ladies, ladies!' cried Quayle. 'I'm sorry. Another half hour, please' — whereupon they jumped to the floor (with slight reluctance, I thought) and went out. It would have been easy to put the wrong construction on that odd scene but one was his wife and the other a friend of hers.

In asking his questions, Quayle revealed a confrontational attitude. His was the robust, conservative voice of American foreign policy. I sensed that he had limited knowledge but was determined to improve it. I also felt that he had suffered a good deal from criticism for his lack of understanding of foreign affairs, and now desperately wanted someone to back up his own ideas. When we finished, he said, 'Well, good! That entirely confirms what I thought' — but I said something to warn him that he should not think he knew it all.

When I visited the States again a year later, he asked to see me once more: a different office, a different photographer, and Quayle a different man, tired, worried and already ground down by the burdens of office. This time he had detailed someone to prepare questions for him to ask me, but he did not want me to know this, and had tried to memorize them. From his expression I could see that all the time he was trying to read his mental list of questions, and not listening to what I said but relying on the note-taker and on being able to read a cleaned-up version of my replies later.

Every visit that I made to America was rewarding. In one year I made three trips, then two in each of the next two years, and three more later — ten visits in all. Always I travelled as a guest of the CIA, who would inform fellow agencies such as the FBI, Naval Intelligence, the State Department and others of my impending arrival, so that they could book some of my time if they wanted it. These trips were organized in a clandestine manner: hotel rooms were booked in other names and nobody was supposed to know who I was. But gradually, as my name and presence became more familiar — and particularly after publication of my book *KGB: The Inside Story* — standards were allowed to slip. Instead of being debriefed in five-star hotels, I simply moved from one office to another in the main building of the CIA, surviving on sandwiches and disgusting coffee from machines. 'What's happened?' I once asked in mock-complaint. 'You used to fly me first class and keep me in luxury. Now I go club class and work on concrete staircases.' Their explanation was that, with the appearance of the book, I was no longer a secret person and there was no need for me to remain in hiding.

The CIA headquarters at Langley, Virginia, about half an hour out of Washington, struck me as a fascinating place. During the day there were always dozens of people standing on the steps outside, drawing desperately on cigarettes, as no smoking was allowed inside the building. Every lavatory cubicle was equipped for people in wheelchairs, with a door that opened automatically at the touch of a button: few people in wheelchairs worked there, but some government regulation demanded that they be universally provided for.

I liked almost all the people I met in the CIA. The overall intellectual standard struck me as lower than in the British service — for the British, needing fewer people, can afford to recruit only those with really good brains. In the CIA some were very good indeed, some less so, but almost all were generous, kind and cordial, with their hearts in the right place. Yet I also found the Americans more critical about their superiors, and more inclined to gossip about them: there seemed to be much more irritation with authority than in Britain, where the easy, unconfrontational attitude to leadership made relationships easier. Such prejudices as the Americans had were the result of ignorance rather than propaganda, and they had a positively Teutonic respect for rules and regulations. People kept asking, 'What is the KGB instruction for such-and-such a situation?' and I would say, 'Now, look, there are endless rules and regulations in Soviet Communist life. But what the intelligence service needs above all is vision, imagination and spontaneity. It follows that there can't be rules for every situation. People play things by ear, and rely on traditional solutions, not all of which are on paper. And when definite instructions exist, they are generally ignored.'

That used to surprise them. Yet often they showed a high degree of brilliance, as in a two-hour session on illegals. In a large room, a number of people sat in a semicircle, and officers responsible for that side showed immense knowledge of their subject, remembering names and personalities of individuals, who had done what, and when. In this field, at least, the CIA's professionalism was striking.

One senior intelligence officer with responsibility for Soviet affairs cast doubt on all my information about Operation RYAN. His theory was that the whole thing had been no more than a deception exercise by the Soviet leadership: certainly he had tested and studied every aspect of RYAN most cleverly, and I was impressed by his thoroughness and knowledge. In the end he came to believe in the reality of the Soviet leaders' paranoia, but he remained sceptical about some aspects. He claimed, for instance, that in the Able Archer exercise, and the reaction to it, the levels of preparedness were not what one would expect before a real nuclear attack: he said that when Americans observed the actions of Soviet troops inside Russia, and checked signal intensities, there was no hard evidence of anything extraordinary.

That made me explain how I had understood RYAN. It was not so much that the Soviet authorities were expecting a nuclear attack at any moment. Rather, they were trying to create a system which would be able to react instantaneously to any future attack — to have their system in place. I explained that Moscow had become worried by the Star Wars initiative: if the whole of the United States was shielded by an umbrella proof against intercontinental missiles, might not the American nation become so overconfident and aggressive as to resort to a sudden assault?

Sometimes, in an attempt to liven up my lectures, I told the odd joke — but it was not always successful. One day, for instance, I brought out the one about the American sent to Russia as an illegal. He has been thoroughly trained and prepared, his identity documents are faultless, he speaks fluent Russian, he dresses like a Russian, crosses the border without difficulty and tries to settle down. His work, however, is not a success, and one day, drinking with his friend Vanya, he complains about his fate. 'Vanya,' he says, 'what's wrong with me? Don't I speak Russian perfectly?'

'Yes, John, your Russian's brilliant.'

'And don't I play balalaika well?

'Like a dream, John.'

'And don't I drink vodka by the tumblerful, just as you Russians do, Vanya?'

'Oh, yes, you can drink.'

'So what's wrong, then?'

'Just one drawback, John, you're black.'

The story might have gone down better if the audience had appreciated that it was supposed to be funny. But another, a typical KGB joke, was easier to spot.

A gala session in the KGB's Dzerzhinsky Club. There are over a thousand senior officers in the hall. Lined up on the platform are the most important bosses, and two of them, one older, one younger, are sitting together, chatting during the speeches which, as usual, are of crippling tedium. The older man says, 'Ivan, I've spotted the CIA spy in our ranks.'

'Really! Which is he?'

'Row eleven — just in the middle there, with the blue tie.'

'But how can you tell?'

'From the old proverb. It's very simple: "The enemy never sleeps".'

*

Work and travel abroad did much to stop me brooding about the family; but the problem of recovering them remained my chief preoccupation, and it was a big moment when the first genuine letter from Leila found its way through, in the winter of 1989-90. When I was telephoned and the caller said, 'We've got a letter from your wife,' my first reaction was that it could not be spontaneous, and that there was no point in hurrying to get it. But when I suggested that this missive, too, was probably inspired by the KGB, the caller said, 'No, no, it's quite different. Please come in.'

The envelope was addressed in crude fashion: 'ENGLISH FOREIGN OFFICE — For Oleg Gordievsky' was all it said. But a battery of Finnish stamps showed clearly where it had come from. Inside was a wonderful, genuine letter, six pages of single-spaced typing, the first true communication for four and a half years. Reading it gave me a tremendous thrill: not just to learn that all the family were well, but to find that Leila was her normal forthright self. 'Stop all that nonsense about not ringing,' she had written. 'Call whenever you like, and I won't say anything silly.' The letter must have been smuggled out to Finland by courier, and when we managed to identify the man, I got someone from the station in Helsinki to go and thank him on my behalf.

Galvanized by this revolutionary development, I began to ring regularly, once a fortnight at a fixed time; and during every call I included some arguments about why it would make sense for the KGB to reunite the family. On another front, the Foreign Office told me that a member of the British Embassy in Moscow would visit Leila and take along any parcel I sent. I rushed out and bought beautiful clothes for the girls, padded jackets especially, and sent them off.

To be sure that Leila was at home when the Embassy representative went round, we worked out an arrangement that would pin her down. During one of my telephone calls, I would fix the precise date and time of the next and the messenger would turn up at the moment the second call was due. As luck would have it, I happened to be in New Zealand when the day for the first call came along, and I had to make it at 8 a.m. one morning, sitting at the desk of the head of the New Zealand security service. Everyone was excited, but at first we could not get through. 'All right,' said my host calmly, 'we'll keep talking, and the girls will keep trying.' So we did, and suddenly, after half an hour, we got a connection. I ran across to the telephone, and there was Moscow, echoing through the satellite. As we chatted, I said to Leila, 'D'you realize, I'm in Wellington, New Zealand. I'm ringing from the university, because they invited me to lecture here.' I duly set a date and time for our next communication, and the first secretary from the Embassy went round on the dot, taking the clothes I had sent, together with five thousand pounds in cash and a large supply of roubles. The money was enough for Leila to pay off the remaining debt on the flat, and to top up her monthly allowance for several years.

The first secretary was charmed by her, and vice versa, and they agreed to meet again. But somehow this good start came to nothing. In spite of making various plans, the Embassy did not manage to deliver a second parcel I sent, and various invitations from the Embassy never bore fruit. Leila and the diplomat met again, obviously under surveillance, but when they planned a third rendezvous, to hand over the parcel, the KGB moved quickly to declare him *persona non grata*. Although the foreign secretary, Douglas Hurd, managed to delay his departure from Moscow by six months, through a personal appeal to his opposite number, Edvard Shevardnadze, the diplomat did not see Leila again until she reached England eighteen months later. In telephone conversations she was disappointed and angry.

We also had problems with two long letters I tried to send via the Foreign Office. In writing to her, my natural sense of mischief rose to the surface in the form of an inclination to tease the KGB, and I referred to them sarcastically as 'the clerks' and 'the executioners' (in early nineteenth-century Russia a clerk was known as an 'executor'). The letter was passed to the British Embassy in Moscow, for onward transmission, but the Ambassador, Sir Bryan Cartledge, read it and refused to pass it. According to Foreign Office dogma, you must always be polite, flexible, courteous…and I was being openly contemptuous. The letter was therefore returned — whereupon I sent it through the KGB after one of my meetings with them at the Foreign Office.

At least Leila started to write letters regularly, addressing them to me at an anonymous postbox in London, and she described various events well, among them the death of my mother, which took place in November 1989. I knew that she had been ill, but not what the trouble was, and it was bitter for me that I could not see her before she died, at the age of eighty-two. Towards the end of her life she had been much influenced by my sister Marina, who had taken a hostile attitude towards me. My mother, not understanding the political complexity of the modern world, had to go along with what her daughter was telling her, but I would dearly have liked to let her have my version of events.

By May 1991 the liberalization of the Soviet Union had reached such a stage that Arif and Katya were allowed to travel abroad for the first time in their lives, and they took their little son with them to Italy to spend a couple of weeks on holiday with friends in Pisa. We formed a plan that I should join them for a day or two, so I filled an old suitcase with things for my children and flew out, only to find the weather appalling, with Pisa barely visible beneath sheets of rain. The Italian security service were warned that I was coming and, because they were worried that the KGB might be using Arif as a decoy, they surrounded me with full protection.

It was a joyous moment when I met my in-laws in a cafe, and I was amused to see Arif wearing an ancient brown sports jacket which I had left behind six years ago — an indication of how severe the shortages in Moscow still were. We took a taxi to a nice, authentic restaurant, and after a splendid dinner we decided to walk back to where they were staying. We had gone only a few yards when Katya said, 'Oleg, look out, we're being followed.'

'Relax,' I told her. 'They're only there to protect me. You did well to notice them. But you never spotted them in the restaurant — five men all sitting at one table.'

Next day we were taken on an excursion by Katya's hosts — an attractive, sexy woman and her husband. Afterwards, to say thank you, I tried to invite them both to lunch at a restaurant, but they insisted on giving us lunch in their house. We bought a couple of bottles of wine and had a party there. We were all delighted by Pisa, which is so small that one can walk everywhere; and another bonus was that Arif and Katya discovered that there was a direct rail carriage all the way to Moscow, so that it was no trouble for them to take my suitcase back with them.

By then many kind helpers had taken up the battle for the family on my behalf, not least Nicholas Bethell, the politician and author, whom I had first met while still working at the London Residency. With his prominent public position, and his wide experience in the field of human rights, Lord Bethell was an ideal advocate, and between us we concocted a plan whereby he should call in on Leila during a visit to Moscow in September 1990. The ruse worked to perfection. To make sure she was at home on the day, I warned her by telephone that someone would come to see her on 30 September. He telephoned her that morning from his hotel, explained who he was, and went round within an hour, risking arrest by the KGB whose minders were as usual parked in force outside the block of flats. In the event they did not try to intervene, and Bethell conducted what he described as a 'spirited interview'. This he published a week later, in the *Sunday*

Express, in the form of an open letter to Gorbachev, quoting Leila at length on the villainies and treachery of the KGB. He also published two glorious colour photographs which he had taken of the family, and these alone gave our morale a powerful boost. Whether or not the diatribe had any influence on events, it is impossible to say, but I was, and remain, profoundly grateful to Lord Bethell for his efforts on our behalf.

At the start of 1991 I began predicting that there would be a *coup d'état* against Gorbachev and his regime. I could see that members of the Central Committee were being pushed to the wall by the march of political development, and that soon only two courses would be open to them: either they would fight back, or they would have to surrender and disappear. Since they were not the type to give in, the only possible outcome seemed to be a coup, and, indeed, on 6 January 1991 I forecast just such an event in a big article in the *Sunday Times*. My only mistake was to predict that the coup would succeed.

When it started, on 17 August, at first things looked very black. The man behind it was Kryuchkov, whose aim was clearly to re-establish the old order and with it the supremacy of the KGB. Yet only two days later everything swung round with dramatic speed. Kryuchkov was arrested, and the liberal-minded Vadim Bakatin became chairman of the KGB.

When these hectic events began, the *Sunday Times* invited me to act as a consultant for the week, and I spent some frantic days in their office, armed with my Russian radio and a portable telephone. Then the unbelievable happened. One day as I sat there, the telephone rang, and a man from Independent Television said, 'We think your family are about to be released. Bakatin, the new head of the KGB, has just given a press conference in Moscow and said that they can go.'

Before I could take in the news, the man was asking me if I would go straight round to the ITV studios to be filmed. Life became like a circus, with unbelievable events occurring all over the place. As I walked up the steps into the studios, I dialled Leila in Moscow, only to find that people from ITN were already at our flat, shooting film there, so our conversation was filmed simultaneously at both ends. I could hear her doing her best to be careful, and not let her hopes soar too high, because she knew that the KGB could easily change its mind. 'But if it's true,' I said, 'when will you come?'

'I don't know,' she said coolly. 'There's no particular hurry. Perhaps next week.'

What had happened, it turned out, was that the new British Ambassador, Sir Roderick Braithwaite, had got in touch with Bakatin the moment the situation changed, and had reminded him of the Gordievsky problem. Then at the press conference Bakatin revealed that he had decided to satisfy the Ambassador's request. When the journalist Olga Belan — an old friend of Leila from her days as a reporter — asked him if he could reveal how he had reached his decision, he replied, 'Oh, well, all right. I felt that it was an old problem which should be resolved. When I asked my generals, they all categorically said, "No!", but I decided to ignore them, and regard this as my first major victory in the KGB.'

Next morning, Friday, Leila got a call from Ovir, the visa and permit department, asking why she had not come in to collect her passport — as if they had been awaiting her visit for days. A passport being an unrealizable dream for 99 per cent of Soviet citizens, this was an amazing question. Leila suggested, 'Tomorrow?', but since that was Saturday she agreed to go in on Monday. By an extraordinary coincidence the British Prime Minister, John Major, was in Moscow that week with his wife Norma, and one of Leila's last engagements in Russia was to take the children to tea with them at the Embassy.

Her flight to England on 6 September, and her arrival here, both proved spectacular. A television team was on board the aircraft, and the air crew celebrated a red-letter day with champagne all round. At Heathrow we had made careful arrangements to keep things under control. The Foreign Office insisted that Leila should give a brief press conference, but I had worked out a scheme for throwing the media off our tracks and had gone on ahead to wait for her at the fort. Since any car could have been followed by motorcycles, we had laid on a helicopter for the cross-country journey, and as soon as she had spoken to the press, she and the children were bundled on board for a short flight to the south coast.

There I waited in a state of breathless anticipation. By then, in September, the nights were closing in, and dark was falling before the party arrived. Then, as I stared into the sky, one of the stars grew brighter and brighter, until it resolved itself into the nose-light of the approaching helicopter, which swung down to land outside the fort.

Out came Leila, much as I remembered her, but the girls had changed practically out of recognition. All the same, they both looked lovely, in T-shirts with little rucksacks that I had sent them. I think Maria recognized me faintly, but to Anna, who had last seen me when she was four, I was a stranger.

Out came bunches of flowers and bottles of champagne, and soon another reception-cum-celebration was under way. The stewards — the same as when I arrived in England — brought simple presents for the children. Then a Landcruiser and driver appeared, and we all piled in: there was not much luggage, for the travellers had had to leave almost everything behind, but the back of the vehicle was filled with flowers.

So we motored for an hour through the dark. Towards the end Maria began to feel sick — and then, in the drive of the house, we saw the one sight we had hoped not to see: a journalist and cameraman waiting for us. In spite of all our precautions, one newspaper had outwitted us. I was furious, and let fly at the intruders.

In and around the house I had put up yellow ribbons — an American tradition to celebrate return and reunion after long absence. I had bought the nicest possible sheets and pillowcases for the girls, with pictures on them. Above all I had left lamps switched on in every room: the real family reunion, and a grand distribution of presents, took place in a cheerful blaze of light.

Chapter Sixteen – The Reckoning

Not until 1994 did we solve the sixty-four-thousand-dollar question of who had given me away. For years four main suspicions had plagued me. The first was that the leak might have derived indirectly from my initial contact with Lazlo, the Hungarian sent by the British to my flat in Copenhagen: I feared that Yelena might have inadvertently said something to arouse KGB suspicions. The second possibility was that Michael Bettaney might have deduced that I was the source who gave him away: perhaps he had passed my name via some intermediary to the KGB. The third conceivable channel was Edward Lee Howard, the former CIA officer who defected to the Soviet Union in 1985: he, too, had been in a position to know my identity. Finally, it seemed possible that the leak had sprung from the trial of the Norwegian spy Arne Treholt early in 1985. For complex reasons, the West German security service had run checks on me, and asked the Danes if I was a fully identified KGB officer. The Danes replied that I had been while I was working in Copenhagen. But earlier, in 1982, to make things easier for the British, who were trying to get me a visa to work in London, they had reported that I had *not* been fully identified as KGB — and it seemed possible that the anomaly had been picked up by moles of the East German Stasi, who passed it back through Berlin to Moscow.

Yet in the end all these fears proved groundless. Prolonged analysis by the British services also failed to produce any clue about where the leak had been. My Judas, it turned out, was the American intelligence officer Aldrich Ames, known to his colleagues as Rick, who was arrested for spying for the Russians early in 1994 and later sentenced to life imprisonment. Little did I realize, when I met him twice during 1989, that on 18 May 1985, the day after I was recalled to Moscow for interrogation, he had received his first payment, of ten thousand dollars, for putting the KGB on my trail.

As a senior officer in Soviet counter-espionage, he sat in on several of the briefings I gave the CIA, and I rather liked him. His face looked gentle and kind, and I thought that he embodied the openness, honesty and decency which are supposed to characterize Americans. What I could not know was that he was a mediocre operator, and had made a mess of his private affairs: he had separated from his first wife, started drinking heavily, and had taken up with a demanding Colombian woman eleven years his junior. By 1985 he had run into debt and badly needed money. Then the KGB officer whom he had been cultivating made a brilliant counter-move, and suggested that Ames should work for him, rather than vice versa. Obviously the KGB promised Ames handsome payment — and what they wanted first was a single piece of really valuable information.

Luckily for him, he was able to supply exactly that. For several years the British had been sending the Americans key information, which I had given them, and the CIA, methodical as ever, had probably collected all these reports in one folder. Ames saw that file, and although — thank God — he never knew my name, he told the Russians that the British had a source with access to the highest level of KGB intelligence. When he, or possibly someone in Copenhagen, added that this source had a strong Danish connection, the trail led straight to me.

I consider myself fortunate. Ames blew my career and life into shreds, but he did not kill me. Several former KGB men, also shopped by him, went to their deaths. By the time the FBI arrested him and his wife on 21 February 1994, he had received over 2 million dollars in Soviet payments. It is clear that if he had brought about my execution, it would not have worried him in the least: when he sat opposite me at the CIA briefings, he showed no sign of unease or remorse at being confronted by a man he had betrayed.

Ames's motives in changing sides were purely financial: mine were ideological and philosophical. As I made clear earlier, one of my conditions for starting to work with the British was that I should not be paid; and although the British government has been kind and good to me since I escaped to live in England, financial gain was never my incentive. Rather, I was driven by contempt for Communist tyranny — and now history has endorsed my opinion that the system was one under which it was impossible for humans to live happily.

In Britain, I have been enormously impressed by the quality of the professionals with whom I have worked in the security services and the Foreign Office: men and women of high intellectual level, well educated with a quick, intuitive understanding of people and their problems. This, I feel sure, is not merely the product of good training, but springs from basic character. In ideological terms, I have found the security and intelligence services far better informed and motivated than the rest of the population, many of whom, even now, seem starry-eyed about Communism and ignorant of its evils. The officers with whom I have dealt all have a high sense of duty and responsibility, and seem to be guided by a special intuition which tells them infallibly what is in their country's best interests. Besides, they are never afraid to take decisions without consulting their superiors — an impressive difference from their counterparts in the Soviet Union.

In the early days of my co-operation I was disappointed that none of my contacts could speak much Russian, but later I discovered that the services — in marked contrast to the bulk of the population — include many brilliant linguists. I know one man, for instance, who speaks both Arabic and Polish perfectly, and another who, besides being trilingual in French and German, is equally at home in Finnish. My case officer Andrew spoke German, Russian, Czech, Serbo-Croat and Swedish.

Of people in general, what has struck me most is that the British are infallibly kind and friendly: they expect the best of you, and on meeting you take it for granted that you're a good fellow. This, again, is an immense difference from Soviet life, which brutalized citizens so badly that people constantly expected to be attacked, and to become victims of scheming or at the very least of sarcasm. I was imbued with such a prickly, defensive attitude when I arrived that I made several fundamental mistakes: expecting a remark to be aggressive or sarcastic, I once or twice let out a sharp answer before I realized that the approach had been friendly.

Other key English qualities, it seems to me, are discretion, respect for privacy, and tolerance towards foreigners. The level of politeness, of courtesy and tact, must be unique in the world, possibly approached in New Zealand, but nowhere else. Also I have often noticed how wonderfully unspoilt and spontaneous people are, retaining their ability to enjoy simple natural things like clouds, sunsets, landscape, sea and flowers. I am sure people were like that in nineteenth-century Russia, but Communism destroyed all spontaneity, making it impossible for people to be sentimental, or to express appreciation.

Of course, the British have some obsessions that Russians find ridiculous: the relative merits of conifers and broadleaved trees, yellow oilseed rape blossom, grey squirrels and Canada geese. Only a prosperous society, without serious problems, could become exercised about such minuscule irritations. I remember a countryman in Norfolk complaining that the quality of life was deteriorating because Happy Eater restaurants and streetlights were springing up everywhere. If ever he had to spend a few weeks in the Russian outback, he would change his tune and positively clamour for such amenities.

And dislikes? Only trivia. Why does Radio Three close down so soon after midnight? Why do people persist in eating off the wrong side of their forks? Why, at dinner parties, are serious subjects of conversation deferred until coffee comes round — by which time everyone is too tired to think straight?

Looking back, I have no regrets about switching allegiance to the West. On the contrary: far from ruing my decision, I am only sorry that I did not make it earlier, immediately after the Soviet invasion of Czechoslovakia in 1968. That was the event that determined the course of my life, and I wish now that I had responded to it more promptly. What I do regret very much is that I let myself be outsmarted by the KGB in 1985. Not only did the disaster destroy my family life: it also ended my active career prematurely. I should have liked to go on bridging the gap between two worlds right to the end of Gorbachev's time in office, explaining the phenomena of change to the West.

My greatest sorrow and pain were that I was cut off from my family for so long, and so missed six irreplaceable years of watching my daughters grow up. Still worse, my marriage to Leila did not survive our separation.

In those six years we had grown apart, and, much as I longed to weave the threads of our lives together again, it proved impossible. The KGB had worked to poison Leila's mind against me, telling her lies about how I had taken up with a young secretary, and so on; she herself, though putting on a brave face and dismissing such allegations as rubbish, did not know what to believe, and had been badly hurt by the rumours.

She had also been much distressed by my failure to tell her that I was working for the British: although she never said so, I believe that she found it a sign of less than full trust on my part, and she felt — quite rightly — that I had deceived her. Also, she thought it a cruel and irresponsible act for anyone in a position as risky as mine to marry and have children. Her predicament in Moscow had become so unpleasant — exposed, alone, the wife of a traitor, shunned by former friends — that she inevitably came to feel, if not hostility, at least a desire to punish me.

Thus when we began to talk on the telephone, she sounded as if she really wanted to join me in Britain, and to reunite the family. Later, though, it turned out that this was not true. What she wanted, first of all, was to escape from the Soviet Union because life there was hard and difficult: she wanted the children to have a better life and a better education. She also wanted to live in the West, and to be able to visit Russia from time to time. Above all, she wanted to come and show me that she was no soft, pacific victim, but a tough character fully able to criticize my actions and maybe prove that I had been wrong all the time.

Having deceived me on the telephone, and in some of her letters, she arrived here in a critical mood, showing hostility and demanding explanations. I did not like this, and I hoped the mood would pass. I strove to combat it by showering affection and presents on the girls: I took them on holiday to America, to Rome, to the Canary Islands, and gave them expensive toys like computers. They, for their part, had got

461

wind that I was in some way an important person. Yet nothing could change the fact that, over the years of separation, they had become closely attached to their mother, and that she had deliberately kept them dependent on her.

In the end I was forced to acknowledge that a combination of my own actions, our separation and the efforts of the KGB had destroyed whatever nice feelings Leila may once have had for me: there was nothing left, and no basis for becoming married again. In 1993 I therefore approached a solicitor to arrange a settlement of our affairs. I think, in a way, we were both emotional casualties of the Cold War.

On the credit side of working for the West, my life became immensely more exciting and rewarding than it would have been if I had slogged on in the KGB. Moreover, I succeeded in my main aim of damaging Soviet Communism, and of limiting its power to harm the West. I never dared dream that the whole system would collapse in the way it did, and I certainly do not believe that my own small efforts in any way hastened its demise. Nevertheless, events have vindicated my claims that it was a truly poisonous system, and the West now sees how terrible it was.

As for my standing in Russia, I never hoped for any understanding or appreciation there. It was more important to me to be honest to my own conscience and to the West. After seventy years of Communist propaganda, people in the Soviet Union had become so heavily indoctrinated that they regarded the Party and the KGB as national institutions and anyone who attacked either must be a traitor to the nation. This being so, I could not expect anyone to understand, still less condone, what I had done. But then, when Communism suddenly disintegrated, I found that a few enlightened people began to appreciate my behaviour, and from 1990 one or two journalists started to express approval in newspaper articles.

At the same time, other people launched virulent attacks — not because they disapproved of my actions but because they had failed to do anything themselves. Because I took a decision they wished they had taken, they were belatedly filled with jealousy and irritation.

I still firmly believe that my decision to help the West was my only option; yet I have often wondered why so few members of the Soviet foreign policy Establishment — the KGB, the GRU and the Ministry of Foreign Affairs — defected during my working life. The main reason, I believe, is simply that the Soviet system was so efficient: the whole apparatus of the KGB, its personnel departments, the Cadres Abroad department of the Central Committee — all this huge apparatus for selecting the right people to go abroad, and then indoctrinating them, worked well. For one reason or another, those chosen were not liable to take big ideological decisions. Some were tied by the size of their families: they had so many relatives that they did not dare leave that number of hostages behind. Others were intelligent but blinkered, and wanted success within the system that had produced them: the idea of publishing a book abroad, or being useful to a foreign government, did not appeal.

Mikhail Lyubimov epitomized this type. Although highly intelligent, and full of warm feelings for Britain, its literature and traditions, he yet retained many crazy leftist ideas. In 1976 and 1977, after he had served in London, he could still discuss Trotsky with serious interest, and in spite of his experience in the West, he remained seduced by the idea of becoming a KGB general. His dream was to become a well-known literary figure, able to recite reams of English verse, and yet to be an important KGB general — an impossible combination.

Of maybe fifteen people who defected during the past thirty-odd years, most went for entirely mundane reasons: one because he had lost a secret KGB document, another to escape his wife, another because he wanted a more comfortable life, and so on. I believe I am one of the few who chose to co-operate with the West out of purely ideological convictions, and who deliberately planned to do so over a long period.

In saying this, I do not mean to boast or claim any credit. Rather, I thank goodness for the various slices of luck that enabled me to see the truth, and to escape from the indoctrination process before it was too late. The first was that I learned German early, and got the chance to read Western newspapers when I was only twenty-one. By this means I found out a great deal about what was happening in the world, long before my contemporaries had any chance to do the same. Another crucial factor was my stay in East Berlin: seeing the Wall go up, and witnessing the hatred and despair that Communism inflicted on ordinary people, showed me that the system was both illegal and criminal.

During my twenties I developed a romantic, idealistic attitude towards recent historical events. The last people who had tried to beat off the Communist threat, and protect the country from totalitarian occupation, had been the White Russians who fought in the Civil War — men like Admiral Kolchak and General Wrangel. When I realized what colossal efforts they had made and began to identify with them, they became my heroes.

Then, while serving abroad, I remembered that the British and French had been allies of the Russians in the two world wars, and I decided that, in a way, I could regard myself as a surviving White Russian officer who had remained faithful to the old oath of the *entente cordiale*, right from the beginning. Once I had decided that it was undignified and dishonest to serve the Communist regime, my mind was made up.

I believe now that it is only in the West that Russia can save itself. The other nations of Eastern Europe — Poland, Hungary, the Czech republic, Slovakia and Estonia — are falling over themselves to join Western alliances, to adopt Western economic and political systems. Russia, I am convinced, will have to do the same. She will have to build not on the experience of the Communist era, which is totally discredited, but on the experience of the old, pre-revolutionary Russia, which was much closer to the West.

In these pages I have frequently ridiculed the KGB for its incompetence, its dishonesty and its failure to grasp the realities of Western life. Nevertheless it was a highly dangerous organization — a huge and typical Soviet department with an enormous budget and many thousands of officers. Even if out of every hundred officers eighty or ninety were useless, the remaining ten or twenty could still pose a serious threat. During my time in London, for instance, the station included many duds, but there were also a few highly gifted men — Mikhail Bogdanov, Yuri Kobaladze, Leonid Nikitenko — with the ability to achieve real breakthroughs on the intelligence front. The KGB did not need that many good agents. The damage done by Aldrich Ames was immense. In Britain Geoffrey Prime and Michael Smith were similarly dangerous; and if Michael Bettaney's overtures had not been rejected, he, too, could have caused a disaster.

I believe that my own main contribution lay in my ability to report so fully on the KGB. The information I provided gave the West a big leap in its knowledge of the KGB, of the Soviet system as a whole, and of the KGB's place within the system. In particular, I gave details of the KGB operation in Britain: even information about where the organization was weak proved helpful, as it enabled the British to save resources. I can say, without exaggeration, that my information saved taxpayers several million pounds, not merely in Britain, but also in the United States, Germany, France, Holland and the Scandinavian countries. Because

I was producing day-to-day intelligence from the KGB, as well as the texts of annual reports and plans, the British, paradoxically, knew more about the situation in the KGB station in London than did Moscow. This knowledge of KGB methods and mentality made life easier for MI5 and MI6, and enabled London to form a clearer picture of the KGB's work against the British Embassy in Moscow.

By exposing Michael Bettaney (the only member of MI5 sentenced to gaol in the history of the organization), I believe I contributed substantially to the security of Britain. The information which I gave about the illegals — their training, the development of their identities, their methods of operation — led to a number of arrests in the 1980s and 1990s. I also gave many details about areas with which I was not directly concerned: I spirited out an annual report of the KR Line (penetration of the British intelligence community), and provided so many new facts about Line X (acquisition of technological and scientific secrets) that MI5 were later able to arrest Michael Smith, who is now serving a twenty-five-year sentence.

On the wider political front, I was able to give Western intelligence officers a far clearer account of the mentality of Soviet leaders than they had ever had before. I exposed the tendentiousness of KGB political reporting, as well as the organization's imperfect objectivity and poor analysis — all of which increased Moscow's misconceptions about the West. I also revealed that it was the International Department of the Central Committee which dictated Soviet foreign policy. (Until then, the Foreign and Commonwealth Office had believed that policy was set by the Ministry of Foreign Affairs.) I provided much information about Soviet policy towards numerous other nations and geographical areas, not least the Arctic, the Antarctic, and the world's oceans. My revelations about the KGB's 'active measures' — attempts to manipulate

Western public opinion — helped Britain and the United States to make sound judgements.

Through my activities, the British government and MI5 received confirmation that their policy towards Soviet espionage in Britain was proving effective. Their new policy of setting a 'diplomatic ceiling', and fixing a limited number of 'slots' for Soviet diplomats, critically weakened the KGB in Britain. There was an immense difference between the situation in the 1960s, when there had been 120 Soviet spies in London, and that of the 1990s, with only thirty-six. Security in Britain became much better than in other Western countries — and my presence as a British agent was itself protection against any possible penetration of the London government or intelligence organizations.

All these factors, I believe, significantly increased confidence within the British intelligence community, and within the Foreign and Commonwealth Office.

As for my own future — that looks Western too. As I write, I am still under sentence of death in Russia, so that any swift return is out of the question. As time passes, my roots in England go down deeper, and the chances of settling back in Russia diminish. All the same, I should love to travel in my homeland, and see some of the places to which I have never been, among them Armenia, the lands between the Volga and the Urals, and the ancient towns encircling Moscow known as the Golden Ring.